MW01469387

ARMAGEDDON
U.S.A.

0109-CAMP

ARMAGEDDON U.S.A.

A CHRONICLE OF AMERICA'S GENOCIDE PHENOMENON AND ITS CULTURE OF DEATH

Ronald Campbell, Ph.D.

0109-CAMP

Books by Ronald L. Campbell

TRANSPERSONAL PSYCHOLOGY:AN INTEGRAL

ENCOUNTER WITH SELF AWARENESS

A SOUL JOURNEY INTO ETERNITY: A TRANSPERSONAL

FABLE ON SELF TRANSCENDENCE

THE CONCEPT OF MAN IN INTEGRAL PSYCHOLOGY

Copyright © 1999 by Ronald LeRoy Campbell.

Library of Congress Number:		00-191070
ISBN#:	Hardcover	0-7388-1114-9
	Softcover	0-7388-1115-7

All rights reserved. No part of this book may be reproduced or transmitted in any form or by any means, electronic or mechanical, including photocopying, recording, or by any information storage and retrieval system, without permission in writing from the copyright owner.

This is a work of fiction. Names, characters, places and incidents either are the product of the author's imagination or are used fictitiously, and any resemblance to any actual persons, living or dead, events, or locales is entirely coincidental.

This book was printed in the United States of America.

To order additional copies of this book, contact:
Xlibris Corporation
1-888-7-XLIBRIS
www.Xlibris.com

CONTENTS

0109-CAMP

ACKNOWLEDGMENTS

The author wishes to express his appreciation to his transpersonal psychological mentor, Dr. Haridas Chaudhuri for his guidance and insights over a period of twenty years. Additionally, he is indebted and grateful to the transpersonal insights and Integral psychology of Mirra Alfassa and of Aurobindo Ghose.

I am particularly indebted to anthropologists John Collier Jr., Dr. John Adair, and Dr. Laura Thompson for instructing me in the more subtle aspects of anthropological knowledge and research.

To my wife Carmen goes my greatest appreciation for her patients and understanding on this 28 year writing and research project of inquiry into the transpersonal nature of humanity.

PREFACE

FUTURIST 22ND CENTURY COMMENTARY: In the waning days of the American empire, Archaeologist Renaldo Campbell uncovers a secret time vault which contains manuscripts written by his ancestor, 20th century Psychologist and Transpersonal Anthropologist, Dr. Ronald Le Roy Campbell, who lived through the tumultuous 20th, and 21st century social destruction of the United States of America.

All of his manuscripts are not intact and what are preserved are fragments written over a period of time; but enough has been preserved to demonstrate the historical validity of the concept of America's Death Generation and its culture of Death which ultimately destroys the United States of America.

Campbell's manuscripts are about America's death generation and its culture of death. It examines the reasons for its emergence into modern life. Its asks the question of how does a culture of death manifest in American society.; and why is this death generation emerging from the depths of social despair and corruption to create a whirl-wind of destruction and chaos that currently spreads throughout the entire American culture as a Genocide Phenomenon. Sad and pathetic is this death generation which gives birth to a death barbarism which sows the destruction for their entire people's sociocultural reality.

From these lost writings comes the startling expose of the decline and destruction of a great people and of their death throes before being cast into the trash cans of history.

Read carefully and you will find in these documents his evaluation of seven causal factors which precedes the imminent social destruction of America which the author sees creeping upon his people. Examine how he perceives America can renew itself.

Dr. Campbell's lone voice calls out from the wilderness of social despair by focusing on the essence of America's lost integrity which all people lose before their people's final collapse as a social entity.

Ultimately the death generation and its culture of death rode a mighty surge of self-destructive force which historically is called the Genocide Phenomenon. The Death cadres claim victory and America's culturecide become a fact and a footnote in the historical process of another extinct culture.

CHAPTER 1

GENOCIDE PHENOMENON: AMERICA'S EXTINCTION PERIL CRISIS

FUTURIST 22ND CENTURY COMMENTARY: In the waning days of the American empire, Archaeologist Renaldo Campbell uncovers a secret time vault which contains manuscripts written by his ancestor, 20th century Psychologist and Transpersonal Anthropologist, Dr. Ronald Le Roy Campbell, who lived through the tumultuous 20th, and 21st century social destruction of the United States of America.

All of his manuscripts are not intact and what are preserved are fragments written over a period of time; but enough has been preserved to demonstrate the historical validity of the concept of America's Death Generation and its culture of Death which ultimately destroys the United States of America.

The lost fragments of the writings of social scientist, Ronald Campbell have been compiled in this book with some brief modern 22nd century commentary on the subject of the death generation and its culture of death.

Possibly the rediscovery of these historical documents, written in an age of violence and open rebellion, will initiate a thorough and critical reexamination of the phenomenon of the death of American Culture and its concurrent theme of the immanent genocidal death of the human species. These are extinction factors that any person of discernment will recognize with painful objectivity in the modern age.

Twenty Second Century

The 22nd century is a time of death for the human species and it is not known for certain whether Homo sapiens shall survive or if the extinction peril Campbell spoke of with such passionate concern will fully engulf modern man.

The mass destruction of modern civilizations in the War's of terror and the plagues of destruction which followed, have presently decimated several billion of our species and we cry out in terror that we may be the last of our kind!

It is not known if our last grasp will be today or tomorrow but most astute observers now feel our specie's destiny call into oblivion! Additionally psychological terror abounds and many of our people refuse to have children and scream at their future by committing mass suicide as our greatest philosophers cry out in astonishment at the plight of the human race while our theologians whimper in the darkness of their sterile doctrines of nonsense. They know now that God has truly abandoned them and even some doubt if he ever existed.

Only our mystics stand firm and challenge the human race to transcend themselves by meeting the challenge of God's call into Eternity; but naturally everyone knows these kooks are mad and their thought imbecilic and absurd!

It is a time of sadness and melancholy for time's past. The wisest among us know that we are living in the end times and that destiny calls the race to transcend itself or perish! But who knows the way out of these terrible times; the escape path has been blocked and the people cry out in madness that God himself has deserted us. We are truly lost children of the death generation and there is no hope for us.

Death stalks us daily and madness surrounds us. Death terrors are the ingredients of our daily life style. No one knows the way toward the light of truth and who among us has the courage to follow that light if it should suddenly appear. Presently we are the dead following death as our guide. Darkness is our creed and truth a myth of forgotten glory that probably never existed; oblivion is our destiny as a people and our only personal goal out of the darkness of living.

History has called us and the immanent extinction of the human race is upon us. Very few of us now have the capacity to reproduce and what children are born are mutants of the worst kind; because in their madness they are cannibalistic against their own kind.

Is there any hope for 22nd century man or are we truly doomed to give the planet up to another species as the 20th century sage Aurobindo predicts if humanity fails to meet the challenges of destiny?

Campbell states that the immanent destruction of the human race faces us and that unless we transcend our lower human natures we will destroy ourselves in wars of expediency and thus our species will become extinct!

We cry out in agony about that statement. Has our time come? Is the human race doomed to extinction? Can this peril be stopped? We cry out but Eternity answers not as our people suffer the living death of a thousand pains.

"God where are you? Lift us up or we perish! Our

species cries out for deliverance from itself. Hear our call because we are doomed if ye answer not."

But enough of that futility, because God is dead and his churches are now but museums of death and his ministers pedophiles and promoters of children's tales of terror. They are the dead talking to the dead for our scientists now tell us that our species is dying. The remnants of our civilizations are entering their death throes and no hope exists for the living except death and oblivion!

So this introduction is an obituary to the death of the human race yet somehow I wish my predecessors had listened to my ancestor one hundred and fifty years ago. If they had only looked into their hearts and minds and let their inner truths guide them they would have walked into Eternity with glory instead of the whimppy death that now awaits humanity, individually and as a species. Campbell, in chapter one, speaks of the culture of death which afflicts 20th century humanity.

THE CULTURE OF DEATH

American's are living at a time in the historical process when their will to live as a people and as a species is becoming submerged within a cultural death wish called the Genocide Phenomenon. Few of us indeed are able to walk away from this extinction peril without feeling its terrible foulness. But most of us are thrust unwillingly into this new era of world uncertainty as death and destruction becomes the motto of the day as we gradually, day by day, join the death generation and its culture of death!

Yes, today we are living within the anguish and social malaise of the death of America as its social attitudes and life energy die before our very eyes. Daily we wither up and waste away in panic and desperation as we die to ourselves and to our country.

We live within the shadow of the social destruction of the United States of America. All that we hold dear and honorable is caught within the death grip of the Genocide Phenomenon which overtly manifests as a destructive culture of death with its war time horrors of massive racial genocide and vast culturecide tragedies that is gradually destroying the world and American society.

The culture of Death is also covertly a latent specie's suicidal death wish which has allied with the primordial fear-anxiety syndrome and its accompanying social malaise of alienation and estrangement of man from himself, society and nature! This culture of death is, however, also a process that is overtly and covertly affecting the military-industrial complex, our governments, educational, corporate and family structures, as well as the average working man and his children's world views; and above all it is the force that is destroying the cultural integrity of American life and its future destiny. American National Character is wilting and changing under its impact as our national mental health crumbles and changes drastically as man the free becomes adjusted into a new technocracy personality mode that allows him to be corporate, business, governmental, educational, men-drones for the new world orders.

Western industrial society and its scientific rationalism is imposing its new agenda of technocracy upon free Americans as the two great western traditions of Christian and humanistic thought dies to itself and loses its character and convincing power. Tillich has characterized this trend as one which is destroying our highest values and freedoms. He says:

> During the last hundred years the implications of this system have become increasingly clear; a logical or naturalistic mechanism which seemed to destroy individual freedom, personal decision and organic community; and the analytic rationalism which saps vital forces of life and transforms, including man himself, into an object of calculation and control. [1]

This book approaches this culture of death from many sides and attempts to understand what it is and the dangers it poses for the survival of America's integrity as a nation and its position as a champion of individual freedom. It inquires into the loss of American individual freedom and its changing national character by presenting seven causal factors that are pulling the nation and individual man deep into the culture of death.

Additionally, this study questions if Transintegral Psychology's contention is true that this culture of death taps deep into aspects of man's unregenerated evolutionary past that still lies buried within each of our unconscious as a residual from our collective species consciousness. Some authorities say that this deep dark force activates a regressive counterforce to the progressive America way of life which leads us into the culture of death. Is contemporary mankind plunging into the dark ages of humanity's primordial past by this immersion fall into the dark recess of humanity's unconscious species consciousness? If the facts are correct then contemporary humanity's regressive behavior creates a barrier to its bright evolutionary future? Possibly humanity may not be able to take that next progressive and immense leap above the human species normal mentality into its higher human potentiality to transcend itself, thus the species is in grave jeopardy! This death force within humanity may destroy the species Homo sapien in modern times. It is the resurgence of the still unregenerated humanity's unconscious primordial past overcoming his future greatness and its name is the Genocide Phenomenon and its overt force is the Culture of Death and its operants are the death generation and its cadres of death!

C.G. Jung concurs with Transintegral psychology's primordial fear-anxiety syndrome that anxiety is a person's reaction to the invasion of the irrational forces from the collective unconsciousness. It is a fear of the domination from our animal ancestry that still lies in an unregenerated form within our individual and collective species consciousness.[2]

This death force of darkness is emerging within the land of the free–a culture of Death so fierce and ominous that the weak tremble and the strong shake and the bewildered wither in fright and anguish. Its depth is so vast that there is no escape from it and there is no future without it and its victory cheers are uttered daily by the leader's of the death generation as America the beautiful withers and wilts in anguish as its people gradually succumb to this American death plague.

This culture of death is overtly and subtlety destroying the very fabric and substance of American socio-cultural life, even as its covert side destroys our psychological viability and inner strength by its emergence of the negative side of success and world economics, the dark side of love, the abnormality of mental health, the fear of death and of life. Its force lies revealed as the cultural facade crumbles and breaks down as conflicts are exhilarated as values change within the socioeconomic, political, religious, racial and philosophical spheres of social influence. Conscious and unconscious prejudices become raw in conflict, tension and alienation. We are also experiencing the disintegrating results of religious prejudice and of racism and strong ethnocentrisms such as the polarization between the black is beautiful countermove against the WASP arrogance. The changing times have also excelerated the economic conflict among the poor and the rich, and sexual discrimination between the sexes, now more covert than previously against females as they move forcefully into the market place. And as our century progresses the generation gap between the young and the old gets worse until now our youth can gun down old women on the streets and cheer in elation for their deeds! But perhaps our greatest class struggle is now in the process as millions of middle class people fall down into lower class status. [3] All these causal factors of the primordial fear-anxiety syndrome represent dualistic nuances of this primordial fear-anxiety syndrome force which constitutes the exigencies of the life of American culture. Its overt side is rapidly causing the socio-pathological disintegrating of our culture with its overt emergence of the death generation in all socioeconomic classes and its covert death cadres, with its concepts of mass genocide, overt and covert murders, social degradation and humiliation of certain social classes and ethnic groups, along with its ideas of social culturecide. The growth and supremacy of the culture of death are rapidly approaching us as our age approaches the end times and the nation covertly trembles in fear and trepidation!

WHEN DID IT ALL BEGIN?

The life force of the America ebbed and collapsed in the dying years of the 20th century. No longer did the people have any self integrity nor had their cultural values any power to instill in them a true purpose to live by. No longer had the Nation any will to live. A great nation's spirit perished in the 20th century of turmoil and challenge.

How could the spiritual integrity of the United States die while preserving itself as a political entity? Perhaps rapid culture change with its technological innovation, allied with explosive developments of technology could not keep up with the conventional concepts of morality and integrity. Some say covert science, allied with secret money interests and an alien agenda is setting up "America the beautiful" in an insidious plot to undermine America's integrity as a nation and as a moral force in the world. But perhaps the true and tried got lost in the quicksand of emotional despair at a world gone mad and out of control! Perhaps the disastrous increase in the world population and the death of religion and its replacement by situational ethics cast the death throe over people no longer in control of their destiny. Many critics say that the country had simply fulfilled its social mandate. Its stiffened social norns simply strangled its outmoded social model which simply collapsed as the culture died!

Perhaps the greatest challenge that the American people could not face, perhaps would not meet, was the task of changing themselves to meet the new challenges. When rapid culture changes occur they affect the social psychology of people which activates the Primordial fear-anxiety syndrome and affects everyone on the conscious-unconscious levels. In America a social malaise and alienation occur within individuals and social groups because the success-failure complex emerges overtly. To succeed in America is to breathe the free air of accomplishment; but to fail in America is to join the death generation! Why? Because it is a fact that each American must have faith that he will be a success in life; yet this faith is a vague conviction that I might succeed, maybe! At its best it becomes a craving for individual meaning and is locked into a truism which says that I must be all that I can be and be the best of that which I am able to be and I must walk that lonely mile alone into fame and fortune or be damned! I must accomplish something in life or my birth is meaningless and my existence futile and my future dismal. If I fail I will die alone, having accomplished nothing, reviled by everyone, exiled from my family and in desperation and self-condemnation I will live my life in alienation and social malaise and those who see me will be justified in condemning me. A failure I am and a failure I will die and let no one tell you otherwise!

Today masses of Americas are falling into failure and fear as they join the death generation. Thus the great nation of the United States of America slowly eroded from the consciousness of the American people.

Oh, the American people remain but their great culture died that day of infamy, that secret time when all cultures die that slow agonizing death of no return. Most Americans didn't even know it had happened. So engrossed were they in the materialism play games of the day that they were oblivious of the death of their spirit. It was as if their courage and integrity gasp its last dying breathes as the fiddler played the latest statistic on drive-by shootings, as they cheered wildly for the winner of the latest pennant battle. It was in such a silent moment of culture death that the copse of their culture gradually stiffened and perished.

Oh the copse is still standing, the people are still saluting their flag and the games go on as the American mouths the words of truth, honor, duty and equality to all!

Poor fools, they don't know they have died to their ideals.

They no longer remember their oaths of integrity to themselves or to the world. They don't realize they will die a slow and painful death as the country enters into it wake and morns its past glory and wonders where it all went too.

They cry tears of remorse as they face a death of no return. The America they loved and cherished lies dead and broken and will rise no more. Those whom morns know this in their deepest understandings and cry bitter tears of repentance. There is no redeemth repentance, no going back, no returning to what might have been. They now must turn to the text books for answers about how, why and when, the great American Culture of the United States of American died?

Can they find answers in dry text books and learned speeches about something no one really understands? No, it must be searched for in the heart and soul of America. It must be examined and pieced together carefully, truthfully and with exact attention to grasping the elusive ethereal force called the spirit of the American people.

Is there any hope for the American people? Can the end be postponed or perhaps transcended by some socio-cultural revival of hope that Americans can grasp? Perhaps we should inquire further into this spectacle of death that is engulfing us and smothering our integrity and morality.

GENOCIDE PHENOMENON

The Genocide Phenomenon is a death theme but also a social process that is now part of the 20th century historical process. It is a culture of death that is presently gripping the world and particularly the United States as its principal prey and victim. It is a diabolical force that is plunging modern societies into a dark age from which none may escape its death touch. It is a cultural force which has its overt death agencies and covert death recruits from all stations of life. It is a culture of death so insidious that it covertly has infiltrates our cultural value systems with its hidden primordial fear-anxiety syndrome and overt dragon's complex so that we daily die from it strangling grip yet know it not! The Genocide Phenomenon is the force that has caused massive cases of world wide culturecide and genocide, that is, the death of societies and cultures which may lead eventually to the genocide of the human species itself. It is the culture of death that will kill America!

The Genocide phenomenon is occurring world wide in its overt and covert form; but this book will examine only the emergence of the death generation within American society by presenting seven integral causal reason for this phenomenon and discusses some solutions to the death pangs of America and its present social and pathological Madness.

The death generation, world wide, has overt and covert memberships, that is, it has its dictatorships and its secular totalitarian priests of death, its overt killers, political terrorists, bureaucratics, political scoundrels, death scientists, corporate presidents, and perhaps even your next door neighbor. But this force is often subtle and seemingly overtly full of life with its Priests of joy and its teachers of enlightenment and its agenda of social upliftment and only rarely do you spot them as your friendly pedophiliac priest or your death master educator, or smiling television minister who is fleecing the devoted and often pure of heart out of their well earned gold. This extinction force also includes, in many parts of the world, politically organized death cadre members which also includes large masses of the passive population who have overtly succumbed to the allure of the death message as well as those large social masses of victims of social manipulation who have either been enslaved or been forced to overtly and covertly accept the culture of death concept for self preservative sake, with its existential mood of self-alienation, desperation and social defeat. [4]

SEVEN CAUSAL FACTORS FOUND IN THE GENOCIDE PHENOMENON

There are seven basic causal forces and many minor factors supporting the Genocide Phenomenon's appearance within the contemporary historical process. An integral interconnectiveness supports these causal forces so that we may not truly grasp the premises of the Genocide Phenomenon intellectually or emotionally until we study all seven of these causal factors and come around full circle at the end of the book; only then can we psychologically and intellectually internalize the genocide phenomenon's meaning to ourselves and our age.

PARADIGM CRISIS-CAUSAL FACTOR ONE

Hypothesis 1. Today the scientific world exists in a period that Thomas S. Kuhn calls "the emergence of the crisis in the scientific community." [5] It is realized by a vanguard group of scientists that science needs to develop new concepts and paradigms that can give new explanations about man in the world.

Theory in its basic concept is a series of two schematic labels that have been demonstrated to show a meaningful relationship with each other by factual evidence or hypothesized constructs. And when we speak of the human condition and sociocultural reality and rapid socio-cultural change we must examine all these factors together in order to understand the Genocide Phenomenon. The rationale for this point of view is that human experience is psychocultural, involving a creative synthesis of cultural achievement and psychobiological activity in relationship to the social and physical environment. The human organism, cultural concepts, and material objects, all belong to the cultural dynamic realm and must be integrally understood; and not to do so risks the destruction of life as we know it as the extinction peril consumes America!

Man in the 20th century lives in a world which exists at a

critical transition period in the historical process. Civilization and its socio-cultural paradigm structure is now in the process of dissolution through a process called the Genocide Phenomenon which is a vast process of inner psychological and outer social dissolution that has mankind in its grip and will not let it go until the human race has perished into oblivion! The process of world turmoil is causing a post industrial resurgence of medieval death barbarism to emerge within many contemporary human societies. World conditions are chaotic and social disruption is rampant, causing psychosocial disharmonies to be a commonplace occurrence throughout the nation states of the world. It is a fact that each culture psychologically codes its inhabitants within their prescribed world view which so conditions each person to its truth that if you disturb that culture beyond the acceptable limits of its tolerance you will have a pathological breakdown of the inner and outer person's personality sanity of the inhabitants of that specific societies. American culture is now undergoing this process of dying to itself as its cultural values and social structure, religions and sciences and technology collapses upon themselves.

AMERICA IS DYING

The first death blows have manifested in Western culture and especially in America where our culture, society and total way of life disintegrates and decays before our very eyes. It is an epochal crisis that calls America to its doom as its sensate culture based on the concept that true reality and value are sensory and that nothing exists beyond what we can hear, see, smell, touch and taste dies to itself. Thus American's materialization of this concept in its sciences, and philosophy, its law and ethics, its economics and politics and social institutions and its modicum of religion, now rests on the quicksand of cultural destruction and disintegration leading ultimately to the collapse of the entire American system[6]

We are now facing the entire collapse of all of the important aspects of ""American life as the organization and culture of Western society becomes sick in body and mind as Western Man comes to the end of a brilliant six-hundred year long sensate day as the post industrial age commences. [7]

Today, thus, is a time when religion becomes dust on the unread bibles and faith becomes pious mouthings of morality and misunderstood ethics. It is a time when the Death of God becomes manifest as the churches become mere social clubs and the spirit of man is led downwards into the pit of despair! It is a time when high priests seduce young altar boys and young maidens are deflowered on the high altars by the elite priests of God and no one cares! It is a time when anti-abortion is on the lips of the church as they utter their last hurrah of a church dying to its self. It is a time when God almighty deserts his churches and the cracks of the religious edifices are heard around the world.

When we speak of the dissolution of entire nation states and vast culturecide tragedies, that is, deaths of whole cultures, we are also saying that these cultural systems internal and external structures with their world views and conceptual and psychological paradigm systems internally collapse generally before their final demise or conquest. This book will address this causal factors as one of the basic reasons for the emergence of the death generation and its culture of death into American life as our cultural's paradigm system collapses. A new cultural model, the psychocognitive culture theory, will be presented in this book, along with new theories about human nature that may begin the process of cultural renewal in America.

But, additionally we must understand that with the dissolution of western civilization and our descent into the dark ages again is not just a social-political happening. The fields of science upon which our civilization rests, are itself at the edge of self destruction themselves as their old models of science gradually collapse. New scientific models are needed desperately if we as a people are to survive or prevent the coming wars of terror!

One of the basic integral factors of the present world crisis is its lack of an adequate paradigm about the nature of man and of his evolutionary potential. The anomaly that is man has finally caught up to itself and now modern man stands before us either as a shining saint or a glaring beacon of death who will uplift us into his glory or exterminate us by trying to remake us into his death image.

Additionally each society and cultures needs to develop a post-industrial social paradigm models or they face immanent social and psychological collapse and disintegration. When our world view collapses or no longer has any true meaning then the social system disintegrates before our very eyes.

But will our scientists and cultural leaders make the needed revolutionary leaps into future scientific and socio-cultural paradigm shifts? Probably not, because they will not change or can not change! They cannot leave life-times of merit and applaud for their scientific endeavors. Additionally we must understand that socio-cultural changes must come from within the hearts and minds of the members of society. It cannot be imposed entirely from above unless its social substance already exists within the consciousness of the people.

Yes this insidious danger of self-destruction lurks on the sidelines of social life as the structure of the scientific world view collapses. It leaves the scientific intelligentsia with crumbs in their hands and half truths on their lips and despair and despondency in their hearts.

It is an end of an age and they cry out in bewilderment and weep bitter tears over the corpse of the old world view. What will take its place? No one knows and those who have a hint of the new way to go are pariahs in the scientific community for they represented a course none are willing to follow. Is there no hope for America? Surely our scientific leaders can save the day and rescue us from our self-destructive nature. Today, however we find that even the sacrosanct authorities of the 20th century, science and its technology, lie naked and prostrate-prostituted to covert Machiavellian death powers. Indeed a pessimistic social critic could cogently argue that science and its technologies have already destroyed the ethical basis of civilization. [8] It can also be argued that our generation and its scientists have been captured by a death force called the Genocide Phenomenon which has recruited our scientists as members of an elite death cadre. Archibald MacLeish has even put forth the thesis that after Hiroshima the loyalty of science was to its own truth and its new creed is the law of the possible-regardless of anything. [9] Since Hiroshima, scientific technical expediency is often a covert arm of nationalistic industrial-military complexes and one-worlders who wink with tacit collusion at military adventurism-with the results that veiled doctrines of manifest destiny daily feed the armed conflicts of our troubled times. Contemporary world events, with its faceless genocidal slaughter and mindless violence, have caused humanity to become death automatons who accept conflicts and genocidal wars as standard accepted practices. But now such facts serve only as beacons of death for emerging ideas concerning new world orders.

The present era cannot overcome the social and psychological crisis caused by false subjectivism and a personality system dominated by a vitalistic-egoism unless a dynamic theory about the nature of man and his relationship to the universe is created. This book will present new models—and new hypotheses, concerned with helping the species understand the nature of culture and consciousness and present new psychological model of humanity which will allow us to understand ourselves better and give us a choice to transform ourselves into a higher and more noble state than we exist in at present. Transintegral psychology, the fruit of an Integral or Transpersonal psychology developed from concepts of Psychology East-West presents several theoretical models to explain the human condition, reconciling and integrating the concepts of mind, culture and personality. For example, the psychocultural evolutionary theory discusses the diachronic evolutionary process and postulates that the "evolution of consciousness is the central nature of terrestrial existence." [10] The Psychocognitive culture continuum theory defines the synchronic relationship between consciousness and culture. It is through changes in the Aurobindonian transpersonality model that evolutionary changes occur in the species and evolution takes place within the psychocultural process.

It is only through new biological-social transpersonal models based on scientific concepts that humanity will be able to transform their lives and cultures into dynamic modes of humane living.

If such a concept of humanity is not accepted and socially implemented soon humanity may perish as a world-wide species. But there is also the possibility that if a holistic paradigm is not soon developed the present socio-ideological structure may collapse without having been replaced with a more than adequate mode. This new theory must be an appropriate and authentic reflection of man's natural potential in the 20th century. It must integrate and internalize the latest research findings in the various fields of science. It must address itself to the challenge of the present age.

The new paradigm concept must include dynamic new theories about economics, ecology, physics, the nature of the human species, and contain new scientific theories which can revitalize all the sciences and give us dynamic clues concerning life itself as well a creating a new transpersonal science of mankind.

RAPID CULTURE CHANGE-CAUSAL FACTOR TWO

Hypothesis 2. The second causal reason for the Genocide Phenomenon's emergence into modern life are the facts of rapid culture changes of social norms and family structures, massive industrial changes and developments, and drastic changes within the social organization and institutions.

THE CAUSES OF THE WORLD CRISIS

What are the causes of this world crisis? The human species is the basic cause of world turmoil so ultimately you must study human nature to understand rapid culture change since there is always an interconnective linkage between man, culture and nature. Transintegral psychology says that the ultimate causal agent of the world crisis can be found by examining human nature. To understand human nature we must investigate the emergent quality of mental evolution and the ever changing psychocultural systems which the human race lives within. This study puts forth the concept that man, culture and consciousness are united together into a psychocognitve continuum of interacting movement. This is a process in which man cannot act without producing movement in the natural world or in the cultural realm or within the personality of man. This interaction goes on within the spectrum of animal existence, culture and the environmental womb of nature. All combine in the drama of the emergent evolution of consciousness. To understand how this Psychocognitive cultural continuum works we must examine the Titan T-Psi hypothesis which postulates a causal linkage, called by Transintegral Psychology the Cognitive-transcultural synthesis that exists between man's personality and his psychocultural reality. The global tensions caused by the emergent evolution of consciousness, the psychological dysfunction and false subjectivism and lack of a viable 20th century theory of man are all connected together with the Psychocognitive process. Additionally we must study the disharmonies of man's multidimensional personality systems. and how they affect the conscious-unconscious cultural process.

   If we do not understand how this mind-culture process operates then we cannot create a useful and viable theory for man in the 20th century. We must know how the human animal conceptually interacts within the womb of culture yet maintains his freedom of self-actuality and self-transcendence. The mechanism must be investigated that allows the inner cognitive aspect of man to create cultural phenomena yet be captured by this creation and to be molded and enslaved by the ideals of the social system. Just how does the personality-dynamics operate on the inner and outer states of consciousness and project it self on the social scene which becomes perverted by the death generation? Answers to these question will be addressed as you read about the Genocide Phenomenon.

Only secondarily will we find our answers in the study of the socio-cultural causes of the world crisis. But answers to these studies will allow us to develop a partial solution by creating a new and dynamic paradigm or species theory for the human race. It is only through such a theory that we can understand ourselves and stop the secondary causal agents of rapid social change that is pushing mankind to a crucial juncture of the historical process. Throughout the world we presently find social chaos and rapid culture changes are causing massive social upheavals. The world's socio-cultural system is being gradually pushed out of equilibrium by biotic and climatic forces, war and conquest, epidemic disease, acculturation, and social subordination. [11] We now exist in a post-industrial age which has not yet developed new and dynamic values and social techniques to support the exigencies of the age. The industrial-Lockean world view is collapsing on the social, scientific and psychological fronts as American National Character changes.. Additionally social and psychological chaos has gripped the social masses as massive cultural changes alters their economic, social, and emotional world views while some nation states and cultures have become extinct.

It is said in the annals of time that a nation has a time of birth, childhood, adolescence, maturity, old age and then death. American culture is at the tail end of the death sequence. It has been found wanting and is being judged by its own people and guilty is the verdict and the death sentence has been given. The present times are merely the lengthy appeal process and it is unknown yet when the final death blow will fall.

We are all walking in the dream time of denial and our consciousness is one of forgetfulness and disbelief and we are bewildered by life itself and none may hold our hands for comfort because we are the death generation and only death can embrace death.

Today's global crisis is a 21th century phenomenon. The human race, additionally lives in an age that has an inadequate world view. It is an age of doubt, existential anxiety and loss of faith in man, God and human progress. This cynical era refuses to believe in anything except corruption, sex, food, money, comfort and pleasure and that the world will eventually become worse since no hope exists for the future. [12]

Additionally, worldwide ecological unbalance, ozone depletion, toxic pollution, political and economic uncertainty, along with the destruction of nation states with its accompanying resurgence of organized genocide and ethnic hostilities perpetrated, by the Death Generation, demonstrates that we are in the midst of an extinction peril so grave that the fate of the human species is held in the balance.

Now nature herself, seemingly joining degenerate humanity death wish, is on an rampage with her uncertain weather patterns accompanied by massive famine, ozone depletion which may be may cause massive mutations to occur worldwide, and unusual diseases. Additionally third world Nuclear proliferation seemingly is leading the human species toward an apocalyptic end to 20th century humanity as human hope is buried within the pit of our stomach as suicidal humanity bows down to its wish to become instinct!

The industrial-technological era presents no palliatives-no technological solutions to the dilemma of man in the 20th century. No, ultimate technological solution exists to save mankind from his own self-righteous folly. On the contrary, mankind seems to be fated to see a continuation of our present technological mentality that will continue to control and run away with us-while corrupting whatever slim ethical and moral character we have salvaged from modern technocracy machine-age expediency.

The results of such technological expediency are now causing a contemporary resurgence of death generation barbarism and a return to the mentality and morality of the dark ages.

Our progressive technological sophistication instead of uplifting us to the heights of humane social living and cooperative social endeavors has only allowed portions of mankind to enslave and commit genocide and culturecide on a mass world scale, ostensible in the name of ethnic cleansing and of the moral upliftment of the third-world peoples but in actuality for political and economic aggrandizement of certain nation states. Indications now are that reconstitute DNA genetic engineering and electronic surveillance technology will further enslave the masses of the world so that finally the darkest hells of the most vivid imagination will not be able to compare to man's future destiny.

Future historians, if any survive the seemingly imminent self-genocide wars, will remark, hopefully, that the 20th century was the tail-end of that barbaric period labeled the medieval dark ages and more than likely they will agree with Nobel prize winner in literature, Herman Hesse that today's humanity" . . . belongs to those whose fate it is to live the whole riddle of human destiny heightened to the pitch of a personal torture, a personal Hell." [13]

The death generation occupy all stations of life and face us daily either as smiling mailmen with death on their minds or as mad serial killers, smiling politicians or elite death scientists whose aura of holy than thou overwhelms and infiltrates our entire modern existence. But often the death fiends are our trusted and friendly pedophiles priests or the cordial corporate presidents or our sacred children who randomly slaughter us in drive by shootings in the name of gang death politics.

We are the last generation who shall speak of love of liberty and truth and justice and those who come after us will point to us as the deluded ones who are the source of madness from the past and they shall say that our only redeeming value is that soon we shall all die and that our madness will finally perish off the face of the earth and they shall rejoice in this thought!

Time is not on the side of America. The vicissitudes of the historical process have called our people and we have rejected the message of hope and justice and love of life itself and we have judged ourselves and our neck is now in the noose and little separates us from our impending death as a people and a culture except that the rope may break or that the calvary shall rescue us or that a timely upsurge of public remorse may start a new and dynamic cultural revival fire that shall inflame the nation so that it may become itself once again by rejecting the death generation's agenda for them.

Are we up to it? Only time will tell if America will rise up from the ashes as a phoenix bird and become what it purports to be or can the corrosive systems of America's death pangs be altered? Can America emerge into a new 21st century with hope? Will Americans have a courageous spirit of knowing the truth about themselves while at the same time possibly transcend the present despair of death living?

America is now living in the death pangs of its great culture. This is a fact of modern living; this is the truth of the hour; this is the future now impinging on the present!

When did it all begin? Well, some social critics say that the social culture began slowly dying when the extended family collapsed with the death of the American agrarian society. The final death blow came with the disintegration of the nuclear family. This was accompanied by the export of jobs and technology overseas and the lowering of workers wages at home as America's industrial base collapses even as massive immigration into the country was allowed to continue!

The back of the working man becomes broke when it is discovered his labor cannot compete with the foreign twenty cent an hour labor forces; then the great American middle class falls and collapses into the lower underclasses, and culture death is on the wings of time.

Death is on the wings of time and no man truly stops the inevitable. No nation realistically stands up to its destiny while its foundations lay rotting on the exigencies of the genocide phenomenon as their people lay on the sands of ignorance, indolence and moral depravity. No nation can withstand its own corruption; it own secret flow of truth!

SUBJECTIVE ERA-CAUSAL FACTOR THREE

Hypothesis 3. The rationalistic-individualistic age of the past several centuries is coming to an end and a subjective era of individual and social subjectivism is emerging, as the third causal factor for the emergence of the Genocide Phenomenon. This is indicated by the trends in art, poetry, political and economic changes taking place on a wide world scale. This subjectivism, however has temporarily been side tracked by a false subjectivism, a Genocide Phenomenon, that has been captured by the vitalistic life surge of the covert primordial fear-anxiety syndrome which embraces unregenerated humanity– an extinction peril of primordial proportions which is causing the world wide tension, wars and Nuclear confrontation crisis. Man's Unregenerated vital-emotional forces, linked up with technological industrialism, has given vital life to this subjective aberration of human nature. This false vital subjectivism, allied with gross materialism and technological innovation, as causal agents of vast sociocultural change, has caused a malfunctioning–a psychological dysfunctioning within the human personality system as a modern death generation emerges into modern society. The proper balance between the outer objective consciousness and the inner psyche and the dimensional-social personality systems no longer exists and it is not functioning properly. As a result a deep anxiety, a primordial fear-anxiety syndrome has developed within the human race–a crisis of self-esteem and a lack of a proper individual and social identity consciousness has occurred in the species Homo sapiens. Humanity cannot shake off the grip of this false subjectivism and its insistent demands yet it finds no satisfaction in fulfilling its concepts. [14]

PSYCHOLOGICAL DYSFUNCTIONING-
CAUSAL FACTOR FOUR

Hypothesis 4. A psychological dysfunctioning of the human race is the fourth causal factor in the present world crisis. The proper balance between the outer objective consciousness and the inner psyche and the dimensional personality systems no longer exists and it is not functioning properly. As a result a deep species anxiety develops within the human race–a crisis of self-esteem and a lack of a proper individual and social identity consciousness occurs in the species Homo sapiens.

Symbolically and existentially individual man and women are thrust into a time of disquiet because their outer natures are so out of tune with their inner essence that social violence and an inner quiet desperation yield up such a sense of despair that life holds no meaning and death no allure! It is a time when mankind cries out in bewilderment at his lack of authentic living and he wonders what curse is he born under.

It is a time when truth dies and morality becomes dead words of poetry which one smells occasionally on the way toward debauchery and degradation. These are activities that one calls recreation and the revival of the spirit. For what is spirit now but the dead soul that clings to life while reciting its liturgy of death. Yet the drum rolls on and the music plays and mankind attends its own funeral unknown to itself.

Additionally because the 20th century stresses the almost exclusive concentration on man's outer objective mind an intensification of egoistic tendencies and psychic disharmonies develops in the mass of the world's populace. One of the reason is that when you are conditioned to believe in a certain way and the social norms and realities change you enter into culture shock! If certain core values change such as the concept of rugged individualism and its autonomous sense of self reliance, which have traditionally allowed Americans to operate as an independent person, changes substantially, and society no longer values this concept, the people who personify traditional values are now deviant persons! Society now punishes those individuals for displaying autonomous behavior in school, work and play. All of our heros of rugged individualism now are punished and often personality dysfunction occurs, individually and collectively among great numbers of the populace. Eventually new personality concepts of natural character may develop but in the meantime whole populations of individuals will exist in anguish and turmoil. They no longer fit into the world of technocracy and our death master's ideal of what a worker-drone's personality ought to be like.

This psychological dysfunctioning of the personality has allowed the vital-emotional consciousness, dominated by its desires and passions to enslave the mind and uses mental ideals to become servants and instruments to this era's false vital subjectism and its primordial fear-anxiety syndrome. This enslavement is causing a deep seated sense of frustration and an existential void in man's being. Humanity cannot shake off the grip of this false subjectivism and its insistent demands yet it finds no satisfaction in fulfilling its concepts.[15] In its pathological form this existential void becomes a species death wish.

The massive cutting down of the world's rain forest demonstrates our species death wish in graphic form. Daily we cut or burn down rain forests the size of the state of Connecticut; forests which provide the world's oxygen supply and provide a natural biological arena for finding of new drugs and medicines for ourselves. This act of self-pain and self destructiveness demonstrates that within the species consciousness of humanity resides a suicidal death wish which the human species embraces with enthusiasm as it manifests as a world-wide Genoçidal Phenomenon. Additionally the ozone depletion, partly the responsibility of modern industrial usages of certain chemicals, will in the near future decide the fate if not the survival of the species Homo sapiens.

PRIMORDIAL FEAR-ANXIETY SYNDROME-CAUSAL FACTOR FIVE

Hypothesis 5. This study postulates that man, culture and consciousness are united together into a continuum of interacting movement. This is a process in which man cannot act without producing movement in the natural world or in the cultural realm or within the personality of man. This interaction goes on within the spectrum of animal existence, culture and the environmental womb of nature. All combine together in the drama of the emergent evolution of consciousness. The psychosocial nature of consciousness has beneath the surface of its interacting a primordial fear-anxiety syndrome that activates within normal social life but rapidly accelerates when vast changes occur with in the socio-cultural arena.

Within American culture this process of rapid culture change allied with soulless technology is now destroying and altering much of what we hold dear in our social orders. It has brought into existence a overt-covert biological-psychological force called forth from deep within the biological nature of the species; this is the primordial fear-anxiety syndrome which supports and feeds the fears of self alienation and destructive feelings of imminent doom which permeates modern society beneath its sensate social institutions and value structures. Lewis Mumford speaking to this situations says:

> People whose course of life has reached a crisis must confront their collective past as fully as a neurotic patient must unbury his personal life: long-forgotten traumas in history may have a disastrous effect upon millions who remain unaware of them. [16]

One of the overt manifestations of this causal primordial fear-anxiety is the spectacle of the Genocide Phenomenon, with it mass killings and annihilations of cultures and languages, etc., which has appeared midst modern 20th century humanity as an overt and covert death wish force of cultural action! It has emerged slowly with the slowly dying industrial age as this era's individual-istic-rationalistic age is captured by a false social trend.

Because of this mass culture change—a vast transitional phase in the history of social evolution, modern man's self-image is tar-nishing, his psychosocial goals diminishing, his life-force erod-ing—in short existential being seemingly for modern man has per-ished. We live today In an age of unprecedented social and tech-nological progress. Man's identity and continuity with existence are broken—having been replaced by intermittent fits of psycho-social anxiety and despair. Social critic and psychoanalyst Erick Fromm says in this regard that:

> The common suffering is the alienation from oneself, from one's fellow man, and from nature; the awareness that life runs out of one's hand like sand, and that one will die without having lived; that one lives in the midst of plenty and yet is joyless. [17]

Man of the 20th century no longer has the steady confidence that made up his yesterdays. Instead mass alienation from himself, his social orders and the progressive evolutionary process is his almost daily lot. Alienated man drifts in a meaningless world over which he has little control. Twentieth century thinkers have aptly described the situational aspects of modern existence as a sense of loss and disenchantment with the glamor of materialism and technology while experiencing a horror of "the death of God."[18]

EVOLUTION OF CONSCIOUSNESS
CAUSAL FACTOR SIX

Hypothesis 6. The fifth causal factor is the biological human evo-lutionary process of consciousness which is constantly occurring within the nature of human consciousness. It is the biological emergent evolution of human consciousness which has presently reached a crisis stage and is causing a tension of mental and emotional anxiety as infrarational man seemingly evolves into a higher stage of rational consciousness.

This book thus addresses itself to the study of this process by presenting several hypotheses of a heuristic nature from the discipline of Transintegral Psychology and transpersonal anthropology These hypotheses explore the emergent evolution of consciousness in human societies as a product of human history. One hypothesis is the Psychocultural model of human psychological evolution as an emergent quality of mind through dimensional spacetime; that is, it presents a diachronic evolutionary view of the psychological evolution of culture and consciousness. Another hypothesis presented is Campbell's Transpersonal Psychocognitive culture Continuum theory that postulates the synchronic relationship between culture and consciousness. The functional human biological energy system that stands behind the evolution of humanity's consciousness is the Kundalini hypothesis which we will discuss in one of the following chapters. The focal point to all these hypotheses is the concept of human evolution as a historic occurrence and as a process through which humanity transcends itself. The evidence is not all in concerning the actualities of this process. Some scientists using a Darwinian approach rest on the natural selection process of unregulated biological-evolution, organically and mentally. Other scientist such as Wallace, the co-discoverer of the evolutionary theory with Darwin feel God is the author of evolution as does Campbell. Sri Aurobindo and the paleontologist–priest, Teilhard de Chardin, also affirm the divine force behind the evolutionary process.

Transintegral Psychology speculates that mankind stands today at the crossroads of history–at a crucial juncture within the historical process. A new order of transpersonal reality–a psychomental biological evolution of consciousness is emerging through the evolutionary process. The exigency of this mental and sociocultural process has caused a mental and emotional anxiety tension to appear within the species as rational man evolves into a higher state of consciousness. The Frenchman Satprem states that"

Everywhere about us we see this proselytizingl shattering of all the old forms: our borders, our churches, our laws, our morals are collapsing on all sides. They are not collapsing because we are bad, immoral, irreligious, or because we are not sufficiently rational, scientific or human, but because we have come to the end of the human! To the end of the old mechanism—for we are on our way to something else. The world is not going through a moral crisis but through an evolutionary crisis. We are not going towards a better world—nor, for that matter, towards a worse one—we are in the midst of a MUTATION to a radically different world, as different as the human world was from the ape world of the Tertiary Era. We are entering a new era, a supramental Quandary. [19]

Campbell as an transpersonal evolutionist conceives that the human species is a self-transcending force that has the potential to become demi-god like in statue and being. He conceives that the species Homo sapien has evolved organically, culturally and in conscious self-awareness of itself and the universe. Campbell stresses that man is an unfinished evolutionary creature who is incomplete and full of contradictions yet is a species who is actively searching for his optimal development. [20] The next step in the evolutionary process is that mankind must actively participate consciously in the evolutionary process. It will not occur automatically but only as an pro-active evolutionary force acting in unisons with universal destiny. If mankind cannot actively participate in its own evolutionary process then the species Homo sapiens will perish from the face of the earth through its own death wish manifested as the Genocide phenomenon.

The human species is a creature of the universe and has the capacity to rise up as a transpersonal force along a wide spectrum of altered states of consciousness through unity with the universe. But to do this man individually and species wide must overcome and transform its human lower nature or the lower forces of creation allied with man's untransformed barbaric lower propensities will lead to mass destruction and possible species extinction. Campbell, is quite emphatic about mankind's propensity to wallow in his lower nature. He stresses a way must be found to balance each person's dysfunctional personality system. The psychological dysfunctioning of the human species and the evolutionary crisis are interconnected and the survival of the species and the emergence of the death generation are symptoms of the death throes of the species Homo sapiens.

Twentieth century man lives in an age of discontent, social crisis and cultural disintegration, but Campbell says these happenings are merely the outer symptoms of the inner thought patterns—the inner states of consciousness of the world populace.[21] The evolutionarily process is a continuous continuum. When the aspirations and psychosocial ideas of the world masses are discontented with present institutions and forms of societal organizations, then a great anxiety and mass alienation appear with a culture's ideological system. This discontent occurs because normal humanity is itself something abnormal in nature. [22] The evolution of consciousness has developed to the point that life and social systems can no longer be supported by humanity without a dynamic inner change of mind. [23]The felt need of the human race is an urge to make an ascension into a higher state of being. A vast self-actualization—a vast self-transcendence is taking place. According to researcher Aurobindo, at each crisis of human destiny humanity touches a point of tension, called by Campbell, the Psycho-Armageddon Factor, and either success occurs, or a collapse of defeat takes place or a repose of unprogressive quiescence becomes the result. [24] Within this historical process that mankind is presently facing is concealed the choice of man's destiny. A fantastic privilege and a promise lie within this evolutionary process. Dynamic self developments and immense self-exceeding can take place if man the abnormal can rise above the provisional order that passes for this normality. [25] The modern age of crisis is an era of promise for human growth on the species level because all human nature has within itself the power to exceed itself by conscious evolution.

All change has its dangers and great promises. When new structures are being build and old formations destroyed, and reformulated, a danger exists that no progress will emerge, or something undesirable may develop or loss by default may occur or oblivion becomes the answer. Mirra Alfassa says that mankind's very existence as a species will depend upon how it faces the present crisis. If humanity faces the problems and resolves them with courage it will rise to a new statue of supramental superman. If Mankind fails to face this evolutionary-existential problem because of his social and psychological blindness or because of his shortsightedness of the problem or lack of courage the species may be annihilated from the face of the earth. [26]

Mankind now holds human destiny in its hands. Species extinction or the emergence into a new species consciousness awaits the decision by the "race." Humanity now sits at the edge of a new age or at the annihilation of the old. The final leap is now being marked by an acute tension and crisis created by the old established forces resisting and the new suprarational consciousness that needs to be born.

We are now within the dynamics of this process. Mankind must rise to the challenge by consciously emerging into the tide of evolutionary history. If the human race does not have the will or capacity to consciously change its nature, then the dynamics of this moment will be aborted. The death barbarism of the human race may allow the Genocide Phenomenon's exigencies of international terrorism to reign nuclear destruction upon the planet or enslave the populous as serfs to the new world order of Masters and slaves.

Humanity, however, has within itself an innate possibility to transcend itself–the result of a mutation several millions of years ago, which has coded mankind to have the capacity to consciously expand the consciousness of the species. This latent biological potential is man's birthright and humanity today, according to the Psychocultural evolutionary theory, must consciously transcend its lower nature and realize a progressive conscious emergence into higher and vaster altered states of consciousness–into a new supramental species consciousness.

OVERT DEATH GENERATION AND THE FATAL NEANDERTHAL FLAW

Hypothesis 7. The most important causal reason for the emergence of the Genocide Phenomenon is the inherent fatal flaw within some members of the species called the Neanderthal flaw. Individuals who have this fatal flaw often become death masters or become members of the death generation people. They exist in the lower reaches of human infrarational consciousness and have impulsive urges to enslave their fellow mankind, thus enters the death generation. Individuals who have this Neanderthal flaw exist in all stations of life, social classes and cultures. They have an excessive compulsive need to control other people and to set up totalitarian dictatorships, government bureaucracies and corporate structures if the opportunities presents itself. They are the insidious force that threatens America's destiny and the freedom of every American. and the very existence of a free world. They are the objective death generation which will bring a thousand plus year reign of darkness upon us which may result in the extinction of the species Homo sapiens. They are the evil people who in their narcissism believe that nothing is wrong with them and that they are psychologically perfect and that destiny has chosen them to recreate the world in their image. [27]

The roar of these human barbarians is the battle cry of 20th century. Unregenerated primordial man has again risen from out of the ashes of a dying rational era and the earth quakes with his deeds. Mankind is dying by the millions on their spears of barbarous war time expediency and contemporary Ethnic Cleansing!

Man the 'wise," the hominid spectacle of the age is wilting, shrinking from his potential glory–failing his evolutionary task to transcend his lower nature and dynamically enter into a higher evolutionary process because of this Neanderthal flaw. But it is a flaw that most of humanity has outgrown through the evolutionary process; yet a strong minority, existing in the millions, yet who are numerically small worldwide are emerging in today's world.. They are dynamically strong with the will to power which is psychologically stuck at this excessive compulsive power control point. They need and want political, economic, and social power. They need to subordinate others to their will and they are ruthless and determined and a-moral in their power behavior. They will not stop until success is won or they die in the process. They are the fanatics that will either enslave us or cause the extinction of the species. Success or death is their motto and they will not stop until America and the world submits to their new order of things. They are the death masters and they will increase in number the death generation until all of us succumbs to their culture of death.

WHO ARE THESE PEOPLE?

The perennial battle of the centuries has been fought with these Neanderthal flawed people. They are often charming and subtle and embrace you with their wit and language. They are often the cultural innovators who lead you down that proverbial path into the rose garden of despair and enslavement. Yes, they are your smiling pedophile priest and may even be the leader of your neighborhood patriotic organizations. They exist in every station of life and professions and they want you to be their followers and to fawn over them and to emulate them and to allow yourselves to be enslaved by them, even as you embrace them in the joy of suddenly finding a long lost friend.

Is it easy to spot them? No it isn't. Oh, you can spot the cruder ones-the Bible thumping demagogues who intellectually exist only two steps above the reasoning of the corner imbecile and who are themselves in danger of failing kindergarten class if they had any true education. Yes you can spot the local skinehead because of his distinctive markings and observe the local used car salesman in his daily rounds of selling fine merchandise. But can you spot the handsome face of fame and fortune as it quietly leads you down that primrose path which seduces you into corruption; or recognize your spiritual leader for what he is as he gently pats you on the back; or can you see clearly recognize your holy than thou political death leader whose backbone is money and his politics is corruption. Oh, his words of morality are honey and truth as he leads you, ever so gently into his web of deceit, even as he places the shackles of slavery around your neck. Thus, every day a death leader leads you into his den if inequity, even as you adoringly thank God quietly for his very presence!

Yes, you can only recognize them with difficulty by how they overtly act, because these people will occupy both sides of an argument, both side of a conflict, both side of morality and depredation. Historically hundreds of thousands of early Christians died for their truth yet their descendents carried out the most horrible carnage of slaughter-house inquisition genocide upon humanity in the name of that very truth. One observes a St. Francis of Assi as living at the height of transpersonal truth and Pope Borgia who observes "God has give us the Papacy, Let us enjoy it" as he engages in incestuous sexual relations with his daughter and son and engages in poisonous murderous carnage at his will. Historically the Christian church burns St. Joan of Arc yet in the same breath makes her a saint. Observe an Emperor Constantine who can murder relatives and Christians with one hand, then embrace them with another as he create his new Catholic Church, even as he is assassinating and slaughtering the original Christian hierarchy and their sacred writings so that he will have his way with Christian truth. [28]

Duplicity is their original name and they will put your neck into the harness of corporate and world harmony and you will yield to them or break. America cry because your freedoms are at stake and your soul is about to be put in bondage and your very sense of being free and dynamic will be taken away from you and no one will stand up for you because you will have joined the death generation.

Additionally, note that genocide is upon the winds of time presently and no nation, no culture has the exclusive franchise on the death generation because the death generation is manifesting throughout the world!

Some critics of world events are questioning why and how modern man has arrived at such a state of world affairs. Many are speculating about the survival of the species and questioning how to persuade the human race to acquiesce in its own survival. [29] Modern social critics are now beginning to feel that the answer may lie in a reexamination of the concept of human nature. Some of these critics are taking a new look at man's rational abilities and wondering why supposedly reasonable humanities behave so unreasonably. They ask why recurrent historical phenomenon seems to have no reasonable causes. [30] Konrad Lorenz even speculates that for every "gift" that man has achieved, such as the faculties of conceptual thought and verbal speech, that man seems to have paid for them with a dangerous evil as the direct consequence of each blessing. [31]

Other critics speculate that the species may have some un-known mental or psychological flaw hidden within itself or some inherent self-destruct mechanism-almost an unconscious racial death wish. These critics speak of man's "carnivorous mentality," of his being subject to phylogenetically adapted instinctive be-havioral roles, or they categorize man as existing in a state of "schizo-physiology," that is being unable to coordinate between phylogenetically old areas of the brain and the neocortex areas thus causing human neurotic and psychotic disorders in the race. Some people sidestep the causes and just say that war and aggres-sive behaviors are natural to the breed. Death and violence to them are the biological facts of life and if the human barbarian roars, so what. Let him do what he is able to do because he is a member of the death generation. Let him fulfill his destiny; let

him be what he naturally is, a biologically coded killer who has
destiny by the tail and might and death justice on his side.

Concepts such as these reflect an almost sinister acceptance
of unscientific concepts-the idea of the innate depravity of humanity, the acceptance that mankind is an innate-genetically coded
killer and that there exists no hope for the race-so let us be merry
until the movement of oblivion arrives! It is said that:

> Nothing seems able to disturb the immobility of things
> and all that is active outside our own selves is a sort of
> welter of dark and sombre confusion form which noth-
> ing formed or luminous can emerge. It is a singular con-
> dition of the world, the very definition of chaos with the
> superficial form of the old world resting apparently in-
> tact on the surface. But a chaos of long disintegration or
> of some early new birth? It is the thing that is being fought
> out from day to day, but as yet without any approach to
> a decision. [32]

PSYCHOLOGY OF EVIL

Is there a psychology of evil that lies just beneath the surface of the
human consciousness? Psychiatrist M. Scott Peck feels that there is
genuine evil loose in the world today. It manifests individually
and within groups of people ; yet its origin, he says, lies within
human pathology and its candidates have mental illness. Evil, therefore, for Dr. Peck is a specific form of mental illness; yet he also
observes that these evil persons are quite common and appear quite
ordinary to the superficial observer in daily life. [33] He counsels us
also that evil is also that force which kills the human spirit without
actually destroying the physical body. [34]

Erik Fromm also speaks of a malignant narcissism which infects
the human race; a force of evil which develops through a long developmental process of choices. This force manifests within evil persons

as a willfulness strength which has remarkable power which these people use to control others. Fromm broadens the definition of necrophilia to include the idea of individuals and organized groups who want to control other people and make them dependent on themselves and to discourage their capacity to think for themselves in an unpredictable world. The goal of the people, whether they are neonazi's or death cadre members or a corporate technocracy manager, is to control other people and make them into obedient automatons and ultimately to make them card-carrying members and victims of an emasculated death generation and thus rob them of their humanity. [35] But in America this death hypnosis is done by cybernetic capitalism and its huge centralized enterprises to provide bread and amusements as they psychologically manipulate the death generation victims through human engineering. The subtlety of this approach uses very malleable and easily influenced people who do not fear authority. It is fired by corporate death masters whose view of reality is based on unlimited consumption and unlimited control of nature; godlike in statue, these death masters know that anything in human nature can be controlled. No longer does independence, private initiative and a person's right to be the captain of his own ship and individual destiny mean anything. [36]

Transpersonal science addresses the question of evil and man's inhumanity to man from an evolutionary perspective. The evil person individually and the Nazi SS mass murders are infrarational men who on the evolutionary scale are morally just above the animal stage of evolvement. They may be brilliant intellectually, as some of our atomic scientists have demonstrated, but they are children of the human race who have never existentially developed their species' moral, ethical, and religious natures. They represent a species position, called the Neanderthal Flaw that most of humanity have partially grown out of and they must be stopped or the human species will become rapidly extinct within the normal life time of most readers of this book.

Members of the overt death generation are infrarational people who have the fatal Neanderthal excessive compulsive control flaw which guides their social and psychological behavioral craving for social control over people and through such actions plunges our social age into the dark ages once again. But the death generation also comprises the victims who have succumbed to its paralyzing and hypnotic influences which dominates them, destroys their freedom of social and intellectual expression and often their economic livelihood. But worst of all, it destroys their sense of self worth by alienating them from themselves, society, nature and the self transcending force of the human spirit. And ultimately it will enslave them and make them servants of a totalitarian technocracy social system which will consist of a new world order that will embrace the planet.

In the mean time the human slaughter goes on, the genocide, the mass ethnocide, the extermination of millions of human beings to war time expediency, the dissolution of countless nations, while mankind sleeps in the oblivion of its helplessness.

Most social critics, however, share the conviction that we must understand human nature while sharing together the disillusionment at the turn of world-events and at the death of the concept of human progress. They have been forced to come to grips with such questions as "Is man a doomed species?" They question whether all of man's higher aspirations are insignificant in the light of the emergence of the death generation? Is his struggle from up out of the primordial dimness of his animal past and all of his great accomplishments mean nothing? Is man an irrational instinctive killer? Does he have as part of his nature a refined but thinly veiled aggression behavior complex?"

If mankind's nature is coded for aggression can the human race really save itself or are the ever increasing wars and killings an indication that man really is an instinctive death killer-a killer who cannot help himself? Is man a programmed aggressive creature who instinctively is a veiled predator-striking out at the only prey worthy of his abilities-Homo sapiens man, a member of his own species. If man is instinctively a killer and the human race cannot evolve out of this condition, the future of the species is very dim and all hope has vanished for mankind.

The repercussion of this wilting of human hope-the agony of the dying race finds expression today in the search for reasons out of this 20th century dilemma. And in the hope that solutions can emerge-an almost death-grip reach for the rope to throw to the species facing self-extinction! Possibly that rope is the fact that "the end of a stage of evolution is usually marked by a powerful recrudescence of all that has to go out of that evolution." [37] In the meantime the Genocide Phenomenon continues and the human race is held in it grip forcefully.

COLLAPSE OF AMERICA

It is rather obvious that the immanent collapse of the American social order is happening before our very eyes on the economic, social, political, religious, industrial, cultural and personal levels.

The chief cutting edge is the death generation's ascendancy to political and economic power as they preside over the destruction of those they consider inferior to themselves and which they consider are rightly sacrificial victims to the new world order. If they succeed the world will plunge into a very dark middle ages of barbarism and terror that will make Attila the Huns ascendancy to power seem as if he were a boy scout.

It is a fact that America's victims of the death generation are the harbingers of the message of doom for their people and way of life. Perhaps anthropologist, Jules Henry, is correct when he says that " . . . our culture is an avalanche of obsolescence hurling itself in the Sea of Nonexistence". [38] Is American society and culture about to committee suicide? Have the death blows of culturecide gone so deep that we must begin to write America's obituary?

SOCIAL DEATH OF AMERICA

It is a fact that what does not exist on the conscious and unconscious level psychologically within a culture or person cannot manifest as overt social actions! The psychological health of a culture fails when the primordial fear-anxiety syndrome as an emotional and psychological illness strikes from within and manifests as overt outbreaks within the social fabric.

When a plaque of sickness attacks a people their young and old die first but when a culture dies from within from its own hands it is a sign of cultural and moral decay of the worst kind. But as with cases of physical illness the social illness first appears overtly in the lives of the old and young as a symptoms for all of us to see. But if the psychological core is rotten then the malady will be so insidious that none shall perceive it until they themselves have caught the malady of death and become part of the death generation.

When the genocide phenomenon death winds blow a fatal malady called the extinction peril occurs then culturecide strikes a nation from within, the end is in sight for that culture. Culture death is on the wings of time and its prey is America as this source of destruction eats away at the vitals of the people of that doomed culture and it is called a reign of death or the Genocide Phenomenon.

It is easy to say that a reformed social order is what we need. It's easy to stand up for morals and integrity and holler and scream for justice. But it is difficult to achieve these ends when the corruption of the day carries a teenagers name and a parents disgrace and we find that human integrity is meaningless. It is difficult to call for honor when there is none. And it is even harder to rise into the flame of truth where only falsehood and doubt exist while death is facing us daily and species extinction is our future. Yes my friends, the genocide phenomenon lies before us and we have it by the tail and we cannot let it go; and our curse is that this generation will bear the burden of finding the solution to evil and death, life and the redemption of our very inner self's. We can't shirk this duty because eternity has us by our right hand and Armageddon by the left hand. Our feet are stuck in the sands of time while our breath is hot with pain and our consciousness sunk deep into despair and all of us are caught in the end times as our souls swirl within the whirlwind flames of our discontent as we reap our destiny as a person and a nation.

REIGN OF DEATH .

The death essence of our nation reveals itself subconsciously to our children as they mature and become Mama and Papa. The Nation's children are our reign of death which descends upon the multitude through the actions of their death children; the end is in sight America and no man can stop what he sees in himself and his children, especially when their children are mere imitations of the inner alienation and desperation of Mama and Papa!

We have but a moment left before our people dies to itself as our cultures perish from the face of the earth. It will be written on the pages of time that our people died a cowardly death of indulgences and plastic illusions as we perished from the face of the earth. Yes, Death accompanies us as we walk hand in hand with the cadre's of death, the cutting edge of the Genocide Phenomenon.

Yes death is upon the nation and crying and anguish and remorse only pushes us toward our inevitable end of cultural extinction and possible physical extinction as a nation and culture. The possibility also lies before us of the demise of the species Homo sapien on a world wide basis.

The question before us my friends, is there any hope for our nation, culture, and species?

My friends, there is always hope, and this book is written so that an exception will be made in our case and that a last minuet reprieve will save the day; and that we individually and as a nation shall walk into the sunset of life with our heads held high. Honor and integrity shall reign supreme as the safety of the race becomes secure in our hands.

But will that happen? Probably not, for how can you still the waves of the ocean at high tide? No, the damage has been done. All that can be done now is to analysis the situation and hope that a new wave of culture change will revitalize the nation, our culture and our integrity as a people.

If this does not happen, then, there is no hope and this book is but an obituary to another dead culture that emerged into existence, grew into childhood, then adolescence, plunged into maturity and then died a feeble and desperate death upon the pages of time! This book, if it survives the coming Wars of Terror, will be but another rare volume, somewhat in the line of a rare Greek or Egyptian book that miraculously survived the burning of the libraries at Alexandria, Egypt in the era before our own.

Let us not weep bitter tears but stand up and face the issue of the survival of the Human race! There is some time left, yet it flows so rapidly past us that I fear that no one can see it, let alone grasp that last thread of hope that lies before us this very day!

THE REST OF THE BOOK

We will examine the seven causal factor throughout the book but first we will examine the nature of the death generation and the death cadre's personality structures.

CHAPTER 2

THE DEATH GENERATION: THE EMERGENCE OF THE GENOCIDE PHENOMENON INTO AMERICAN SOCIETY

FUTURIST 22ND CENTURY COMMENTARY: The death of an age often comes slowly-almost imperceptibly, yet with certainty its roar and death cry precedes it; and woe to those who cannot understand or hear its approaching signs.

Historians tell us that 26 high civilizations preceded the modern age and that many ancient human species have perished from the face of the earth. Do you think that contemporary civilizations and mankind are the exception to the rule? Do you really think that the species Homo sapiens is superior to its ancestral forms or to other species of mankind that perished in antiquity or became extinct before our modern species emerged?

Man the tool maker, the thinker, the being who has conscious awareness of himself and a potentially bright future ahead of himself now has also the capacity to destroy himself and his world and is doing so in random abandonment of his rational sanity. Apparently humanity has not the morality or wisdom to transcend his lower primordial nature and find unity with the universe, society and himself! Twentieth century man has placed himself on the extinction list!

The beginning of the end times for America the beautiful commenced when an elite political force, allied with covert money interests, in the name of national security and morality, legally disarmed the average American citizen of his guns. Two hundred and seventy million private arms were melted down. Immediately the American people became serfs to covert powers they understood not!

It was at that point that America's cultural paradigm began collapsing. Agrarian truths no longer fitted the social situation and the collapsing truth of American Industrial life was exposed as unworkable myths that kept the underclasses in their place in the hope that they too might rise into another higher class level through hard work and merit. America no longer believed in itself As the social mobility class structure collapsed and millions of Americans fell socially downward, the new elite class stood arrogantly on the body of the large underclass that lay prostrate beneath their feet as the common man became obsolete.

With social obsolescence came the subtle and covert belief that a serious decrease in the general population was necessary, no absolutely necessary; thus, many mysterious diseases of the late 20th and 21st century began to take their toll and the world rolled onward while the world of mankind took one step backwards and ultimately the human species fell into obscurity and extinction! Man the wise voluntarily crawled into a dark culture of death with its repression and genocide and its covert use of human cloning.

Twentieth century breakthroughs on the biological front, with its covert development of human cloning and its use as a political, corporate and military weapon, only added to the death of American society. Its uses in the 21st century by covert forces are surely causal factors in the great wars of terror that followed.

Social scientist Campbell describes below the mode of thought of 20th century man before the wars of terror began. While he is known primarily as a psychologist and social critic we also find within his writings his concern for the future evolution of mankind. This undoubtedly reflects his 20+ years experience as a teacher of physical anthropology and his concerns for the future of humanity.

From a historic prospective please note that this is the first time Campbell states that the twentieth century is a reemergence of the dark ages. Previously he implies that the 20th century ought to be included under the middle or dark age's category. Below he addresses himself to the phenomenon of the death generation which preceded the wars of terror.

THE DEATH GENERATION PHENOMENON

The Death generation is a phenomenon of the 20th century and its members exist among all stations of life, within all social classes and among a variety of culture's world-wide. They all belong collectively to the culture of death and they are the harbingers of the death of America and ultimately to the world as we know it. When this death culture becomes dominate in the life of American society it will embrace the population into a sphere of death reality that will break the spirit and life force of the present culture of life.

Why is this so? It is because of the continuum of mind-consciousness and social-behavioral awareness is unitive force that exists within the sphere of consciousness-culture. It is a fact that man, culture and consciousness are united together into a continuum of interacting movement which is ever an unending process. Specifically this is a psychocognitive process in which man cannot act without producing movement in the natural world or in the cultural realm or within the personality of man. This unitive interaction goes on within the spectrum of human existence, culture and the environmental womb of nature. All combine together in the drama of life and when the theme of death consciousness and its culture of death becomes active it enters into the inner dimensions of man's consciousness and his culture.

We live within an era of American Cultural life in which the old puritanical concepts of being on the right side of God has perished with the death of God. And we know deep down that our cause is no longer just and that our motto "In God is our Trust", is now our epithet for destruction. Just as our traditional culture gives conditional love to our children and emphasize work and disallows pleasure all for the sake of developing goodness and integrity in the sight of God, so with the loss of puritan faith Americans now know they have taken a wrong turn as their life force ebbs and dies for all the world to see. We have entered into the culture of death because the puritan weakness within our culture's system has manifested throughout American life. We no longer believe in ourselves and grasp for our safety the primordially fear-anxiety syndrome as our safety net. Presently we are but pale shadows of our ancestor zeal for truth and justice and achievement through hard work and integrity. Our ancestors could conquer wilderness and build cities because they believed that they were right. And individually, as long as his gardens and farms flourished and the walls of his cities rose his zeal slackens not. Hardship will not faze him and even small setbacks only harden his resolve. Bank failures or a drought only tell him he must work harder; but against overwhelming defeats when he can't see the causal relationship between his moral relationships and his behavior, then he is helpless and goes down for the count.[1] And so collective America lies paralyzed in its own discontent as the genocide phenomenon pressed America the beautiful into a deep, dark culture of death which daily recruits the masses into its foul system of defeat and death.

Additionally an insidious aspect of this situation is that many card-carrying members of the death generation are honest people but also unconscious members of the death cadres, even while they consciously cry out for the salvation of America! But the fact is America that you must save yourselves first from yourselves. The death of America lies not only on the corrupt backs of our death masters but also on each and every person's shoulders and if you will not change for the better America you will write your own epithet as you sink deeper and deeper into the culture of death.

Observe yourself America in everyday life where one spouse has a voracious hunger for power and produces a warped dictatorial rule of one marriage partner over the other. Often a sadomasochic relationship develops in the marriage with its destructive effects on the submissive mate and children; even incestuous parent-childhood relationship seemingly are common within America's death culture. But what also happens daily in America is the pathetic submission of persons of superior humanity and intellect to efficient death governmental and corporate bureaucrats because of their passivity and fear to be their own person and to act as an American.

The death theme has so permeated our culture that one can daily observe a husband embarrassing his wife in front of their guests through the use of a joke, by using cutting and cynical witty remarks; or often a discontented wife insinuates that she is a superior sexpot yet how inadequate her mate is in bed. Meanwhile our children shout with glee as they shoot innocent children and old women down in the streets. They celebrate life by bestowing death on their sacrificial victims which kills America daily by immersing them into psychosocial despair as our death children rape, beat, kill, and maim Papa and Mama and they rejoice in those activities. So America you are separated by degrees only from your political and corporate death masters as you gradually become death generation members!

The culture of death is especially strong in the interplay of power and control, with its fear and submission activists of the Fear-anxiety syndrome. This interplay manifest whenever people are thrown together in marriage, business, social or professional situations, in civil service, the military or any where people are dependent upon each other. Business offices throughout the nation are places of intrigue and power conflicts. Power drives cause one man to plot against another or to ferment teapot revolutions to unseat another or even one's own boss, the symbol of a domineering mother or father of childhood. Daily the battle of the sexes occurs in business offices. Women often resort to verbal attacks on those in high places, sometimes using sex to get ahead; or because of the unfair barriers against them rise quickly by being as unscrupulous and uncaring as their male counterparts. When the women runs the office she may unconsciously represent a mother figure to those who compete for her favors. [2] The culture of death, thus, is everywhere and nowhere and yet all of us live within its foul breath daily.

When the subconscious aspects of the genocide Phenomenon becomes a foul dragons breath we find one generation turns against another. William Irwin Thompson put it cogently: " . . . Our advanced technologies of child rearing and police control seem to have brought us back to the mythic situation in which Cronus tries to devour his children and the children think if they castrate their father they will be free." [3]

The death generation is now manifesting throughout the world, covertly at high levels of corporate and governmental levels and overtly in the streets of America as the confused death generation youth kill and maim the average citizen with drive by shootings, bombings and home invasions. Often this death cadre are terrorists who strike at governmental and civil targets and speak through the blood which spills down the streets of their madness. Now America has internal terrorists who bomb federal buildings at random; seemingly as a type of civil war among death generation personnel. Additionally on the street level serial killers roam our streets killing at random overtly and at times covertly and no one is safe from these death squads because we are in the death pangs of the death of American Culture and our obituary is now being written.

THE EMERGENCE OF THE DEATH GENERATION

The emergence of the death generation in the early part of the 20th century signals the end of the industrial age and the commencement of the post industrial technocracy that is mechanizing society and controlling it by computers [4] which is presently attempting to embrace the entire world in various forms of new world orders and in particular is reorganizing America in its image.

As Zbigniew Brzezinski states it, "In the technotronic society the trend would seem to be towards the aggregation of the individual support of millions of uncoordinated citizens, easily within the reach of magnetic and attractive personalities effectively exploiting the latest communication techniques to manipulate emotions and control reason." [5] This is the end times which Aldous Huxley spoke about in his book,"Brave New World, and Orwell's 1984 surely portrayed as the terrible end that America is rapidly heading towards!

The human element is slowly being tamed and domesticated to be part of the total industrial-governmental machine by psychological conditioning and other more esoteric devices as well as through the use of presciption and street drugs. But behind this emergence of new social forms and concepts is a culture of death with its overt and covert cultural dimensions which permeates the subconscious of the species as a primordial fear-anxiety syndrome which alienates and dehumanizes and estranges each one of us from ourselves and each other and nature. And when this fear syndrome subconsciously becomes institutionalized as a core values its dragon complex breaths destruction within a social order as it becomes a covert death dualism which hides behind concepts of success, triumph, hard-work, rugged individuals, self-reliance but manifests its hidden self as the opposite of its other more positive half. It is a destructive force that often requires its human sacrifices such as the Kent State massacre and the death sacrifices of our youth on the throne of foreign war adventurism and the millions that die yearly through modern diseases that all of modern science with its yearly spending of billions of dollars, seeming can't understand or cope with let alone cure! The psychologist Rollo May talks about the dragon breath as it affects us. He says:

> Let no one think for an instant that we in our vaunted civilization have gone beyond the primitive human sacrifices. We sacrifice our youths not by the dozens, but by the thousands. The name of the god whom we appease is Moloch. We have sacrificed 50,000 of our youths in Vietnam, and if we add up the Vietnamese, the sacrifice goes up to several millions. Our Moloch's taste fits the age-old forms: it is for virginal youths. Our Moloch is greedy—which means we have much inner aggression and violence to project. [6]

Transintegral psychology calls this the tri-causal force behind psycho-cultural life. On the cultural level this is called the dragon complex which devours one with its black fire as it kills millions in civil and war time expediency and when the dragon breath blows white fire untold thousands are enslaved and dehumanized or made into dehumanized workers and technocractic serfs to overt and covert governmental powers who themselves must find meaning in life by triumphing over their downtrodden masses.

Often the dragon complex operates subconsciously by hypnotizing its victims without killing the patients who lives on to suffer or triumph another day. Within American culture the dragon complex has institutionalized itself in all phases of American society. It is found everywhere as a cultural core value and is the Genesis of the Genocide Phenomenon..

When it becomes a devouring negative force in American life then the T-P Titan factor enters into alliance with the primordial fear-anxiety syndrome as a culture of death that holds in its grip the death of America to itself. When it roars it becomes the Genocide phenomenon and it is the ghost of America's future.

The Titan force is always operative in society but when it combines with the primordial fear-anxiety syndrome, an all consuming negativity of alienating of oneself from the central core of your being, and from your fellow human beings and most tragically of all from nature, then you are prime candidates for the death generation.. The dragon complex allied with the primordial fear-anxiety syndrome are the forces that severs your link with your transcendent soul essence and is the dragon's breath that kills your human spirit and it is the force that enslaves modern man.

When the vicissitudes of terror emerge into contemporary times the cutting edge of the Genocide phenomenon appears within modern society. It is a terrible phenomenon. Surely, this occurrence is an aberration, a type of social insanity. But the facts are that because of today's social change exigencies, with its massive social repressions and bureaucratic machine technology, humanity is enslaved body and soul. The result is chaotic culture decay which manifests as a horrible extinction peril. Now the human species itself faces possible extinction overtly and the perceptive know we are the end generation or death generation. By end generation I mean the last generation before the death of a cultural age takes place.

DEATH SCIENTISTS

America has even produced a formal culture of death as its scientist-high priests of nuclear fiery death, become the elite leaders who pronounce through their work that the death of the world may occur unless America's truth reigns supreme. It has been estimated that 50% + of America's elite mathematicians, chemists, physicists, biologists and physicians, etc., and their technicians, and university research and consultant's talents have "been put out to pasture on the rank grasses of death". [7] And that even physicians and biologists do research on biological warfare which is designed only for the mass exterminations of people and that even anthropologists and sociologists do systems analysis, i.e., the study of radar systems, the integration of weapons, machines and people as they also examine the personality make ups of missile and bombing crews; while our economists determine global strategies for economic warfare, weaponry economics, logistics, etc.

For the past 50 years our death elite have been training the most acute brains in the country as a death cadre or as sometime called the elite of death which we support in relative luxury. [8] This elite cadre of death are part of the end generation but are also card carrying members of the death generation

The modern times are witnessing this end generation destroy American culture and mutilate what is sacred and holy to their grandparents. They revel in this destruction; they sanctify their actions by appealing to common street sense and feel that they are right and worthy to step on dead and dying social customs and norms which are putrid and stand as barriers to their uncertain future.

In contrast to the death generation is the culture of life which seems frightened and confused, inarticulate and wondering "where it will all end;" but the forces of death are confident and organized and stomp on the wolly-minded and scattered Americans as their impotence destroys them as they fearfully cower in their "homes of safety" as death struts among the streets and homes of America. [9]

DEATH GENERATION THEMES

A generation emerges in an age in which self alienation, social nihilism and separation from nature is causing a generational rupture in its psychological nature. A primordial fear-anxiety syndrome rapidly emerges as support to the human Genocide Phenomenon as some generational members become card carrying members of the death generation.

The concept of death to this extinction peril generation is an euphoria feeling of elations which gives life meaning to them as they wantonly gun down children in the streets and rape old women in dark alleys.

But for the organized members of this death generation the genocide Phenomenon is a theme of life . It gives them the opportunity to embrace social repression as a fact of social renewal. It signals a new life in the world because ethnic cleansing is the fascist mentality that signifies life and morality to them. It is the beacon of death truth which allows the true believer to contact the essence of its authoritarian force by rejecting free life and happiness through adhering to an insidious modern scientific technocracy that molds the life directions of this century. And these truth holders know they will be the elite that will save the world from its chaos.

When technocracy's authoritarian policies are your friend and companion life has significance only as a theme of death control which you call life truths. The death of social systems is your goal and your aid when terminating enemies or victims; the extinction peril is your ultimate tool which you embrace in your life long quest, that is, until your life force ebbs and flows into the grime ripper's hand; then your death smile is your final triumph against life.

When the death cadres control Life and direct their authoritarian social control over the masses, the death generation reaches its final goal, and they know in their heart of hearts that they have finally triumphed over life and that the death god has won; and in that fact each death member rejoices, for they are a beacons of death light because they are a members of the death generation.

Rejoice all you candidates for the death cadre, for in your life work you shall triumph, because the death theme shall uplift you into the darkness of eternity's darkest hell and its dark illumination shall uplift you into the elation of its agony and despair and ultimately you will be the cause of the death stroke to the human species.

You shall destroy your fellow human beings in fits of triumphant joy as you slaughter, main and rape and the world cheers you on; and yet you will reap the whirlwind as you become full fledged emissaries from hell. But you rejoice in that fact because you are the death generation and death is your creed, gore your substance, and its joy is the euphoria that you feel as you run with the tide of genocide.

You feel in your heart that you are the cleansers of mankind and the upholders of the laws of nature and you glory in that fact. Weakness and biological degeneracies, stupidity and human failures are your justifications for your social actions. Ethnic cleansing is your goal and the betterment of the race is upon your lips as you slaughter your way through history. You are the sociopathic that sees nothing wrong in slaughtering families and raping ethnic women so their men folk will exile them for their sexual impurities.

You are the death consciousness of a modern world gone Mad. You are the truth of a degenerate 20th century and you know in your heart that history will vindicate you as you march triumphantly over the land with death in your right hand and the truth torch held high in your left hand as you shout your righteousness slogans, even as your foul breath scorches the land. You are the death generation and nothing but death and dying races and dead cultures will satisfy you in your march to glory.

Beyond the facts of death and destruction that you accomplish you must act to cleanse the world. If you do not stand up to this task, then the Genocide Phenomenon will wither up and shrivel away and the death generation will have failed in its noble task of remaking the world into the dark glory of New World orders.

CULTURE OF DEATH

The concepts of death and defeat and hopelessness and passive anguish have become a culture of death that is gradually taking over the positive energy of the nation. The culture of death is still covert for most people but whole segments of society have embraced the inevitable fact of the Genocide phenomenon and wait passively for their end in the meaningless contemporary life. They are the dehumanized masses who are alienated from themselves and society and nature and above all from the transcendence of their very person. But above all they are people whose believe structure rests on social truths and technological concepts that have died but they missed the wake and still believe the corpse is alive and well. But in the meantime these passive death generation masses die to themselves little by little each day as time moves them into bewildered walking dead who look alive but died to themselves long ago. Another group of young death generation members who are more vocal and rebellious strut the streets of our nation with a chip on their shoulders and death in their hearts and they will not passively die to themselves only; they will take many with them to the death lands as they cry to high heaven of their agony and of the meaningless of life gone sour and they will make their mark and none shall rejoice in that fact.

Some members of the death generation are seemingly the unholy ones who talk of the hypocrisies of religion and materialism but know only pain and death and despondency and cry out for salvation from themselves; yet find solace only in riotous living, drugs and death themes. For they are the death generation and they know in their hearts of hearts that they stand on the quicksand of the future and that behind them lies nothingness and before them oblivion!

And they care for nothing, not their own children left abandoned to grandparents or for their offspring's drug destroyed bodies, nor for the millions left dead on the battlefields for corporate profit or national honor. For how can death itself produce life.

The death generation's offspring represents the diseased side of society and their rotten apples will be our future and none shall rejoice but all shall be uplifted into the inequity of the meaningless spectacle of the culture of death.

THE DEATH CHILDREN

A reign of death is upon us called death children. They are our children who reflect what we are inside. Their desperation, their pain and agony are our cries; our agony, our search for meaning and substance in life.

Our children's blood flowing in the streets is our tainted blood of rejection and social abuse which refreshes them daily as they go about their pillage of death!

Oh woe to a people who bleed through their children, who hold death linkage with their seed so strong that their children symbolically are surrogates for the frustrations and agony of life of their parents.

Our death children know intuitively where their affections originate because they neither respect nor treat with civility their parents who they see as their oppressors, rapist, physical and emotional abusers, who have committed the ultimate horrendous crime of bringing them into a world they never asked to enter. They neither ask for life nor respect it and their only answer to the sanctity of life is to destroy it in drive by shootings and by murdering their parents and raping their grandparents and by burning down their schools and vandalizing their parent"s sacred halls of education.

On the street level Graffiti is their sacred scriptures and heavy metal their songs of heroism and death their motto. And their method of communication is through Rap lyrics that tell the death zombies to rape and victimize women and to kill cops. For life holds no meaning to them and death signifies only an end to their earthly suffering because they are the Death Generation.

Mighty are they and fearsome is their demeanor for they are the death children. They are as the leaves in the wind and they fear nothing, for their parents are canon fodder to their guns and they reek of death and destruction for they are the death children rising out of their parent's mistakes to spread their death and destruction upon their fellow mankind.

They are everywhere and nowhere. You cannot identify them by the foulness of their breath or the ugliness of their form , because they often are beautiful of form and seemingly angel like and courteous and respectful, yet they are the seeds of your destruction and the genesis of your future because they will tramp on you and defile you and spit in your face as they stomp on your genitals, lest any more death children emerge from your seed. They are you in your most depreciable form and they are papa and mamma as you really are emotionally and psychologically. But they cannot hide from you what they are as you conveniently do. Their corruption manifests upon the winds of time and they will have their day and you are their victim and your fate rests in your children's hands, America!

Cry as you may America, you shall not escape their hands. They shall throw back upon you all your perversions and all your misguided aspirations for they are the death children and they have no mercy for you who pervert them and made them what they are! Cry America, cry for your misdeeds, cry out for your salvation and face the facts that the chickens have come home to roasts and nothing can save you from yourselves or your death children.

There is a time of dying and this fact is as true for cultures as it is for human beings. The old saying that nothing lasts forever surely applies to the nature of cultural deterioration. For a culture is in some sense a living organism which comes into being, has its childhood, adolescence, maturity , middle age and old age and then perishes from the face of the earth. Can any one point out a cultural descendants of an ancient Egyptian, Babylonian, Roman, etc. Very few cultures have survived from the ancient world. Even the few culture that have some continuity from the past such as the Chinese, and Hindus are not culturally the same as their ancestors and usually do not use the ancient languages such as Sanskrit, or ancient Chinese. As for the ancient Egyptian or other ancient cultures they are dead; and as for their languages we usually do not know how they were even pronounced. Once a culture's language is lost the culture as it was known becomes dead and eventually becomes extinct or emerges into something different from the original culture. Often most of the people themselves perish and become extinct as many tribal groups in Brazil have done in this century, along with the extinction of over 15 +languages.

THE BEGINNING OF THE END

The 20th century is the century of death for the American culture. It is the beginning of the end and those who live through it morn the death of their way of life much as they would the passing of a friend and companion who died in the youth of his being because he lost his way and none could save him because he was beyond help. He did not have to die. He did not have to succumb to the disabilitating malaise of cultural disintegration. But he did and cry and morn as you will the facts of life are that your friend is dead and nothing can bring him back. Nothing! Cry America for your obituary is now being written!

Oh mourn America, lament in agony and cry for the lost youth of your young, because there is yet so little time left; the last minuet of the last hour is ticking now and none know for sure if death or redemption awaits the hand of life that is called mankind!

Some say why must the death children's parents bare the blame for the depravations of their death children? Why can't we just destroy these rotten apples and start over again? Why can't a new course be laid and a new beginnings commence and a new start emerge so that a new generation can be born to decency and truth and American honor?

Why, oh why America, can not the grace of God descend and

save us from our death children? Because America, the death children are you acting out your most perverse fantasies and when they kill and main they are killing Mamma and Papa with glee in their hearts as they rejoice at the touch of death and salute life through death which is their rallying cry against life and humanity. Change what you are inside America or face yourself through your death children!

There will be a time when it will be said that America died during the last days of the twentieth century and their children plunged the death knife into the corpse of America as they personally committed the coup d'e-tat upon American life and its aging population. They rose up as a mass in rebellion and stomped on all that was holy and beautiful and thus the United States of America perished from the face of the earth and no one mourned!

Is there no hope America? Are Americans doomed to live out their lives within the terror of the death children's obsessions? Only you America can answer that question, only you collectively and individually can make the decision to transcend your lower natures; remember in your hands lies the future of America!

AMERICAN WORKERS AS MEMBERS OF THE DEATH GENERATION

The American worker is a case in point. From childhood until he enters the work force he is conditioned on concepts of democracy and freedom of choice that emphasizes that he must exploit all his resources of his personality as a duty to himself and for the culture and that even the survival of the nation partially rests on his or hers shoulders. It must be recognized that Americans are supposed to have an inexhaustible reservoir of drive and personality resources and they must exploit their personality always to their best advantage. If you do not do this then you have failed as a man or woman. To fall short of one's potentialities is considered a symptom of neurosis. [10]

When they enter the work force they find they have entered

a dictatorship that needs them to do tasks that impoverish their personality and kills them a little each day and they must obey or not work.

Immediately they learn that all rights of American citizenship are denied them, including freedom of speech and that company spies surrounds them and they must become as if they are robots obeying its technocratic master or lose their jobs. Ultimately it come to a situation, as Harvey Swados, puts it that"the worker's attitude toward his work is generally compounded of hatred, shame and resignation.' [11]

"In industry the person becomes an economic atom that dances to the tune of atomistic management. Your place is here, you will sit in this fashion, your arms will move x inches in a course of y radius and the time of movement will be .ooo minutes".

Added to this dilemma is the fact that the worker must renounce his very self or get few of the material rewards that his social conditioning makes him hunger for, almost on pain of being unAmerican if he does not buy, buy! [12] Thus American's innerself becomes perverted into an outer drive to obtain a high and rising standard of living; so that now this cultural imperative becomes a moral law which becomes a part of America's conscience. But the work necessary to gain these coveted goods becomes but one " . . . dreary interlude between nourishing hours with one's family.' [13] Our worker cannot rely on his alienated working companions who by now have become living machines who use each other and who [14] may be company spies as all of them are alienated-selves because all of them have sold their soul to the company and thus have no authentic self any longer; [15] also the worker receives little solace in a comradely group interaction because such groups are inherently replaceable and much like the interchangeable gear that characterizes all workers; for it is a fact that all his comradery groups can be replace by a similar one at another job. But even here he must be careful because workers who change their jobs too much are looked upon as a symptom of emotional disturbance. [16]

Thus at work he is a covert victim of destabilizing his very inner self. [17] Erich Fromm makes the point that when you sell your self you become a thing which has no self, thus you are as alienated as an alien to your very self and no longer experience your self as the center of your world and as a creator of your social actions: All your actions now stem from the social rules of the job and now you are an estranged slave to those master rules; [18] thus estranged from yourself you must flee from that enslaving job in search of the perfect job but if you changes your job too many times you are considered as psychologically unstable because industry is hostile to workers who move to often and try to keep them though higher wages, fringe benefits, and seniority; yet paradoxically industry always tries to lure outside workers to their new plants because they know worker have no loyalty to the job. So you have an industry that is two faced and knows that most interchangeable gear workers main theme is "Why do you give a damn, bud?" which is the worker's creed of the day and do you think the company cares about their canon fodder workers? [19] Why? Workers, in essence, are members of the death generation and if they have to die because of black lungs in the coal mines or of radiation sickness or of asbestos poisonous, so what! The work must go on and workers are interchangeable gears and when they are no longer needed they are eliminated through down-sizing, since firing is such a nasty word. Added to this is the fact that U.S. international corporations owe no allegiance to their workers or the United states or to the U.S. economy, but to themselves and their stockholders. Break the back of the unions , down-size and throw the middle class workers into the lower classes so they can better be controlled is their covert goal. Export technology and jobs so the work force will become members of a third world county and know their place. This idiocy is the death masters motto of the day and know this America, these people, the fired workers and the companies that fire them, are card carrying members of the death generation! [20]

Added to this problem is the American's workers' fear of becoming obsolescent in a rapidly changing job market that needs you to change careers at least three times and find 13 plus jobs during your work life in an era that fires their managerial work force at aged 40 and casts into job oblivion the common working man beyond the ages of thirty-five so that he may die in poverty and cultural deprivation.. This obsessive fear of becoming obsolescent now is a common element in the emotional crisis in America because human obsolescence is to become dead and to be a victim of the death generation, even as you join their ranks. Added to this fact is that America's industrial system forces its workers to do jobs of minimal self interests and by thus fitting their work force in this mold destroys and impoverishes their personality stability and these workers thus become spiritually useless to themselves. [21] American workers compensate for this personality impoverishment by seeking a high-rising standard of living or by changing their jobs. Job changing covertly is a process of easing the deep narcissistic wounds and pain that the meaningless work process forces on him; and he hopes against hope that he will find that perfect job, much as a sick man painfully shifts his body on his bed of pain to find a more comfortable position. [22] Naturally he never does and in the agony of his plight he dies a little every day and his spirit withers and dies as his personality becomes totally impoverished because he has now joined the death generation and knows it not!

Today the American worker faces his total social and psychological destruction when he loses his job and becomes obsolescent; his personal extinction peril has arrived and he immediately dies inside as he faces the oblivion of his work career and the destruction of all he holds dear.

He is now the filth that America has discarded and maligns because often he is homeless and a bum and represents all that is terrible and unclean in America as America blames the victim and casts him out of their memory as a necessary waste by-product of a productive society.

Recently in a radio program in Detroit the listeners said they feared automation of industry next to fear of Russia or of Nuclear annihilation. And the loss of jobs through automation produced various sorts of fears in them such as fear of change, and technology itself and of displacement and unemployment and of fear of machines and science in general. [23]

It is a fact that American workers, on facing company automation, have gotten sick on the steps of their work place and others have developed various illnesses caused by fear of new work operation; and we know that mature women have cried in rest rooms, fearful of losing their jobs, as they realize that they are now useless and thus have become dead to the world and themselves. [24] Truly they are members of the culture of death.

So it is understandable that when a person is under extreme stress or has personal problems his outer ego facade may crumble and he may be in danger of psychologically breaking down. This factor is exhilarated if the socio-political and religious values are collapsing and the social order itself is dying or within extreme culture change.

The worker knows that he is filth beneath the soles of his death masters' feet. All he has to do is observe members of his fellow workers as they near retirement age and see them discarded before they can get their pension by a grateful management for their life services. Our toiling workor only has to look into the anguished face of a man who is fired days or weeks before his 30 year retirement and now faces a bleak life ahead with no pension or talk to a service man who is being discarded before he can retire. It is also the policy of companies these days to go out of business or to be dissolved when bought up by a larger conglomerate and thus cheat the workers out of any pensions. Often when the worker retires they cheat him on the amount of his pension; but what of it. Why should your death masters be concerned with the discarded lives of worthless workers; Morality and ethics and honor mean nothing when it comes to dollars and cents and the workers know it. No matter that this worker toiled in the steel miles and worked along side other workers who fell into the hot steel or that he faced the terror of his fellow worker being decapitated beside him.

It is of no concern to corporate America or to governmental agencies that this workers has given his all, his sweat and blood and his very body to industrial injuries.

In fact, industrial worker injuries are a convenient way to discard workers in America. Workers cannot sue their employer because under worker compensation law industrial worker injuries will take care of their own, which means they take care of your medical needs and if you sue them you get a pittance for your injuries and in many cases lose your job. And they do this by casting them out to die and swivel up as their social self and sense of worth collapse them into a death generation member. The total fraudulent level of this debasement of American workers stinks to high heavens and adds to the death of America. Cast your loyal worker off America because he is a nobody now and cleanse yourself of his stinks and rejoice in the fact that he will die soon and you won't have to tolerate a worthless drone who is about to die because his social self is now dead and he faces individual and job oblivion soon and will walk alone to his death as a card carrying victim of the Death Generation.

DEATH OF THE PURITAN ETHIC

Ethics as we know it died when the Protestant work ethic died sometime in the 20th century. Oh many people still mouth the ethic and make speeches about our superior work abilities but the people no longer hold it dear in their hearts of hearts! Yes., we still have true believers and a large mass of the population that only half believe the myth and the rest who have rejected the concept but still feel guilty about breaking this core value. We even have millions of citizens who totally reject the protestant work ethic and live off welfare. Oh, we have a small minority who yell and rant against welfare recipients, especially second and third generation welfare people who live off of the largeness of the nation, just because of the puritan ethic. But most of the rest of us just holier a while and forget about it because in our heart of hearts we know that when all the jobs are gone we will be joining the welfare group reluctantly. But even as the job loss continues throughout the country, federal legislation is being passed to throw people off the welfare roles and to limit any governmental help to a certain period of months.

Perhaps with the recent export of jobs and technology overseas everyone recognizes that idle hands conditioned to work now hold in their hands the funeral flowers of death and none rejoices because the wise among us know that people revolt or become revolutionaries not to gain more of what they have never had but to protect what they are losing. Cry America, because you are being set up and you will die inside in the agony of your despair even as the boots of the death masters give you their grace!

But why did America's work ethic die? Nobody knows for sure but we will discuss the situation in more detail in a later chapter on workers of America. But some say that when free and independent farmers were herded into factories by economic necessity, as the working man was economically driven off the land and that he no longer was an autonomous and independent human being and that had something to do with the work ethics death. Well perhaps, but others say that maybe Corporate America broke the workers heart and will and degraded him and turned him into an interchangeable gear; into something that was discarded and thrown away if he became damaged goods or refused to give him a job when he refused to become a walking slave zombie to the death lords of industry? In any event our worker no longer believe in the work ethic and its use as a manipulative tool to get maximum work out of the work drones! But remember America, when you have no pride and respect in your work achievement you become dead inside and alienated from yourself and you now become prime victims for the death generation.

WHITE COLLAR WORKERS

White collar workers have entered into the outer portal of the administrative wing of corporate America. They are of a more refined cannon fodder than the blue collar workers but expendable material also to corporate exigencies. But the higher echelon of these executives are the mechanism that controls the masses of workers and that fact alone makes it necessary to fit them into an elaborate intercultural social order that rules America. To be a member of the enlightened order of managerial bliss one must sell his mind and soul to the masters of industry and be sincere and forthright in all his actions toward them. He must be a company man to his core as must his wife and their social and individual lives must revolve around the company center of the universe, that is, their corporate masters.

They will be thrown into a type of age-grading into managerial groups initially since all of the newly graduated college recruits will be basically the same age. They will be processed along a treadmill process that will take all the years of their lives. The top 15% will make it to the top of the corporate ladder and the rest will stay on their course, climbing up ever so steadily, because there is never is any level plateau where they can rest. And they will never be able to free themselves from the grating primordial fear-anxiety syndrome and thus they stand naked before their inner selves as possibly inadequate to this tasks and must suffer alone and in quiet desperation. Contemporary times finds many of these executives being discarded in middle age and thrown out in the streets to the wolfs of corporate necessity as America downsizes and expands its corporate industries overseas. But this fact does not matter in corporate death politics because there is a dual sense of honor in the corporate structure, that is, loyalty and respect is demanded by the corporate death masters from their subordinates but their death employees are expendable cannon fodder and no sane corporate death master should morn the figurative cutting of discarded throats when the exigencies of the moment demand it.

White collar workers are not picked for their brilliance or innovative force of personality or their rugged individualism and self reliance but for their conformity to the rules of corporate life and for their ability to be a team member and take orders. They must fit into the concept of a group mentality , thus if you are an individualist you are not wanted! If you are too bright or insightful you are unwanted. Oh, they play fast and loose with their propaganda with America's concept of individuality and self-reliance but they lie through their teeth as they march their white collar drones into the corporate machinery to be processed and socialized into following a dictatorial mentality which will rule them throughout their lives. Oh, on the managerial level they don't work a forty hour week but must gladly and cheerfully work 80+ hours if called upon. The damage done to wives and children is meaningless to the death masters but is an covert indicator of the loyalty of the worker. A man must do what he has to do even if he must sacrifice his loved ones to fulfill his compulsive need to climb the corporate ladder; he must do it. But the facts of the matter are he must, because he has no other choice. The rising executive must willingly sacrifice himself and his family to the overall company's good or be suspected of being disloyal and not to be made of the right stuff. Our company man is on a treadmill and he must go forward and upwards or he has no job. He must be satisfied with paper awards and congratulations for his achievements; but, gradually he will be rewarded more substantially by his corporate masters at each new level of achievement by an increase in salary and office status awards of better furniture, etc., but he must be a company man! He must pick the right wife and his children must go to the right schools and he must live in the correct neighborhoods and drive the appropriate car. His loyalty is to the corporate structure and his eyes must be always be on the subtle nuances of company directions and procedures. In return the company will transfer him from city to city every three years or so during his upward social-company mobility so that his life revolves around company personnel and mandates.

It is an interesting fact that our rising executives must become mobile, not only in terms of geographically moving from one company location to another and also by rapidly making new friends at each new company location; but he is also mobile as he moves ever upward within the company executive structure which is nowhere and everywhere and exists wherever his corporation exists worldwide. What this means from a functional social class position within the culture of his corporate world is that he must discard his old friends and acquaintances as he moves upward from one corporate class structure to another. This social reorientation is in contrast to the working class social relationship with close relative and friends which are based on long years of shared experiences and rests on the vicissitudes and exigencies of life. It also explains their reluctance to change jobs or migrate from one city to another unless absolutely forced to do so because of job loss. [25]

The white collar executive, however, has a problem when he moves upward into another social class of the corporate hierarchy, that is, he must discard his old friends and acquaintances and fellow workers left behind. He must do this because he must or he stands revealed as inadequate managerial material because any corporate fool knows that a rising person must dissolve relationship from people who are liabilities and forge relationships with people who can help them. So by definition you cannot be identified with the losers and taint yourself with the putrid smell of failure! If you cannot be corrupted by throwing away earned loyalty bonds and made to defecate on ethical relationship concerns you are not made of the right material. You must voluntarily accept the corporate ethics and situational ties of your temporary corporate class positions, or you must be cast out of the death masters domain. They will not accept you if you cannot dissolve your deep emotional ties to your birth family or to your emotional past or to your original lower-class status. You must leave home literally and spiritually so you can become one of them, that is, to become a death master! [26]

The rising death master must leave Mama and Papa and brothers and sisters and friends and acquaintances of lower-status behind. Often he must leave his church and clubs, cliques of his youth and family and be initiated into the higher echelons of corporate America! But these facts of abandonment and betrayal on the rising executive part is still not enough of sacrifice in the bootcamps of corporate America. When you rise from one corporate class status into another one you must also repeat this same death master absurdity again and again against your fellow workers and their families, because this is a test of your loyalty to the company store and you must do your duty or perish. [27]

Some authorities suggest that the promoted executive and his wife gradually sever their relationship to old friends and subordinates. The corporation wants to minimize resentment so our new death master apprentice must find logical reasons for not joining the group at coffee breaks or lunch . Additionally he must miss any bowling or card session occasionally and then more frequently until everyone gets the message! If he is invited to the home of subordinates the invitations should be accepted but never reciprocated unless he invites the whole group of subordinates at once and after a while all such interactions ought to cease once and for all time. And of utmost importance to our rising death master is his wife's social behavior at this time. She may not understand the death rejection and betrayal tests and situational ethics of office organization. She must be patiently counseled or she become dangerous if she insists on keeping close friendships with subordinate wives. Her friendships will be watched and if not severed will show that our new death apprentice is not a master of his own home and this fact will jeopardize his Job. In the dictatorship of corporate America, traditional ethic and morals is the enemy and if you cannot look upon your fellow workers as things to be manipulated and used, with no regard for common decency, then you are suspect and cannot be a death master; you cannot rise into the ranks of corporate truth. [28]

It is a fact that the death masters relies not exclusively on the overt behavior of their employee-apprentices but utilize psychological tests which can tell them in decimal figures his psychological health. They will find out his degree of radicalism versus conservatism, his social judgment, practical judgment and of his hostility to society, and the amount of perseverance he has and about his personal sex habits. [29] Whether you will be put on the shelf or promoted may now depend upon the psychological test you have to take. For years Sears would never promote a person into the upper brackets until the Board chairman consulted the tests. [30]

There is no place for you to hide from Big-Brother. A death apprentice's soul, not only belongs to the company, it is the company. And as our man on the rise identifies with its inner essence you will find only degrees of differentiation between his inner personality and the company's brilliance of existence. Additionally his social self also belongs to them and his very being and livelihood rest on his performance with corporate guidance; and the primordial fear-anxiety syndrome has him and he must do what he has to do or perish or be thrown out into the cold hard world of American life where he would have to rediscover his individuality again. He would have to face himself and at all cost he cannot afford to do this. It is better to live in corporate slavery then find himself because by now his corporate life is his tribal identification. He rejoices in that fact and is blessed by his superiors occasionally as he rises in corporate truth. The grace of his corporate death masters uplifts him and he knows he is succeeding in the new all American way and thus he has paid his dues and is a card carrying member of the death generation. But in his heart of hearts he knows that he is a failure to the traditional American way of life and a traitor to his inner self's sense of self-esteem. He knows, however, that he can never go back home to traditional America. This lost corporate soul must now cry inwardly as he gives a desperate resignation sigh of a drowning man who can only grasp at the tinsel stars of his corporate enslavement to give meaning to his life and his betrayal sacrifices as a corporate drone!

THE DEATH CADRE

FUTURIST COMMENTARY: The 20th century has seen the emergence of organized death cadres among many societies overtly and covertly. Their overt rise marks the beginning of the wars of terror which continue today in the 22nd century.

The concept of the death cadre will be fully discussed during the next chapter but it must be understood that these cadres are but the overt manifestation of the unrealized aspiration of a great number of the populace. They are always with us as part of humanity's unregenerated dark side and when civilization and truth and honor fails the dark hordes of humanity's evolutionary nature rise up and enslave us and destroy us and make of us fiends from hell. They have destroyed civilizations and cultures from the beginning of time and they are always with us in our darkest moments and covertly hide from humanity in its greatest moments of destiny! When they gain government control they are the future Attila the Huns and the Hitlers and Stalin's and Himmler's who now masquerade as lowly clerks and actors and harmless fellows whom we meet along the ways of life. But when they rise, death and destruction surrounds them and humanity weeps!

When they gain control of the various world's Industrial-military complex they have caused mass culturecide, that is, the death of entire societies; with this process comes loss of languages and socio-cultural reality which have perished in the death throes of countless societies, along with 100 million people in the western world who have suffered organized genocide in this century alone; so that humanity reeks with the blood of the human race yet mankind conveniently forgets its crimes as it rushes full speed ahead toward species doom.

Today we are looking at a spectrum of organized mass killings as well as the seemingly chaos of random killings by children with death guns in their hands and murder in their hearts. But behind this overt situations is the death of western civilization and third world countries as the new death age engulfs us and remakes us and allows this black plague of death to become the new motto and new age icon. For we are the death generation and only our deaths or our salvation from ourselves shall decide the question of the future of the human race.

No place is safe, no harbor gives safety from this malady, because this destructive force lurks from within the very heart of mankind and is presently manifesting within western civilizations and certain third world countries.

When the American public has no fury against the genocide they see daily in their television sets taking place in Bosnia, then they are tacitly setting themselves up because the cadres of death know they have won and their people are ripe for the death marches that they will eventually inflict upon their own people. In this sense death has triumph as the dead soul of America lies as a corpse before the world as easy pickings as America sleeps in its oblivion of death.

There is no place to run to and no place to hide because the species Homo sapiens has come to an evolutionary impasse. Until the species rises up beyond its present mentality and transforms its lower natures, it will be in peril; a peril of awesome proportions called the extinction peril is upon us which no man can forestall, no nation can stop, no religion can pronounce against.

If the human race cannot rise above its lowest degradation then it will sink into it and then all is lost. All will perish in the darkness of the coming wars of terror!

You are the death generation in your person and species. You are the terror that faces yourself and that terror is making your lives miserable. So face yourself or perish by your own hand.

It is a fact that when you covertly accept death concepts, instead of life, that you set in motion grave unconscious forces which can manifest as psychosomatic illnesses, accident-proneness and other individual acts that can injure you short of outright suicide. You become covertly aggressive against yourself. So your death wish may be subtle or not so subtle and you may be accident prone or become morbid and depressive or go through a series of strange maladies. Often people have unconscious guilt about dead loved ones and have a powerful unconscious desire to be reunited with that person. [31] It is a fact also that the psyche will often unconsciously deny a situation and the individual mixes up his signals which often leads to disastrous decisions which in turn may destroy the creativity and accomplishments of a man even of superior abilities. [32] As our culture collapses you will find whole populations of these people joining the death generation. They will regress, as if they were helpless children who are seeking the protection of a trustworthy and benevolent father. Childhood conditioning will push whole population into following a Death leader who is strong and amoral but whom they think they can trust and who will then arouse their hostility and fear to create a warlike spirit. His empathy with this mass mind will diminish their mass depression and feelings of hopelessness produced by inner discontent and maladjustment. Through the use of mass propaganda he will brainwash the near total population. Remember that in American culture success equals love and when one person controls another this factor says that emotionally and unconsciously that the leader "cares" about them. [33]

The master death leader, Hitler, the German Pagan Messiah, says that all propaganda "must be so popular and on such an intellectual level, that even the most stupid of those toward whom it is directed will understand it. Therefore the intellectual level of the propaganda must be lower then the larger number of people who are to be influenced by it." Goebbels, Hitlers propaganda minister said "It is the absolute right of the State to supervise the formation of public opinion." Such propaganda must also instill fear this death master said. "If the day should ever come when we {the Nazis} must go, if some day we are compelled to leave the scene of history, we will slam the door so hard that the universe will shake and mankind will stand back in stupefaction." [34]

PSYCHOLOGY OF EVIL

According to psychiatrist M. Scottpeck there is a psychology of evil. and it practitioners are quite common and usually appear quite ordinary to most observers. They are the mother of three next door or the deacon in the church on the next street. They comprise, as Martin Buber points out, as people sliding into evil and those who have been taken over by it. [35] Evil, thus is a force which we find in the Genocide Phenomenon and within the death generation and within the nature of each person and it has to do with killing! It may take your life or anothers overtly but it first kills the spirit by destroying your sentience, awareness, mobility, growth, autonomy and will. It will kill all or be selective of any of these attributes without killing your body. [36] It seems to be a force that kills your liveliness from within you or from some outside people force; yet its force is characterized by the fact that those who manifest its force refuse to acknowledge it. And these people live down any street in America and may be rich or poor and are not designated criminals; in fact they are probably "solid citizens"–Sunday school teacher, bankers, policemen and Mama and Papa who are active in the PTA. [37]

They are you as you attempt to adjust to the realities of the world. They are every American who used to have an ethical character which wants to do a good job well but do it successfully with goodness. Why? Because Americans have build into their character structure an insistence upon a relationship between what we do and what we get out of life. We don't look at how a person is born but at what he has made of himself. There is not one of us who does not feel in his bones that he can walk in the halls of greatness and hold up his head as a worthy American. [38]

But these people are also ones who have slide into the death generation. Oh, some are disguised as good guys who cover up their bad impulses by a facade of affability which effectively covers their sadistic impulses. [39] But there are others, who number in the millions, who have lost their faith in the American dream.

They are the poor ones who know that no matter how hard they work they cannot get ahead if they don't have pull, and realize this fact because life is a racket. And they hold the cynical obverse concept of believing that success and effort is no longer the American way. They have become card carrying members of the death generation. They are the rank and file people who are killing America inch by inch; they are you and me who have lost our moral keystone to an orderly American world. They are Americans who have neither vision nor humility and lack the will and purpose that made America great! They are the alienated ones who have neither bitterness nor a genuine hatred of those who have brought them into the culture of death. They belong to an America that exists in the limbo of cynical grabbing-politics or belongs to a business community in which ethics has ceased and moral responsibility is passe. [40] They live in a culture of death that is waiting for an American fascist who is strong enough and amoral enough to lead his death followers into the new death millennium.

These ordinary Americans are not designated criminals but they commit crimes against life and liveliness; and their crimes are so subtle and covert that cannot be classified as crimes. Scottpeck makes the point that even criminals who are in jail, although destructive and usually repetitively commit crimes, have an openness to their wickedness; and as these criminals point out they are the "honest criminals." They stress the truly evil ones always reside outside of jail; a point the Scottpeck feels is generally accurate.[41] He says that evil is committed by the self-righteous people who will not undergo the discomfort of self-examination. He speaks to the point when he give us an example of a boy asking his father why he called grandmama a bitch? The father grabs the boy and washes the kid's mouth out with soap, and in the name of discipline an evil has occurred. The faultless father scapegoated the kid or as the psychiatrists call it projected his evil feelings onto the son. The father saw the profanity and uncleanliness as existing within his son, not himself, yet it was the father's own filth projected onto his image of his son's actions and in the name of discipline he assaulted his son but felt "what a good parent I am." By his action the father became a member of the death generation!

Hitler, the arch criminal, projected his own internal hate onto the Jews and his evil became an exercise of political power which resulted in the Genocide Phenomenon. Today other death cadre killers duplicate this madness and the other death generation fiends seek to impose their will overtly and covertly through political acts of coercion against humanity. Naturally they stand on the stump and proclaim they do these things to destroy the evil they see all around them instead of destroying the sickness within themselves. Naturally some of these death generation criminals are psychopaths or sociopaths who kill and commit crimes yet feel guiltless because they lack a conscience. Some of these creatures are so reckless they don't cover their tracks very well and are classified as "moral imbeciles" but there seems almost a serene quality of innocence to their lack of concern. They seem to be as happy inside jail as when outside committing their crimes. [42] The majority of death generation members are not sociopaths but cover up their unregenerated natures from themselves by lying to themselves. They are absolutely dedicated to preserving their self-image and to seem to the world as morally pure. And naturally while they seemingly have no motive to be good they wish the world to think of them as "good people." At all costs they must think of themselves as perfect people; yet they do have a conscience and know the evil they do yet at the same time try to avoid that awareness by sweeping their acts of evilness under the rug of their subconsciousness.

The perceptive person, however, will see the smile that hides the death agents hatred and smooth and oily manner that covers his fury and observe the subtle glove that covers his mailed fist. He will observe his maliciousness of evil that lies thinly beneath his expertise at disguises and then he will know the uncanny game of hide and seek [43] that our death masters use on us. It is a fact that this game is played daily in the offices and board rooms of corporate America, in the mills and factories and governmental agencies of America and absolutely every Sunday in our churches and holy places.

Beneath the personality facade of the death generation is a fear of life itself and only by embracing death and evil can they find life tolerable. And in this fact they are not far from the average Americans fear of death which places him within the genocide phenomenon.. Death is a tabu subject in America. Old age and sickness or being crippled in body or mind also cannot be tolerated as subject matters for general conversation. These potential death generation members must stand back from it because the submerged death theme is the opposite of life and they cannot face that fact; yet its death theme embraces them daily in their sleep and awake they cling to a death's opposite, the life principle, in desperation and fear. When you fear something so much you can't think about it or talk about it, it always lurks just below the surface of your consciousness and you develop anxieties about your competitive life and destiny and your fear betrays you in your everyday life yet its anxiety becomes normal and natural to you. If it were taken away you would feel some how cheated by life. You must have the thrill of conflict and touch destiny through suffering which makes you feel alive and dynamic and American! Some of these Americans are already covert members of the death generation while the rest suffer the ignorance and anxiety of daily life until they either transcend their lower natures or enter into the Genocide Phenomenon.

The primordial fear-anxiety syndrome embraces them in holy terror and drives them and forces them to keep up the pretense of wholeness and goodness that covers up their evil action against others. They cannot be exposed to the world or themselves or come face to face with their own evil. Daily and hourly they live their lives in fear and terror so chronic and interwoven into their very being that there is no hope for them. [44] They will perish in the hells of their imaginations yet let them not gain political power or the fires of hell will encircle humanity.

Today we find an overwhelming mood of outright rage at life, even a fear of life itself and the feeling that life is becoming almost too burdensome and tormenting to be endured and suddenly you have covert recruits for the death generation's agenda of death over life, tyranny over freedom.

When you have no clear cut vision of the future then you live in the present or the past. But what if the past is unclear and the present is a hell through which the drama of life is played by an idiot speaking words of nonsense while pretending to love himself yet all the time covertly destroying all that is true and holy within himself? When you observe just such a person you have come into the presence of a card-carrying member of the death generation!

Nothing is truly sacred to the death generation but destruction and death and their only truth is that they have lived before the spectacle of death and momentarily triumphed, that is, until death itself shall end their misery through suicide, murder or accidental drug overdose or through mass executions for treason, which they face if they fail in their idiocies of pseudo-grandeur.

The death rattle is in their throats and death is upon their lips and they expect a short life and revel in the concept that they stand alone before life itself and curse it because they are the death generation and they fear nothing, even death itself.

Yet it must be said they do fear one thing and that is life itself! For life demands of all of us certain things and woe to those who ignore its demands! So it may be said that the death generation is running away from life itself and they know it not yet but they cry out inwardly for salvation from themselves and hope against hope that their inner cry will be heard and that some miraculous hand will rescue them from themselves; but in the meantime they project their childhood hates on innocent targets as psychotic acting out which provides temporary relief from their unbearable repressed violence and inner tensions. [45]

PSYCHOLOGY OF EVIL

Dr.Scottpeck feels that the concept of evil as a disease, that is, as the ultimate disease, obligates us to scientifically study it and officially name it as a psychiatric disorder. He speculates that it ought to be possible to place it as a subcategory under existing broad category of personality disorder which stress the denial of personal responsibility. But even within these broad categories another subcategory entitled "narcissistic personality disorder" can be created. He says that evil people constitutes a specific variant of the narcissistic personality disorder and that we must study them in depth. [46] He states that in addition to evil person's aborgation of responsibility which characterizes all personality disorders there are four specifically distinctions to identify the evil person by such as:

(1) They have a consistent destructive scapegoating behavior which is usually quite subtle.
(2) They have an excessive yet often covert intolerance to criticism and other forms of injury of a narcissistic nature.
(3) They must maintain their public image and self image but also have a denial and pretentiousness of their vengeful motives and hateful feelings.
(4) They have an intellectual deviousness and may have a mild schizophreniclike disturbance of thinking. [47]

DEATH GENERATION EVIL

There is a force of anger and terror so vile that when it infects you a change in character takes place and you become a member of the death generation! Its energy and force taps the unregenerated aspects of the dark primordial forces of the species consciousness and what is covertly present joins with overt terrors of evil and creates mass movements of the Genocide Phenomenon. It is a dualistic force, that is, it comprises an oppressor and a victim who then may join his initiator as a passive or active purveyor of fifth and degeneracy. It is a Genocidal force so vile that its members can committee mass killings and impose ridged brainwashing techniques on their victims and yet this genocide force frees them to feel in their hearts that they are pure and grand and represent the forces of goodness and justice in the universe.

Historically we have seen these grand champions as infamous Atila the Hun, Hitlers, grand Christian Inquisitors and official death murders of the Christian Church, and as faceless technocrats in varieties of repressive regimes the world over. When the Turks massacred a million plus Armenians at the beginning of this century they felt justified in those actions, as did Hitler when he killed through genocide 20 million plus victims as sacrificial offering to his pagan destiny; or a Stalin who became a Grandmaster of the death cadres and delighted in killing his own people in the millions. In contemporary time Bosnia's ethnic cleansing and Cambodians killing fields of mass genocide are the beginning of the end for the human species.

All of these victims are us in a symbolic sense. They are our brethren in suffering and death; they are a part of our species fabric who even today symbolically cries out to us through our subconscious species consciousness with a warning of coming events and for justice!. They are still connected to us because the victim and the saved are part and partial of the same species consciousness and the same evolutionary force. We can't escape from each other. They speak to us from the grave and their voices of warning speaks to our unconscious of the ominous genocide phenomenon that is about to engulf us. It is a fact that these victims of man's inhumanity to man were but the water to prime the pump of a massive extinction peril that will soon decimate the planet and emerge us into a new dark age that will murder all civilizations on the planet and create an elite of vile and sadistic death technocracies that will cleanse all of humanity of any decency and goodness it still has left. Oh, woe are the signs America! America are you next?

The brethren of death are with us today. Yes that is a fact. Today they are with us again, that is, the unknown brethren of death and destruction are covertly waiting in the wings, throughout the world, to save us from ourselves. They are mighty and strong, although clearly hidden from the masses, and they know their duly and shall fulfill it. Oh, you can't run away and hide from them because this terror is hidden within you and me and you actually may be one of our future oppressors unknown even to yourself. The dark night of our primordial past still lurks within you and it is mighty and terrible and it has you by its hand and cry as you may you are a part of it and can't run away from yourself. This evil is part of your unregenerated human nature and it is constantly with you and haunts you constantly and may overwhelm you at any time and when it does you become a card-carrying member of the death generation. And if you are vile enough you become a candidate for the death cadre corps and will be the mass execution of the human species.!

America now is your time to be counted. The evil that is in you can be changed. It is not something permanent and cast in cement. It is not something that was created at the beginnings of time. It is not something you cannot combat with knowledge and internal strength. It is something you can grow out of and it will respond to the higher influences of humanity and evolution.

The human species now lives within the killing fields of humanity. How you respond will determine the fate of the human species. Mark well my words America; our nation's time of destiny is now; shrink not from your duty to yourself, America and the future of your species.

CHAPTER 3

THE DEATH CADRE

FUTURIST COMMENTARY: Covert death cadre organizations are a fact of life in the latter part of the 21st century. They are efficiently organized and ruthless in their goals and the creed of death is in their hearts and truth and morality upon their lips. They know that destiny is on their side as they plot and scheme and kill and massacre their way into political power. One hundred million die in the early wars of the 20th century but when THE DEATH CADRES finally gain total political control billions die in their ovens and guillotines of inequity. Then the horrors of death become a statistical national honor as countless lives are sacrificed upon the altar of death almighty as sacrificial lambs to the new world orders.

CADRES OF DEATH

The death generation does not just consist of the cutting edge of chaos committed by children with automatic weapons. There is also a cadre of death generation bureaucratics who have eugenics on their breath and organized mass genocide in their hearts; and they are mighty and hateful and death is at their finger tips and they will achieve their goals of "cultural renewal or else; and they will not stop until the death rattle itself takes them.

But in the meantime they find joy in life through the anticipation of the death of all that you hold holy and in the hope of cleansing you individually and collectively of your entire life force as a person and as a nation! They are the death generation's intelligentsia and upon them rests the future death of a great nation and they will succeed even as the death rattle surges from their throat!

Our modern century has seen these death cadres strut upon the stage of life as they cut down millions through their programs of mass genocide and social reform. The chief Death Master historically is Hitler-the pagan messiah, who kills 20 million people in his ovens of death even as he personally tortures his enemies as they hang on meat hooks in his dudgeons of death.

Yet all the while he presents a public demeanor of love, strength and goodness which represents all that is true and worthwhile to the masses as they adore and adulate him and uplift him to a state of demi-god. Even now his life and dreams are held in the hearts and minds of many adoring followers, overtly and covertly, on many fronts of the new world's orders. One exGerman solder recently said "If Hitler were to call me again, I would go to Stalingrad–with joy." [1]

On the other side of the death card is Stalin, the Death Master, who starves twenty million of the country men to death to bring about Russia's collective farms while simultaneously murdering and killing millions in his Siberian death camps. Yet even today you have Russians marching in parades carrying his pictures and honoring him by wishing he was still in control.

Why? Because millions of covert members of the death generation must embrace order and death truth by identifying with their arch-demon death leaders.

It is a fact of death politics that the death champions and their sacrificial lambs must love each other in their embrace of death. They must each taste the flavor of death and stare into each others eyes adoringly just as a tiger's prey looks into the tiger's eyes adoringly through the hypnotic gaze of the tiger!

But you ask, "What of the overt victims who are not hypnotized by the killer?" Yes, truly they are the victims of life, especially when they are powerless. Do you think the California Indian population who perished in genocidal fury from a population of 200,000 in 1849 to 20,000 poor souls 20 years later went willingly to their deaths; or can you conceive of the terror of the young Indian maidens, who as late as the early twenty's of the 20th century, were rounded up and sterilized in Santa Barbara, California. Do you think they willingly committed genocide of their race. Do you think the mass genocide of the American Indian masses lays easily on the conscience and history of the great American republic? Do you think the slaughtered men, women and children, victims of the MyLai massacre voluntary died; or that the evil of these death generation solders can be easily forgotten by America? Today the death screams of 30,000 victims, thrown to their deaths into the depths of the ocean from airplanes, by Argentina death squads calls to the world for justice.

We are the death generation America and the death bureaucrats are still with us committing mass genocide in the killing fields of Cambodia, Bosnia, Rwanda and in the death squads of Argentina, Guatemala and El Salvador and on the street of America; the future bodes bright for the death cadres; for death is upon the winds of life and billions shall perish at their hands as the death generation fulfils its mandate to uplift life through death!

THE INSTITUTIONALIZED
DEATH GENERATION

The death generation often becomes institutionalized as overt governmental bodies or as covert forces within governmental structures or as secrete death cadre societies waiting to take political control if the opportunity presents itself.

The question is are there overt or covert death cadres waiting to take control of America. Possibly yes, perhaps no! Ask the conspiracy buffs! But understand this fact that the dark night of the human unregenerated humanity is a death force always lying just beneath the surface of the human species consciousness. It is waiting to take control and remold humanity into its authoritarian concepts of reality.

To be a member of the death generation and specifically the death cadre requires only that you have a latent sadistic or masochistic drives or an urge to control people or a feeling of superiority over other people or at worst an excessive compulsive need to force your truth upon humanity. You may even be a member unconsciously because you feel ardently that God is on your side and you must save the world from itself. Thus, all who are not with you are against you and you cannot allow your idea of evil to live, in fact, to not destroy this evil is to fail God and yourself.

You may also be a death cadre member because you must uphold the purity of the race, not knowing that races are only temporary episodes in time.

Possibly you feel you must uphold your group's morality as its ethics and truth guides you to oppress and murder and committee genocide and ethnic cleansing; and you know in your hearts of heart that you are morally right and correct and God and nature is on your side, because you are a member of the death generation.

You may be a member of the death cadre because our society is confused and you can't guide your children correctly by telling them what is good or bad or how to behave in a specific situation. You can't tell them because you don't know yourself and you suffer for that reason and you know you are setting a bad example for them and you cry inside as you know that you are a contributing person to the success of the death generation and are now a hidden card carrying member of the death cadre!

Hitler and Stalin are perfect examples of the death generation becoming organized and systematically poring its filth of death on humanity . Today neo-nazi's and other reincarnated covert groups await in the wings to again roar the challenge of the human barbarian and proclaim death to the lowest and glory to the superior ones as they go about their deliberate slaughtering of the "inferior races".

The human barbarian is about to start the organized phenomenon of genocide as he once again talks with his sugar tongue to the sleeping masses and roars his honey pronouncements for all to find cover under a variety of new world orders called by various names.

The death generation has many members among the political, economic and bureaucratic classes and when they become organized as a death cadre they become mighty and terrible and roar together with a purpose that strikes terror in the minds of mankind.

Modern Cambodia is just such example. A great and ancient civilization perished on the killing fields of Cambodia. But the people's inner drive and life force expired before that small band of militant revolutionaries herded people from their cities as they massacred millions of people in the countryside

The sad fact is that they were massacred by a numerically small cadre of the death generation. Massacred by their own people; human beings whose agenda called for the destruction of Cambodian culture and the killing of millions of their fellow citizens in the name of their enlightenment so they could form the perfect society and stamp out corruption and deceit and allow truth and goodness to triumph.

One wonders whether this social reorganization is but just a prelude to coming national and worldly events. Because it is obvious that given the right opportunity certain groups of people will rise to the occasion and become, in effect, an organized death cadre.

Nobel prize winner Lorenz says that such people can be imprinted by demagogic leaders who triggers innate impulses to violent aggression that can threaten the survival of humanity; a fact that the organized death generation is well aware of and content to utilize. [2]

Naturally the Cambodians did not overtly know that these

fiends from hell would committee culturecide and genocide on them or that initially any one who could read or write would be executed or that before them lay the total destruction of their society and that most of the population would die in the death marches.

Do you think the death cadre's will tells you these thing before the fact. No, they will talk of national honor and justice and family values, and of national self-interest and how the people must be organized so that justice can prevail, while at the same time they are stripping you of your civil rights and privileges through executive orders that are unconstitutional but will do so in the name of combating the drug epidemic or the lawless element in society.

They must do this because the death cadre is international in scope and instinct and will be stopped only by their deaths or until you lay prostate beneath their feet with the death rattle in your throat and eternity on your lips.

To accomplish these ends the organized death cadre's must have a weak, disorganized and confused society as prey. The Cambodians are a case in point; from a psycho-political point of view, they perished because their culture had no inner drive or functional integrity left so they became victims of their own ineptitude. After long periods of civil wars, after the end of the 2nd world war, they covertly lost their will to live as persons and culture. Some unconscious negative force, perhaps a death wishes, seemingly was working covertly within a great people as they unconsciously carried out a policy of self-destructiveness. 3 It is a fact that after great destructive episodes a reactive phase of apathy, widespread discontent and depression spreads on a people; 4 thus they as a people failed the challenge of history and death were their reward. A great people died that day yet the truth is that inwardly their death theme seemingly attracted the fiends of death to their door as millions went to their grave in agony and turmoil. America are you next?

IDEAL DEATH CADRE

The ideal death cadre is one who rejects life and nature, ideas and the dynamics of everything that has life and substitutes them for abstract ideals, objects or things of death. Their speciality is the present and everything they produces through their senses are but things or objects. He must become a machine. Sex is but a love machine, feelings are now nothing but sentimentally, peek experiences and intense elation now are only fun and excitement.[5]

The death cadet's love and tenderness is channeled toward gadgets and machines, and death concepts. He is now a dead machine and his world one of lifeless artifacts. Lifeless food and synthetic organs become his world and he is controlled by it.

Life to him is bound up in the technical controls of machinery that control men which he surrounds himself with and his greatest goal is to become the Robot that can't be distinguished from living men. If he could clone himself-he would do so.

The death cadet lives in a world of "no-life"; a death world which he embraces as he transforms the living world into a stinking and poisonous place which feels good and pleasant to the Death Generation.

The bureaucratic death cadet could cares less if the earth is destroyed within a hundred years. Technical programs cannot and will not be stopped even if they crush the life out of the planet. [6]

The death cadet sacrificed his children in ancient times to the Gods; today he offers up all life to the Death God that lies within his heart. Erich Fromm makes the point that it makes no differences even that he may operate from ignorance of ecological facts, because, within his nature lies a necrophilous element that prevents him from making use of any objective knowledge he realizes.

The death cadets often are nuclear scientists who design weapons to destroy all humanity. They and their political leaders gamble with life itself while they calmly speculates whether fifty million dead is an acceptable casualty figure in an atomic war.

Death and dying are a "truth high" to the death generation! Can you expect our youth not to embrace death through drugs, drive by murders and seemingly sacrificial torture murders of young children, when our elite leaders promote liberty through death, love through living a life that embraces death and the annihilation of the human race as its ideal.

Freud stressed often that man's repressions often return and one can see that a death cadet attraction to death and decay appears as malignant anal character. [7]

The genocide propensities of the human species has ample historical president. Tamerlane's pyramid of skills, Peter the Hermits slaughter of the Jews on his way to liberate the holy land, Hitler's killing of six million Jews and the slaughter of 15 million other people in his ovens of iniquity, an action by which he offered up his death victims as sacrificial lambs in the name of his new world order. Surely Stalin's starvation of 20 million peasant farmers and the additional millions that died in his death camps shows mankind's genocide tendencies. Today within Rwanda one tribal group has just massacred 700,000 people in tribal animosities and surly Bosnia's genocide falls under ethnic cleansing imperative's that is blatant genocide.

RANDOM KILLING

But beyond organized killing is the death fact that American faces daily in drive by shootings as its teenagers become killers of American civilization. Whether you are death children randomly killing, or administrators of countless bureaucracies, what you really want to do is to control people; one way or the other you wish to impose your desires and commands on other people. But above all you want to experience the thrill of death as life flow through your fingers of death as you breath in the intoxication of might and power and realize within your heart that you are a man of might and terror!

BLOOD REVENGE

Death on the streets of America has many ends and causes yet the fact of our children killing other human beings is a decent into nihilistic death politics at its worst. When they kill randomly they are the fiends from hell that must feed upon their own kind to feel alive and dynamic. When they kill specifically as a proactive vengeance against another gang then they enter the arena of Blood revenge. This aspect of the genocide phenomenon is a world wide spectacle of widespread vengeful aggression of individuals and groups. It is a death institution found practically all over the world from East and Northeast Africa, West Africa, the upper Congo, Polynesia, in Corsica, New guinea, and among frontier tribes of northeast India, bengal and among early America's mountain clans and in today's death children gangs. [8]

Blood revenge is a type of death consciousness that requires a death of a child gang member, a member of a family, clan or tribe to kill a member of a corresponding unit if one of his own people has been killed by them. The crime , however, will never be expiated by the punishment of the murderer or his gang organization, because this killing act does not end the killing sequence. The very act of killing the aggressor in turn obliges the members of the punished group to continue the blood revenge scenario ad infinitum. This endless chain of blood revenges have historically led to many extinction of families and larger groups. [9]

Our world lives within an era which exacts vengeance upon its peoples. The classic example is the lex talionis of the old testament which threatens to punish any misdeed up to the third and fourth generation. This ideas also lives within the law of the Yakuts which says "The blood of a man, if spilled, requires atonement." The children of the murdered, thus took vengeance upon the children of the murderer, even until the ninth generation. 10 Today our death-children gangs demand respect by taking blood revenge as a mode of social life. Our future death master will also require a blood sacrifice as they masscre the human race into acceptable death master goals.

Historically all people live in the control mode of life. Yet America has a pluralistic, religious, and social order. Yet, even here groups are vying for the power and if the opportunity presents itself millions will perish as a new structure of social order fulfills its social, racial and economic mandates.

There is no place to hide! There is no safety sanctuaries, no place to run too, no ultimate comfort zone!

Future death generation scientists will insert computer chips on your body which tunes into sky satellites which can track you wherever you are. They will put microchips in cars and along the highways which will communicate with the automobiles computer and the chips in the automobile to track you from their sky satellites. And if the death cadre's wish they can automatically shut down your automobile's motor individually or stop all moving vehicles over a wide geographical area. They will control you by traffic and monetary controls and you will be restricted to living within assigned areas of the country.

There is no place to hide from the death generation! They may even connect you to more sophisticated devices that allow them to hear and see any event in your daily life as well as to monitor your thought patterns.

You are the death generation in your person and species. You are the terror that faces yourself and that terror is making your lives miserable., because you are the death generation. Face yourselves or perish at your own hand!

FUTURIST COMMENTARY: Most of the historical records of Campbell's era were destroyed in the 21st century wars of terror. But we believe the author was referring to the united states government of the year 2001 which initiated a program of placing micro chips in the hands and often foreheads of U.S. citizen seemingly for the expressed purpose of stopping illegal immigration into the country. Civil war resulted, especially after it was discovered that hundreds of thousands of legal and illegal American citizens were being executed in the hundreds of concentration camps set up around the United States to contain the illegals, and that the government was covertly allowing gang members to rape and loot in night raids, seeming searching for drugs and illegals, but in actuality their purpose was to disarmed the citizens of their guns.

This was the time of the terrible American civil war which took place as The Death Cadres launched the invasion of the Americas; before it was over 38 million Americans perished in the death camps and America the beautiful perished from the face of the earth!

When order was restored a public hanging for treason, of the leaders of this government, took place at high noon, Oct. 1st, at 11:59 A.M. in Washington D.C. in the year 2,010. Campbell speaks to the theme of the death cadre concepts below:

On the governmental levels, trust and honor and the pushing of authentic family values are on some of their lips while in their hearts lie schemes of oppression and plans for the technological planting of microchips into their victims so as to better protect them against themselves and guide their freedoms of actions and thoughts. For these members of the death generation are the organized end of the spectrum of the culture of death and one step above the street generation of death, for they have plans of human redemption that embraces eugenic and ethnic cleansing and they hold in their hands a scheme of death so horrendous that life itself cries out for redemption from this scourge of degenerate humans who are so holy than thou that even God himself cannot speak to them; yet they glibly speak covertly of the holy honor that is theirs of uplifting the race toward the perfection of bureaucratic wholeness.

On the covert governmental and sociocultural levels they revel in the wholesale destruction of all that is sacred and holy and insert into the life currents the death of nihilism, confusion and ultimately slavery as the human sheep become too weak and confused to protest their destruction and enslavement. Remember always that in the absence of political freedom all your liberties are destroyed. [11] And in the name of public safety they will disarm you and put computer chips on your hand for identification which records all your life activities to their central computer and allows them to track you by sky satellite wherever you hide, and soon you will be but a number among all the rest of the slaves that politicians call their constituents and government bureaucrats their stooges.

Then they will break the back of your socioeconomic classes through exporting jobs and technologies out of the country and you will be landless American peasants who bows and takes his hat off to the lowliest government official. And in your shame and degradation you will have become a casualty of the organized death generation and you will weep and wail but your chains will be too strong to break and your strength sapped and you will die a number among numbers as prey to the death generation. And if you are no longer needed you will die a genocide victim on their guillotines and perish in their ovens to provide dog food and fertilizer for the betterment of human society.

But what can one say of their unholy plans that rests on terrible blueprint crimes of the past and on a pathology of death. In actuality they live in a confused present and in their minds the future rests on a pathological past which they would again make our future.

THE DEATH CADRE'S NEED TO CONTROL OTHER MEN

The most destructive flaw in the human personality of the death cadre is their propensity to control others. This surge of power or will to power seeming comes from a vital emotional drive which has been perverted by some member of the death cadre; in these men this natural sense of allowing their self to experience the world through accomplishments which develops into a perverse certainty about his or her's place in the destiny of the group. If the situation warrants it some power driven death cadre members become dictators who require all people under them to adhere to their truth and dogma and to be controlled by the presence of such a truth on the pain of death.

America's democracy lies in its death pangs whimpering and crying as the shrewd death cadre's manipulate the mass mind through the press and mass education. All of our noble and idealist leaders have been replaced by shrewd money-makers who now control the vote through political machinery and through ownership of the press and television. This insidious control influences the mass mind so much that it has ceased to think as the 30 second political TV spots condition the death generation to do the bidding of their death masters.

The death cadre controls the press so that most cities have only one newspaper; and the press is now free to notice only what they want to report and in any detail that suits their fancy. So now you have a situation that condemns any truth to death by just being silent about it. In a controlled press where is your freedom of speech or how can you protect yourself by using your constitutional rights if you don't have the money to back yourself up? [12] When they have laws that allow them to confiscate your property based merely on the accusation that you are under investigation how do you defend yourself as a penniless person? Also Congress has attempted many times to water down and destroy the 4th Amendment of the United States constitution so that police can enter America's homes at will and seize what they will. If the death cadre's are successful America the beautiful will become a vast totalitarian monster that will pollute the world with its madness.

The death cadre is on the march and through money control and by manipulating the voters they have made our elections into a preconcerted game, a farce perpetrated upon the mass mind called popular self-determination. And whom do they elect to our high offices but unscrupulous and non-intellectual politicians who will do the bidding of the Death Masters in the name of truth, honor and the will of the American people. [13]

There will come a time when the Death Cadre takes over the

political reins directly. No one can stop them because they will grow on the soil of degenerated democracy and conquer it.

Then the death barbarization will set in as the greatest democracy the world has ever known dies and becomes a horrible military giant of barbarism and death that shall bring about the entire extinction of the human race. [14]

All who live within the narrow domain of this certainty must live out their self-realizations within the confines of the controller's dictates. Malinowski asserts that once a people enter into an anti democratic action it tempts nations and people into the road of imperialism and dictatorships and military ventures and that violence will breed violence and engenders anti-democratic morality because of its efficiency,

Once the organized death generation realizes how efficient ruthlessness and quick decisions are and how effective obedience to a supreme command is, then the hell with public opinion, voting deliberation and any consideration given to the conscience of either individuals or groups of citizens. [15]

The modern age is now seemingly being affected not by one or several dictators but by a death cadre, a fifth column within American culture and within western civilization in lesser degrees. For convenience sake this destructive influence is called the death generation. They are the dark night of humanity's lower unconscious rising into the social order and overtly presenting themselves to humanity to demonstrate what the species has to change within themselves.

Thus in some subconscious sense all of the present generation are the death generation and the elite of this force who are the cutting edge of self-destruction that faces our nation, seemingly draw their energy and force from the unregenerated dark forces of humanity's unconsciousness. But America remember that the death generation must fulfill itself; for death is its middle name and truth but a variety of death pangs!

One does not question what one knows instinctively. One only acts and lives through its expression and its social actions. Ordinarily this fact of life has its positive nature and if a person does not live his own truth then he is a phony and divorced from his inner reality. Yet the facts of life are that only a unique minority in this life follow their positive inner feelings; only a few human beings within the great masses of populations are their own man.

Why is this so? Why are the masses of mankind driven by truth's foreign to their own nature? Perhaps the main argument is that most men are sleeping zombies and are dead to life itself. They follow their social conditioning. They live their culture's imperatives, their church's dogmas, their subculture's rules and often are driven by their lower natures.

On the sociological level there is the fact of cultural determinism which embodies various rules which guarantee's order and security and allows co-operation and social action under states of peace and progress. But within all cultural systems are certain concepts and rules that foster discrimination and oppression and may become inimical to freedom and in rare instances annihilate freedom for death concepts and actions.

Harold D. Lasswell in his classic book "Psychopathology and Politics points out that often there is a close relationship between a person's psychological nature and his political thinking. And that logical thinking alone cannot explain a person's action even where logic is adroitly used and that an individuals or government's logic that certain actions are in your own or your nations best interest may be dominated by illogic, fantasy, covert urges of revenge or paranoiac persecutions. [16] Generally such negative rules are based on concepts and doctrines outside the experiences of individuals but dictate claims of superiority, privilege and power to the true believer if he believes and acts on these rules of oppression. And it is to be noted that such false social doctrines of hierarchy and discrimination have to be associated with organized mechanism of physical violence and terror. And inevitable you find that any group which perverts the rules of freedom must use violence to pervert a culture's freedom rules. They must abuse you by constraints on your freedom because you will not willing give up your freedom unless it is taken away from you or you are deceived and tricked, manipulated and controlled and thus disarmed you perish or submit to the tyranny through your ignorance and naivete.

But you ask why would Americans stand for this; or what is the aspect of American social character which would allow this to take place? Is there some part of American character that allows our citizens to ignore the obvious, even when it faces us? Primarily the problem lies within concepts of rugged individualism and self reliance ideals connected with contemporary unconscious fears about the future. Americans are running scared on the social and unconscious levels and so long as they are left alone in their individual social space they will cower in their holes of despair and think pleasant thoughts and hope for the best. So don't ask them to stand up for their constitutional rights because they will try to ride out the storm of repressive governmental laws and regulations and pray that somehow they and their family and friends can survive the future social upheavals. Why? Because their social individualism is an ancient social rite.

It must be remembered that Americans have not changed some aspects of their national character much since The Frenchman Tocqueville's classic ethnography on American character and American Democracy in 1831. He viewed our politicians as political cowards and the American population as no better. But he admired our courage to the point of recklessness when Americans searched for personal fortunes and admired our independence but stated Americans really cared little for people outside their family or the narrow coterie of friends which surrounded them. He makes a specific point which characterize America's present attitude toward themselves and which reflects on America's attitude toward the homeless and other failures of the American system. He says:

> As in ages of equality no man is compelled to lend assistance
> to his fellow-men, and none has any right to expect much
> support from them, every one is at once independent and

> powerless . . . His independence fills him with self-reliance
> and pride among his equals; his debility makes him feel
> from time to time his want of some outward assistance,
> which he cannot expect from any of them, because they are
> all impotent and unsympathizing.(Vol. 2, p. 786.)

The organized death generation realizes this and know how to behaviorally manipulate you and how to divide and conquer and are sociologically wise and will use already developed mythologies, doctrines, knowledge about American National Character, and dogmas which have been accepted and have already molded countless peoples to culturally and spiritually condition themselves to passively submit to the death generations oppressions. [17] They will use psychological principles to manipulate Americas by exploiting their misery, thus using American cultural ideals against "Americans and will use hate as a uniting bond and take advantage of each person's inner hostility to incite people so they can put forward their ideas for radical changes as they covertly embrace death to the ignorance of the average man as they toast their successes to the extermination of ignorance and inferiority in the United States of America! [18] They will play on America's obsessive preoccupation with thoughts of imminent annihilation through a Nuclear Holocaust. They know that even with a tentative peace with Russia and the destruction of the Soviet Empire that America's phantasms of atomic destruction is still ruled by the Great Nightmares of fear which stupefies with terror American's from all walks of life. Even though all desire peace they cannot think of how to acquire it and find it easy to brood on war and death and to know in their hearts of hearts that only death lives in the future. [19] Everyone knows deep down now that some third world county will drag us into species annihilation and that our only future is death, death, death!

Generally you will find that rules that develop through education and through lessons learned within a culture's context or have a long tested tradition based on co-operation and ethical dimension are rules of freedom. Usually such rules of conduct may produce high degrees of discipline and performance but generally do not become rules of tyranny or oppression.

But there comes a time when a great corruption enters into the life of a people and their culture and then the civilization dies from within and death lies upon the winds of time and the stench of death lies just beyond the next curve.

It is a fact that political regimes and sociocultural philosophies are born into existing systems and they find meaning through growth, maturity and death. Each period will have its brilliant creativity and surely it's cycles of violent unrest and death. [20]

Why you ask does this have to occur. Well the answer must be sought in psychopolitics and from within the psychological nature of man; but realize this fact that when the individual inner man is dead the outer man is a zombi who has no life force, no strength of character, no inner force that allows him to exist.

But the wisest among our people know that if they transcend not their nihilism that the future is lost and the human race shall perish in their own misery and that their life will have been for not and even they unconsciously want to feel that their insignificant lives have some meaning and that their death signifies something, even if no one recognizes that fact!

But for most of them there is no past or future, only the present which stands on quicksand and represents the agony and meaninglessness of a life that seemingly should have never been! They have no hope and no guide to the future and they wish for none for they are the death generation and they fear no man alive and would just as soon waste you as spit in your face.

For death is joy to them and through taking life that gain meaning and significance. So to them human sacrifice is a holy act and sanctifies them to life itself and yet through their misery they call out for salvation from themselves. But who will give it to them? Know ye not that they are their parent's children and nothing can be done for them. Can one rotten apple help another ?

Can one lost generation save another? Can the lost save their children who are perishing before their very eyes?

It is written that truth and honor rests not on lies and deceit and that death is no answer to perversity and change! Can the dead cleanse their ranks of filth; no I say let the truth of the matter be decided in the arena of the possible and let the truth of eternity decide the future!

It is a time of action but also of reflection and the cleansing power must come from within each individual and nothing can be done to right the present if we do not have the resolve to elevate ourselves into the ranks of honor and truth. Great cultural changes of a positive nature will not occur until an inner resolve takes place and this is matched with positive overt outward action based on inner psychological balancing.

Crass materialism has destroyed the fabric of our society and the next step is the dissolution of its material structure; because our society rests on shallow concepts of reality and dying naive and childish religious myths, all of which are contributing to the death throes of our dying social order. Can something that is dead resurrect something that is dying? Even the religious spirit seemingly is failing us and has not the power to revitalize our dying culture or help the death generation.

Why? The religious spirit is something akin to artistic talent. It is either there or non-existent; or so weak that its flicker's of light has no strength or duration! But above all religion has been so perverted and constitutes such a mass fraud that even the naive can perceive the deception. Why? Because the evoutionary minds of the age will not accept nonsense and lies based on deception and fraud. It is time that the mature minds of society grew up and began to seriously interact with the reality of the situation and started to march in tune with the Cosmos. Yet it is seemingly a fact that this awareness is still on the unconscious level with most of mankind.

CAPITALIST REALITY AND
THE DEATH TECHNOCRACY

The psychological aspect of modern industrialism and capitalism that allowed individual Americans to amass wealth and use it as power was felt to lead ultimately to economic harmony in American society at large. Yes these striving caused intrasocial isolation and hostility in economics but it was believed that America was enhanced by such strivings for self-aggrandizements and the country was content and embraced this system. And the country did prosper and Americas material standard of living increased. But monopoly capitalism has arisen and its needs are for drone-boys to manage the store and America quakes as its national character wilts and dies to itself. The death of the independent, autonomous, rugged individual who is self reliant and a resourceful farmer or businessman is finally admitted. The small farmer and independent business man are daily dying in America as the lockeian concept of capitalism dies and is replaced by mega international technocratic corporations and governmental agencies who neither want nor need self reliant autonomous individuals to operate its large industrial and governmental agencies. The yes man, the subservient worker-drone who knows his place, the inter changeable gear-man who can fit in any where he is wanted, is now the industrial drone-boy of the hour. [21]

Work is no longer done for its intrinsic meaning but has become a job done for wages or salary as individual workers daily lose their sense of self-esteem and social purpose as his innate feeling of self-strength crumbles into inner and outer social anxiety. The worker-drone now has only money and its acquisition as an accepted criterion of success and prestige and he is always anxious and afraid. He has caught the dragon complex by the tail and is on its vicious circle as he stands on the quick-sand of his work career! If he loses his job or career he loses everything. He may become homeless or fall down the social class scale. Our worker drone must at all cost be successful because he never knows if his neighbor has more wealth or that he has achieved an unassailable job security thus he can never get off this treadmill of keeping up with the Jones. Tawney writes that job security is always out of the control of the worker, thus job security is always on our worker-drone's mind. Tawney says, "Thus the actual economic developments, particularly in the monopolistic phase of capitalism, work directly against the assumption of freedom for individual endeavor upon which industrialisms and capitalism are based."

But American National Character does not die easily because individual Americans can't let go of the assumptions of individualism, despite their contradiction with the work situation. The primordial fear-anxiety complex becomes operative now as individual middle and lower middle class workers redouble their efforts to gain security and to invest in property, annuities and the American dream. Anxiety for success is the motivation for their constant defence of the American dream, lest it stop before they "have it made." Why? [23] Americans have no permanent sense of ego security. Their sense of purpose and self-being rest on the success complex which rests on the back of the primordial fear-anxiety syndrome. Take away success from an American and you have a broken man or women. To fail in "America is to fall into disgrace and non-being. To fail is to face the death of your very personhood and you will die subtly daily to this fact rather than go down into total defeat. No horror of war, even of total annihilation itself is worse for an American than to fail in life. To fail in America is to become a bum who even your Mama-boss will not condone. Ah, but your death masters know all this and do they press this point on your job and take away what little sense of integrity you have left and ultimately they will crush you as they downsize and you become an all-American failure bum!

Corporate institutions have developed world views as a countershock against our old cultural ideals of who we are as individuals, and how we ought to relate to each other as social creatures. Thus dies independent man. He is being replaced by alienated and desecrated men who are enslaved by giant bureaucratic technocracy that views people as expendable numbers who must conform to their new order or they do not work. And when these people are no longer needed they are thrown to the dogs as necessary industrial casualties and forgotten.

Rollo May has said that "anxiety is a pervasive and profound phenomenon in the twentieth century". [24] But this anxiety was largely covert prior to the advent of the atomic era in 1945. It is interesting that Linds' study of Middletown in the 1920's found no overt anxiety but his later study in the third and fourth decades of our century show definitely overt anxiety throughout the social order. [25] Thus the primordial fear-anxiety syndrome emerged overtly within American life. But a thorough study of the social data shows that the entire social order is permeated with hidden anxiety. This is evident in the compulsive work of workers and businessmen who seemed to be running for dear life to earn money, and the pervasive struggle to socially conform, even as they live a compulsive social gregariousness in all their social activities. Even their leisure time is programed with organized activity.

Pascal describes the symptoms of covert anxiety as "the constant endeavor of people to divert themselves, to escape ennui to avoid being alone, until 'agitation" becomes an end in itself." It is interesting that only one citizen in Lind's original study noted this covert anxiety of his fellow citizens when he said "These people are all afraid of something: what is it?" [26]

In the 1930's the Lind's again studied Middletown and found conscious anxiety present; and the Lynd's observed that all the citizens had one thing in common, that is, " insecurity in the face of a complicated world." [27] Investigation showed that this anxiety was not totally because of the economic depression but because of the confusion of social roles which each individual was facing. The people of Middletown they wrote,

> is caught in a chaos of conflicting patterns, none of them
> wholly condemned, but no one of them clearly approved
> and free from confusion; or, where the group sanctions

are clear in demanding a certain role of a man or woman, the individual encounter cultural requirements with no immediate means of meeting them. [28]

Rapid culture change patterns were bringing overt anxiety to all the citizens of Middletown. The Lynd's observed, quite rightly, that "most people are incapable of tolerating change and uncertainty in all sections of life at once." [29] Modern research surely demonstrates that some people are unable to maintain their sense of well being when social changes come too rapidly. Generations of anthropologists can certify to the fact that when you are plunged into another culture you may hold on to your composure but you may also go into varying degrees of culture shock or become temporarily depressed or even become temporarily psychotic or suffer intense emotional problems or just be so freaked out that you have to immediately leave that culture. Modern travelers surely bare testimony to this fact . Some travels can't even make it beyond the airports of the foreign country being visited. Other world travelers cannot tolerate the foreign culture and go into culture shock and must leave that culture. Fortunately most Americans travel in sanitized groups that stay in English speaking hotels and travel in groups outside of the hotels to specified tourist spots. where they interact with English speaking guides.

In Middletown the people's tendency toward the changing social norms was to retrench into rigid and conservative social and economic social ideologies. Today you see this happening with conservative Christians and with the present Pope within Catholicism. [30]

When you have massive social anxiety within a society the possibility of fascism and subtle forms of industrial-corporate authoritarianism may develop which relieves this anxiety.

Today Americans live within a technocracy in which industrial society is integrating its anachronistic gaps into a higher organizational integration. It is up-dating, modernizing, rationalizing and planning its efficiency of large-scale co-ordination of men and resources. It seeks to extend to all areas of human life and mold free Americans into social organization that matches the precision of our engineering mechanistic patterns. These techniques of the entrepreneurial talent are now applied to orchestrate all human beings into the industrial complex so that politics, leisure, education, entertainment and cultural activities, even unconscious drives of protest against technocracy become integrated together into a vast sociocultural pattern of conformity to technocracy's aims and goals. All these facets now fall under technical scrutiny and purely technical manipulation and are designed to create new social organizations which support modern technocracy. [31]

Jacques Ellul makes the point that the technological age requires predictability and exactness, thus technique must prevail over human beings. This is a factor of necessity because for technocracy it is a matter of life or death that it reduce man into a technical animal who becomes a slave to technique. No autonomy in humanity is to be allowed and he is to be manipulated either negatively by scientifically understanding human nature or positively by integrating mankind into the technical machine framework that enslaves America. [32]

In order to accomplish human integration into the technocracy all human life must now be guided by a central core of experts who concern themselves with large-scale public necessities while their subsidiary experts apply the public pressure and pass laws pertaining to the personal aspects of life such as mental heath, child-rearing, sexual behavior, and recreation so that all of the human life style becomes subordinate to technocracy.

In addition technocracy has a multi-billion-dollar brainstorming industry which seeks to anticipate and accommodate and integrate into its social planning any new social patterns, even before the public is fully aware of them. Your secret death masters, thus, have plans either to adopt or to reject or to disparage new social themes before the sleeping public knows what's going on. An example of this was Herman Kahn's Hudson Institute's developing of strategies to integrate hippies into our social life and to look into the possibilities of programmed dreams for the general public. If the death Master deem it necessary to legalize now illegal drugs it may be that dream palaces and LSD sanitoriums will cover the land as our death masters tighten their sharpened tentacles of control over a slumbering America.

The roots of technocracy lies upon the basic concepts we have spoken about when America came into being. Obviously it is entangled in the scientific world view which is used to justify the death leaders reliance on technical experts. Beyond science there is no appeal and our corporate Masters rest their case on sensate materialism which rests on scientific methodology.

Theodore Roszak has made the point that because of technocracy's immersion into technological progress and scientific ethos it has become ideologically invisible; even while it values and concepts of reality become "as unobtrusively pervasive as the air we breathe." But in the meantime it consolidates its power as a transpolitical phenomenon, that is despite its most "appalling failures and criminalities", only because every body is paying attention to antiquated categories of political parties, etc. The technocracy thus appears as" a grand cultural imperative which is beyond question, beyond discussion. [35]

The concept of small and independent but dynamic free enterprise entrepreneurial systems has died a quiet death in America as the corporate structure takes over 70% + of the employment of people. The concept of the independent autonomous man of business and means who are the backbone of the republic lies quaking in its death throes.

The original concepts of industrialism and capitalism rests on many factors but of supreme importance is the idea of the force and power of free individualism, that is, the rationale for modern industrialism was the free and autonomous individual's right to amass wealth and employ it as power. [36] Tawmey makes a point that an individual's self interest and "natural instinct" for aggrandizement were apotheosized as legitimate social and economic motivations in life and society. [37] The original industrialism of the last two centuries was based upon "the repudiation of any authority [such as social value and function] superior to individual reason. Individual man, thus could follow his own interests and ambitions free from central powers who would subordinate him. [38] Today modern "industrialism is the perversion of individualism." [39] Monopoly capitalism now has a damaging and disintegrative effect on each person's relationship to himself and to his fellow men. [40]

But the most insidious thing about this happening is that its totalitarianism is subtle and has become progressively more subliminal by charming us into conformity by exploiting our conditioned allegiance to the scientific world view and by manipulating our needs for creature comforts and security. And the most dangerous part of all is that these death chiefs of technocracy do not see themselves as agents of a totalitarian control but rather as conscientious managers of a grand social system which is incompatible with any form of exploitation against humanity. [41] But Tillich says:

> During the last hundred years the implications of this system have become increasingly clear: a logical or naturalistic mechanism which seemed to destroy individual freedom, personal decision and organic community; and analytic rationalism which saps vital forces of life and transforms everything, including man himself into an object of calculation and control." [42] It is a fact that these agents of the death cadre want you to believe three basic and interlocking principles: "1. The enigma that is man has been solved and it is purely technical in character. Scientific analysis by specialists have impenetrable skills to solve all social and economic problems through personnel management and mechanical gadgetry. "If a problem does not have such a technical solution, it must not be a real problem. It is but an illusion . . . a figment born

of some regressive cultural illusion." 2. Science has compiled 99 percent of human needs and through rational social controls we can fulfill all our human needs. If friction appears within the technocracy then it is nothing more than a "breakdown in communication." 3. The social experts know our deepest needs and desires and can provide for our needs. If you have any doubts seek them out and you will find they are on the payroll of our state and/ or corporate structure . All the certified experts who count belong to headquarters[44]

Robert S. McNamara, in his book "The Essence of Security" states quite succinctly the above point He says:

Some critics today worry that our democratic, free societies are becoming overmanaged. I would argue that the opposite is true. As paradoxical as it may sound, the real threat to democracy comes, not from overmanagement, but from undermanagement. To undermanage reality is not to keep free. it is simply to let some force other than reason shape reality. That force may be unbridled emotion; it may be greed; it may be aggressiveness; it may be hatred; it may be ignorance; it may be inertia; it may be anything other than reason. But whatever it is, if it is not reason that rules man, then man falls short of his potential.

Vital decision-making, particularly in policy matters, must remain at the top. This is partly, though not completely, what the top is for. But rational decisions-making depends on having a full range of rational options from which to choose, and successful management organized the enterprise so that process can best take place. It is a mechanism whereby free men can most efficiently exercise their reason, initiative, creativity and personal responsibility. The adventurous and immensely satisfying task of an efficient organization is to formulate and analyze these options. [45]

While profiteering within the capitalist technocracy Is a central incentive this goal no longer holds it primacy since our largest industrial enterprises can count on a steady stream of high earnings; therefore the basic trend is toward large-scale social integration and control as an end in itself. It desires the rationalizing of the total economy. [46] Now we must deal with the paternalism of expertise within our cultural-economic system because our death Masters want greater and greater control over us since that is the efficient way to operate.

America's civil service and other public institutions are modeled on the British systems. It may be that our future death master will also adopt the following British ideas. In a documentary study of the British Health Service [47] they felt too much lay interference and wanted the service to be placed only in the hands of professionally competent administrators. And naturally they wanted only the most up to date hospital facilities. But in a straight matter of fact manner they proposed that in the future they felt their psychiatric faculties would have the job of certifying "normal behavior and have the power to do the adjusting to "abnormal–unhappy and ineffectual citizens–to the demands of technocracy. Does this mean that our future death cadre will use psychiatric manipulation to mold citizens to the world views of the Death Masters?

Further: the NHS felt that population control would also be in their hands, which meant additionally they would administer a "voluntary euthanasia" program for the incompetent and unproductive elderly. It is interesting that Dr. Eliot Slater, editor of a journal of psychiatry felt that even if the elderly retain their vigor " . . . they suffer from the defect of an innate conservatism." As quoted in the "Times Diary " he said, "Just as in the mechanical world, advances occur most rapidly where new models are being constantly produced, with consequent rapid obsolescence of the old, so too it is in the world of nature." [48]

The NHS would also have a program of compulsory contraception for adolescents who would have to apply in later life to the NHS for permission to have children. The National Heath Service, thus would additionally have the job of evaluating the genetic qualities of prospective parents before they had permission to beget.

This is your future America. Governments and political parties may come and go but the civil service technocracy goes on for ever. And they will force their will on the nearly pathological passivity of Americans dead to themselves.

Recently technocracy has begun a new program to extend its influence throughout the world, that is, within the last quarter of a century the technocratic corporate structure has begun to export jobs and technology overseas to take advantage of foreign child labor and 20 cent an hour labor forces and to prepare for the New United World Order. The result on the American scene is that the final death blow to what remains of American worker independence has slowly happened. The back of the working man is broke as his high paying jobs migrate and workers are thrown out of jobs, often at early middle age. Even high and middle management jobs are abolished for many men beyond age 40. Some beg themselves back into the corporate system at greatly reduced pay while others become as homeless as those who sit in squalor in shacks in the Appalachian mountains and on the streets of San Francisco. And the sad facts of life are that according to the Stanford Research Center that 19 million Americans will be homeless by the year 2,000.

A sad facts of life is that a miner, with possibly a 4th grade education and who can barely read or write but who is thrown out of work will never work again! But an even sadder fact of life is the worker with a high school diploma and even college graduates whom are thrown out of work in early middle age before they have reached even their earning potential are casualties of the new American way! But who cares. Expendable we all are to our corporate death masters. And if we protest too much or cause passive aggressive revolts we are enemies of the people and if large groups of us protest too much, all the better. The death cadre's need an excuse to clamp on a more sinister despotic dictatorship than now prevails. And they will do so in the name of public order over subversive public unrest. The laws are already on the books that will set aside the constitution when we have a national emergency. Cry America while you are manipulated and set in your place!

America is seemingly headed for a two class system of the elite and the lower classes workers who must work for minimal wages if they are to eat!

But the ultimate death stoke to our founding fathers capitalist illusions is the fact that our death masters, the wealth managers, and their political cohorts allied with the elite of modern corporate America, do not own the corporations they run. They control them and essentially their motto is the hell with America's stock holders if they try to influence business management beyond their permissible allowance. Recently a stockholder with $1,000,000 worth of stock had to finally sell her stock because she was impotent to make her influence felt within the company. America's stock owners are powerless absentee landlords whose authority has been usurped and America no longer is the land of independent free enterprise as the non-autonomous man becomes afraid and terrified of his future.

Today the alienated individual man is a caricature of his old self of dynamic individualism and now he is but a broken means to an end for his corporate bosses and their political cohorts and he must take his crumbs where he can and be grateful he is allowed to grovel in the dirt for what ever sustenance is thrown his way. He is an expendable human commodity and shown no mercy. Grovel America in the mud because America the free is obsolescent, as your American corporate death masters yell in no uncertain terms.

DEATH CRY

Death is the cry of the day and everyone rallies to its cry for the wisest among us know in their inner hearts that their time has come and the near future is unknown and that if they survive the death marches of the future they will be broken and crushed beyond recognition. But they don't know what to do about their lives and are confused and bewildered about their social and psychological situation, because death is upon the winds of time and in the depth of their subconscious being they know their time has come and they must face themselves by conquering their lower natures or perish on the wings of the death wind! But will they rise to the occasion? Will they face themselves and expose themselves and transform themselves? No you say! But they must or else all is lost!

But from within the still depth of humanity emerges a weak and feeble idea; " despair not humanity, the sage of life within us says, for all is not lost, all is not yet destroyed, all has not perished".

"Within the human spirit lies a source of eternal life that all may touch if they but desire. Touch that source and all will be well, touch that source and humanity's redemption from itself will commence as the golden age of the species emerges into the dawn of a glorious tomorrow."

Do we have to face the issue of freedom or death? Do we have to assert ourselves, face ourselves or perish? The chooses are grim but do we have any choice. Do we really have enough time to table the issue and hope everything will work out?

The cynic will say it is already too late, the optimist will assert that humanity has progress in his bones and will survive all the vicissitudes of life and evolution and triumph as a species.

But the death generation has already chosen and death is on their breath and murder in their subconscious and cruelty upon their hands. For nothing can help them but actionless death and the hate that motivates them. All those thus infected shall perish from the face of the earth. The only hope lies in the rest of us who stand on the side lines. Are you ready to do your part? Can you arise to the occasion?

Can you take the bull by the horns and declare that come what may your inner fortitude and goodness of character will triumph over the odds of defeat. If you can join the human race and transcend your lower natures and stand up for progress and assert your right to say we of the human race will become better than our lowest members and we will become more godlike and walk consciously into eternity.

The forces of life are upon the planet earth at this time and the species trembles and subtly moves on the subconscious level. For a choice is being given us to walk into the sunlight of a bright life or to fall into the abyss of the death generation. What is your choice America, life or death?

The death cry of the species screams to us from throughout the world. We have reached a point in the history of humanity in which a choice is being given us to transcend our lower evolutionary flaws. We must move into our highest human potential and become greater and vaster than we are presently. But our negative half dwelling, within our species lower subconscious natures, is manifesting in strength throughout the world as its cutting edge, the Neanderthal flaw men and women, are now emerging worldwide as the death generation and its executive branch is the death cadre, a factor we all own within our natures. Presently they emerge within a cross-cultural corps of a controlling death generation, representing all that has gone wrong with the species Homo sapiens! They are all of us in a symbolic sense facing themselves in a testing pattern against the rest of evolved humanity. If they get their way collective humanity will have lost it integrity and will perish as a species; we are presently the lost one who will cry the death scream which will descend upon us all as the Genocide Phenomenon!

In 1915 the futurist Aurobindo said " . . . The world is preparing for a new progress, a new evolution. Whatever race, whatever country seizes on the lines of that new evolution and fulfils it, will be the leader of humanity." [49]

We are in the midst of that titanic battle now America and history is waiting for your answer! But perhaps before we discuss further the negative aspects of America's failures we should in-

quire into the evolutionary crisis we are wallowing within presently. Perhaps we should also discuss the nature of the evolution
of consciousness and the gigantic cultural changes America and
the world is flounder within presently. the next few chapters will
address these situations so that later on in the book we can better
understand the nature of the culture of death which has America
by the throat.

CHAPTER 4

AMERICA'S CULTURE OF DEATH

FUTURIST COMMENTARY: Extinction is the ultimate end of all social systems. This is a fact and it is folly to believe that American culture shall escape the enviable fate of all cultures–death! The last 500 years has seen the death and destruction of thousands of cultures throughout the world. In many cases the inhabitants of many of these cultures became extinct through the overt or covert hand of genocide and in cases where some inhabitants survived their cultural organization and languages were lost.

It is a sad fact that humanity has within its personality system a runaway perversion that allows it to kill fellow members of the human race and exterminate them and degrade them and think nothing more of these acts than one would crushing a bud beneath one's feet.

Campbell, the social scientist, comments on the fact that the 20th century is really a time of darkness instead of the pseudo light of modern progress which it is portrayed to be by the controlled presses of the world. He sees this century as one of barbarism and death that rivals the dark days of the church's inquisition. He laments that the 20th century is a return to the dark ages as the forces of humanity's unregenerated unconscious sets the mood and creates the death knolls of the human race and its cultures. He says:

It is a sad day America when we must recognize the fact that the race of man is still struck in the dark mud of his primordial death consciousness and that America in particular has entered into a culture of death. America the beautiful has descended into the abyss of the culture death and none may say for certain if its truth light shall prevail or that the death destiny that now faces it shall not strangle the hope of the world into its oblivion of death!

It is a fact that our nation nows faces a peril of death so hideous and fearsome that if it does not perish in the coming battles for its integrity it will bears the scars of this titanic struggle for generations to come. It is not just a struggle against America's obsessive fear of annihilation by a foreign power but is a descent into the dark corners of America's unconscious. It is a battle for the minds and hearts and for the very soul of American life and its integrity. It is the pivotal battle of the century and America you are now called upon to show your colors and to become what you purport to be. There is no middle ground in this struggle. You cannot sit out the battle. You cannot run away from yourself. You cannot be an idle bystander hoping you can ride out the storm to safety; because there are no safe ports and no quiet harbors and no place to hide from yourselves. America this is your time of destiny. Stand up and transcend your faults or perish in the coming wars of terror!

America now has in its hands the capacity to annihilate the human race and it rejoices in this fact. The death masters have taken on the mantel and powers of God himself and they will succeed or take the planet itself down in a fiery annihilation that lies beyond our most fearsome imaginations.

Today additional individual adolescence nations also shout daily with glee because as kings of the mountain none may touch them and that they may dictate policy and truth to the rest of the world of mankind as they clutch their nuclear weapons of terror; even as certain third world nations rush to create their own models of the fiery death. Additionally, other equally ignorant Death Master Nations, who also have the "Bomb", threaten with equal bravado that none may dictate to them because history is on their side and that if they are restricted in any manner their bombs will annihilate all enemies of the people. Thus the age of nuclear terror is upon us and it places another notch on the gun that kills American culture and ultimately the world.

The greatest danger to America, however, is the enemy that dwells within each American as daily it manifest as a psychological projection into our outer culture from the dark inner natures of every death generation American. When there is no hope for the future a culture dies from within as its people gradually perish from the face of the earth. When a culture has an obsessive fear of annihilation by a foreign power it dwells within a culture of death! But when a nation begins to fear the enemy from within itself then it has entered the death pangs of its history. When a culture dies individually within the heart and minds of individual Americans the end of America is in sight.

When death faces America constantly, all challenges, joy, and humor flows out of a culture as the spectacle of death takes over and insidiously destroys what ever fiber of morality and ethic remains. It manifests everywhere. But when it become formal American foreign policy and rests on concepts of death so hideous that one would think that only fiends from hell would speak in such terms, one knows America's obituary is being written. And when America's pure knight of honor and integrity dies to itself all is lost. Today the joy and a challenge to America's youth stands on the mantel of death, a step has been taken that no man can undo. It is pure idiocy that our scientists and statesmen imagine that national honor may require us to incinerate hundreds of millions of corpses to maintain freedom and justice! President Kennedy has said that:

> . . . . I still exceedingly regret the necessity of balancing those hazards {from the fallout consequent on aerial bombing testing} against the hazards to hundreds of millions of lives which would be created by any relative decline in our nuclear strength. [1]

Corruption takes over in America as idiot Death Masters and other incompetent people use top-secret classifications to hide their bungling and idiotic errors; hidden technologies are developed that allow hidden factions to do what they will under the clock of secrets and national defence. It is but a moment from the war's of terror America. Beware!

There comes a time, which no man can predict with sureness, when the spirit of the nation and culture flees to the hills of despair and dies in agony alone and in disgrace and its whimpers are heard by no man because in the arrogance of his pride he has no ears to hear and no comprehension of his coming demise. And if he could hear he would reject outright any news of the pending death of American life and spirit.

Woe to a nation who, in the ignorance of the night of their falsehood, rejects the signs of the times and instead rejoices at their freedom for degeneracies and its euphoric thrill and its touch of culture death as it defecates on all that is holy in America. Such fools surround us daily as they laugh over their triumph over superstition and ignorance. What they think is life is death and they do not know that they are dead men walking through life as a zombies who are controlled by the dark forces of their unconscious and are still guided by the dead hand of outmoded tradition; and when they partially wake up they are taken by the deathmaster's hand into the camps of the culture's morticians and given uniforms of war and political worth to wear and thus documented are embraced within the ranks of the dark ones who preach peace and truth, love and justice. Now as a card carrying member of the death generation they are a purveyor of truth and modern ideals and by upholding the agenda of the dark priests from our culture of death they too contributes to the death generations ultimate goal of truth through death, life through patriotic dementia.

CULTURE OF DEATH

All sciences and cultures have overt and covert theoretical designs that map their world views and conceptual realities. During long and often short periods of time the exigency of the historical process causes these ideas and themes to be altered, lost, destroyed or as in the present era to become dysfunctional along with certain aspects of the grand paradigm conceptual scheme. When cultures change, dynamic alterations occur in the concepts of individual identity and national character, thus setting up grave psychological disturbance within the social character and unconsciousness of a people collectively and individually.

When both of these processes happens a social crisis of great proportion occurs within the world's order as the society's sciences, religious concepts and codes of conduct, and general life forces wane and gradually die a death of agony and populace disbelief.

When a culture dies a great people's spirit also dies along with it and woe to their inhabitants who inadvertently commit mass culturecide; for their tears of death create a gap in the human experience. America, none may stop the death pangs of what is dying to itself.

The crisis of cultural death has appeared within American society. The country's cultural life force is wilting and dying to itself and the death force is so insidious that though the death rattle is heard it is discounted as an aberration. The perceptive among us realize that American society's time has come and that there may be no hope for old glory. We morn for the loss of all we hold dear and honor what is dying to itself within American society. We hope against hope that old glory can be resurrected in a revitalization of American culture. We pray that American's life force will emerge out of the present social malaise so that we will not see the ship of America go down into the sea of oblivion!.

This crisis has seven integral causal agents which are discussed throughout the book. The connecting theme which runs throughout the discussion concerning these causal factor is the concept of the Genocide Phenomenon as it refers to the death generation and the human condition but more particularly to the death of the American culture and American's national character. An examination of this cultural disease will show that it affects America on all social, economic, industrial levels and philosophical levels throughout the entire social order. It is the social cancer that is killing America; no American social institution has escape infection!

In this chapter we will begin dealing with aspects of the death of the psychocultural womb of culture through which we breath and have internalized in our subconscious natures as Americans. We will leave to another chapter to discuss the constituent elements of the nature of our culture but instead concentrate on several core values as they have developed historically and examine the contemporary changes that have occurred to them.

We will look at the culture of death in terms of basic American values and how a shift in the actualities of these cultural values and motivations can start the destruction of American cultural life. Remember that the seven causal factor are interconnected and a discussion of any one factor will always be incomplete.

It is also necessary that this chapter define the original American cultural values and its philosophical cultural bases so we can later discuss the process of culture change and its repercussion on each person individually and socially.

WHAT IS WRONG

Americans don't know the full extent of how or why society is breaking down but they do know something is wrong with us as a people and as a nation. This book attempts to explain how and why American society is dying and if there is any hope for the patient. Before we get into the nature of culture and its process of change let's start our investigation by looking at some of America's core values as they developed historically so that we can examine them as they are now in their changed form This way we may understand ourselves better and perhaps get a clue as to not only what ails us but also how we may cure ourselves individually and as a family and as a people. We cannot understand the social changes now taking place if we have no understanding of the original social concepts upon which our social order is built. This information is necessary also if we are to understand the real nature of culture and consciousness which we will discuss in greater detail in later chapters. Additionally such information will help us understand the cultural variables necessary to understand the modern dilemma of culture change in relationship to the evolution of culture which may give clues to where the present era is heading.

AMERICAN WORLD VIEW

American culture has a world view that provides a frame of reference for organizing life's activities that explain the how and why of daily existence and gives significance and meaning to each American's existence. A large part of this frame of reference is unconscious and so internalized from childhood that it is unquestioned and looked on as the only right and moral way of perceiving reality. An indepth study of the nature of socio-cultural reality as it relates to culture and personality and culture theory and culture change will be undertaken in later chapters of this book. This chapter will deal only with the historical process of some of the core values of the American world view and of the scientific paradigm models that support American social life and integrity.

WORLD PROGRESS IN AMERICAN LIFE

The idea of progress is inherent in this world view, thus most Americans know the world is progressing forward into a better state as the world thinkers and scientists steadily accumulate human knowledge and methods. Americans also think that each person is an autonomous entity who has the inherent power to uplift himself into a progressively higher and more noble state of being. They know that nature has an order to it and that scientific observations are always objective and that it is natural for people to desire to own private property.

Today Americans live under the seventeenth-century Newtonian world machine paradigm that took shape some 400 years ago. Naturally it has been refined and modified but retains much of its early vision as its shadow influences our every move and thought process. [2]

The modern world view rejects ancient concepts by saying that history continues in a straight line and each future stage represents an advance over the preceding one, thus as Jacqques Turgot said in 1750 that history is both progressive and cumulative. Life is lived within constant change and movement that is progressive, even if occasionally progress is uneven or retreats a few steps it will still move progressively forward toward the perfection of life on earth and for the creative fulfillment of the human species. [3]

Today, after a period of 300 years we are living with the ideas of three architects of the mechanical world view, that is, with the ideas of Francis Bacon, Rene Descartes, and Isaac Newton.

With the publication in 1620 of Francis Bacon's Novum Organum, Bacon laid the groundwork for the modern world view by stating that, "Now the true and lawful goal of the sciences is none other than this: that human life be endowed with new discoveries and powers."[4] He emphasized that through science humanity would "enlarge the bounds of human empire, to the effecting of all things possible." [5] Thus through the objective knowledge of science mankind would take "command over things natural—over bodies, medicine, mechanical powers and infinite others of this kind." [6]

Next Renee Descartes, a mathematician laid the groundwork of the mechanical world view by stating that the world can be reduced to mathematics. He states that " . . . it gradually came to light that all those matters only are referred to mathematics in that order and measurements are investigated, and that it makes no difference whether it be in numbers, figures, stars, sounds or any other objects that the question of measurement arises." He felt that through mathematics that " . . . such a science should contain the primary rudiments of human reason, and its province ought to extend to the eliciting of true results in every subject." [7] He goes on to say that mathematics " . . . is a more powerful instrument of knowledge than any other that has been bequeathed to us by human agency, as being the source of all things!" [8]

So at one stroke Descartes turned all nature into simple matter in motion and reduced all quality to quantity and announced that only space and location mattered." Give me extension and motion," he stated, "and I will construct the Universe." [9] No longer was the world messy, alive or chaotic, because everything had its place and all relationships were harmonious and worked with precision. They presented to humankind a faith that the world could be known and man could be its master. [10]

Isaac Newton discovered the mathematical methods for describing mechanical motion by explaining that one law could describe how a planet moves or how leaf falls from a tree; thus he subjected all nature to the laws of mathematics. Newton states that "all the phenomena of nature may depend on certain forces by that the particles of bodies by some causes hitherto unknown, are either mutually impelled toward each other, and cohere in regular figures, or are repelled and recede from each other." Newton's three laws state "A body at rest remains at rest and a body in motion remains in uniform motion in a straight line unless acted on by an external force; the acceleration of a body is directly proportioned to the applied force and is the direction of the straight line in which the force acts; and for every force there is an equal and opposite force in reaction." [11]

The mechanical world view thus came into being and dealt exclusively with material in motion that was cold, inert and made up entirely of dead matter. God was given credit for creating the universe but was retired from the science as unnecessary and then entirely forgotten. Dostoevski spoke for the age when he said "If there is no God, everything is possible." [12]

The mechanical paradigm soon became accepted because it

was simple, it was predictable and it worked in the real world. It also explained how the universe functioned and could be ascertained by scientific observation and mathematical formulas.

What it didn't do was predict the chaotic behavior of persons and their erratic thinking patterns.

The solution to this dilemma was the concept that society was only misbehaving because they were not adhering to universal natural laws that govern the universe. If science could figure out just how these natural laws applied to human being's, it was calculated that social institutions could apply them in short order. Thus, was born the idea of seeking human perfection in this world; history, therefore, is now a progressive journey from disorder and confusion to a well-ordered and predictable social state when viewed from the Newtonian world machine.

Two men developed concepts that showed the relationship among society's behavior and universal laws. John Locke showed how the workings of government and society fell under the world machine paradigm while Adam Smith brought the economy under the wing of this new paradigm model.

Locke concluded that society was chaotic because its traditions were based on irrational traditions and customs that originated from the theocentrism from the ancient past. He concluded that religion had to go because by definition God was unknowable and must be removed as a social prop for government. He only conceded that each person could believe in God but it was bad policy to put God in government affairs.

God is removed from the affairs of humanity and man is alone for the first time in the universe. Mankind is now mere physical phenomena who are cold, mechanical bits of matter interacting with other bits of matter in a mechanical universe. Formal religion is looked at askance because as Thomas Jefferson says, "In every country and in every age the priest has been hostile to Liberty; he is always in allegiance with the despot, abetting his abuses in return for protection for his own."

Humanity could create their own meaning for existence and

Locke proclaimed that pure self-interest was the basis for the establishing of the state and that in particular society must emphasize the protection and allowance of property acquiescence and values.

Man lived in a materialistic and individualistic society; man was a social atom and his purpose in life was to amass personal wealth and self-interest was his moral imperative and the only basis for society. Government's purpose was only to allow persons the freedom to utilize their power over nature to produce wealth and to subjugate nature so that people might acquire material prosperity for their creative fulfillment. [13] Locke emphatically stated that persons must become "effectively emancipated from the bonds of nature." [14]

Locke insists that mankind is good by nature and only acts evil when there is a scarcity and lack of property because people are by nature acquisitive; therefore if wealth can be increased social harmony will spread and uphold society. He feels nature provides enough raw material so that all mankind can fulfill their self interests of material acquisition and that this self interest will not conflict with others. Above all he insists that the world is a gift to the industrious and rational people and those who can apply reason the best shall benefit the most in life. [15]

Locke is emphatic in presenting the idea that the ownership of property, which means value that is extracted from nature, is not only man's natural right but a duty that one has to generate wealth. Locke insists that "land that is left wholly to nature . . . is called as indeed it is, waste." [16] Nature thus has value only when we mix our labor with it and make it productive. Locke states that each person should "heap up as much of these durable things (gold, silver, and so on) as he pleases; the exceeding of the bounds of his just property not lying in the largeness of his possession, but the perishing of anything uselessly in it." [17]

Modern man and America in particular embrace Locke's concepts so much so that the individual is reduced to seeking the meaning of life through the hedonistic activities of production and consumption, thus our dreams and desires take the road in pursuit of material self-interest.[18]

Adam Smith developed an economic theory that reflects the mechanical world view of Newtonian paradigm. In his book The Wealth of Nations, he says that just as there are natural laws that rule the heavens so there are laws that rule economics. He states if humanity obeys economic law's prosperity and material wealth will accrue and growth will come to the people. The functions of governments are to not interfere with these immutable natural laws of economics. Specifically governments ought not to put regulations and control over the economy or they will stifle this laissez-faire economy, that is, the idea that by leaving things alone so people can act naturally and unhindered in their economic lives.

For Adam Smith humanity's selfishness is a virtuous activity and through such activity's scarcity will be overcome. Smith, thus, removes morality from economics and states that any attempt to do so interferes with the "invisible hand" that asserted the natural law that governs economic principle in the market place. This natural principal governs the economical process and automatically allocates jobs, capital investments and good's production. Humanity, through rational reason can discern this principal. He insists that free, unfettered trade and competition between acquisitive persons, living in a continuously expanding market is what makes the world go around

Humanity, according to Adam Smith, is basically egoistic in pursuit of material gains and subordinates the rest of their desires to satisfy economic goals. Man individually does not have to make ethical choices but only use utilitarian judgment when he pursues his material self-interest. [19]

The mechanical world view achieved its greatest triumph in 1859 with the publication of Darwin's On the origin of species. Social philosophers like Herbert Spencer seized on the more superficial trappings of this concept by asserting that this theory was proof positive that progress exists in the world. Social Darwinism was thus born and the concepts of natural selection and the survival of the fittest provided support for the mechanical world view that enlightened self interest leads to material well being and to social order.

Survival of the fittest is reinterpreted to mean that all mankind is engaged in a relentless battle with other men and those who survive pass on their superior traits to their offspring and are better able to protect their material self interests. Evolution is the means through which a progressive social order is increasingly brought into manifestation with each succeeding generation developing better means to maximize their own self-interest through material needs.

The world view of the mechanical age accepts the notion of progress to create a more material environment. Its sciences are designed to reduce nature to consistent principles or rules: its technology is the application of these rules. [20]

Mind is reduced to matter and subjectivity eliminated by putting man and world within a system of objects linked together by universal relationships. Scientific knowledge is the only legitimate knowledge. [21] The materialist, thus, uses science, to deny human subjectivity by declaring that men are objects, that is, the subject matter of science, yet he doesn't see himself as an object because he is an objective beholder and can contemplate nature as it is.[22]

Man, thus is a rational person who can arrive at autonomy in his social, intellectual and emotional life. Mathematics is the chief tool of reason through which man creates "autonomous reason" as Tillich calls it or as Cassirer's phrases it "mathematical reason. Autonomous reason will make it possible to master physical nature, including the human body, which will be mastered and controlled by means of mechanical, mathematical laws.[23] "Mathematical reason is the bond between man and the universe." [24] And with the liberation of reason in every person a period of universal humanity and a system of social harmony will develop. Within this system no person need feel isolated because if he courageously pursued his interests they will fall into an accordance with his fellow men. [25]

The mechanical view of the universe walked, hand in hand, with the first Industrial Revolution which replaced the energy of man and animals by the mechanical energy of steam, oil, electricity and the atom. Small and medium-sized industrial enterprises were developed and managed by individual owners who exploited their workers while they personally became members of the middle and upper classes and masters of their homes and destiny. Ruthless exploitation of indigenous, non-white population, took place as domestic worker reforms occurred and eventually in the first half of the 20th century the working class rose from its abysmal poverty to a comfortable life style within industrial society. [26]

The mechanical paradigm, according to the historian Walter Schubart exists in the age of the Heroic culture mentality in that man views the world as something to be conquered. Humanity must put it in order by human organizational effort. Mankind, thus, does not live peacefully in the world but strives against nature, because he has self-confidence, and self-pride and a lust for power that looks on the world as at a slave. He will master it and mold it and create a world according to his plans.

The heroic man has indeed broken down the power of the former religious rulers and political powers and has succeeded in mastering nature and has become economically stable as he walks into the rational world view. The modern rational man has relegated the dark and diabolical forces of man's nature to the dark middle ages by explaining them as cunning schemes of deceitful kings and priests. [27]

The heroic man looks not to heaven but uses his lust for power to conquer the material world by using empirical tools of science. Secularization thus becomes his destiny and heroism is his life feelings and tragedy his end and final destination

This world is dynamic, nothing is static and man will challenge any power, even the strength of God. He is always maximally energetic, active, tense. He has to be the master of the earth and indeed he has changed the face of the earth and is even now pushing his plans for the total conquest of nature. [28]

The historian Nikolai Berdyaev calls this age the humanist-secular phase that is leading toward a new dark middle age, that is, the twentieth century is a transitory era that is witnessing the death of an age and its disintegration of civilization into a future dark age.

In the mean time man is the measure of all things and values because man is the center of the universe. His purpose is to develop the free, creative forces of humanity. He is to face and test his freedom unhampered by outside forces except his own senses, self-control and reason. All his actions are a liberation from superhuman controls and are dedicated to the glory, power, and creatively of self mastery. [29]

THE MODERN AGE AND THE UNITED STATES

F.S.C. Northrop makes the point that the social soul of the United States of America is an Anglo-American cultural system based on the philosophy of John Locke and supplemented by that of David Hume, Bishop Berkeley and other English empiricists; and is based especially on the sciences of Galieo, Huygens and Newton's Principia.

Northrop says that the American Declaration of Independence, The Constitution of the United States, American concepts of property and property legal statutes, conceptions of the rights of man and of government, etc., is an almost a verbatim articulation of the philosophy of John Locke.

On the economic front America's economy and ethics are based broadly on the concepts of Adam Smith, Malthus, Ricardo and Jevons, along with the utilitarian ethics of John S. Mill and Jeremy Benthan, that rest on Locke's concepts of economic and ethics.

Northrop says even the Protestant religion of America is an

enunciation of Locke's concepts of religion. Max Weber also points out that Capitalism is the counterpart of calvinist theology which regarded wealth not as just an advantage, but a duty. Business is not to be regarded as perilous to the soul–summe periculosa est emptionis et venditionis negotiatio, but acquires sancity. Labor is now a spiritual end and covetousness is no longer a great danger to the soul; in fact poverty no longer is meritorious. Money making and piety are now natural allies which develop diligence, thrift, sobriety, prudence through hard work and progress. [30] For the Calvinists success is the one visible sign that the worker is one of the chosen ones. [31] This concept finds expression in Benjamin Franklin's autobiography when he answers the question of why money should be made out of men by quoting Prov. xxxii. 29, "Seest thou a man diligent in business? He shall stand before kings". [32] Thus was born the capitalist work ethic which transcends business astuteness by requiring the person to obey the rules of work ethics as a duty to life itself. [33] In fact, the summum bonum of this social work ethic, with its concept of earning money and then more money without any spontaneous enjoyment of life is devoid of any eudaemonistic or hedonistic admixture. Your work is done purely as an end in it self and the acquisitions of money and property are the ultimate purpose of life. [34]

Anglo-American democracy assumes that each person is capable of controlling himself and can regulate his personal conduct, thus governmental control must be kept at the lowest possible strength. This concept rests on the idea that each citizen has a strict conscience which rests on categorical imperative of right and moral conduct. This code will control a person individually and regulate one's fellow citizens. [35]

Northrop concedes though that the total culture of the United States contains aspects of other cultural systems such as remnants of Indian pre-colonial culture, the Aristotelian-"Thomist Catholic Church and an emerging new culture that transcends the Galilean-Newtonian-Lockean culture that is based on up to date natural science grounded on modern science. On the whole although the major cultural system in the United States is the Lockean-Protestant-Individualistic-Businessman-Atomistic Operational cultural system that represents Locke's tabula rasa of the human soul or personality. [36]

Thomas Jefferson, the writer of the declaration of Independence, in a letter to a young law student, gives us a glimpse of the genies of the literary influences that underlie the cultural imperative of American culture. He advises him that from dawn to 8:00 A.M., to read the physical and natural sciences, religion, ethics and philosophy. He preferred the empiricists and materialists. He recommends reading John Locke twice, especially his Essay concerning Human Understanding and Conduct of the Mind in Search after Truth: also he recommends Dugald Stewart's Elements of Philosophy of the Human Mind, Condorcet's great Outlines of an Historical view of the progress of the Human mind, and Kames's Essays on the Principles of Morality and Natural Religion. From 8 o'clock to noon he tells him to read Cole's Institutes, that deals with endless legal arguments against the imprisonment of commoners and their maltreatment and of the extralegal liberties against them.

From 12 o'clock in the afternoon until one o'clock, Jefferson instructs his young friend to study political works, especially Locke, Sidney, Priestley and Malthus. In the afternoon he is to read history written by Greek and Latin authors in the original, On Burke and Roberston on American annals and on Gibbon's Decline and Fall of the Roman Empire. In the evening the young law student ought to turn to literature, rhetoric and oratory and study the criticism of style in felicitous phrasing and imitating the oratorical effects of Demosthenes and Cicero by practicing among his friends. [37]

Jefferson, the writer of the Declaration of Independence, sets the stage for our country's mind set by seeking the equality of man based on scientific findings [38] and sought a rational and materialistic source for man's intellectual equipment by rejecting revelation and theological assumptions. Jefferson viewed man's mind as an extension of his nervous system and felt that science would eventually yield up all of man's secrets. Man's genius lay within the flesh and blood structure of his nervous system. [39]

So ultimately a materialistic psychology is the basis of American democratic fervor, that rests on the unswerving confidence in mankind's limitless capacity to surpass himself in all human endeavors. [40]

This materialistic psychology rests on sense experience alone. The dichotomy between the mind and body enuniciated by Descartes and other thinkers of the seventeenth century supports this concept At all costs irrational experience is suppressed by a preoccupation with rational, mechanical phenomena. [41] Sensations are the foundation of human development and find expression in the French intellectuals that Jefferson knew so well from his life in France. Cabanis, Condorcet, and tracy and of course Locke, whom a century before stated their position succinctly in his book, Essay Concerning Human Understanding. He rejects unequivocally any possibility of innate ideas, and puts all learning within the domain of the senses alone. He says "Let us then suppose the mind to be, as we say, white paper, void of all characters, without any ideas." From sensation "all those sublime thoughts that tower above the clouds . . . take their rise and footings." A similar concept is produced by Cabanis, in his book Rapports du physique et du moral de l'homme, whom Jefferson felt was "the most profound of all human compositions," in that Cabanis states there is no separation of sensory and spiritual actions. Even Condorct, in his great work, Outlines of an Historical View of the Progress of the Human mind, says that "The first great advance in thinking was Aristotele's conclusion that all ideas, even the airiest abstractions and intellectual flights, originate in man's sensations." [42] From the Englishman William Godwin's book Enquiry Concerning Political Justice, Jefferson, accepts the concept that Godwin and his French contemporary's assert that the root of all experience was sensory. From the English biologist Hartley he accepts the function's concept of vibrations as the core of all sensory action. Thus one of the fathers of our country has set the tone of modern America in sensory categories that is now leading to the Death of America.

AMERICA'S SENSORY CULTURE

America's life force is sensory. In fact, sociologist Pitirim A. Sorokin sees the modern age as a dying Sensate Culture. He states that Sensate culture is based on the concept that true reality and value are sensory; and that there exists no reality beyond what we can hear, see, touch, smell and taste. The Sensate concept is an articulation and materialization found though out "American culture in its science and philosophy, religion, its laws and ethics and politics and economics, social institutions and its fine arts."[43]

Sensate culture also rests on the progressively linear theories of science and of the evolution of the human species. The historic process is viewed as if it were a progressive advance along the highway of life, with some deviation and detours from caveman to superman. Sorokin says that all twentieth century linear theories are but midget variations of Hegelian, Comtian, Spencerian, or Marxian models of progress-evolution. [44]

Science is the basic cornerstone of modern social orders and objectivity is its icon god and the truth of reality rests on the scientific method.

AMERICAN NATIONAL CHARACTER IN 1831

American national character is thoroughly engrossed with the concepts of materialisms and lopsided in its preoccupation with amassing wealth and status and prestige rests on each person's rising standard of living. This was a fact of life in 1831 when Tocqueville visited us and still embraces us today in its death grip. This preoccupation with materialistic accumulation now leads us into the arena of the Genocide Phenomenon.

It is interesting that though Tocqueville admired our peacefulness, our justice and independence yet he was saddened by our flaws. He thought us "the most prosaic of all peoples on earth, a fact that bored him to death. He felt American politicians were political cowards and the general population as well. He felt Americans were empty-headed, and in mortal dread of being different from their neighbors. He considered us lopsidedly occupied with material enjoyments and making money. But he admired our courageous pursuit of personal fortune but saw that beneath this materialistic bravado lived a fear of life that imprisoned Americans into social and political conformity. He found Americans lived with fear of having any deviant opinions. [45] Tocqueville writes:

> "When I survey this countless multitude of beings, shaped in each other's likenesses, among whom nothing rises and nothing falls, the sight of such universal uniformity saddens and chills me, and I am tempted to regret that form of [aristocratic] society which has ceased to be. . . . (Vol. 2, p. 825.)"

AMERICAN PEOPLE

Americans have long considered their country as a utopia just waiting to happen. It is a privileged place to live. To be born an American is to receive the grace of providence and every American who walks on this sacred soil has the obligation to fulfill his innate nature for God and country and to keep the land free and undefiled by foreign and negative influences! When the cold war between Russia and the United states was strong many Americas proposed that we bring twenty thousand Russian University students annually into the United states for two years of study. Why? Naturally they would return to Russia so full of love and admiration for the United States that no war between us would be possible! [46] When General Patton circulated an order to his troops prior to the invasion of Europe in 1943, in order to uplift the morale of his troops, he spoke also as an American:

When we land, we will meet German and Italian soldiers whom it is our honor and privilege to attack and destroy. Many of you have in your veins German and Italian blood, but remember that these ancestors of yours so loved freedom that they gave up home and country to cross the ocean in search of liberty. The ancestors of the people we shall kill lacked the courage to make such a sacrifice and continued as slaves. [47]

Do you think any of Patton's solders questioned his order or the premise upon which he spoke? His soldiers were Americans and they did their duty even if many were descended from German or Italian nationals. Why? Because they were first, second or third generation Americans whose ancestors had left their native lands to become Americans.

The soldier's parents and grandparents and greatgrandparents left their native cultures and rejected old ways to accept new ideas and concepts of living and their children were born in America and became socialized as Americans and embraced American's culture, language, customs and eventually threw off the authority of their immigrant fathers. Yes Papa was even rejected as ignorant, old-fashioned and in significant ways, alien. He became a source of shame and opprobrium as his children recognized that Papa was not an appropriate role model or a guide and exemplar. But Mama, was retained as an emotional source of love and food and succor; but all of Papa's children knew that to grow up like Papa, who at best was only a half-American, was to become a failure, a fact that even the father recognized. The strange fact is that even by this act of rejecting father the first-born generation Americans were not entirely creating a new social norm because native born families were doing the same thing since the exigencies of the new industrialism kept Papa away so much from the family that Mother now became the Mama-boss!

Papa now was a weakened semi-relative who eventually becomes almost a non-entity in American family life.

The English anthropologist Geoffey Gorer considers the first-born generation break from their immigrant Americans of major importance in the development of American National character. It must be remembered that in 1860 American had a population of 30 million people which consisted of slaves, old folks, parents and children. During the next 70 years another 30 million young immigrants crossed the ocean to America. In American cities the immigrants outnumbered native born Americans. Even as late as 1940, eleven and a half million white Americans were foreign born and about twenty-three million Americans had foreign born parents. The significance of this fact is that they were not a small group fitting in to a larger social order but the immigrants were in size large enough to change the society they were moving into in certain significant ways..

The significance of this fact is that the immigrant population was large enough to bring about a change in the American national character which was predicated on the fact that Papa was rejected as a guide and model as a private solution to personal problems of acculturation into American society yet this very fact became an act that reverberate in every family in America to this day because mother-dear became Mama-boss and as the family authority figure who gave only conditional love which was based on the child's obedience, thus, Americans acquired a feminine consciousness which rests on conditional love based on temporary success patterns. The symbolic act of rejecting Papa as a moral authority, so as to be accepted into American society, also symbolically reenacted America's colonists rejection of England and King which brought independence from King George, the father figure.

This fact is very important if you are to understand a core American value. America by rejecting Father England's authority was also culturally rejecting authority which was coercive, arbitrary, morally wrong and despotic. This fact is reflected in America's constitution through which authority is jealously circumscribed through balanced checks based on the principle of divided power so that no person or group can gain excessive authority. America through this act reinvented the ritual Freud spoke about when downtrodden sons collectively killed their father but pledged among themselves to established the legal equality of the brother by rejecting the dead father's legal authority and privileges. [48] But even though father England is dead he is still part of American national character covertly. Each American male has rejected Papa-dear, along with whatever country of origin his ancestors came from but the new father-figure on the internal scene is feared and resented. The "unnat'ral old parent" as Dickens stated in 1843, lives on in Americans unconsciousness as the authoritarian father who is hated and loved, copied and mistrusted, admired and resented, despised yet looked up to with a sensitive ambivalence which never falls into indifference. [49] Remember this fact though, that when Cain slew Able, from a biblical point of view, he did it over jealousy of a fathers' love.

The American declaration of Independence and the American 'Constitution declares a compact that guarantees freedom and equality of all Americans. It is a common renunciation of all authority over people, that is a rejection of father's envied and hated privilege. [50]

Americans psychologically are emotional egalitarians, technically toward all men but emotionally to other whites only and any subordination of one man to another is repugnant and legally forbidden. American's believe that any authority over people is morally detestable; and you must at all cost resist such unAmerican urges. Americans are suspicious of people seeking authority and are ever vigilant and look askance at governmental office holders. They consider them as potential enemies and usurpers. [51] A weak government is always preferred over strong authority. Americans feel that authority is inherently bad and dangerous, therefore any governmental" . . . authority must be as circumscribed and limited as legal ingenuity can devise." In all cases governmental office holders must remain under constant scrutiny and be considered as potential enemies. [52] "Authority over people is looked on as a sin, and those who seek authority as sinners." [53] Any person who exercises authority over people are suspect unless they do so only to improve their social portion or to make money. The people who desire military careers as officers are also suspect! Aside from a few families in the south and southwest, in which military careers are quasi-hereditary, most of the main body of graduates of West Point and Annapolis are appointed as acts of political patronage performed by senators and congressmen for poor men and women of ability. If any young person of ability who enters the armed forces without such appointment or because of any family tradition in peacetime, intending to become an officers, he or she would be looked at askance and will immediately be suspect to be unnaturally lusting after power! But even the military as a whole is suspect and not only must remain under civilian control but eternal surveillance of officers and their men must be constant and seriously watched President Truman's firing of General Mcharthur is an example of this paranoid fear of run away military arrogance and the placing of the military above civilian rule. The drafting of civilians has always been felt to be the proper counterweight to total military thinking and it has additionally always been used by parents and Judges as a type of reform school for deviate youth to be straighted out and taught proper respect for the American way! Recently a totally professional army of solders below the officers' rank has been created and the fears of the country has been aroused and most people look askance at this development yet don't want their sons and husbands to fight foreign wars and military adventurism! With one side of their mouths they lament our professional boys being killed in foreign adventurism but out of the other side of their mouth they say "fools–they volunteered and got what they deserved because they are now nothing but mercenary troops." The armed force's starting wages are equal to many civilian jobs now and large bonuss are given for reenlistments and thirty, forty thousand dollars plus can be accrued for college education if you only listen to the military's fraudulent ads about "being all you can be", by entering the armed forces to be a professional solder for honor and money! In the meantime some Americas have begun to not trust the government and its mercenary troops and have begun forming armed civilian militia in many states while many States are stating their sovereignty against Federal governmental authority.

EQUALITARIANISM AND SUPERPATRIOTIC IDIOCY

It is important to understand that where power becomes authority or seems to doing so or there is a fear that it might take control, then America's hackles rise and danger signals occur and Americans start putting powder into their guns. For example, the latest idiocy is that some superpatriots think a covert shadow American government is in collusion with the United Nations to invade America with secretly placed U.N. troops stationed on U.S. bases in the United States while our diminished army is out on another foreign military adventurism. In their newspapers you constantly see their photographs of United Nations equipment being transported throughout the United States as they report on the U.S. government training foreign pilots to fly black unmarked aircraft. And naturally you wonder what's going on? Naturally the United States government always patiently explains we are only training Nato foreign pilots like we have been doing for years. Congress in response has declared that no United States troops can be put under United Nations command and that they will no longer fund American troops doing United Nations business!

This all sounds so idiotic, if it were not an old American trait! Paranoid apprehension of foreign contamination has been endemic among minority groups throughout the entire history of the United States. The basic difference between early superpatriots and the present variety is only the source of the enemy. In the early days of the Republic the source of corruption and contamination was the British Empire or later anti-Catholics sentiment suspected the Vatican of intentions of a sinister nature. Interestingly, America has had only one Catholic president who was assassinated before he served one term! Naturally the majority of Americans never shared such unrealistic beliefs. Generally these fringe lunatic groups identified the enemy as within the country, that is, as Negroes, Jews, Catholics, or the Internationally-minded Eastern seaboard upper class. But when the cold war began the hostile danger now was the Soviet Russia, communist China and their associates and allies. Finally there was an enemy who actively engaged in sabotage, subversion and spying and suddenly the superpatriots delusions had little discrepancy with the majority of American citizen belief system. Now here was a real danger. Every one knows these things happen. Last week the French president accused American CIA of corrupting his government. This week an CIA operative is accursed of killing a husband of an "American women in Guatemala. So Americans know real dangers when they feel it! Now the latest lunacy is the perceived danger from the United Nations; while other idiots say the real danger is the flying saucer scare. Such prophets of doom claim one in every forty Americas have been implanted with sophisticated electronic devises of spying by hostile Alien, extra Terrestrials.

Another conspiracy concept is presented by Col. Cooper,an exmilitary intelligence officer, a siblings of various armed force officers and a son of a retired army general. It is said that he says in his book,"Behold the Pale Horse", that on the basis of secret intelligence reports that the extraterrestrials contacted President Truman initially but made a secrete treaty with President Eisenhower to set up joint-secret underground bases throughout the United States and the World in exchange for giving our government Alien technology. Other conspiracy people say such factors have allowed Russia and United States to set up bases on the Moon and Mars which are maned by stolen American children! They claims that no President since Eisenhower knows the true extend of the development of this secret shadow government which wants to set up a new world order with the Extraterrestrial as emperor, with a small upper class of humans beneath them who shall rule a united earth while the rest of the world populous become slave workers for their Alien death Masters.. Some people claims an inter-governmental war has been going on for years with murders and counter murders continuously occurring between and among conflicting governmental agencies, as some in house-patriots fight this insidious take-over in which prominent world citizens are murdered but replace by human clones who will follow their death masters every command. They asserts the entire cold-war scenario between Russia and the west was a set up to get the needed funds to build those secret bases with additional billions coming from drug monies from drug trafficking which has been cornered by the CIA world-wide. What idiocy!

On the other hand you have Col. Plhilip J. Corso who says that " . . . in Roswell in 1947, the landing of a flying saucer was no fantasy. It was real . . . "(Corso:3,4:1997) He goes on to say that, "Today , items such as lasers, integrated circuitry, fiber-optics networks, accelerated particle-beam devices, and even the Kevlar material in bulletproof vests are all commonplace. Yet the seeds for the development of all of them were found in the crash of the alien craft at Roswell . . . " Is this nonsense? Yet col. Corso is a former Pentagon Official, aid to General Trudeau, army Intelligence head, and formerly on the staff of general MacArthur, and who finishes up his career after retiring from the army as an aid to Senator Strom thurmond, a member of the Senate Armed services Commitee.

Now to muddy the waters a little more we have President Reagan when he was in office who was asked to explain his U-turn concerning the evil empire of Russia he answered that what made common cause was space. More specifically he stated, " . . . a danger from space to all the nations on Earth."

He spoke of his fifteen hours talk and five hours of private conversation with General Secretary Gorbachev which took place in 1985. Reagan said " . . . I couldn't help say to him, "Just think how easy his task and mine might be in these meetings that we held if suddenly there was a threat to this world **from some other species from another planet outside in the universe.** We'd forget all the little local differences that we have between our countries and we would find out once and for all that we are all human beings here on this earth together." (Sitchen:.308 1990)

Gorbachev's statement on February 16, 1987, recalled his discussion with President Reagan in words almost identical to those the American President had used. Additionally he said.

"At our meeting in Geneva, **the U.S. President said that if the earth faced an invasion by extraterrestrials, the United States and the Soviet Union would join forces to repel such an invasion.**

"I shall not dispute the hypothesis, though I think it's early yet to worry about such an intrusion." (Sitchen: 309:1990)

President Reagan when he addressed the General Assembly of the United Nations on September 21, 1987, speaking of the need to turn swords into plowshares, said:

"In our obsession with antagonism of the moment we often forget how much unites all the members of humanity. **Perhaps we need some outside, universal threat to recognize this common bond.**

I occasionally think how quickly our differences would vanish if we **were facing an alien threat from outside this world."** (Sitchen:311:1990)

"As reported at the time in *The new Republic* by its senior editor Fred Barnes, President Reagan, during a White house luncheon on **September 5, sought confirmation from the Soviet foreign minister that the Soviet Union would indeed join the United States against an alien threat from outer space;** and Shevardnadze responded, "Yes, absolutely." (Sitchen:311:1990)

President Reagan in a Chicago, May 1988 meeting with members of the National Strategy Forum raised the issue of the secret threat, when he told them of wondering, **"What would happen if** all of us in the world discovered that we were threatened by an outer—a power from outer space—from another planet."(Sitchen:312:1990)

Is this all nonsense? Let's hope this is all idiocy. I for one don't like these scenarios; even if they were true it grates against my scientific sensitivities and my emotional nature's silent communion with nature!

All this makes an interesting science fiction movie, I guess, but this idiocy runs throughout some superpatriots groups as they arm themselves for the coming fight against these delusional dangers. Now most states have armed militias.

The English anthropologist, Geoffrey Gorer, found it difficult to talk with these superpatriots in a social situation. He felt they showed psychopathic characteristics with their incapacity to tolerate anxiety. Some of them, during the cold war said it would be worth sacrificing three quarters of the population of the United states to destroy the Soviet Union. [54]

Small groups such as these have never been able to influence United State policy, therefore their hatred of each administration is rabid. Great malevolence is voiced against any President and his family and they are treated as traitors and as consciously furthering the surrender of the United states to Communist or presently to covert shadow governments who are allied with their death master aliens. Each existing government is seen as a vast conspiracy and dominated by "internal persecutors" who murder and kill covertly as the occasion demands. [55] Well, so much for lunacy fads except to say that probably the next wave of absurdity will be we are being covertly invaded by little green men who abduct us from their flying saucer but whose homebases are not outerspace but the inner earth; a nonsense which was first started probably as a joke by Admiral Bird, in his first interview after returning from the south pole, many years ago, but has now achieved almost a cult status. (The Hollow Earth. Raymond Bernard.)

AMERICA'S BECOMING

President Johnson, in his inaugural address sums up certain American concepts that still hold sway over the hearts and minds of Americans. He says:

> It is the excitement of becoming–always becoming, trying, probing, falling, resting, and trying again–but always gaining. In each generation–with toil and tears–we have had to earn our heritage again.

If we fail now, then we will have forgotten in abundance what we learned in hardship; that democracy rest on faith, freedom asks more than it gives, and the judgment of God is harshest on those who are most favored.

If we succeed, it will not be because of what we have, but what we are; not because of what we own, but what we believe.

In the remainder of this chapter we will examine some of America's basic concepts or building blocks upon which America stands. We will examine only a few of the basic changes in our culture's basic orientation that are affecting our cultural process and examine the other factors throughout the rest of the book. Major changes in the capitalist concepts and business orientation, in concepts of scientific and cultural objectivity and the change from a rational era to a subjective psychological cultural process are causing an identity crisis and trauma in American national character as the basic cultural core values change within the American cultural process.

AMERICA IS A BUSINESS CIVILIZATION

America is a nation build on the principles of shared political and judicial powers and upon the equality and independence of citizens and upon the sacredness of property which classifies America as a Business Civilization. It is also built upon ideals of hard work, thrift and the competitive struggle which allows Americans to achieve their own unique success in life, that is, their own particular American Dream. Competition and business and social achievement allow each person to feel a type of king of the mountain mentality. Inherent in America's cultural life force is the concept of tension, fear and anxiety as the citizen gladiators fight out a constant and perpetual battle either to gain political or economic power-control or to keep themselves into power or just to maintain social status. The primordial-fear-anxiety syndrome is built into our political and social systems, since the Varible Uncertainty Principle underlies the social and national life of our industrial technocracy.

On the social class dimension and the family front the same battle constantly goes on to maintain jobs, social positions, social status and respectability and success. Nothing is certain and at any moment in Time an economic depression, or loss of job may destroy your social position or your future livelihood. It is a fact of life that today your life's work may be annihilated by your job being exported overseas, or your family may fall from middle class to lower class status economically and socially. Families may even lose their homes and all their material processions and end up wandering the streets as beggars.

This controlled chaos that is American life is a system of competition so fierce that it preoccupies American life entirely, almost as if they were on a roll a coaster ride from somewhere to no-where! America is at war with itself constantly and the casualties are ourselves because our future is the Genocide Phenomenon.

America's linkage with the primordial fear-anxiety syndrome began at its inception as a nation. When we severed our ties to England and eliminated the monarchy we became a nation without a head. Governmental unity depended upon the balance of power. We created a pact of brothers, none of whom could become the strong father, thus each viewed himself as primus inter pares.

The country from the beginning was held together by pitting of group against group in healthy and unhealthy strive; city against city, state, against states, the federal government against states, south against North, West against East, The congress against the Executive, the House against the senate, the Navy against the Army , Harvard University against Yale.

The president of the United States, although the commander-in chief in war time is in peace time little more than the head of a political party who becomes the victim of bard attacks constantly. [56]

The competition for social status in the United states is a fierce contest upon which rests the emotional and psychological health of the population. We have a social class mobility system of five to nine social classes, unlike some other cultures which have rigid class systems or even castes in which you are born into and within which you will die..

In terms of social anxiety the system allows a person to rise up from one social class to another based upon his merits and abilities. It may take three generations and masses of money to reach the upper class but it can be done and is constantly being achieved. Naturally when you are on the top you can only fall down to a lower class status, which happens all the time also. But this game also goes on with large masses of classes in competition with one another. Presently we are witnessing millions of families which are falling from middle class status to lower class status. Many of the millions of families or their descendents who rose up from the lowers class status after the great economic depression to middle class status are now falling back at an alarming rate into lower class status; they fall with deep despair and are embraced within a negative emotional crisis which takes from them their very essence of their humanity. Because of their fall from "grace they will die disgraced in the eyes of their contemporaries and in their deepest hearts they will know this final defeat will brand them forevermore as social failures and even death will not give them solace.

Within the family all things must be earned. Children must earn the love and respect of their parents, which in part dependents upon their social success outside the family arena. Nothing is ever certain and successes in life rests on each person's effort and achievements and to be a person of worth and respect is to be a successful person. No one escapes this social and moral obligation, even the super rich, because each person's success in life is a matter of competition and becoming king of the mountain in your field is to be recognized as being a chief among your peers.

But within the childhood arena great pressures to succeed causes the primordial fear-anxiety syndrome to manifest early because our social norms and mores are rapidly changing and the kids stand upon quick sand of uncertainty and no one knows how to teach them the right and proper way to go because even their parents are lost and bewildered and throw up their hands in desperation and defeat. So the children now learns from their peers and some of our children have joined the death cadres as they murder and hunt down their victims so they can kill them in cold blood. Now surely they follow a different drummer!

POLITICIANS

Politicians are tolerated and not suspected if they go into politics for their personal advantage, that is, to earn money or improve their social position but if they have sinister reasons to search out and grab political power then America is outraged! This is one of the covert reason why President Nixon was kicked out of office in mid term. Americans do not like people who are lusting after authority that is not given to them constitutionally. The immigrants and less assured groups and less assimilated population, for example, loved and trusted President Roosevelt as a father and felt protected by his benevolent authority. The rest of the country saw only a President who held office four times in a row and liked doing it and thus was a menace to the country. [57]

By law an American president can only serve two consecutive

four year terms. A better system would be to allow any president only to serve only one six year term! America handles the situation by constantly alternating between strong and weak presidents. It is fact, according to American folk understanding, that a strong president represents a moral threat; but a weak president can bring the country close to anarchy because constitutional provisions prevents any other group from exercising authority. [58]

The American people always think of the governments as they, never we. The covert function of government is always to increase its authority and the public's duty is to resist the ever encroaching governmental controls and its creeping socialism. This is because government by definition is a necessary evil which at best must be a type of umpire who must prevent contestants from taking any unfair advantage of their competitors. Governments' function is to be the arbitrator in private enterprise which is a quasi-religious moral attitude behind the American way of life. Ah, this very fact of American life rests on the fact that the threat of violence covertly plays a major role in American life, and in its commercial, industrial and political life. Violence is every where. One minute a death child is gunning down a babe in arms in the street, the next minute some one is assassinating the President of the United States just as another women is being raped, a fact that occurs every few minutes nationwide. But the fact of the matter violence is institutionalized as part of the primordial fear-anxiety syndrome and social actions are always predicted upon the fact that violence could erupt at any time if a political machine doesn't get its way or if a striking union doesn't win or you could lose your job if you do not do as your death masters desire! Daily you see business threatening to leave a city or state if taxes are not reduced or if they don't get certain concessions. When they win cities and states gives them what they want and often large amounts of cash is accrues to the companies. Nonconforming business and professional men are kept in line frequently receiving threats of physical violence. But although morally America condemns these practice, there is always a sneaking admiration for people and organizations that get away with these fear terrorism tactics. This is personified in our action and detective movies and films of violence and murder in which private and public humiliation of victims daily feed the perverse appetites of the general public. The public eats up this violence because unconsciously they are a violent people. Oh, they are not antimilitaristic because they don't like fighting and violence but because they detest authority. Americans can't stand being pushed around and ordered about by officers or governmental officials. In Vietnam this was amply demonstrated by the constant deaths of officers perpetrated by ordinary solders throwing handgernades at them. Returning veterans from world war Two had greater and deeper animus against their own officers then they had against the Japanese. In psychiatric interviews veterans fantasies showed retaliation against former officers in which they were humiliated and snubbed, and the most common fantasy was the scenario of the exsolder, now an employer, refusing to give a job to his ex-officer who now was a humble civilian suppliant. [59]

No, American shows no distaste for fighting and violence. What Americans don't like is being controlled by business, corporate, governmental and military authorities which is always morally bad. Control over your own destiny or natural resources, goods, chattle-power and money is good and proper; but even here Americans suspect individuals who monopolize national resources. When this happens legitimate power is being transformed into illegitimate authority and Americans will not tolerate this yet seem lately to be powerless to stop it. In the early years of this century anti-trust laws were enacted as personal attacks against Capitalists such as John D. Rockefeller. Now these laws are used against powerful trade-unions leaders and corporations. [60] It is a fact that Americans will detest a mercantile technocracy dictatorship as much as they are now covertly resisting becoming slaves to their future death masters! The only question is has contemporary America any backbone left? Will they succumb to corporate control? Modern "industrialism is the perversion of individualism." [61] Tawney surely points out that the apotheosis of individual self-interest and his "natural instincts" for self aggrandizement of old fashion industrialism runs counter to modern corporate death politics and management.[62]

An interesting factor of American life is that people in authority must seem as if they are ordinary people, that is, conspicuously plain citizens. They must seem as if they don't belong to the elite and develop or act as if they have the same interests and mannerisms of their fellow citizens. They must act as if they are one of the boys. They must be glad-handed, extravert, and know the first names of their subordinates and be democratically obscene in their language. President Nixon's use of obscenity was legend, though only covertly and discreetly spoken among his close cohorts. Our death politician must seem to not hold the veiled mail fist of authority. [63]

Why must the superrich hide their wealth and power from the average Americans? They do so because respect and awe are generally the emotional responses to personified authority; but these are painful emotions to Americans and they are as carefully avoided by them just as any shame-face feeling are by the Japanese. But when Americans must face people or situations which might evoke such feeling they use levity, incongruousness, or elaboration which allows them to be reduce in status the feared authorities so that such feelings of awe or respect is unnecessary. The present scandal rag magazines harassment of the English Royal family is an instance of the efforts to reduce power and wealth down to the human level of absurdity and equality. [64]

Americans can feel awe and respect for abstract things, such as flags which represent freedom and democracy or feel awe toward the Liberty Bell, The Lincoln Memorial or the Allamo. But emotionally they cannot respect power and wealth person's unless they are brought down to their level emotionally.

There is a great American tradition which allows the great tycoons to amass their great fortunes and ride roughshod over his rivals and employees but once his fortune is achieved he must begin to give away his money. Oh, the facts in may cases belie the actualities but this is what America expects. Inherited wealth and power has always been considered dangerous for the county and the wealth ought to disperse or dissipate their wealth. This wealth is especially felt to be a handicap for their children. If a child has nothing to strive for he will suffer by not being a true American. If you live on accumulated wealth or family reputation you lose all motivation and lose out by not personally seeking the American dreams and thus are unAmerican. To be an American is something to be earned not bought! Ideally the great-grandson of a very rich man should be starting over financially and otherwise just as his great-grandfather did. This is because the upper-class wealthy have nowhere but go but to fall down the social ladder. How can they progress? They all fear this social falling process, thus they become dangerous to the country because they will always fear that some group will be hostile to wealth and high status or that some minority group will deprive them of their security or that the central government will weaken their hold on local sources of power. They will fear heavy public taxation or that federal medical and education or welfare programs will eat away their wealth. [65]

PAPA-DRONES

Americans, however, do not feel awe or respect toward their fathers. Oh Papa-drone, the emasculated father wants to be the feared and respected patriarchal figure but he is limited by the negative sanctions against the exercise of authority over another human being. Even if his temperaments of authority is strong his wife, his neighbor or his community will not support him. It is as if in an analogous situation that the father has the state's Executive authority, the mother the Legislative and the neighbors and the school teachers, the Judiciary authority. Symbolically the child is the public and he plays off one authority against another and uses these checks and balances to keep his freedom. Papa-drone lost all his authority years ago when he immigrated to the United

States and became an incomplete American whom his children couldn't imitate, must not, if they were to be successful Americans. So Papa-drone now no longer expects his sons to be like him, or stay in the same social class as he is or even to have the same profession. Papa-drone cannot be a model on which his son's will emulate. Oh, he ought to help them improve their position vis-a-vis the neighbor's children and teach them to hunt and fight and above all he must support and exemplify any moral precepts and rules that Mama-boss and the generally female schoolteachers support. His children and especially his sons will have a feminine consciousness and he will be from early childhood on, have developed an open conspiracy between Papa-drone and himself to thwart or sidestep the feminine concepts of domestic and social behavior. The code words are always "Don't let your mother catch you" . Father and sons seem to have a happy rapport based on this shared masculine resistance to Mama-bosses demands and exigencies. Yet it must be said that in some families this solidarity is broken by rivalry between them for Mama-bosses affection and it burst out in full force at adolescence. Now the father-drone must give the son the use of the family car or the choice of TV Programs, [66] although this practice have been side check generally by giving the kid his own TV. set. Yes, the cult of Youth holds America in its grip of idiocy as our children emerge into the Genocide phenomenon and now only find life meaningful if they can gun down reflections of themselves in the streets.

All Mama-bosses in America have arrogated or historically have had thrust upon them the dominant role of child rearing which in other societies has been held by the father, or shared by both parents, a fact which has created the feminine consciousness of America. The very character of American children and adults rests on Mama-boss and her influence on the youth of America. [67]

America creates moral consciousness and character by training children to an ethical viewpoint by giving rewards and love when they conform to arbitrary moral standards yet by withdraw-

ing love and inflicting punishment when our children fail to conform. The children internalize these standards which are operative even when the parents are absent as these internalize controls
become part of the total personality and become a conscious-
unconscious conscience of each child. [68]

Mama-boss in America instill a feminine consciousness upon
her children; which is reinforced by an almost totally female school
teacher system. Women school teachers are perceived to be harsher
and shriller than Mama-boss because their teachings are not tempered by love. Little Johnny carries within an encapsulated, ethical, admonitory, censorious mother in all his relations with or
among other people. They either follow or are revelling against
moral Mama-bosses rules and prohibitions all the days of their
lives. Rules tell him when it is proper to fight or stand up for
himself, what is properly for male sexuality and drinking and
above all is the injunction to be successful all the days of your
life. Without success Mama-boss has no love or respect for you
even if she can't tell you how to achieve success. And cry as you
may, no reality other than success will make you feel as if you are
a man of American success.

The male may try to escape from women's influences in general, and Mama-bosses controls in particular and even have great
resentment about the emotional situating he finds himself in
through out his life. But he can't ignore his conditioning because
the insistent maternal conscience is a specific aspect of his personality. And when he rebels and throws off the politeness, neatness, modesty and cleanliness which are obviously concessions to
feminine demands he has pangs of guilt. But he tries by going to
stag poker games or fishing trips to balance Mama-bosses inner
voice.

But boy-drones can't fight mother too aggressively because
her very being is also tempered by love and understanding occasionally, yet he know fully well the wheedling and deceit that
also accompanies Mama-bosses behavior! [69] It is a fact that most

boys will reach and pass through adolescence under almost undi-
luted Mama-bosses authority.

Mama-boss is finished with her children's formal education
usually between sixteen and twenty one which ideally consisted
with them leaving the maternal home and often the town in
which they were raised. When her daughters are married Mama-
boss is not expected to play any part in the marriage except as an
honored guest occasionally. She cannot help her daughter in raising her children since child rearing rules will have changed too
much since she was a mother. Mama-boss's graduated son must
pass out of her life. He must leave her, revere her, and forget her
and generally have as little as possible to do with her.

The other side of the coin of American life is the image of the
clinging mother whose great emotional attachment to the son is a
menace in every boy's psychological life because of its vampire like
possession tendencies. Every male has a hidden fear of being pos-
sessed by his clinging mother thus, adding to each son's ambivalence toward women in general. [70]

MODERN TIMES

In the year of our Lord 1995 the cultural malaise began to be felt
even by the masses and its finger of death began to eat at the
vitals of the culture and confusion reigned as the acid of cultural
death became even obvious to the dullest citizen and they wondered how and why they no longer felt whole and progressive and
looked forward to a bright future. They spoke of family values
and wondered how the family structure had collapsed and speculated on the process of getting back to where our society had started
from! Yet all the while their pervasive discontent silently seeps up
from the culture's unconscious as it pushes them to silently arm
themselves because even they in their ignorance will not face death
willingly. Private armies exist now in most states and even cities
and states are now claiming Federal lands as private citizen silently
arms themselves in unprecedented numbers.

Yes, death through self-defense is their only answer to the death challenge because these social critics emphatically feel that the death generation comprises all stations of life and that the death decay is widespread and contagiously lethal.

The first causal factor of the genocide phenomenon rests on the concept of the grave Neanderthal flaw in the consciousness of some of the human species which factor is that our post industrial age has been captured by a social malady called the Genocide Phenomenon. The overt facts of this socio-cultural disease is the manifestation within the world arena and particularly in America, of an overt-covert Death Generation, the death cadre members, who have manifested the first casual factor, the Neanderthal flaw, which are half of the overt effect of the Genocide Phenomenon. This overt death cadre is a conscious culture change operatives who are bringing about massive social changes overtly and covertly as they take over America and the world for their new world order. The other half of the overt effect is the actual change in direction and motivation within the core themes of American sociocultural life most of which are overtly manipulated toward a new world order of technocracy.

The hidden half of the Genocide Phenomenon is the covert primordial fear syndrome of defeat and social depression, that is the hidden side of Americas success syndrome that has tore the heart out of American life and given her an identity crisis and destroyed her value systems and alienated Americans from themselves, society and nature!

Today most of America's population is living within the psychologically conditioned values of rugged individualism and self-reliance while the rest of the socio-economic, educational, corporate, scientific life stress the very opposite of these themes, even though they mouth them seditiously. We have a social situation that now stresses the group and denigrates individualism and self reliance. The mass psychological dislocation of American National character and its personality dysfunctioning finds manifestation as an unconscious fear syndrome.

We will discuss this fear syndrome in other chapters when we

speak of the individual activities of social destruction that are occurring daily in America.

America's will in the meantime is being destroyed as we have
been thrust unwillingly into an arena of rapid socio-cultural change
in which our society's old core values and world-view are collapsing but are not meeting the new challenges of the modern age;
and even the new emerging scientific and cultural value concepts
which are developing as the bureaucratization of society occurs
are found to be not only incompatible with our old sensate culturally conditioned industrial world view but aid in the destruction of dying America. The new scientific concepts belong to the
new age and as yet we cannot personally or as a nation reject our
old ideas and their scientific paradigm models since our technoc-
racy-industrial world view rests entirely upon these ideas; and
these modes of psycho-social reality are us in the most vivid sense
of our very essence as a person and a people. The country has
radically changed yet the Protestant Ethic has not. [71] We have
been so socialized and conditioned since childhood and emotionally and mentally are like Popi, the cartoon character, who
says, "I am what I am." But gradually as we accept the new scientific pictures of a dynamic non-sensate world view our paradigm
dies to itself, possibly in global disaster.

Americans are lost in a maize of social confusion and psychological doubt through the exigencies of the post industrial age
and the contemporary remaking of human society. We do not
know where we stand as people or where we are going as a society
and we don't realize yet that we will never know the answer to
these questions until the new post industrial age is well established.

AMERICA TODAY

We have had a brief review of our culture's beginnings and saw
how we became what we are today. The country is today experiencing massive social changes which contains massive assaults on

Americas National character!. We must understand that phenomenological and existentially that when a person begins to experience psychological and social trauma because of culture change these feelings and mental shocks become personal psychological wounds.

America you are now living through this traumatic process. So when we talk about these psychosocial wounds as personal anguish it is because it helps us get a clear feeling of the social chaos in relationship to traditional values and norms. It is a fact that when we examine our hurts and feelings as anguish and alienation and can see ourselves within this psychological process we can focus more clearly later on the theoretical aspects of our malady. It is as if we are approaching the problem from within the pain and through such an examination we existentially feel and explore until a clear focus of the problem and its theoretical and cultural aspects is presented to us as the dynamic present; and as we acknowledge the pain on the emotional and intellectual dimensions as part of our self, we also acknowledge ourselves as humans within the sociocultural reality of the genocide phenomenon.

Our psychosocial wounds are a reaction against a social system that is collapsing and a world view that is outmoded and which rests on a faulty understanding of human nature and the human species' psychological ego system. Additionally, man of the eternal spirit, has been lost and as his personality dysfunctional hurts increases he cries to the high heaven in fear and anguish over his lost nature. He is a pathetic creature now-half alienated man and still half animal crying fearsome moans of desperation about something he can't quite grasp but knowing full well he is dwelling in misery. But why? He instinctly feels he ought to be happy and content but he is not and as he licks his wounds of despair and alienation he cowers in the corners of his defeats by accepting his loneliness as part of human nature.

It is a sad fact, however, that only through the loneliness of anguish, transintegral psychology says, can some members of the species burst its self contained shell of social and psychological limitations. Humanity must want to be a conscious part of human evolution; only then will each personally be a person of the hour and stand up and proclaim that," I am a man of the earth and a daughter of the mountains of life, and I claim my birth right as a transcending member of the human species." Only then America will you be wholesome and dynamic and the leader of mankind.

What is certain is that it is an age in which the death generation emerges as isolated and alienated individuals but also as an overt and covert organized social forces that may eventually bring about the entire annihilation of the entire human race.

When we speak of a change in values we are really talking about a shift in the core values of a culture's world view, that is how we view ourselves within society, nature and the cosmos. A culture is a system that has interrelated parts that are basically harmonious to themselves generally. In particular there are always discordant aspect within cultural system but if the culture is functional it will at the worst limp along by piecing together it discordant parts best as it may.

When we examine the nature of culture in later chapters we can go into greater detail than now. But understand that if you have certain core values such as the concept of rugged individualism and its autonomous sense of self reliance that have traditionally operated in each of us to allow us to think and act as an independent person but suddenly the culture no longer values this concept but instead punishes those individuals for displaying autonomous behavior in school, work and play, thus individual personality dysfunction occurs personally and collectively among great numbers of the populace. Eventually new personality concepts of natural character will develop but in the meantime the population of individuals who still believe in the American way will exist in anguish and turmoil.

SUBJECTIVE ERA

The individualistic-rationalistic era is now in the middle of a process called the subjective era. It is a world wide phenomenon that
is drastically changing the rational-sensate world view and is causing fear and anxiety the world over. We will discuss this interesting
factor in the next chapter.

CHAPTER 5

AMERICA'S DEATH SUBJECTIVISM

FUTURIST COMMENTARY: THE GLOBAL CRISIS OF SUBJECTIVE CONSCIOUSNESS

There are periods in the history of mankind when the very social fabric of life rises up and seemingly protests and mankind finds itself at a juncture in the historical process. The 20th and 21st centuries were critical turning points in the life process of the human race. The scientist, Ronald L. Campbell lived though these trying times and attempted to analysis the social problems and psychological dysfunctions of his times. In this chapter he speaks of the subjective era that preceded America's second civil war.

In the year 2,005, in the midst of a savage war to establish a united fascist state throughout the Americas, a strange mystic-scientist appeared in Yucatan, Mexico, and acclaimed himself to be Quetzalcoatl, an ancient Toltec Messiah.

Immediately, Mayan Indian and Nahua speaking Aztec Indians rallied around this strange prophet who spoke their languages and who appeared to have miraculous powers of mind over matter and command of advanced technological sciences. Lost buried libraries of Mayan, toltec, Mixtec and Axtec codex's were uncovered. Thus emerged the first of many 21st century Indian National Universities who taught lost sciences and dynamic social programs which began in the Indian areas of Mexico initially but almost immediately spread like wild fire throughout the Americas.

Quetzalcoatl, as had the prophet Wadoi, a Paite Indian of the 1890, spread his concepts throughout the Indian Nations. Always he spoke in their native tongue and when Indians no longer knew their ancient language he miraculous taught them how to speak them again.

Quetzalcoatl also had a powerful command of english through which his charismatic personality won hundreds of thousands of ordinary Americans over to his side in most extraordinary ways that announced to the world that a superhuman personality had emerged into the world arena.

By the year 2,010 Indian empires had established political control over large areas of Mexico and central America, and the traditional Inca areas of South America and well as in areas of the United States and Canada. Most notable is the emergence of a dynamic Inca empire as much of western Spanish America died and faded into oblivion.

The fascist Government of the Americas, now situated in Washington D.C. and Rio De Janeiro was so busy fighting for control over the Americas and engaged in the civil war in the United States that they ignored the mad Indian scientist in remote Mexico until it was too late. Indian armies, allied with Mexican patriots who now fully embraced their Indian heritage, took back what was historically theirs as they fought the invading American Gringos and their Mexican allies.

The Dakotas, Montana and areas of the West also became Indian nations again as American Indians reasserted their legal and sovereign control over Indian lands once again. And as in early colonial days, hundreds of thousands of white and black, Americans fled their civilization and became adopted Indians. In the latter days of the 21st century, when the Wars of Terror began again, and after several billion people had perished from the face of the earth, millions of white and black Americans once again fled to the safety zones of the Indian nations.

Almost immediately, with the help of Quetzalcoatl and his superior technology, mighty Indian nations took additional control of most of the rest of the western areas of the United States and created new and advanced nations.

How could a mad Indian scientist accomplish all this against a powerful United States technology? The simple fact is this prophet did not come alone and had at his command a sophisticated technology and strange air craft and weapons that paralyzed the American empire and they sued for peace; and when the American Fascist government was overthrown the New reformed Americans Empire accepted the fact that the Americas now had numerous politically active Indian Nations. These states were tacitly accepted as parts of the empire, although in actuality they were politically autonomous.

How could all this happen you ask? Our historians answer that America's subjective era didn't succeed in overcoming its false subjective and negative tendencies and the culture collapsed into a dictatorship! Campbell speaks to this subjective issue as he discusses the subjective cultural era.

The evolutionary animal still carries within his nature a substantial amount of his subhuman origins. This fact dominates humanity's physical and emotional natures but strongly influences the species' mentality. [1] During the process of cyclic social evolution when one era is ending and another emerging the potential exists for an easy transition or tumultuous one to take place within the evolutionary process.

Presently a transition from a semi-rationalistic-individu-alistic era to a subjective era is taking place. A false subjectiv-ism, however, has taken control of the purer form of social subjectivism. This false subjectivism has emerged because the emotional life force inherent within humanity–the vi-talistic life surge of unregenerated humanity is causing strife and conflict on a world wide basis. The vital-emotional mind of humanity is still not much different from that of his ancient ancestors and is infrarational in nature. [2]

This infrarational false subjectivism is the theme of the day–the unconscious world view of the modern age. Briefly, before discussing subjectivism and false subjectivism, we must clarify the idea of life power in us, the vitalistic and dynamic nature resident in the human species.

VITAL-EMOTIONAL LIFE PRINCIPLE

Transintegral Psychology says the vital-emotional life principle in humanity has as its aim to allege its existence, to possess, increase, to expand and to enjoy life. Its goal is to grow and pleasure and power is its motivation for existence. This principle uses force, intensity and extension to make a place for itself in the world primarily. It desires to dominate the earth and to possess, produce and enjoy the world for itself and the human species. [3] This emo-tional desire is individualistic and seizes on the family, social and national life to fulfill the vitalistic life urge. In the family the individual gains satisfaction through possessions, joy of compan-ionship and self-reproduction. His gains are the possession of spouse, wealth, servants, estates and the reproduction of himself in his progeny. Often his life purposes impinge on his offspring. He also gains satisfaction from the mental and vital pleasures and emotional affections of domestic life.

In society a wider field of vital exchange and self-aggrandize-ment offers itself through gregarious pleasures and achievement of social goals. In the nation and its constituent parts, a wider field still presents itself and power, fame and leadership fulfill the vital rage of self-aggrandizement. If the higher reach of fulfillment does not manifest in the life of the individual then the modern phenomenon of wanting to participate in the social events occurs–a feeling that one is doing one's part by participating in the democratic or political process. It is through such actions that the individual can feel and share a sense of participation or a fictitious image of participation in the power pride and splendor of an intensive collective activity and vital expansion of being. [4]

In all the above examples the vital life principle is at work. It is operative on the competitive side of our nature but also associated with the cooperative dimension–but predominate over it. [5]

When this vital force is carried to its ultimate extreme the arrivest emerges. This character uses his family, society and nation as a prey to be devoured, or as a thing to be dominated or conquered. Sometimes, however, the individualist becomes the adventurer and reverts to a primitive antisocial feeling and becomes a nomad. He becomes a solitary antisocial person who looks on society as an oppressive prison to his expansion–to his subjective express of existential being. Society in this case is no longer an instrument or a sympathetic field to be utilized and conquered for self-aggrandizement. [6] Presently the death generation has emerged and death and self-extinction faces this generation!

The individualistic-rationalistic era is now changing into a subjective age and unfortunately a false subjectivism is also occurring. Let us now investigate the new emerging subjectivism first, then inspect the concept of false subjectivism.

SUBJECTIVE ERA

The psychocultural evolutionary theory says that after an era of semi-rationalistic and individualistic cultures a subjective period eventually takes place. The rationalistic period serves as an era of critical reason, largely destructive to past infrarational falsehoods and standards that are no longer alive or dynamically relevant to the needs of the populace. [7] The individualistic period thus serves as a radical attempt by mankind to discover scientific laws and humanity's relationship to nature and the universe. [8] Example of this is found in Europe in olden times where a potent physical science developed that has uncovered laws of the physical universe and developed economic and sociological concepts on the physical principles of the human animal. After a while it is realized, however, that man is a mental and emotional being as well as a physical creature—but more mental than anything else. A realization takes place that although the physical environment and man's physical being affects and limits humanity it is the human race's psychological nature and social needs that determines the economic and social institutions of the human animal. To understand life, man, and society, a subjective psychological introspection is needed.

A scientist must transcend the limited critical and analytic reason methodology because to understand a social situation the individual must become actively self-conscious and not merely self-critical. Eventually what occurs is that the rationalistic ideal begins to subject itself to intuitional ideals, and aspires toward self-consciousness and self-realization.[9] A new concept of living develops in which the laws of physical nature are replaced by a new theme that emphasizes the will and power active in the species on the outer and inner dimensions of humanity. [10]

The 20th century has seen the beginnings of this subjective age—the transition from the rationalistic and utilitarian period that individualism has created, to a subjective age of society. Old intellectual standards are changing and 19th century materialism is giving over to a novel vitalism that takes various forms such a Nietzche's theory of the will to be and will to power as the causal agents of the law of life. New pluralism and pragmatic philosophies develop that concentrate on life and the pragmatic scenario because they seek to interpret human reality with force and action instead of understanding and knowledge. [11]

The new intuitionism is wide spread in modern times and finds reflection in the art, music and literature of the world as an ever deepening subjectivism. The dynamic objective literature and art of the past no longer command the mind of the age. We find now an increasing psychological vitalism in the arts that seeks to penetrate the subtle psychological impulses and tendencies of mankind. [12] It is a subjectivism that seeks the hidden inner side of things rather than a search for the objective canon of nature. In education, the subjective theme is objectified by the goal to bring out the student's own intellectual and moral capacities. [13] Its task is to touch the child's inner impulses that the inner creative senses can be developed rather than conditioning the student by imposing s stereotyped formula on his struggling and dominated impulses. [14] Even contemporary views on criminal behavior and punishment have a subjective turn now. We don't want to just imprison, hang, terrify or torture physically lawbreakers, but attempt to understand them and make allowances for their inner deficiencies, environment or heredity. [15] In science one sees a turn from the objective in physics to the subjective concept of Heisenburg's theory of indeterminacy and in the recognition that the scientific observer himself influences the object under study.

We see also this subjective side in the phenomenological analysis of behavior and life, and in transpersonal analysis of behavior and life, and in transpersonal psychological research that has discovered that the division between matter and the inner being is not absolute. Science thus now attempts to extend exact knowledge into the psychological and psychic realms. A recent example of sciences acceptance of subjectivism is the recognition of the discipline of parapsychology as a legitimate science by the American Association for the Advancement of Science.

In religion one sees the trend toward rejection of the heavy hand of ritualistic tradition and in the attempt at a revival of its strength of the spirit. [16]

The subjective age influences the mass consciousness of entire societies, as it is presently doing with the culture of death but also affects the individual along one of the personality dimensions that corresponds to the four parts of the subjective self. In the life process of man one finds that the search for happiness and contentment establishes itself along one of the aspects of man's personality self. The search, for example, for an authentic sense of self identity may identify itself with the physical pleasures. It may also identify with the emotional self and its desires, impulses will to power, self-aggrandizement growth and egoistic fulfillment. The life process in the mental and moral being may stress inner growth, power and individual or collective perfection as the goal of life.

This type of subjectivism can develop into a subjective materialism, pragmatic and extroverted for a while but eventually goes inward to gain the satisfaction of power, joy and forceful vital will-to-be feelings. Beyond this stage is a subjective idealism that stresses the inner fulfillment of the religious, aesthetic, intellectual and ethical fullness of being. A trend toward mysticism, occultism and the search for the inner self takes place. Subjectivism, at this point can provide the means for the self-realization of the inner being personality, the authentic self existing behind the physical, vital and mental ego structures of the human personality. [17]

Subjectivism we have seen regards everything from the point of view of containing and developing self-consciousness. The law of life is within ourselves. It started with a self-creating process that was subconscious, then half-consciousness and eventually developed an awakened consciousness. This consciousness is a potential and a promise of increasing self-recognition, self-realization, and self-shaping. The dynamic impulse of subjectivism is to find the authentic self, to see its insights and to live out its goals internally and externally by an internal imitation that awakens this self. The subjective insight takes a complex view of human nature and recognizes, for example, that reason and intellectual will are not the only means to understand and realize ourselves. After all reason and will are effective forces of the self.

Will is a force for self-shaping and affirmation and reason a mean for self-recognition. [18]

The goal of subjective man is to perfect his individuality by a process of free self-actualization from within but at the same time to respect, aid and be aided by the same free development in others. Man must harmonize his existences with his culture while developing his species potential and emergent mental capacities. The psychological law for social orders is to perfect its cultural imperatives by a free development of its social themes but to respect and to aid and be aided by the same free development of other communities, nations and sociocultural units. [19]

OBJECTIVITY IN CULTURE AND SCIENCE

If we are to understand the American social crisis today we have to realize that many of the core values developed by Western Industrial society upon which our social order rests are invalid or only partially true because of the changing times. The great battle now being fought between scientific materialism and subjective life concepts is because the two great traditions of Christian and Humanism have died and lost their convincing power. The basic concept of social and scientific objectivity, for example, that supports America's basic core value of social reality, the sciences, and modern technocracy society is also falling apart but in its dying grasp wishes to enslave America through its technocracy and psychological manipulation of the masses, thus emerges America's culture of death.

We know now that objectivity is nonexistent on the subatomic levels as science and society in general enters into a scientific and social subjective era which has been captured by a false subjectivism which rejects the concept of objectivity.

The myth of objective consciousness claims that scientific consciousness is cleansed of all subjective distortion and personal involvement. From this elevated state of scientific knowledge we discover objective knowledge . All the natural sciences are built upon this bedrock and for any field to become scientific it too must become objective.[20] Objectivity to the scientist gives science its keen critical edge and cumulative character. [21] And as Americans we live and breath in a scientific culture in which objectivity grips us subliminally in all we say and act. The very soul of our society adheres to the mentality of the ideal scientist and we seek always to adapt to it dictates. Its ideals surrounds us with its myriad images and pronouncements during every waking hour and we know to be successful in life means to be objective. [22]

The concept of an objective science which our scientific industrial order is built upon is now questioned. Michael Polanyi, for example argues, . . . " there is no such thing as objectivity, even in the physical science".[23] But this idea has grave consequences for our scientific modern technocracy.

The modern social technocracy, however, has made of scientific objectivity a cultural icon which has made of objectivity society's commanding life style. To be modern means to be objective in regard to your self, others and society objectively. And if you personally cannot do this you must act as if you are an objective observer and treat all cultural situation in accordance with the dictates of objectivity. [24]

Science's objectivity has been called into question, especially on subatomic physics levels. Heisenburg's theory of indeterminacy demonstrates that science cannot predict the actions and movements of subatomic particles. The old physics will not work on the examination of subatomic matter. In fact, scientists now know that separate and objective observation of data is not only not possible but such observations it is now known influences the observed data by the mere fact of the scientist's proximity to the scientific experiment. Doing modern physics is now like doing complex metaphysical problems of mysticism. The basic cornerstone of scientific life, modern physics , which traditionally has been the model emulated by the social sciences for it objectivity, now belongs to scientific paradigm models more akin to mysticism then to traditional scientific methodology; gone forever is the solid rock of objective perceptions and the rational world view of Locke and of our early American founding fathers.

We will discuss this problem more in detail in the chapter on Paradigms crisis. But the counter culture pose a curious question now that science has never faced before.

This crisis on the social level has entered into a curious phase in that the counter culture has even questioned the validity of the conventional scientific world views and undermined the foundation of the technocracy. Science is no longer seen as an undisputed social good but now science and scientist are somehow felt to be the enemy. [25] In fact whole segments of America's intelligentia has rejected scientific objectivity as a fact and ran away from this idea as if it were a plague by accepting the concept of objectivity only as a mythology which a people and culture have invested meaning and value. [26] As part of the subjective era we are presently living within many diverse groups of transpersonal transcendentalist have come into existent. Transpersonal emphasizing the personal individual with his higher mystical nature and transcendental signifying a nebulous transcendence that leaps above sensate knowledge to that mysterious but generally unknown source of all life.

We are living in an age in which witches run lose and devotees of Krishna prance and jingle not only in Times Square but also in Moscow, and shamans, exorcist, wandering bards, and gurus cast their shadow against the death of scientific materialism. [27] America's counter culture through drugs, LSD experiences and mystical practices have rejected sensate culture. Ex Harvard University Psychologist Leary now talks about a bizarre form of psychic Darwinism which encourages the LSD trippers to join the new race of man still in its evolutionary process. He says "the sacrament that will put you in touch with the ancient two million year old wisdom inside you"; it frees one "to go on to the next stage, which is the evolutionary timelessness, the ancient reincarnation thing that we always carry inside." [28]

Additionally American intellectuals has been influenced by

Zen Buddhism, college students have become Tibetan Buddhists or followers of Hindu gurus as we enter a world wide subjective era of inner self discovery. Some youth created Jesus movements which tied rock and soul music together which speaks to feelings but not thoughts. It emphasized testimonials and gifts of tongues but above all it emphasized the individual person as being filled with spirit. Jesus in now the friend and inner guide and subjective strength who takes them through adversity and torture love and bliss. [29]

Within the Christian churches new religious revivals–Pentecostalism which anthropologist Kgor Kopytoff calls a "rapidly emergent institutions" have developed. [30] These believers look for a transforming experience which is central to New Testament theology. Such experiences, it is reported radically change individuals through the subjective religious experience of the Baptism of the Holy Spirit which they feel transforms their life. [31]

This transcendental state has even effected governmental agencies, for example, a major aspect of the worldwide subjective era started internationally in the political era of German National Socialism which rejected Judaic Christian truth, ethics and morality for the mythological elements of German pagan past and Adolph Hitlers ideas of "the magical relationship between man and the whole Universe." [32] Adolph Hitler and his associates were pervaded by mythic imagery, mediumship and occultism and the rejection of western science. [33] Herman Rauschning states Hitler said in his presence that "the aim of human evolution is to attain a mystic vision of the universe." [34] It is interesting that Jung found that his patients were dreaming of images of Wotan, the traditionally deity associated with German military nationalism, years before Hitler came to power. [35]

The German leadership became mystical and pagan under the personality of Hitler's hypnotic magnetism. Secularized leadership and objectivity and the movement of Germany away from supernaturalism toward sensate materialism stopped when religion and politics were united within the subjective world view of the German fuhrer, Himler and the inner groups of occult Nazi's. All of Germany was held under the sway of the new German Messiah whom Chamberlain proclaimed was the " . . . awakener of souls, the vehicle of Messianic powers . . . Here is the new leader sent by God to the German people in their hour of greatest need." [36]

It is said that a day of subjective destiny occurred to Adolph Hitler as he viewed "the spear that had pierced the side of Christ" whom he considered to be an Aryan God. The German Messiah Hitler describes it below:

> The air became stifling so that I could barely breathe. The noisy scene of the Treasure House seemed to melt away before my eyes. I stood alone and trembling before the hovering form of the Superman (Ubermensche)–a Spirit sublime and fearful, a countenance intrepid and cruel. In holy awe, I offered my soul as a vessel of his Will. [37]

The German nation accepted Hitler; the subjective politician was able to capture the subjective feelings and aspirations of his people as they moved from the rational-sensate material world to that of subjective feeling.

Strasser, who felt Hitlers intellectual arguments were based on ideas and books he imperfectly understood, said that when he stood up and threw away his intellectual crutches and boldly let his inner subjective spirit talk, Hitler then became transformed into one of the greatest speakers the world has ever seen. Strasser says:

> "Adolph Hitler enters a hall. He sniffs the air. For a minute he gropes, feels his way, senses the atmosphere. suddenly he burst forth. His words go like an arrow to their target, he touches each private wound on the raw,

liberating the mass unconscious, express its innermost aspirations, telling it what it wants to hear. [38]

SENSATE MATERIALISM

In the meantime as Nazi Germany becomes controlled by a subjective Luciferic possession America continues to develop a reality structure which is sensate within all avenues of the culture's
social and industrial, scientific structure. But the concept of reality as only sense experience is presently falling on bad times.
Through the use of our modern scientific instruments we know
that scientific objectivity is a farce and that the human species is
not limited by his objective senses but has subtle senses also which
seemingly are connected to all humanity and possibly to the total
universe as well. Human perception is not only not limited to
gross sense perception but is connected to eternity itself, according to many experts.

SUBJECTIVE HUMAN NATURE

The old concepts of materialistic psychology with its concepts of
rational mind objectivity and that the self and consciousness are
nonexistent, lies dead and broken on the new evidence of man's
personality nature. Man is now conceived of as a creature of altered states of consciousness with an unconscious and
superconscious nature that is connected to the rest of humanity
on a subliminal level and possibly to the universe as part and
partial of the innate species nature. Additionally humanity is felt
to be an evolutionary species on organic, cultural and consciousness mind dimensions, that is, mankind is a transpersonal species
that has progressive self-transcending potential. These factors are
all part and parcel of the emerging new world view that is gripping America. Later chapters will go into the scientific proofs of
these assertions. But realize this America that the foundation of

your culture's world view has collapsed and you are daily crying and in anguish because of that fact.

FALSE SUBJECTIVISM

The individual and the social order as it emerges from an individualistic age often develop a false egoism within its natural character. This subjective drive expresses itself as a will to be, a will to power and desire to find one's authentic individual or social identity. This drive can produce a false subjectivism. "The man who is born to be a dictator is not compelled" cried Adolf Hilter before the assembled correspondents from the world press. "He wills it. He is not driven forward, but drives himself . . . . The man who feels called upon to govern a people has no right to say, "If you want me or summon me, I will cooperate.' No! It is his duty to step forward." [39]

It is possible to sidestep false subjectivism if man, individually or collectively, recognizes that the authentic self is not the ego or that a country's national character is not the essence of the"race" and that a culture's basic personality is not representative of the super race or superior to imagined "inferior races," nationalities, etc. If concepts of manifest destiny are sidestepped, then an understanding develops that mankind is one species occurs and the subjective era can develop normally. If, however, the vital-mental tendencies get out of control then the primary power that is man demands its due and a false subjectivism develops. [40] Often this false subjectivism develops pseudo racial concepts.

"I am founding an Order," Adolf Hitler confided to Rauschning. He was speaking about his plans to extablish the Burga where the secnd phase in the breeding of a new race was to take place. "It is from there that the final stage in human mutation will emerge–The Man-God!" [41] "This splendid Being will become the object of universal worship." [42]

The reason for this is that the half-infrarational man needs three things for life satisfaction. They are power if the opportunity presents itself, creative self-fulfillment of all human faculties, and the enjoyment of human desires. [43]

The vital life power in man must assert itself and expand and possess and enjoy its existence. Power, pleasure and growth of being are its sense of reality. Two powerful impulses move it, however, one, a self-assertive individualistic urge and two, a collective assertion that works by strife but also by mutual assistance and unitive effort if the opportunity presents itself. It uses these coexistent, co-operative and competitive endeavors to gain its goals. [44]

The vital urge in life has its legitimate place in the life of the individual and society. When prevented fulfillment, however, a perverted monstrous barbarism emerges–a horrendous death generation creature of the night who devours and destroys mankind and nations in the name of vitalistic and egoistic life demands.

Walter Stein, companion to Adolf Hitler when they viewed the "talisman of power, the spear of Longinus, the spear that pierced the side of Christ, gives us an interesting example of how a death Master is born. Stein tells us that Hitler stood before the spear as in a trance in which some dreadful magic spell had entered the vital barbarian Hitler. His eyes shone with an emanation of alien force as he swayed on his feet and became engulfed within a ghostly ectoplasmic light. It seemed as if his physiognomy was transformed by some mighty spirit which inhabited his "soul" and was creating an evil transfiguration which embraced nature and power [45]

As Young stein observed the future pagan messiah he recalled the legend that the spear embraced both good and evil and he wondered if this youth, the future killer of million of human beings, was now the personification of the "Spirit of the Anti-Christ. [46]

August Kubizek, in his book "Young Hitler" gives us an insightful example of how this death force worked within the personality of Hitler. Kubizek says:

0109-CAMP

"Adolf Hitler stood in from of me and gripped my hinds and held them tight. He had never made such a gesture before. I felt from his grasp how deeply he was moved. The words did not come smoothly from his mouth as they usually did, but rather erupted, hoarse and raucous. Never before and never again have I hear Adolf Hitler speak as he did in that hour."

"I was struck by something strange which I had never noticed before, even when he talked to me in moments of greatest excitement. It was as if another being spoke out of his body and moved him as much as it did me. It was not all a case of a speaker carried away by his own words. On the contrary; I rather felt as though he himself listened with astonishment and emotion to what burst forth from him with elemental force. . . . like floodwater breaking their dikes, his words burst from him. He conjured up in grandiose inspiring pictures of his own future and that of his people. He was talking of a Mandate which, one day, he would receive from the people to lead them from servitude to the heights of freedom–a special mission which would one day be entrusted to him." [47]

Hitler, the Death messiah of the subjective age, believed in his personal destiny because he was the Death Prophet or herald of the new race of "Supermen" whom he believed would emergence within the Aryan peoples of the Twentieth century. They would have superhuman magical powers; and he felt that he personally was on the threshold of developing such faculties and magical powers which would be a foretaste of coming events when the great unseen forces of the etheric world became available to man. The Fuhrer felt, that as a man of destiny, that he was a Godfather to a new elite race of supermen about to emerge within the twentieth century. They would be masters of time and space. he said, "what today is known as history we will abolish altogether." He stressed that "Some men can already activate their pineal glands to give a limited vision into the secrets of time. But the new type of man will be equipped physically for such vision in the same manner as we now see with our physical eyes. It will be a natural and effortless gift." [48]

This concepts of brotherhoods based on the purity of the blood became the goal of subjective German National Socialism. Hitler emphasized that "Creation is not yet completed. Man must pass through many further stages of metamorphosis." But for the German Messiah the end result of the future new man was a glorious being of intrepid countenance and superhuman strength, who has intuitive powers which transcended mere intellectual thinking. He has a type of superhuman picture consciousness with magical faculty of imagination. These God-men, according to the Death master, would be so powerful that lesser mankind will be powerless to disobey them and that even the "spirits between heaven and earth would obey their commands. Supermen thus would become the elite of the earth and no earthy power would prevail against them. Hitler the subjective Death Master says. "They will be the Sons of the Gods." The Death Master goes on and says that" . . . All creative forces will be concentrated in a new species. The two types of man, the old and the new, will evolve rapidly in different directions. One will disappear from the face of the earth, the other will flourish . . . This is the real motive behind National Socialist Movement!" [50]

For Adolf Hitler the superman became objective fact. The Nazi superman, the elite of the race and lord of the kingdoms of the world exists as a fact of life to the Fuhrer. In a confession to Rauschning, the Nazi Gauleiter who defected later to the Allies, he discusses the mutation of the German Race. Adolf Hitler says:

> " The Superman is living amongst us now! He is here!' exclaimed Hitler triumphantly. "Isn't that enough for you? I have seen the New Man. He is intrepid and cruel! I was afraid of him." In uttering these words Hitler was trembling in a kind of ecstasy. (Hitler Speaks: Hermann Rauschning.). [51]

DEATH ECONOMICS

The present world crisis is also an example of the run away vital life urges as an emergent materialistic economic barbarism of 20th century man. We observe commercial and military interests united in their patriotic aspirations and supporting the national life by creating the most monstrous and nearly cataclysmic wars of the 20th century. [52]

In the name of colonialism, communist doctrines of manifest destiny, ethnic cleansing, capitalistic self-interest, the new world order, fundamental religious concepts, national goals, and arrogance of power, the beast of barbarism—releasing the dogs of war, have trampled the planet in the name of civilization's "best interests."

Today we find that our vital death barbarian, that is the Genocide Phenomenon, is now a creature of modern industrial societies and rising third world countries, as well as modern cross-cultural-religious fundamentalism. It is a creature of sociocultures that are complex and whose truth of existence is economic expansionism-economic self-aggrandizement; but is also a creature of diverse religious fundamentalism as well as of atheistic totalitarianism that exists not only in technologically advanced countries but in some oil rich third world countries and covertly in many democratic countries. This false subjectivism called the Genocide Phenomenon does not have to exist. It rules supreme now. It can be overcome and transformed by an emergent evolutionary jump of an awakened humanity. In the meantime economic and vital death barbarism exists and to understand it we must define it more fully.

Looking at economic death barbarism from the individual's materialistic position we find a person who is mistaking his vital-emotional personality for the true self and guides his life by vital-istic desires and urges. The satisfaction of wants and the accumulation of possessions is his aim of existence. The vital man is not a cultured or noble or thoughtful, moral or religious man. He is the successful man. He is the human who must accumulate, arrive, succeed, and possess all his existence. He has to accumulate wealth and add possession on to possessions. The opulence, show and the plethora of conveniences and inartistic luxury represent vital man at his best. This being and his false subjectivism vulgarizes religion or makes its coldly formalized, turns government and politics into a profession and a trade and lives devoid of nobility and beauty. Even creative enjoyment itself is made into a business by this vital man.

Unredeemed vital man view's beauty as a nuisance, and art and poetry as ostentation or a frivolity unless he can utilize them for advertisements. To him civilization is comfort and morality is social respectability. Politics to him represents the opening of markets, exploitation, the encouragement of industry and trade that follows the flag. He conceives of religion as pietistic formalism or as a mean to satisfy vitalistic emotions. He embraces education only as a utility for fitting a man for success in competition in the industrial world. He also values its utility in science for its useful inventions and knowledge that allows him to give stimulus to industrial production and power for industrial organization. [53]

The culture heroes to the vital man are the successful mammoth capitalist, the organizer of industry, millionaire sports figures, multimillionaire rock musical stars and the opulent plutocrat—all the supermen of the commercial age of the 20th century.

Today our semi-civilized societies are populated mostly by modern vital-barbarians. Our contemporary vitalistic barbarian is a partial Philistine. The type of man who mouths the right words, acts out the correct stage roles on the social stage. He is impervious to concepts and ideas and surely embraces no free intelligence. He is innocent of art and beauty and vulgarizes most things he touches whether these are ethics, literature, religion or life itself. [54] He must mimic his social roles—his acting career must reflect the higher sensitivities of the mental culture because he is the vital-emotional man—the vital barbarian. He is thus forced to act out the proper social roles because he has never emotionally and mentally or experientially reached the proper state of consciousness necessary to internalize these altered states of consciousness. He must mimic these social roles that the mental intellectual has by right of his emergent evolutionary consciousness. These Philistines exist in all socioeconomic class structures and no social group is without masses of these barbarians.

One can ask why they are this way but they act the way they do because they are using only the ego-personality of the vital ego. They, therefore, exist only in the life of the senses—emotions are their guide within a life of practical conduct. This is why they are a crude mass of likes and dislikes and prejudices enslaved by convention and habitual thought patterns of their cultures. Their ethical reality is that of the average Philistine man. [55] This mental barbarian is a person whose mental life lives in the lower substratum of the mind. The life senses and emotions are his boss although he has the appearance of an intelligent will he is merely reflecting cultural rules and concepts. This is why when the culture changes rapidly he easiily becomes a member of the death generation.

SENSATIONAL MAN

Our philistine population, however, has a higher dimension of being—a sensational man, although semi-civilized and living in the vital substratum, he sincerely desires to be stimulated from above.

Modern man today is vital or mental in nature but our sensational citizen is a man who lives in the lower substratum of the mind yet is one step above the pure vital barbarian. This man, however, has gotten a glimpse of some higher and nobler urge of the intellect. This type of man—the sensational man, has awakened to the fact that a higher intellect exists as a legacy within itself and that he ought to be mentally active. He should develop an appreciation of the higher arts of civilization and internalize the humanities into his personality make-up. The sensational man wants to do more than imitate the activities of his culture's intelligentsia. The vital-sensational man realizes that he must take into account the higher mental life, and make some intelligent use of his higher faculties. He strives to be knowledgeable concerning ethical problems, social problems, science and religion, art appreciation, etc. He may have no dynamic idea about aesthetics or beauty, but he surely has heard that art ought to be an important part of his life existence. [56] The sensational man is, therefore, the consumer of an extraordinary amount of books, films' videos and tape cassettes, radio and television programs and educational courses. He creates a demand in modern civilizations for these arts of higher mental thinking. He creates a cultural imperative that forces overt commercialism onto the masses to consume these "culture" types of commodity. The acquisition of these cultural items and arts of intelligent thinking or of viewing programs thus becomes a cultural necessity. It becomes a core value to that all modern sensational people, in all modern civilizations, must acquire too if they are to adhere to the driving force of their culture's imperatives. The sensational man, has in essence, remade the old cultural imperatives in his own image so that today's commercialism of the arts, and education has become the core value of modern civilization. The sensational activism is todays civilization's basic driving force. Today the entire American culture (United States), for example, makes its obeisance to sensational drives. Science sells its goods at the public's door while educational commercialism and social activism in the humanities KO tows to this man of the hour.

Our vital-sensational man still exists in the vital-emotional and lower intellectual substratum of his personality. He therefore, must be constantly stimulated to think and be forced to become relevant by the higher intellectual food of his intellectual superiors. All manner and type of sensational pabulum must be constantly fed into him—thus giving his activities color and sensationalism. "An army of writers cater to his needs and if ideas are put before him with brilliance and force and with mental sensation and excitation he thirsts for this general information. He does not have the time nor the desires to coordinate or assimilate these ideas but he likes popularized scientific knowledge, etc. The intelligentsia now can get a hearing from him if they first stimulate or amuse him.

Our sensational barbarian can be stimulated and becomes a ferocious warrior. It is he who in his barbarism successfully brought about in a few days the Russian revolution which the intelligentsia had failed to do in over a century. It was this creature who opposed and then accomplished the enfranchisement of women, who has evolved world classes, who rose up the labor movement and who wages wars of ideas. It is the sensational barbarian who is the precipitative agent for the reshaping of the modern world scene. It is because of their driving force that a Hitler, a Mussalini or a Lenin, achieved their raped successs—their stupefying victories. [57]

Our contemporary vital barbarism is a mass movement of vital mankind who have transcended their previously unrestrained physical natures. But they are still immersed in the throes of a dynamic vital nature which is constantly demanding its due. A semi-rational control exists which restrains our sophisticated barbarian, as there are several types of ego-minds co-existing within modern man's personality. Unfortunately the vital-physical desires are so strongly in control of our sensational man that our age's crisis reflects this barbarian's false subjectivism. This false subjectivism may continue for some time, since a culture and a civilization is merely the reflection of the mode of thought of the majority of a culture's population. Our contemporary age must continue to suffer the throes of the vital barbarian in its adolescence evolutionary trauma. It now must face itself as the Death Generation!

SUBJECTIVE AGENT OF GLOBAL CRISIS

One of the causal agent of the global crisis of consciousness is this age's subjectivism which has been captured by a vitalistic death surge called the Genocide Phenomenon, which is of the nature of unregenerated humanity. The solutions to this false subjectivism rests on the emergent evolution of consciousness, the balancing of the personality structure of man and in the creation of a new paradigm or viable theory of man.

A return to the purer form of subjectivism and a turning away from the false subjectivism would be a good first step. This type of subjectivism affects the individual along one of the personality aspects which corresponds to the four parts of the subjective self. A positive approach to contemporary life surely lies along the search for happiness and contentment from within the inner dimensions of man's personality. Whatever the individual's goal of life is, a positive expression can be obtained within the subjective era. Ultimately subjectivism can provide the way for an inner awakening of the authentic self within man. In fact the dynamic impulse of subjectivism is to discover this inner self and live by its insights. This is because this type of subjectivism recognizes that reason and will are not the only means of understanding human nature. Besides the goals of subjectivism are to perfect man's individuality through free self-actualization yet at the same time respecting this same free development in others. By the same token the cultural order must also have the freedom for the development of its social themes while respecting and aiding others in their social development.

Commentary: Campbell feels that this causal agent is a direct causal factor in the emergence of the death generation's destructive patterns since it causes a rupture between the outer human consciousness and the inner source of human reality. Campbell states:

FALSE SUBJECTIVISM

The individual and the social order as it emerges from an individualistic age often develop a false egoism within its natural character. This subjective drive expresses itself as a will to be, a will to power and desire to find one's authentic individual or social identity. This drive can produce a false subjectivism.

Unfortunately a false vital subjectivism, allied with technological innovation and gross materialism has taken over the above type of subjectivism. Consequently this false subjectivism is causing world wide tensions, wars and Nuclear confrontation crisis as man's vital egoism brings about the third causal factor in the present world crisis. This excessive vital egoism caused by false subjectivism has caused the proper balance between the outer objective consciousness and the inner mind of man to dysfunction. The exclusive concentration on man's outer objective mind has caused an intensification of humanity's egoistic tendencies and a psychological dysfunction has now developed in mankind. Man's vital consciousness has now dominated the mind which has become a servant to this era's barbarianism. Deep seated frustrations and an existential void in man's being is causing an intensive anxiety in the human race. Humanity does not seem to be able to escape from the bonds of this false subjectivism yet finds no satisfaction in fulfilling its demands The vital-emotional man of kinetic force and action must be brought under control or his sensational life drama and will to power and adventure passions will destroy the world. While it is true that the vital man has a turbulent, chaotic and often unregulated life preoccupied with the acquisition of material objects and possessions he can at his best be a great force in the mechanism of evolution. This is because the vital-emotional mentality deals in possibilities and novelty and is always seeking to expand his self-affirmation and aggrandizement of power and profit. He likes for unrealized possibilities and desires to materialize them, possess and enjoy them when he can do so. He also desires the subjective, emotive satisfaction and imaginative aspects of world desires. [58] These factors in the vital man's nature will allow him to overcome his false subjectivism by escaping the enslavement of the vital-emotional forces and become a mental adventurer for social and culture. Because of vital man's poorer force he becomes at the highest intensity of his life impetus a dynamic breaker of social bonds and seekers of new horizons. He may disturb the past and present and create a new social synthesis. He does this by controlling his kinetic vital energies through getting the reasoning intelligence to govern it. With such a balance a powerful formation can impose itself on man's nature and environment and accomplish a strong self-affirmation on the actualities of life. Vital man must be controlled by the mental mind and will to become a good instrument. He must transcend his surface vital ego which is narrow, ignorant and quite limited by his exultation for life expediences and find the true vital. The true vital is the inner vital. It is strong, calm, vast and has no limitations and is capable of great power. It will not emerge unless the total personalty structure becomes balanced and orientated around the authentic self-the psychic being or self personality.

It must be remembered that the vital in man in the life nature which consists of our desires, passions, feelings, sensations and our will desire force as well as our energies of action. The field of anger, instincts and interactions of desire possessiveness is also part of the vital nature. The important thing we must remember is that this vital force is the life force in man and nothing can be done or created in life unless the vital is there as an instrument. Even the transformation process and the emergence into higher states of mental consciousness needs this vital force. If the vital is enslaved to ego desires it becomes as harmful as it can be other wise helpful in the transformation process. The vital must be controlled by the mind even in ordinary life or it brings disorder or disaster as the collective global crisis testifies.

Another point for us to remember is that the mind and the vital-emotional ego systems are mixed up on the surface consciousness, even though they are separate forces in themselves. Often the vital desires certain objectives and a struggle ensues between it and the mind in man. This is a classic struggle! It has been going on for millions of years. It will go on until species extinction or man is transformed. It will continue until the mind gets control and then the authentic self integrates the mental, vital and physical ego personalities around it and then eventually emerges into higher states of awareness consciousness. This classic struggle's present rationale is that the vital-emotions started in its evolution with an obedience to impulse urges. It listened to no reason but used tactics which would further its ends. It doesn't care for the voice of reason and wisdom but takes advantage of the modern custom of justifying action by reason. The vital mind has developed a strategy which gets the reason to find reasons for justifying the vital impulses and feelings. If the mental reason does not fall for this game then the vital ego habitually shuts its ears and does what it wants to do. [59] Of course if the-mental ego is in control then the vital-must do its bidding.

Throughout this text we have been talking about vital-emotional man and mental man but it must be remembered that the majority of the world's population are infrarational beings who exist on the upper levels of the lower mind. Only the intellectuals and a few sages are true mental beings. Most of the human race consists of composite beings who have several personality systems operating simultaneously in the human personality. The average individual's external personality is a mixture of these plural ego systems, and during the day one or the other of the systems takes over the outer surface personality for as long as it can gain and keep control. In the course of a day the dominant control of the personality shifts back and forth many times. When the inner self integrates these ego systems around itself then true existence begins and one personality only lives within the human body. In the meantime we must get the vital to cooperate since it is a force and power on its own and operates quite independently of morality or reasoning. If one attempts to tyrannize it or submit it to harsh discipline it will one day revolt and avenge itself with interest. If the vital no longer insists on getting its way but refuses to cooperate a dryness or a passive neutral state of consciousness occurs. This dryness develops when the vital is quiescent, unwilling but passive and not interested. a neutral state comes into being when it neither is unwilling nor assents but is passive and quiescent.

The involvement and consent of the vital is necessary for all human actions, even the transformation of the personality structure. Until the vital-emotions is transformed no superior life or suprarational stage can be achieved. If it is not transformed then surely species extinction faces the human race because the death generation has taken over.

We cannot understand the Genocide Phenomenon and the death generation unless we understand humanity's evolutionary nature on the organic, mental and cultural dimensions. There is something that evolves and changes on all these levels that is so interconnected that we can't separate them overtly but only intellectually speak of them separately as an indivisible union. Yet the paradox is that we must discuss them , one by one, in order to grasp this scientific Trinity intellectually.

The next few chapter will attempt to place these categories in perspective; only then will we be able to talk about the Genocide phenomenon and the death generation as facets of this evolutionary process that man is apart of yet also a co-creator. But before we get into the subject matter lets put into historical perspective some of the subject matter we will soon examine.

MAN IS AN EVOLUTIONARY MENTAL CREATURE

The first sign of the development of an integral paradigm for 20th century man is that we are again viewing man as an evolutionary mental creature. This concept, a 19th century phenomenon, which died out in the first half of the 20th century, is now being revived as it is recognized that humanity is an evolutionary creature with not only organic, but also social and mental dimensions.

When unilineal cultural evolution or evolution in progressive hierarchical stages was rejected by most 20th century scientists the concept of mental-social evolution died a quick death in the scientific community. The rationale for this rejection was that it was accepted that social change was not primarily connected to an evolution of mentality. Not only did anthropologists reject such ideas but biologists reject the theory of recapitulation as linked with mental evolution, and psychological concepts of evolution fell on "evil days" within the psychological discipline. Animal psychologist ceased to be evolutionary-minded and physical anthropologists became unconcerned with behavioral evolution because of their concentration on evolutionary morphological problems. [60] Even psychologists concerned with studying personality between 1910-1940 preferred not to mention ego or self in their writings, thus effectively doing away with any entity that could psychologically and mentally evolve in time and space. [61]

Today, because of expanded scientific research in the fields of parapsychology, biofeedback research and transpersonal psychology, it is realized by a vanguard group of scientists that man is a self-transcending, evolutionary creature. New concepts and new paradigms now call for new explanations of man. Psychological man is now understood to be a psychohistorical creature, as well as a socio-metaphysical being. Human nature, to be fully understood, must be examined in integral terms that views Homo sapiens as a creature of a long evolutionary process—organic, psychomental and psychocultural. Transintegral Psychology presents the hypothesis that the key to the new structural paradigm is the concept of evolution as a self-transcending process.

PANDORA'S BOX

This concept of mental evolution may open a "Pandora's box" and let loose the past evils and abuses of social Darwinism and the unilinear cultural theory. This is a great danger, especially if future scientific technology develops definitive techniques to prove this hypothesis. The present evolutionary status of the species, therefore, needs to be clarified.

SPECIES CONSCIOUSNESS

Mankind, in the present era, exists within one species, Homo sapiens, divided into racial types that appear to be intellectually, linguistically and physically equal. All are potentially equal in the stream of consciousness evolutional. Transintegral psychology agrees with scientific findings that amply demonstrate that no racial or national community is superior to any other group mentally, psychologically, physically or linguistically. All human kind exists within the higher dimensions of the infrarational stage. All populations exist within a range of altered states of consciousness and are probably statistically equal with the range of mind states. They probably exhibit altered states of consciousness in their population much as I. Q. Variations exist. Now historically this equality of consciousness among groups may not have existed and may not prove to be a fact in the future. Right now, however all social societies seem to be equal in species consciousness in all of its potential. Within the recent historic past while certain cultural and technological differences exist among and between groups, these are the result of historic occurrences, borrowing, and cultural diffusion, that allowed certain peoples at the crossroads of world interaction to gain certain technical and literary sophistications over other groups. History amply demonstrates that even these "high" cultures become extinct, or wane in their power and influence, and often descend into dark ages and even may completely lose their language, technology and cultural sophistication. At any one time one group, nationality, country or radical group may appear superior in some manner or form, but in reality it is riding the tide of the cultural dynamics of the age and will, in due course, face the exigencies of the historical process. From a psychological point of view, however, all people are racially, linguistically, and mentally equal. There is no one group that is inferior as a group. It is possible to take appropriate persons from any group and train them properly in a specific science and it can be demonstrated that the species consciousness is equal in all groups. This applies to culture as a whole when they decide to enter the modern world or gain a certain technological sophistication. All members of the human species belong to the stream of evolutionary consciousness and within all groups exist the total range of psychological types and potentials to enter into the varying dimensions of altered states of consciousness. Within each society an individual may exist in varying dimensions of altered states of consciousness. Some people may even live in very extremely high states of mind. Such geniuses may make dynamic cultural contributions that may transcend the usual cultural diffusion and historical occurrences and borrowing that allow certain cultures to capture technical and literary sophistication over other societies. If large numbers of such individuals exist within one specific society then great social gains and mental leaps can be made for humanity. No scientific evidence now exists that proves that any one culture has a monopoly of large masses of people living in higher states of consciousness. All societies are probably statistically equal with the range of mind states, much an I. Q. Variations exist within specific groups. Scientifically we can verify these states when our technology becomes more technical and sophisticate. Elmer green of the Menninger Foundation says that direct verification of higher mind energy states and their structural arrangements must now be inferred from parapsychological data and from reports of mystic and occultists from various cultures. This is because our electronic instruments are constructed of minerals and cannot quantify the higher ranges of altered states of consciousness because the transducer components are inadequate. Because humans, according to Green, have all the necessary parts and can detect a greater spectrum of energies we must rely on the descriptive analysis of men who have lived in such state of mind. [62] It would be advantageous for science to make a thorough analysis of the literature, both East and West, on the ranges of consciousness described by men who have existed in the higher dimensions of mind. It would even be better to examine living sages who can demonstrate such states of mind. Some scientists, such as Anthropologist Philip S. Staniford, are attempting this type of research and are utilizing empirical subjectivism techniques to duplicate the see higher states of mind. This attempt supplements the empirical findings of biofeedback research, through which we have found that in some way the research subject can control this internal body and mind states. Biofeedback research utilizes electronic instruments to monitor and feed back information to the scientist and the research subject on the minute internal happenings of the subject's body and mind. This transpersonal technique to monitor "inner space" is a development stemming from the research and experiences of psychologist, meditators, engineers, physicists, and physiologists, and draws on electronics and psycho-physiological operant conditioning procedures. Examples of recent research using these techniques are the various projects of Elmer and Lyce Green of the Menninger foundation. In their laboratory in the United States, they have conducted research on autogenic training and biofeedback focusing on alpha and theta brain-wave states, reverie and imagery. Also, with their portable laboratory, they have carried out cross-cultural research on altered states of consciousness and have made physiological studies of yogis in India and in the United States. Luids West, University of California at Los Angeles anthropologist, has also used electronic equipment to study the transpersonal abilities of the Tarahumar Indians of central Mexico. [63]

Through such scientific research social psychology and physiology, will hopefully gain and understanding of social phenomena and man's altered states of internal awareness. Better still they will understand the relationship between consciousness and culture and how the integration of mind, culture and personality are related. We must know these answers if we are to construct a new theory of man for the 20th century. It is not enough that we think we know the above categories are integrally related. We must understand and examine the actual process in detail. This is why when we talk about the new development of a viable model of humanity we must have an interdisciplinary approach to the problem. We must set up research projects that can quantify ego states in a meaningful manner with specific psychocultural processes. Already you have researcher, such as Paul Bakan, with his controversial hemisphere study correlating certain behavioral activities to the left or right hemisphere of the brain. He believes that through the measurement of eye movements called "clems," or conjugate lateral eye movements, that he can judge whether one is an analytical person or a vital-emotional person. He also types people according to alpha waves. [64]

UNDERSTANDING OURSELVES

America we cannot understand ourselves until we walk into the light of our human nature on the yonder path ahead of us. Let's walk together, sons and daughter of the concealed light and talk about human nature some more and perhaps we can come to an understanding of who we are and where we are going and the paths we are treading upon.

When great events occur within social orders we must stand back and observe them so that we may understand the why and shape they are taking and what they signify to our way of life and to each of us personally.

The beginning of this journey of self-discovery will be to examine, in the next chapter, the psychological nature of culture and its relationship to consciousness. Perhaps such an inquiry will place in perspective the nature of culture change that each person must face in America today.

CHAPTER 6

EVOLUTIONARY CRISIS: SPECIES EXTINCTION OR EMERGENT . TRANSMENTAL QUALITIES

FUTURIST COMMENTARY: It is a historical fact that species die out and the human fossil record surely attests to the fact that our predecessors and species of humans who may never have been in direct ancestral line of the present Homo sapiens have perished from the face of the earth. Human beings have no God given right to exist forever; in fact the 22nd century surely demonstrates that the human race is dying and may last no more than several generations more. Our greatest scientists are working to perfect the biological cloning system for humans since much of the human stock, through disease, radiation and choice are no longer breeding stock. Some scientist are even cooperating with the alien forces that are presently battling the remnants of worldly civilization; their hope is that by combining and cross breeding two different stocks of self-aware beings that a new and dynamic race—a new species, if you will, shall come into being. The purist among us reject this absurdity and the battle goes on as the race perishes and grasps its last breath of life.

Campbell, below sets the mood but he also speaks to the human capacity to self-transcend itself and how if individually a person can emerge into the evolutionary force a transformation may take place that will save the human race from oblivion!

In an age in which science is atheistic and agnostic we find that Campbell, the scientist, truly believes that God is the Transpersonal Author of an Emergent force of Evolutionary Destiny! Campbell's premise is that humanity and the Universe are one. The free will of the human species is the deciding factor on whether life or death for the species will win the toss of destiny! For Campbell there is a special concentration of dimensional Consciousness–a supramental force that urges the species on and embraces each person individually if they will voluntarily change through transforming their lower natures by emerging into the higher realms of their destiny. But even Campbell concedes that each person individually must balance and dynamically change his own personality before he can contribute to the survival of the human race!

Campbell presents a new personality model and some of the process of changes necessary for entree into the higher evolutionary ranges of mental and self-realities. All human beings have these potentials, all have these capacities, all can emerge into their destiny; when they do so the universe greets them, the world honors them, the human species cheers them and God-almighty embraces them!

Mankind is presently facing an evolutionary crisis in which is concealed a choice of its destiny. This crisis rests not only upon man's unregenerated animal nature and blocked evolutionary threshold but also comes from a disparity between the limited faculties of the human race's mental, psychological and ethical natures and the technical means of self destruction at his disposal! The human species has reached an age of human development in which great technological advances have bewildered the race and mankind has lost its way. [1]

Is it possible that man is evolutionarily an unfinished animal? Does mankind's salvation from himself rest in some type of evolutionary advance-a further development in the human race? Does mankind act the way it does because humanity is neither rationally nor emotionally as high on the scale of evolution as he places himself? Is it possible that only the rare-few, the flowers of humanity–the suprarational mutants–the Christ, Pythagorous, the Buddha, Apollonius of Tyana, Plato, Aknaton, the rarely balanced intellectuals and geniuses in every field of human endeavors have truly touched authentic rational heights, whereas the rest of humanity is still immature and infrarational in nature and behavior. Can it be that collective humanity has not arrived at a mature adult life stage and behaviorally exists in an immature-like ambivalence of naive submental stupidity and unchecked adolescent emotionalism?

Transintegral Psychology presents a concept that evolutionary man is still a pygmy mentally and emotionally. Man's feet are still stuck in the primordial mud of the unconscious, his mind lying just above the lower level of mentality, his psychoemotional personality still primordial and undeveloped. The human personality is stilted, immature, disharmonious instinctive in motive and activity, orientated toward the pleasures of the flesh and self-aggrandizement.

This being is only kept in check by a thin line of limited mental and psychosocial restraints. Transintegral Psychology's stress is that modern man is still an animal–a thinking and speaking animal, but instinctively a primordial animal. [2]

Violence will surely continue to disrupt human society so long as any of the lower lusts and personality dysfunctioning of human nature enslaves man. Transintegral Psychology, on the other hand, does not support theories that man is innately an aggressive creature, a predator whose instinctive nature is to kill with a weapon. [3] It also rejects Konrad Loenz's contention that man's aggressiveness and often irrational behavior is phylogenetically programed. [4] Man's aggressiveness and often irrational behavior is only phylogenetically based in the sense that man is evolutionarily an unfinished being, an unbalanced and immature creature–emotionally and mentally. Total mechanical-instinctive behavioral responses is only applicable to the lower animal forms. Scientific research findings point out that the examination of animals up through the mammalian class, through the primates culminating in the study of man, demonstrate quite conclusively that innate behavior–controlled by genetic heritage, show a progressive blurring the closer one arrives to man. At the human stage psychological complexity increases and innate responses give way to individual behavioral actions based on individual social experience.[5] Transintegral Psychology, therefore, rejects outright all propositions–unsupported by factual evidence, which stress the innate depravity or the absolute instinctive bondage of man and contend instead that mankind has a potentially bright and infinitely creative future ahead of him if he consciously corrects certain deficiencies within the species. Surely Loren Eiseley's contention is true that man is nature's greatest experiment at escaping the blind subservience to the lower instinctive forces of nature. [6]

HUMAN SELF-TRANSCENDENCE

Can man transcend his present human condition? Transintegral Psychology affirms that this possibility exists because man is an animal in transition. The species has progress in its bones as C.P. Snow puts its. [7] Psychically, emotional and mentally man is an evolutionary animal. The species has an innate ability to transcend itself–an inherent mechanism which allows humanity to emerge into Olympian heights of luminous consciousness. There is an biological species imperative which lies within the genetic makeup of humanity. Its hour has arrived. Its force is upon the waters of time and humanity still sleeps to its destiny while this evolutionary force quakes the world and humanity to its roots. " . . . if a single being among our millions of sufferings succeeds in negotiating the evolutionary leap, the mutation of the next age, the face of the earth will be radically altered. Then all the so-called powers of which we boast today will seem like childish games before the radiance of this almighty embodied spirit." [8]

Many social critics, however, question not only man's ability to control his present human nature but the human animal's ability to change, and some critics assert that man's character is unchangeable. [9] Archibald MacLeish, for example, feels that the present age no longer believes in man and Loren Eiseley feels that the mechanistic view of man pioneered by The behaviorist Watson and developed by Freud and others have created modern man's loss of authority over his own destiny. [10] Many critics would agree with MacLeish's contention that modern man has been conditioned to believe that he has no inner direction power–that he is an empty organism. [11]

Transintegral Psychology contends that man has change built into his psychophysical system. The human race has been on the self-transcending roller-coaster ride since mankind's beginnings– when he burst through the threshold from the dryopithecus ape sphere of existence and emerged into Australopithecince man millions of years ago. Man is at another threshold today and the species Homo sapiens must make a conscious decision for progressive self-transcendence for survival reasons. For the first time in the history of humanity the species must consciously cooperate with his latent human nature or perish as a species. A new dimension of being–a new transpersonal man must emerge into a higher harmonious human state. The new superman must transform the barbarian dwelling with in him and consciously regenerate the present race of mankind. Humanity's goal must be to emerge a being who is to man what man now is to the animal–a regenerated humanity who has arisen into the heights of higher states of consciousness. The human race can be uplifted and changed, but such an evolvement is a long and arduous process of creative evolution— a regeneration of humanity's inner transpersonal nature. Can humanity achieve this change in nature? Transintegral Psychology's affirmative response is yes based on recent research findings in the biological and psychological sciences concerned with altered states of consciousness. [12] The human evolutionary potential is unlimited if success can be achieved in changing mankind's present social malaise.

Commentary: Campbell conceives that any paradigms must be examined in terms of man, science and natural laws and that mankind is inexorably interlaced to the wider cosmos. Man's consciousness is intertwined to this wider Cosmos and man's culture and consciousness are dimensional realties that interface with each other. Thus man, culture and the cosmos are interconnecting categories of existence that can't be separated from each other in any meaningful manner. Campbell states:

EMERGENT CULTURAL SYSTEMS: THE PSYCHOCULTURAL EVOLUTION OF MAN

Hidden within the vastness of primordial time the stream of life emerged on earth eons ago. During the late Pliocence or early Pleistocene eras the emergent evolutionary force brought forth Australopithecus man. This extraordinary birth which projected the human animal into conscious self-awareness and dimensional time began the startling psychocognitive emergence of early man and set in motion the psychocultural process. Homo erectus man and Neanderthal man and Homo sapiens, our present species gradually emerged along an evolutionary sequence as yet not fully understood by the scientific community.

This evolutionary process is still operative today and one of the causes of the world crisis is the fact that the human species has outgrown its present mind state and humanity's life and social systems seemingly can no longer be supported without a dynamic inner change of consciousness.

Man needs to become normal again by a conscious emergence into a higher state of mind awareness. We have already investigated partially the process of how it works and the relationship between consciousness and culture, altered states of mind, and the integral dynamics of the integration of mind, culture and personality. We will examine in more detail below the conceptual framework supporting the above premises.

MENTAL EVOLUTION AND ALTERED STATES OF CONSCIOUSNESS

Commentary: Campbell, although postulating a far future organic evolution of the physical body of the Species Homo sapiens, concentrates on the present evolution of human consciousness which he perceives to be intimately linked to the total evolution of mankind. He says that Transintegral psychology conceives of man as a mentally unfinished evolutionary product–in contrast to the generally accepted notion that human mental nature, if not pathological, is stable and static. The psychocultural evolutionary theory says that mind states are not universally equal and stationary within the species. Just as there are I.Q. variations within a population so there also exist differential mind states within the same population.

Not only are there quantitative consciousness differences between members of a population, but individuals themselves may or may not display the ability to enter into varying states of mind. The data findings of biofeedback research, parapsychological studies, and transpersonal psychology research are demonstrating that humans manifest a spectrum of varying states of awareness. The human animal vibrates or exists among a variety of states of consciousness. These differential mind states may be defined as a qualitative alteration in the process of mental functioning. Altered states of consciousness is not defined by the content of the mind, physiologic change or behavior but only by the varying pattering. [13] Transintegral Psychology says that all normal persons do not live in the same type of consciousness, because of personality differences as well as genetic, social, cultural and environmental reasons. Some people also live in the upper reaches of an infrarational consciousness, some in a rational state, and a few in a suprarational mind state. These mind states may exist simultaneously within a single mental, vital-emotional, or physical ego system or shift periodically during the day into a multiplicity of personality states.

Experimental psychologist Tart says that a variety of states of consciousness exist within the population. He says that some people think in words, for example, whereas others think in images. Some can voluntarily anesthetize some areas of their body, most cannot. Some people recall past events by imaging the scene and observing relevant details, whereas others use complex verbal associations and no images. In terms of practical experience this means that person x may have certain types of experiences that person Y cannot experience ordinarily and cannot ever hope to experience. [14] Seemingly, because of the differential nature of the evolutionary process, the species exists within a spectrum of varying states of consciousness. Transintegral Psychology says however that humanity is genetically coded–through that fortuitous mutation which allowed our ancestors to become mental creatures several million years ago–to progressively emerge into higher and vaster altered states of consciousness. The selective advantage given by that mutation is still with us today, but this potential is still latent in most of humanity. But the fact of the matter is that the evolution of the mind consciousness is linked with the psychocultural evolution of man. But we have reached a point in our species evolution that mankind must become a conscious participant in his own evolutionary process.

THE PSYCHOLOGICAL EVOLUTION
OF CONSCIOUSNESS

Today we are again viewing man as an evolutionary mental creature. This concept, a 19th century phenomenon, which died out
in the first half to the 20th century, is now being revived as it is
recognized that man is an evolutionary creature with not only
organic, but also social and mental dimensions.

When unilinear cultural evolution was rejected by most 20th
century scientists and the concept of developed that culture change
was not primarily connected to an evolution of mentality, the
concept of mental social evolution became unpopular and died a
quick death in the scientific community. Not only did anthropologists reject such concepts but biologists rejected the theory of
recapitulations as linked as mental evolution, and psychological
ideas of evolution fell on "evil days" within the psychological
discipline. Animal psychologists ceased to be evolutionary-minded
and physical anthropologists became unconcerned with behavioral evolution because of their concentration on evolutionary
morphological problems. [15] Even psychologists concerned with
studying personality between 1910-1940 preferred not to mention ego or self in their writings, thus, effectively doing away with
any entity that could psychologically and mentally evolve in time
and space. [16]

Today, because of expanded scientific research in the fields
of biology, parapsychology, biofeedback research, transpersonal
anthropology and transpersonal psychology, it is realized by a vanguard group of scientists that man is a self-transcending, evolutionary creature. New concepts and new paradigms now call for
new explanations of man; psychological man is now understood
to be a psychohistorical creature, as well as a socio-metaphysical
being. Human nature, to be fully understood, must be examined
in integral terms that view Homo sapiens as a creature of a long
evolutionary process–organic, psychomental and psychocultural.
Transintegral Psychology presents the hypothesis that the key to

the new structural paradigm is the concept of evolution as a self-transcending process.

PANDORA'S BOX

This concept of mental evolution may open a "Pandora's box" and let loose the past evils and abuses of social Darwinism and the unilinear cultural theory. This is a great danger, especially if future scientific technology develops definitive techniques to prove this hypothesis. The present evolutionary status of the species therefore needs to be clarified.

Species Consciousness.

Humanity, in the present era, exists within one species, Homo sapiens, divided into racial types that appear to be intellectually, linguistically and physically equal. All are potentially equal in the stream of consciousness evolution. Transintegral psychology agrees with scientific findings that amply demonstrate that no racial or national community is superior to any other group mentally, psychologically, physically or linguistically. All humankind exists within the higher dimensions of the infrarational stage. All populations exists within a range of altered states of consciousness and are probably statistically equal with the range of mind states. They probably exhibit altered states of consciousness in their population much as I. Q. Variations exist.

Certain cultural and technological differences exist among and between groups, these are the result of historic occurrences, borrowing, and cultural diffusion, that allowed certain peoples at the crossroads of world interaction to gain certain technical and literary sophistications over other groups. History amply demonstrates that even these "high" cultures become extinct, or wane in their power and influence, and often descend into dark ages and even may completely lose their language, technology and cultural sophistication. At any one time, one group, nationality, country or racial group may appear superior in some manner or form, but in reality it is riding the tide of the cultural dynamics of the age and will, in due course face the exigencies of the historical process. From a psychological point of view, however, all people are racially, linguistically and mentally equal. There is no one group that is inferior as a group. It is possible to take appropriate individuals from any group and train them properly in a specific science and it can be demonstrated that the species consciousness is equal in all groups. This applies to cultures as a whole when they decide to enter the modern world or gain a certain technological sophistication. All members of the human species belong to the stream of evolutionary consciousness and within all groups exist the total range of psychological types and potentials to enter into the varying dimensions of altered states of consciousness.

EVOLUTION AND ALTERED STATES OF CONSCIOUSNESS

Transintegral psychology conceives of man as a mentally unfinished evolutionary product—in contrast to the generally accepted notion that human mental nature, if not pathological, is stable and static. The psychocultural evolutionary theory says that minds states are not universally equal and stationary within the species. Just as there are I.Q. variations within a given population so there also exist differential mind states with the same population.

Not only are their quantitative consciousness differences between members of a given population, but persons themselves may or may not display the ability to enter into varying states of mind. The data findings of biofeedback research, parapsychological studies, transpersonal anthropology and transpersonal psychology research are demonstrating that humans manifest a spectrum of varying states of awareness. The human animal vibrates or exists among a variety of states of consciousness. Psychologist Charles T. Tart states that:

0109-CAMP

> An overall pattern of psychological functioning, an altered
> state of consciousness (ASC) may be defined as a qualitative
> alteration in the overall pattern of mental functioning, such
> that the experiencer feels his consciousness is radically dif-
> ferent from the nor- mal way it functions. Note that ASC is
> not defined by a particular content of consciousness, behav-
> ior, or a physiologic change, but with overall patterning. [17]

Tart also recognizes an assertion of Transintegral psychology that
all normal persons do not live in the same type of consciousness,
because of personality differences as well as genetic, social, cultural, and environmental reasons. [18] Aurobindo, the formulator
of the basic concepts of the psychocultural evolutionary model
would carry this idea further and state that some people live in
the upper reaches of an infrarational consciousness, some in a
rational state, and a few in a suprarational mind state. He also
feels that these mind states may exist simultaneously within a
single mental, vital-emotional, or physical ego system or even shift
periodically during the day into a multiplicity of personality states.

Experimental psychologist Tart says that a variety of states of
consciousness do exist within the population. He says that some
people think in words, for example, whereas others think in images.
Some can voluntarily anesthetize some areas of their body, most cannot. Some people recall past events by imagining the scene and observing relevant detail, whereas others use complex verbal associations and no images. [19] Tart makes a further point by saying that:

> This means that person A may be able to observe certain
> kinds of experiential data (have certain expert- iences)
> that person B cannot experience in his ordin- ary SOC
> no matter how hard B tries. Several conse- quences may
> result. Person B may think that A is "nutty," too imagina-
> tive, or a liar, or he may feel inferior to A. Person A may
> also feel "odd" if he takes B as a standard of "normal-
> ity."[20]

Seemingly, because of the differential nature of the evolutionary process, the species exists within a spectrum of varying states of consciousness. Transintegral psychology postulates, however, that humanity is genetically coded–through that fortuitous mutation that allowed our ancestors to become mental creatures several million years ago–and to emerge progressively into higher and vaster altered states of consciousness. The selective advantage given by that mutation is still with us today, but this potential is still latent in most of humanity. The executive force of this mutation for human mental evolution is the kundalini phenomenon. It seemingly is the hidden evolutionary force operative within the evolutionary consciousness of human nature.

KUNDALINI PHENOMENON

Scientific study of the kundalini phenomenon is very recent, and considerable research clearly needs to be done. Research is now in progress in a number of countries, including Japan, Germany and Russia, as well as the United States. Some researchers such as Itzhak Bentov believe that the hidden potential of the nervous system is vast and that the kundalini mechanism may well be the next step in its evolution. [21]

Transintegral psychology puts forth the hypothesis that the transforming energy of the evoutionary process is the kundalini phenomenon. This process, however, is not an automatic evoutionary force since it seemingly needs the conscious collaboration of willing participants. In this regard Aurobindo sees man as a transitional being and postulates that the human species must consciously participate in his own evolution. [22] He feels physiological self-alteration can only take place after one emerges into a permanent state of supramental consciousness. Through the mobilization of the kundalini energy, a possibility exists for the transformation of being down to the cellular level. [23] Kundalini researcher Gopi Krishna challenges the entire scientific community to investigate the mysteries of kundalini. The question is will science be able to throw light on the phenomenon?

Seemingly some people open the kundalini force through meditation and other practices, usually within esoteric systems designed to emerge people into higher states of consciousness; but to some people it seemingly opens up spontaneously, although many of these have followed some type of self transformation process on their own. One such person was Gopi Krishna who after seventeen years of regular morning meditation experienced one morning an overpowering awakening of kundalini. The force was so great and the results so dire that he became exceedingly ill. He was forced to give up his work and for 25 years struggled to contain this new force within his ailing body (Krishna;1967).

Eventually he experienced an expansion of consciousness and many considered him an "awakened" person. Once the kundalini power was harmonized and under control he was determined to bring to the world of science the challenge of investigating this energy. James Hillman, a psychologist, collaborated with him on his first book, an autobiographical account of the happenings we have recounted here in brief. Gopi Krishna worked with scientist, until his death, in the United States and in India.

It is only very recently that Westerns have become aware of the existence of kundalini. Even in India, the experience itself and knowledge about it has not been widespread in the population. Anthropologists have witnessed its effects in numerous cultures but have not, as far as we know, related it to kundalini. R. Katz, a psychologist, saw it as a result of long hours of dancing as practiced by the Kung people of the Kalahari desert. In the dance, they say, they warm up the "!n'um" which resides in the pit of the stomach until it rises from the base of the spine to the skull, where the experience of "!Kia" occurs. One tribesman was reported by Katz to have described the experience thus:

> In your backbone you feel a pointed something, and it
> works its way up. Then the base of your spine is tingling,
> tingling, tingling, tingling, tingling, tingling,

tingling . . . and then it makes your thoughts nothing in
your head. [24]

In our own culture, there appears to be a marked awakening of
consciousness, as well as interest in consciousness itself. There is a
turn toward meditation and, as a result of this, an increasing
number of people are beginning to experience kundalini. Often
they do not realize what is happening to them and are sometimes
frightened. Sannella, a psychiatrist and ophthalmologists, includes[15]
case histories in his book "Kundalini-Psychosis or Transcendence?"
. . . and gives us a generalized description of a kundalini experience:

> In a darkened room a man sits alone. His body is swept
> by muscular spasms. Indescribable sensations and sharp
> pains run from his feet up his legs and over his back and
> neck. His skull feels as if it will burst. Inside his head he
> hears roaring sounds and high-pitched whistling. Then
> suddenly a sunburst floods his inner being. His hands
> burn. He feels his body tearing from within. Then he
> laughs and is overcome with bliss. [25]

The kundalini energy usually travels from the base of the spine
upward to the brain area, but it may also travel from the top of
the head downwards. According to Integral Psychologist Haridas
Chaudhuri, [26] it can also be opened at any of the various chakra
centers. Aurobindo says:

> In our yoga there is no willed openings of the chakras; they
> open of themselves by the descent of the force. In the tantric
> discipline they open from down upwards,[27] the muladhara
> first; in our yoga, they open from up downward. But the
> ascent of the force from the muladhara does take place. [28]

Clearly, from a subjective point of view, the phenomenon exists
and is meaningful. If scientific research can establish the objective

reality of kundalini, we must then ask: Can it be controlled, and does it have any significance for the human species from an evolutionary viewpoint as transintegral psychology contends?

SCIENTIFIC RESEARCH ON KUNDALINI

A number of scientists are attempting to devise techniques with which to study and measure kundalini. One such researcher is Dr. Hiroshi Motoyama, a Tokyo scientist who has developed apparatus with which to research psi energy and measure the subtle energy flows of the meridians and chakras. The Motoyama device is an instrument which allows the subjects to be tested inside an earthed (grounded) room which is lead-lined to eliminate extraneous electromagnetic interference. Chakra energy is recorded on a highly sensitive strip chart recorder from subjects who manifest psi ability and from those who do not. Electrical charges are recorded from the forehead, vertes (top point of the head), throat, heart, lungs, abdomen, navel, coccyx, knees and ankles. Subjects without psi ability show slight changes; those with it demonstrate considerable change. Motoyama has also recorded measurements from subjects with fully awakened chakras and others with only partially awakened chakras. The device recorded energy from the chakras both when the subjects were focusing on them and when they were not. The energy level for both groups was lower when the subjects were quiescent. Motoyama also demonstrated that psi energy emanates from the chakra and meridian points during the phenomenon of psychokiniesis. Using the electroencephalograph, Motoyama showed that the psi energy of kundalini radiates from an awakened chakra and flows out from there through the meridian points of finger tips and toes. [29]

An English researcher who lives in California, Dr. Christopher Hills, has combined his expertise in radiesthesia and Yoga to invent a number of devices which he feels can measure the subtle energies of the biophysical phenomenon. He contends that one instrument, which he calls the Kundalini Roomph Coil, can register where a subject's kundalini energy is focused, and allows the user to tune this latent energy so that each chakra, or energy vortex, will open gradually. Hill has written about his devices in several of his books. [30]

Dr. S. Vinekar, Director of Research at the Kaivalyadhama Laboratory at Lanalva near Poona, India, has developed a map of the kundalini process in the human body by using EEG (electroencephalograph) and GSR (galvanic skin response) instruments to record its electrical effects. [31]

The University of Bangalore, India is now investigating the kundalini phenomenon in its government supported study, "Project consciousness". And in Germany, the Max Planck Institute has conducted a biochemical search for the kundalini which involved electrical sensation, inner lights, tingling and convulsions. Moderation of the symptoms over a time period was shown, as well as alterations in the central nervous system. [32]

Some researchers in the United States now feel that the dynamics of kundalini may be analogous to a laboratory-induced effect called "kindling", which is similar to an epileptic seizure and was originally thought to fit the epilepsy model. However, John Gaito of York University, England, believes that in some cases different mechanisms are involved, as the amino acid, taurine, which suppresses epileptic seizures in laboratory animals, does not stop the kindling effect. It is interesting that permanent changes in the neural circuitry system are seemingly caused by the kindling effect. The analogy of the dramatic kundalini phenomenon with the kindling effect-and especially the stimulation of the limbic region of the brain-is significant. With laboratory animals, bursts of electrical activity which spread to adjacent brain regions kindle convulsions. Bernard Glueck of the Hartford (Connecticut) Institute of Living feels that a resonance effect in the limbic brain may be set off by sounds used in mantra meditation. This type of mantra sound is a repeated tonal stimulus which could become rhythmic and convulsive in nature. Some of the kundalini case studies of Lee Sannella occurred after the use of transcendental meditation using mantra techniques. [33]

According to research physicist Robert L. Pecik's kundalini hypothesis, the characteristics of the nervous system's electrical flow undergo a change in control, sensitivity and efficiency because of certain stimuli. He thinks that one possibility is that large sodium or potassium ions are replaced by smaller hydrogen ions for the conduction of electrical impulses. Since the clathrates in blood may diminish as the larger ions are being replaced by the hydrogen ions, for the conduction of electrical impulses. Since the clathrates in blood may diminish as the larger ions are being replaced by the hydrogen ions, reduced mental awareness could occur. The hydrogen ion would carry the electrical energy which causes the kundalini effect. [34]

Much of this modern research is based on the theoretical ideas of Dr. Vasant Rele. In 1926, Dr. Rele read a paper before the Bombay Medical Union which was later expanded into a book called "The Mysterious Kundalini". He postulated that a subject could achieve conscious control of the sympathetic nervous system. He reasoned that the right vagus nerve, which is the major nerve of the parasympathetic system, was the carrier of the kundalini energy. The activities of the sympathetic system's six plexus can be controlled through stimulation of the right vagus nerve at its central connection in the medulla. It is postulated that this nerve can be stimulated by certain breathing exercises which by reflex cause the kundalini to ascend up the spinal cord. This occurs through control of the afferent and efferent impulses of respiration. When breathing attention becomes conscious, and the normally unconscious control of respiration by one of the plexus of the sympathetic system ceases, the kundalini then consciously passes through the vagus and other parasympathetic nerves whose nuclei are in the bulb and midbrain. [35] Rele's case studies show yogis controlling their heart and pulse, stopping the heart and the pulse at the wrist, and giving other demonstrations of skill and strength. [36]

Elmer and Alyce Green of the Menninger Foundation have

done similar research on the physiological psychological areas of self-regulation of autonomic processes. Swami Rama caused the left side of the right hand to increase several degrees in temperature above the right side of the same hand. This demonstration showed exquisite differential control over the neural apparatus which is normally uncontrolled. Jack Schwarz, too, was able to perform similar acts as well as to control bleeding. [37] The Greens have also conducted research on skatipat, by which a fully awakened person can transfer the kundalini energy by thought or touch. The Greens' research shows that a recipient's heart rate decreases several beats per minute at the time of contact. [38]

Finally, Dr. John Goyeche, a psychologist with the Department of Psychiatry at Kurume University in Japan, recorded some psychophysical data during his own kundalini experience while he was working at the University of Manioba in 1972. During a breathing exercise, he had three separate kundalini experiences, each lasting about a minute, within a span of 15 minutes. The polygraph record showed that at the onset of each of these experiences, several things happened, the most notable being the "large localized skin potential response which occurs in the EEG channel, indicative of a sudden sympathetic response". However, respiration rates and heart rate acceleration showed little variation during each experience. Goyeche hypothesizes that the kundalini is a sympathetic reflex which compensates for the critical drop in metabolic level and increased carbon dioxide level. This metabolic drop agrees with the reported declines in carbon dioxide elimination and oxygen consumption in the research of Wallace and Benson. Goyeche also feels that the kundalini bliss experience is similar to that of the high following an intravenous amphetamine injection. [39]

GOPI KRISHNA AND KUNDALINI RESEARCH

Gopi Krishna says that kundalini is a form of bioenergy which drives the evolution of man to higher states of mind. He feels that this bioenergy permeates the billions of living cells as self-charging batteries of prana, of living electricity. Russian biologists, biochemists and biophysicists, using electron microscopes and Kirlian high frequency electrical equipment have indeed photographed this plasma-like constellation. It seems to consist of electrons, protons, etc. and, as an energy body, is a unified organism which has its own electromagnetic field and is polarized. [40] Gopi Krishna feels that the ubiquitous nerves, when aroused, cull this bioplasma from the cells and send it through the spinal cord to the brain. The kundalini activation uses the bioplasmic energy already present in the human organism. Thus, every neuron in the brain, nerve and nerve fiber makes the human body into a dynamo of live electricity. [41]

The director of the Biophysics laboratory at Kazak State University in Alma-Ata, U.S.S.R., Viktor Inyushin, has also conducted research that corroborates Gopi Krishna's viewpoint. The biofield has spatial formation and is shaped by electrostatic, electromagnetic, acoustic, hydrodynamic, and possibly unknown physical fields. Research shows that it consists of ions, free electrons, and free protons (subatomic particles that exist independently of a nucleus). Bioplasma accumulates most intensely in the brain, and the center of the spinal cord seems to be the center of bioplasma activity in the body. There is more bioplasma in the nerve cells than in the blood. Inyushin says experiments with bioplasma demonstrate an organism's ability to change mass into energy. [42]

> A point of view that seems to complement this comes from Swami Amatananda, who says that: The Kundalini's journey all happens in the subtle body, which is a lot like the physical body but is made up of subtle energy . . . it contains all the impressions which create the particularity of this physical body. You could imagine it as a subtle inner glove fitted inside the physical body, which determines and sustains that body's form. [43]

No comprehensive paradigm of the kundalini phenomenon yet

exists. We know it can be awakened consciously through various techniques, occurs spontaneously, or emerges by accidents-in falls, for example. It can have a powerful positive or negative effect on an individual. An awakened person can experience longevity with excellent health, but, on the other hand may develop terrible bodily pains, heat, and deteriorating heath. Even death and insanity are all possibilities. Researcher John White, in a paper given to the American Anthropology Association convention makes the point that:

> The 'white light' experience of the mystics can become the 'ugly glaring light' of a schizophrenic and the 'signs and wonders' performed by saints can turn into psychic phenomena that terrify people who naively venture beyond the limits of their understanding and preparation. Without proper guidance from personal experience, and without right preparation–meaning a healthy, ethical, regulated manner of living that is neither ascetic nor orgiastic–kundalini can become the source of deteriorating health, terrible bodily pain and heat, many forms of mental illness and insanity, and even sudden death. In physiological terms, the pranic stream has gone astray into one two side channels of the spinal cord. [44]

White also makes the point that kundalini research is the first testable field hypothesis of the Psychopysical linages among mind, body, culture and the cosmos that covers the spectrum of anthropological enigmas, psychological, psychic and transpersonal phenomena. He thinks it unifies the physical and biological and social sciences. [45]

Transintegral psychology asserts that the kundalini energy is the basic energy system behind the evolution of the human species and is the link to the human race's transpersonal natures. And that even in its seemingly latent or asleep form it provides the energy that drives and supports each person's individual exist-

0109-CAMP

ence. Future research will hopefully provide us with hard data to support this hypothesis.

Futurist Commentary: The scientist Campbell embraces the evolutionary social-cultural theory of the suprarational intellectual psychologist, Aurobindo Ghosh. This theory conceives that humanity has the possibility to progressively emerge into higher and higher altered states of consciousness.

Campbell contends that the evolutionary causal agent of the global crisis is a biological one since the emergent evolution of consciousness rests on certain esoteric biological facts and partially on the specie's conscious cooperation with the evoutionary process.

THE FUTURE EVOLUTION OF MAN'S CONSCIOUS EVOLUTION

The evolutionary causal agent of the global crisis is taking place because the human race has been brought face to face with a critical decision. Human destiny through the exigencies of evolutionary change is pushing humanity to a crucial juncture within the historical process. Mankind has reached the point in the history of the species when he must consciously desire to emerge into a higher state of consciousness. The species must overcome his lower barbarian nature, transform it and then ascend into a higher dimension of human reality. This stage of the evolutionary process is presently causing an acute tension within the world populous. The dynamics of this process requires that humanity make a decision consciously to transcend itself.

Species success or social survival, racial extinction or emergence into as higher state of species consciousness depend upon the conscious development of the supramental consciousness within terrestrial evolution Those portions of humanity who are emerging into this state of consciousness are fighting an heroic battle of inner purification so that a whole world civilization will be saved from obscurity and destruction. [46]

It is entirely possible that the majority of the species will reject this possibility. Death will be the answer to this refusal since man is an evolutionary creature on the organic, mental and social dimensions. The human race cannot stop evolutionary change! Just as his physical form has evolved and changed in form and function through time we must also realize that this dweller within a time-space continuum exists within a never ending creative evolutionary process as long as the species exists. Life is one ceaseless process of self-transformation.

There is hope for mankind–the species can be saved from extinction–the human race can transcend its animal nature. The evolutionary force is at work within mankind and the shock of the human race's leap from an pure animal nature to human status speaks to us from our subconscious mind. 47 This creative cry–this birth scream, which burst the human animal into conscious self-awareness became the catalyst which is today pushing humanity into the obscure dimensions of altered states of consciousness. The basic theme of terrestrial evolution is an evolution of consciousness. The major fact of the next evolutionary leap is a change of consciousness.

The solution to this causal agent of the present world crisis in consciousness is that humanity must consciously desire to overcome its lower nature and progressively evolve into higher and vaster states of mind growth. Let us now speculate about this future beyond secular man and concentrate on the possible future evolution of humanity . We will briefly examine this process so that we can more fully understand the solution to the first causal agent of the contemporary world crisis.

BEYOND SECULAR MAN

Eons ago life emerged out of the world stuff, the primordial essence, as biologist Julian Humbly defines the life source of the animal kingdom. Hundreds of millions of years later, during the late Pliocene or early Pleistocene eras, mind emerged as a rational instrument. Man became a self-conscious infrarational being. Since the attainment of that epic mind pinnacle a gradual evolution of man's psychomental consciousness has allowed some men to change their natures. They first evolved beyond their infrarational personalities, then through a range of rational altered states of consciousness. Ultimately a few giants, the Christ, Aknaton, Appollonious of Tyana, Lao Tzu, Buddha, and other geniuses emerged into a suprarational dimension. Some men now have the possibility to emerge into a superconscious state of superior human mentality. Empirical research on altered states of consciousness seems to demonstrate that such vanguard states of mental awareness are appearing among our species today. The research findings of Transintegral Psychology also seem to point of the fact that man now has the dynamic potential to evolve into a supramental race. This state is a gnostic mode of consciousness which would be dimensionally ultra suprarational. Ultimately there might even exist the possibility of the emergence of a gnostic species. If Aurobindo's vision is correct then present humanity–man the half-animal, half-mental, half-civilized creature that he now is may exist in the twilight of a dying infrarational age. Our species may exist in the death throes of a semimetal consciousness which is emerging into the heights beyond secular man. It may even be possible that some men have emerged as the vanguard of this new era. Superior rational beings–mutants who through the use of transpersonal techniques may be manifesting a suprarational consciousness, thus creating a dimensional crisis. They may be creating a new beginning which will allow the human species to emerge the supramental consciousness within terrestrial evolution.

Carl Jung says we are now living in an era which is the right time for the metamorphosis of the Gods. [48] Transintegral Psychology says that mankind is such a vanguard person who is undergoing a metamorphosis into suprarational man. The futurist Aurobindo addressing the concept of conscious evolution says that:

Imagine not the way is easy; the way is long, arduous,

dangerous, difficult. At every stop is an ambush, at every turn a pitfall. A thousand seen or unseen enemies will start up against thee, terrible in subtlety against thy ignorance, formidable in power against thy weakness. And when with pain thou hast destroyed them, other thousands will surge up to take their place. Hell will vomit its hordes to oppose and enring and wound and menace; heaven will meet thee with its pitiless tests and its cold luminous denials. [49]

GNOSTIC CONSCIOUSNESS

There may be men who are ready to emerge into a gnostic consciousness. A gnostic power consciousness may emerge out of rational man–transforming all earth consciousness which is ready for this dimensional transformation. [50] When the gnostic consciousness emerges in the vanguard beings the veil between the subliminal and the surface personality will be broken and the subconscious will become conscious while the still deeper inconscious will become a transformed lower subconscious. [51] The higher mind states, overmind and other gradations of consciousness will be carried forth within the new state of awareness and a hierarchy of ascending degrees of gnostic beings may constituent formations of gnostic light and power in earth nature. [52]

The different grades of gnostic beings would utilize their specific powers of consciousness as their particular principles of action. A Higher-cognitive being would act through the transpersonal essence of his thought, the truth of the idea which would be translated into life-action. The illumined gnostic being would have a transcendental truth-vision, whereas the Intuitive gnostic being would have a direct transpersonal contact which is a perceptive unity of action. The overmind gnostic being would have an inclusive largeness of being and doing that is comprehensive in vision with an immediate and dynamic grasp of consequences.

The supramental gnostic being is a person of knowledge-by-identity who uses all the powers of integrate personality to accomplish his purposes. He may have an integral knowledge of the sovereign principle of effectuation that requires no external aid to embody itself. Even here there will be intermediate degrees of gnosis; but thought here is not knowledge or action instruments or force but channels of expression of knowledge. It would have a comprehensive grasp and play of illuminated vision, a direct truth-contact and sense and a play of radiant thought. The Supramental gnosis is self-knowledge and intimate world-knowledge and a self-light of being effectuating itself. [53]

Highly developed suprarational beings who may be unable to sustain such a high degree of mind energy would find their consciousness spectrum location within an echelon of mental levels. These levels would range from the lowest degree of mind awareness to the highest frequency of supermind.

TRANSPERSONAL CONSCIOUSNESS AND ORGANIC EVOLUTION

How will these higher states of consciousness affect organic or the physical evolution of man. It is entirely possible that if such a mind emergence does occur and if favorable mutations emerge on the organic level that a new man could through speciation emerge. A new type of man would emerge from present humanity on a chronospecies dimensional level. It is possible that a new physical form or new morphological human body would not take place. But at the very least a new racial phynotypic or physical variance from the present races could take place. And even a new species could emerge from the single human species on earth now. If any of these things occur it will probably follow the general course that the animal kingdom has followed in the past. Julian Huxley says that by observing the evolutionary process we see that the general biological advancement occurs through a series of steps or through an emergence or a series of dominant types. Each dominant type because of some improvement is able to multiply and spread at the expense of the former dominant group from which it has evolved. [54]

It is impossible to speculate what the phenotype make up of the gnostic beings would be. We can only say that within the gnostic species, race or type, Homo supermentalenus, itself would exist some beings who had transcended most of the present vicissitudes of life and whose supramental consciousness would be unitive in form and structure with the power of a vast universal spirituality. Aurobindo feels that each gnostic being would feel the presence of the higher power in all parts of his consciousness and in every cell of his body. [55] The dimensions of his life would be like a perfect work of art and his spontaneous genius would have an infallible quality. The gnostic individual would live in the world and yet exist out of it but also exceed it in his consciousness. He would also live in his self of transcendence above which would be universal yet free in the universe. The gnostic being as an individual would not be limited by a separate individuality from the universe. He would be a free and powerful individual with a vast depth personality which could create intricate forms of self-expression. His entire nature would be in obedience to the will of the higher self while his personality expression would exist in a balanced psychosocial relationship with the rest of mankind.

Aurobindo says that each gnostic individual and the total collective gnostic beings would have a symphonic communication awareness with each other and the conscious All which hold and contains them in its universal dimensions. Each person would be conscious of itself within every other gnostic person but at the same time be conscious of the same WILL and the same Self and energy active in the collective group of gnostic people. Such a gnostic consciousness and will, aware of its oneness, meaning and identity, and points of diversify, becomes a symphonic movement of unity and harmony mutuality in the existential action of the collective group. This unity rests on an individual unity which has a symphonic concord with all the movements and powers of his being. [57]

The gnostic race-living within the essence of an inner dimensional manhood would also manifest a clearness of vision and a psychic sight which would reflect superhuman perception of worldly affairs. Through this insight they would probably influence a segment of untransformed rational humanity to consciously emerge into the lower reaches of the suprarational mind states. Eventually a series of mental types might exist from rational man all the way to the higher summit of the supermind–the summit where some gnostic beings would exist in the ultimate pure existence of Transpersonal Consciousness.

SPECIES EXTINCTION OR EMERGENT MENTAL EVOLUTION

It is not certain that a new type of humanity will ever evolve on this planet. The world wide tension–the result of the radical inner crisis in the species Homo sapiens may bring the extinction of the species through Nuclear Warfare or ecological disaster, or through the actions of the death generation, or possibly if the death generation wins then the planet will be plunged into a dark age which will last thousands of years, etc. Mira Alfassa says that we are now:

> . . . in the very thick of that battle, facing heroically the furnace of inner purification so that it may not be necessary to pass once more through one of those formidable, titanic destructions which plunge a whole civilization into obscurity. [62]

The chances are about even that our species will prove unfit for the further integration of higher mind states and will perish of Nuclear suicide or because of some unknown reason. Several other possibilities present themselves. One, that our species may become extinct. Two, our species may fail and become only an inter-mediary evolutionary link between the lower animal kingdom and some type of beings who neither belongs to our species nor our genus. A third possibility exist that our present civilizations may only be destroyed through Nuclear warfare while some of our species may survive and a small portion of mankind might evolve into the supermind. It is also possible that a portion of humanity may gain the supramental change while the rest of humanity will emerge into higher states of consciousness. These people would act as the intermediary link between the emerging gnostic beings, general humanity and the lower animal kingdom.

CHAPTER 7

CULTURAL MALAISE

FUTURIST COMMENTARY: The 22nd century is a time of self-doubt and emotional anguish and social destruction. In this chapter Campbell describes the process and themes that exist within the human race's lower subjective natures which contributes to human self-destruction. Campbell constantly emphasizes that the personality structure of the species is unbalanced and unintegrated and needs to become whole and united as a personality process so that the human race as a whole and man individually can walk the long road of the evolutionary gauntlet and successfully rise into his innate potential as a supramental being. Campbell states:

The emergent evolution of the suprarational mind is also causing a renaissance of consciousness and we need to know how to live and cope with the new problems of existence. A new transpersonal science of humanity must be developed.

REASONS FOR THE WORLD CRISIS

From an objective point of view the causes of the world crisis and tensions and resistance to the emergent supermind are caused by seven reasons. The first causal reason has already been partially discussed, that is, the biological emergent evolution of human consciousness is causing a tension of mental and emotional anxiety as infrarational man evolves into a higher stage of consciousness.

The emergent evolution of consciousness within the human species is causing a mental and emotional anxiety tension in the human races. Infrarational man is evolving into a higher state of rational consciousness. This urge is an innate biological instinct caused by a mutation that occurred millions of years ago when mankind emerged in conscious self-awareness from the dark void of nature.

Transintegral Psychology speculates that mankind stands today at the crossroads of history—at a crucial juncture within the historical process. A new order of transpersonal reality—a psychomental biological evolution of consciousness is emerging through the evolutionary process. The exigency of this mental and sociocultural process has caused a mental and emotional anxiety tension to appear within the species as rational man evolves into a higher state of consciousness.

We are now within the dynamics of this process. Mankind must rise to the challenge by consciously emerging into the tide of evolutionary history. If the human race does not have the will or capacity to change its nature, then the dynamics of this moment will be aborted. The barbarism of the human race may allow the exigencies of international terrorism to reign nuclear destruction upon the planet. Humanity, however, has within itself an innate possibility to transcend itself—the result of a mutation several millions of years ago, which has coded mankind to have the capacity to consciously expand the consciousness of the species. This latent biological potential is man's birthright and humanity today, according to the philosopher Aurobindo, must consciously transcend its lower nature and realize a progressive conscious emergence into higher and vaster altered states of consciousness—into a new species consciousness.

Mankind is also living within the instinctual primordial fear-anxiety syndrome which cannot be transcended unless and until the human race has transcend itself into the Gnostic consciousness of the future.

The tide of the evolutionary process has brought the human race up to this point of manifest destiny. Man has allowed this era's individualistic-rationalistic age to be captured by a false social trend, an subjective era, a causal factor which is destroying humanity. The present era cannot overcome the social and psychological crisis caused by false subjectivism and a personality system dominated by a vitalistic-egoism unless a dynamic theory about the nature of man is created.

This causal agent is operative because emergent evolution is causing the individualistic-rationalistic age to emerge into subjective era that has been captured by a false subjectivism. This false subjectivism is a force of unregenerate vital-emotional man. His uncontrolled vital life force linked up with technological industrialism is pushing the species toward possible extinction.

A new model—a new paradigm model must be developed to help the species understand the present era by evolving itself into a higher and more noble being than man is at presently. The lack of such a scientific model is another causal factor that is destroying mankind.

This causal agent is the lack of an adequate paradigm or super theory of man. Without such a model the 20th century human dilemma cannot be solved and even its absence contributes to the world crisis and to the enigma that is man.

Another reason for the global crisis is that the materialism of infrarational vitalism has caused a psychological dislocation, a psychological dysfunction between man's outer and inner personality consciousness. The death generation thus becomes the dominant force in the destruction on of human cultures.

Another causal reason is an inherent Neanderthal flaw within the species that allows men who exist in the lower reaches of human consciousness to have the urge to enslave their fellow mankind.

Rapid culture change is also effecting the species as it struggles to maintain its social and psychological health, thus it is one of the seven causal factors which we must study.

We have discussed these causal factors in the first seven chapters and will continue to do so in the rest of the book The reasons for the present world crisis rest on these seven factors; which even on the common level it is rather obvious that the immanent collapse of the American social order is happening before our very eyes on the economic, social, political, industrial, cultural and personal levels is because of these seven flaws.

THE INSTITUTIONALIZED
DEATH GENERATION

But let it also be known that the death generation often becomes institutionalized as overt governmental bodies or as covert forces within governmental structures or as secrete death cadre societies waiting to take political control. America, your fear of government is justified .Everyone knows politicians live within corruption and Americans tacitly understand how a politician can do something for what he can get out of it, and America generally looks the other way if he is legally sophisticated, that is, so long as he is not a politician for sinister power reasons. But if in actuality he is a politician because of his lust for power then America's pathological hatred emerges against that person or his overt or covert organization. [1] Recently it was reported on national television that private armies exist in 22 plus states, organized especially because of their fear of the Federal government. Are these people part the lunetic frinze or do they know something we do not realize?

The ideal death cadre is one who rejects life and nature, ideas and the dynamics of everything that has life and substitutes them for abstract ideals, objects or things of death. Their speciality is the present and everything they produces through their senses are but things or objects. He must become a machine. Sex is but a love machine, feelings are now nothing but sentimentally, peek experiences and intense elation now are only fun and excitement.[2]

The death cadet's love and tenderness is channeled toward

gadgets and machines, and death concepts. He is now a dead machine and his world one of lifeless artifacts. Lifeless food and synthetic organs become his world and he is controlled by it.

Life to him is bound up in the technical controls of machinery that control men which he surrounds himself with and his greatest goal is to become the Robot that can't be distinguished from living men. If he could clone himself-he would do so.

The death cadres lives in a world of "no-life"; a death world which he embraces as he transforms the living world into a stinking and poisonous place which feels good and pleasant to the Death Generation.

The bureaucratic death cadet could cares less if the earth is destroyed within a hundred years. Technical programs cannot and will not be stopped even if they crush the life out of the planet. [3]

The death cadre sacrificed his children in ancient times to the Gods; today he offers up all life to the Death God that lies within his heart. Erich Fromm makes the point that it makes no differences even that he may operate from ignorance of ecological facts, because, within his nature lies a necrophilous element that prevents him from making use of any objective knowledge he realizes.

The death cadres often are nuclear scientists who design weapons to destroy all humanity. They and their political leaders gamble with life itself while they calmly speculates whether fifty million dead is an acceptable casualty figure in an atomic war.

Death and dying are a "truth high" to the death generation! Can you expect our youth not to embrace death through drugs, drive by murders and seemingly sacrificial torture murders of young children, when our elite leaders promote liberty through death, love through living a life that embraces death and the annihilation of the human race as its ideal.

Freud stressed often that man's repressions often return and one can see that a death cadet attraction to death and decay appears as malignant anal. character. [4]

The genocide propensities of the human species has ample

historical president. Tamerlane's pyramid of skills, Peter the Hermits slaughter of the Jews on his way to liberate the holy land, Hitlers killing of six million Jews and the slaughter of 15 million other people in his ovens of iniquity, an action by which he offered up his death victims as sacrificial lambs in the name of his new world order. Surely Stalin's starvation of 20 million peasant farmers and the additional millions that died in his death camps shows mankind's genocide tendencies. Today within Rwanda one tribal group has just massacred 700,000 people in tribal animosities and surly Bosnia's genocide falls under ethnic cleansing imperative's that is blatant genocide.

But beyond organized killing is the death fact that American faces daily in drive by shootings as its teenagers become killer of American civilization. Whether you are death children randomly killing, or administrators of countless bureaucracies, what you really want to do is to control people; one way or the other you wish to impose your desires and commands on other people. But above all you want to experience the thrill of death as life flow through your fingers of death as you breath in the intoxication of might and power and realize within your heart that you are a man of might and terror!

Historically all people live in the control mode of life. Yet America has a pluralistic, religious, and social order. Yet, even here groups are vying for the power and if the opportunity presents itself millions will perish as a new structure of social order fulfills its social, racial and economic mandates.

There is no place to hide! There is no safety sanctuaries, no place to run too, no ultimate comfort zone!

Future death generation scientist will insert comuputer chips on your body which tunes into sky satellites which can track you wherever you are. They will put microchips in and along the highways which will communicate with the automobiles computer and the chips in the automobile to track you from their sky satellites. And if the death cadre's wish they can automatically shut down your car's motor individually or stop all moving vehicales over a wide geographical area. They will control you by trafic and monetary controls and you will be restricted to living within assigned areas of the country.

There is no place to hide from the death generation! They may even connect you to more sophicated devices that allow them to hear and see any event in your daily life as well as to monitor your thought patterns from a distance..

You are the death generation in your person and species. You are the terror that faces yourself and that terror is making your lives mesurable. Because you are the death generation. Face yourselves or perish at your own hand!

Futurist Commentary: Most of the historical records of Campbell's era were destroyed in the 21st century wars of terror. But we believe the author was referring to the United States government of the year 2001 which initiated a program of placing micro chips in the hands and often foreheads of U.S. citizen seemingly for the expressed purpose of stopping illegal immigration into the country. Civil war resulted, especially, after it was discovered that hundreds of thousands of legal and illegal American citizens were being executed in the hundreds of concentration camps set up around the Unitied States to contain the illegals, and that the government was covertly allowing gang members to rape and loot in night raids, seeming searching for drugs and illegals, but in actuality their purpose was to disarmed the citizens of their guns.

This was the time of the terrible American civil war which took place as The Death Cadres launched the invasion of the Americas; before it was over 78 million Americans perished in the death camps and America the beautiful perished from the face of the earth!

When order was restored a public hanging for treason, of the leaders of this government, took place at high noon, Oct. 1st, at 11:59 A.M. in Washington D.C. in the year 2,010. Campbell speaks to the theme of the death cadre concepts below:

On the governmental levels, trust and honor and the pushing

of authentic family values are on some of their lips while in their hearts lie schemes of oppression and plans for the technological planting of microchips into their victims so as to better protect them against themselves and guide their freedoms of actions and thoughts. For these members of the death generation are the organized end of the spectrum of the culture of death and one step above the street generation of death, for they have plans of human redemption that embraces eugenic and ethnic cleansing and they hold in their hands a scheme of death so horrendous that life itself cries out for redemption from this scourge of degenerate humans who are so holy than thou that even God himself cannot speak to them; yet they glibly speak covertly of the holy honor that is theirs of uplifting the race toward the perfection of bureaucratic wholeness.

On the covert governmental and sociocultural levels they revel in the wholesale destruction of all that is sacred and holy and insert into the life currents the death of nihilism, confusion and ultimately slavery as the human sheep become too weak and confused to protest their destruction and enslavement. Remember always that in the absence of political freedom all your liberties are destroyed. [5] And in the name of public safety they will disarm you and put computer chips on your hand for identification which records all your life activities to their central computer and allows them to track you by sky satellite wherever you hide, and soon you will be but a number among all the rest of the slaves that politicians call their constituents and government bureaucrats their stooges.

Then they will break the back of your socioeconomic classes through exporting jobs and technologies out of the country and you will be landless American peasants who bows and takes his hat off to the lowliest government official. And in your shame and degradation you will have become a casualty of the organized death generation and you will weep and wail but your chains will be too strong to break and your strength sapped and you will die a number among numbers as prey to the death generation. And if you are no longer needed you will die a genocide victim on their guillotines and perish in their ovens to provide dog food and fertilizer for the betterment of human society.

But what can one say of their unholy plans that rests on terrible blueprint crimes of the past and on a pathology of death. In actuality they live in a confused present and in their minds the future rests on a pathological past which they would again make our future.

THE DEATH CADRES NEED TO CONTROL OTHER MEN

The most destructive flaw in the human personality of the death cadre is their propensity to control others. This surge of power or will to power seeming comes from a vital emotional drive which has been perverted by some member of he death cadre; in these men this natural sense of allowing their self to experience the world through accomplishments develops into a perverse certainty about his or her's place in the destiny of the group. If the situation warrants it some power driven death cadre members become dictators who require all people under them to adhere to their truth and dogma and to be controlled by the presence of such a truth on the pain of death.

America's democracy lies in its death pangs wimpering and crying as the shrewd death cadre's manipulate the mass mind through the press and mass education. All of our noble and idealist leaders have been replaced by shrewd money-makers who now control the vote through political machinery and through ownership of the press and television. This insidious control influences the mass mind so much that it has ceased to think as the 30 second politcal TV spots condition the death generation to do the bidding of their death masters.

The death cadre controls the press so that most cities have only one newspaper; and the press is now free to notice only what they want to report and in any detail that suits their fancy. So now you have a situation that condemns any truth to death by just being silent about it. In a controlled press where is your freedom of speech or how can you protect yourself by using your constitutional rights if you don't have the money to back yourself up? When they have laws that allow them to conficate your property and bank accounts based merely on the accusation that you are under investigation how do you defend yourself as a penniless person?

The death cadre is on the march and through money control and by manipulating the voters they have made our elections into a preconcerted game, a farce perpetrated upon the mass mind called popular self-determination. And whom do they elect to our high offices but unscrupuous and non-intellectual politicians who will do the bidding of the Death Masters in the name of truth, honor and the will of the American people. [6]

There will come a time when the Death Cadre takes over the political reins directly. No one can stop them because they will grow on the soil of degenerated democracy and conquer it.

Then the death barbarization will set in as the greatest democracy the world has ever known dies and becomes a horrible military giant of barbarism and death that shall bring about the entire extinction of the human race. [7]

All who live within the narrow domain of this certainty must live out their self-realizations within the confines of the controller's dictates. Malinowski asserts that once a people enter into an anti democratic action it tempts nations and people into the road of imperialism and dictatorships and military ventures and that violence will breed violence and engenders anti-democratic morality because of its efficiency,

Once the organized death generation realizes how efficient ruthlessness and quick decisions are and how effective obedience to a supreme command is, then the hell with public opinion, voting deliberation and any consideration given to the conscience of either individuals or groups of citizens. [8]

The modern age is now seemingly being affected not by one

or several dictators but by a death cadre, a fifth column within American culture and within western civilization in lesser degrees. For convenience sake this destructive influence is called the death generation.

In some sense all of the present generation are the death generation but the elite of this force is the cutting edge of self-destruction that faces our nation. Because the death generation must fulfill itself; for death is its middle name and truth but a variety of death pangs!

One does not question what one knows instinctively. One only acts and lives through its expression and its social actions. Ordinarily this fact of life has its positive nature and if a person does not live his own truth then he is a phony and divorced from his inner reality. Yet the facts of life are that only a unique minority in this life follow their positive inner feelings; only a few human beings within the great masses of populations are their own man.

Why is this so? Why are the masses of mankind driven by truth's foreign to their own nature? Perhaps the main argument is that most men are sleeping zombies and are dead to life itself. They follow their social conditioning. They live their culture's imperatives, their church's dogmas, their subculture's rules and often are driven by their lower natures.

On the sociological level there is the fact of cultural determinism which embodies various rules which guarantee's order and security and allows co-operation and social action under states of peace and progress. But within all cultural systems are certain concepts and rules that foster discrimination and oppression and may become inimical to freedom and in rare instances annihilate freedom for death concepts and actions.

Harold D. Lasswell in his classic book "Psychopathology and Politics points out that often there is a close relationship between a person's psychological nature and his political thinking. And that logical thinking alone cannot explain a person's action even where logic is adroitly used and that an individual's or government's logic that certain actions are in your own or your nations best interest may be dominated by illogic, fantasy, covert urges of revenge or paranoiac persecutions. Generally such negative rules are based on concepts and doctrines outside the experiences of individuals but dictate claims of superiority , privilege and power to the true believer if he believes and acts on these rules of oppression. And it is to be noted that such false social doctrines of hierarchy and discrimination have to be associated with organized mechanism of physical violence and terror. And inevitable you find that any group which perverts the rules of freedom must use violence to pervert a culture's freedom rules. They must abuse you by constraints on your freedom for you will not willingly give up your freedom unless it is taken away from you or you are deceived and tricked, manipulated and controlled and thus disarmed you perish or submit to the tyranny through your ignorance and naivete.

But you ask why would Americans stand for this; or what is the aspect of American social character which would allow this to take place? Is there some part of American character that allows our citizens to ignore the obvious, even when it faces us? Tocqueville says that:

> Each person, withdrawn into himself, behaves as though he is a stranger to the destiny of all the others. His children and his good friends consti-tute for him the whole of the human species. As for his transactions with his fellow citizens, he may mix among them, but he sees them not; he touches them, but does not feel them; he exists only in himself and for himself along. And if on these terms there remains in his mind a sense of family, there no longer remains a sense of society. (Vol.2, p.786)

Primarily the problem lies within American concepts of rugged individualism and self reliance ideals connected with contemporary unconscious fears about the future. Americans are running scared on the social and unconscious levels and so long as they are left alone in their individual social space they will cower in their holes of despair and think pleasant thoughts and hope for the best. So don't ask them to stand up for their constitutional rights because they will try to ride out the storm of repressive governmental laws and regulations and pray that somehow they and their family and friends can survive the future social upheavals. Why? Because their social individualism is an ancient social rite.

It must be remembered that Americans have not changed some aspects of their national character much since The Frenchman Tocqueville's classic ethnography on American character and American Democracy in 1831. He viewed our politicians as political cowards and the American population as no better. But he admired our courage to the point of recklessness when Americans searched for personal fortunes and admired our independence but stated Americans really cared little for people outside their family or the narrow coterie of friends which surrounded them. He makes a specific point which characterize America's present attitude toward themselves and which reflects on America's attitude toward the homeless and other failures of the American system. He says:

> As in ages of equality no man is compelled to lend assistance to his fellow-men, and none has any right to expect much support from them, every one is at once independent and powerless . . . His independence fills him with self-reliance and pride among his equals; his debility makes him feel from time to time his want of some outward assistance, which he cannot expect from any of them, because they are all impotent and unsympathizing.(Vol. 2, p. 786.)

The organized death generation realizes this and know how to behaviorally manipulate you and how to divide and conquer and are sociologically wise and will use already developed mythologies, doctrines, knowledge about American National Character, and dogmas which have been accepted and have already molded countless peoples to culturally and spiritually condition themselves to passively submit to the death generations oppressions.[10] They will use psychological principles to manipulate Americas by exploiting their misery, thus using American culture ideals against "Americans and will use hate as a uniting bond and take advantage of each person's inner hostility to incite people so they can put forward their ideas for radical changes as they covertly embrace death to the ignorance of the average man as they toast their successes to the extermination of ignorance and inferiority in the United States of America![11] They will play on America's obsessive preoccupation with thoughts of imminent annihilation through a Nuclear Holocaust. They know that even with a tentative peace with Russia and the destruction of the Soviet Empire that America's phantasms of atomic destruction is still ruled by the Great Nightmares of fear which stupefies with terror American's from all walks of life. Even though all desire peace they cannot think of how to acquire it and find it easy to brood on war and death and to know in their hearts of hearts that only death lives in the future.[12] Everyone knows deep down now that some third world county will drag us into racial anihilation and that our only future is death, death, death!

Generally you will find that rules that develop through education and through lessons learned within a culture's context or have a long tested tradition based on co-operation and ethical dimension are rules of freedom. Usually such rules of conduct may produce high degrees of discipline and performance but generally do not become rules of tyranny or oppression.

But there comes a time when a great corruption enters into the life of a people and their culture and then the civilization dies from within and death lies upon the winds of time and the stench of death lies just beyond the next curve.

It is a fact that political regimes and sociocultural philosophies are born into existing systems and they find meaning through growth, maturity and death. Each period will have its brilliant creativity and surely its cycles of violent unrest and death. [13]

Why you ask does this have to occur. Well the answer must be sought in psychopolitics and from within the psychological nature of man; but realize this fact that when the individual inner man is dead the outer man is a zombi who has no life force, no strength of character, no inner force that allows him to exist.

But the wisest among them know that if they transcend not their nihilism that the future is lost and the human race shall perish in their own misery and that their life will have been for not and even they unconsciously want to feel that their insignificant lives has some meaning and that their death signifies something, even if no one recognizes that fact!

But for most of them there is no past or future, only the present which stands on quicksand and represents the agony and meaninglessness of a life that seemingly should have never been! They have no hope and no guide to the future and they wish for none for they are the death generation and they fear no man alive and would just as soon waste you as spit in your face.

It is written that truth and honor rests not on lies and deceit and that death is no answer to perversity and change! Can the dead cleanse their ranks of filth; no I say let the truth of the matter be decided in the arena of the possible and let the truth of eternity decide the future!

It is a time of action but also of reflection and the cleansing power must come from within each individual and nothing can be done to right the present if we do not have the resolve to elevate ourselves into the ranks of honor and truth. Great cultural changes of a positive nature will not occur until an inner resolve takes place and this is matched with positive overt outward action based on inner psychological balancing.

Crass materialism has destroyed the fabric of our society and the next step is the dissolution of its material structure; because our society rests on hallow concepts of reality and naive and childish religious myths, all of which are contributing to the death

throes of our dying social order. Can something that is dead resurrect something that is dying? Even the religious spirit seemingly is
failing us and has not the power to revitalize our dying culture or
help the death generation. Why? The religious spirit is something
akin to artistic talent. It is either there or non-existent; or so weak
that its flicker's of light has no strength or duration! But above all
religion has been so perverted and constitutes such a mass fraud
that even the naive can perceive the deception. Why? Because the
evoutionary minds of the age will not accept nonsense and lies
based on deception and fraud. It is time that the mature minds of
society grew up and began to seriously interact with the reality of
the situation and started to march in tune with the Cosmos. Yet it
is seemingly a fact that this awareness is still on the unconscious
level with most of mankind.

DEATH CRY

Death is the cry of the day and everyone rallies to its cry for the
wisest among us know in their inner hearts that their time has
come and the near future is unknown and that if they survive the
death marches of the future they will be broken and crushed
beyond recognition. But they don't know what to do about their
lives and are confused and bewildered about their social and psychological situation, because death is upon the winds of time and
in the depth of their subconscious being they know their time
has come and they must face themselves by conquering their lower
natures or perish on the wings of the death wind! But will they
rise to the occasion? Will they face themselves and expose themselves and transform themselves? No you say! But they must or
else all is lost!

But from within the still depth of humanity emerges a weak and
feeble idea; " despair not humanity, the sage of life within us says, for
all is not lost, all is not yet destroyed, all has not perished".

"Within the human spirit lies a source of eternal life that all
may touch if they but desire. Touch that source and all will be

well, touch that source and humanity's redemption from itself will commence as the golden age of the species emerges into the dawn of a glorious tomorrow."

Do we have to face the issue of freedom or death? Do we have to assert ourselves, face ourselves or perish? The choices are grim but do we have any choice. Do we really have enough time to table the issue and hope everything will work out?

The cynic will say it is already too late, the optimist will assert that humanity has progress in his bones and will survive all the vicissitudes of life and evolution and triumph as a species.

But the death generation has already chosen and death is on their breath and murder in their subconscious and cruelty upon their hands. For nothing can help them but actionless death and the hate that motivates them. All those thus infected shall perish from the face of the earth. The only hope lies in the rest of us who stand on the side lines. Are you ready to do your part? Can you arise to the occasion?

Can you take the bull by the horns and declare that come what may your inner fortitude and goodness of character will triumph over the odds of defeat. If you can join the human race and transcend your lower natures and stand up for progress and assert your right to say we of the human race will become better than our lowest members and we will become more godlike and walk consciously into eternity.

The forces of life are upon the planet earth at this time and the species trembles and moves on the subconscious level. For a choice is being given us to walk into the sunlight of a bright life or to fall into the abyss of the death generation. What is your choice, life or death?

· INFRARATIONAL EVOLUTION STAGE

The infrarational evolutionary stage commenced several million years ago during the late Pliocene or early Pleistocene eras. The psychocognitive emergence of early man through a fortuitous mutation began the psychocultural process. Man's mental evolution was an emergence from a lower hominoid creature with its type of undifferentiated or oceanic consciousness. Through a process of closer cooperative interaction between the mind and situational social realities the evolution of consciousness began.

We know from documented research that man had upright posture or stood up straight and was a savannah dwelling creature prior to the expansion of the brain. There is evidence that this mind expansion was caused by An interaction between toolmaking activities and symbolic thought processes which caused the development of the forebrain in man. Conceptual thought, the development of the forebrain, and the emergence of the concept of separate individuality probably occurred together. A mutation, occurring during or prior to this process, allowed the expansion of consciousness in our ancestral types. Psychocultural evolutionary theory says this process is still going on today.

With the development of the ego sense man became a true individual and a social being by overcoming the bond of nature which welds and holds the animal kingdom within a tight web of instinctive behavioral patterns. Man had to affirm his personality against nature so that he could evolve all his human capacities and gain self-mastery. Man's egoism and self-discriminating mind thus became a force for man's evolutionary progress. [14] Man now became a being who no longer had to react to an instinctive code. Conceptual thought arose at that movement in the dimness of prehistoric time and a member of the animal kingdom left behind his animal relationships and bondage to an instinctive oceanic consciousness. Man was no longer a slave to total natural selection and learned behavior and social heritage became created through trial and error methods. This newly acquired social heritage thus was transmitted from generation to generation. finally brought humanity into a new world of time, space and death. The nature of life that ends in death became a fact. Language developed and learned behavior activities gradually emerged as codes of law, art and social organization. Culture as a supraorganic structure provided a new dimensional social reality which has from that time to the present time allowed mankind to live within a dynamic social system which embraces all human reality.

SOCIAL DYNAMICS

The group dynamics which developed were a spontaneous play from the subconscious impulses and vital intuitions and first mental renderings. The communal psychology emerged not from deliberate intention but from the inner self and partly from the environment working on the communal mind and temper. People were not yet a thinking collective but a species in the throes of the evolutionary process. [15]

To emerge from this type of communal life probably took hundreds of thousands of years since the emergent mental process is a slow one. Slowly small groups of vanguard individuals developed rational faculties; political, religious, and economic communities evolved. Finally about ten thousand years ago, the hunting and gathering stage of existence was left behind by some groups when animal husbandry and agriculture were developed. A sociocultural revolution took place and settled community patterns developed, finally culminating in the emergence of city states. When writing was invented a greater cultural complexity developed and city states emerged into national states, often followed by empires.

THE RATIONAL EVOLUTIONARY STAGE

According to the psychocultural evolutionary theory the true rational-intellectual stage of cultural evolution has not yet arrived. All members of the species Homo sapiens have reached the rational state of consciousness, but rational-intellectuals do not exist in sufficient numbers to create a truly rational social order. Humanity thus lives still in the upper reaches of the infrarational stage of evolution. This is a highly sophisticated level in comparison to Australopithecine culture of early man but it is still infrarational in nature and content.

All humans today are rational beings but most are not rational-intellectuals. Most rational people use physical-mental or emotional-mental cognitive faculties to conceptualize, according to the Aurobindo personality model. The true mental person is the intellectual giant or genius, whereas the average person is a creature of physical and emotional desires who has not learned to use his or her higher states of consciousness. Until individuals emerge into a higher state of mental consciousness most societies will remain infrarational. The emergent evolutionary consciousness is a slow process and totally dependent upon individual development.

Transintegral psychology says that the collective group can only emerge into a higher dimension of cultural mind if the individuals become more rationally conscious. The individual serves a dual purpose by raising nature from the dark unconscious to the superconsciousness and exalts it to meet the transcendent reality. The mass and collective social consciousness is close to the lowest unconsciousness. It has a subconscious and an obscure and mute movement which needs the individual to organize and express it in an effective manner. The mass of humanity still has not transcended psychophysical or psychoemotional mentality. To be human means a vital-emotional animal ego mentalized and humanized by a limited amount of outward thought and knowledge.

We are today, thousands of years after the development of city states, little advanced beyond our ancestors psychologically, morally or mentally. Transintegral Psychology says that the majority of men live in their physical and vital-emotional consciousness except for a few saints and a large amount of intellectuals. This is the reason why humanity has made little progress during the last several thousand years, except in material equipment and technological information. Homo sapiens are perhaps a little less

cruel and brutal and have more plasticity of intellect in the elite
and are quicker in social relations, but that is all. [16]

SUPRARATIONAL EVOLUTIONARY STAGE

While no suprarational men or cultures exist, most near-rational-
intellectual societies have been influenced by individuals living
in the suprarational sphere of existence. Even today, revivalistic
research studies dynamic mystics or prophets who through the
charismatic might of their personality lead whole societies at times
of social stress and disorganization into new eras of social rebuilding. Such individuals are suprarational humans possessing the
emergent consciousness at the peak of the evolutionary tide.

The majority of mankind evolve slowly and contain within
themselves the material, vital and mental man. A small minority
have gone beyond this evolutionary barrier by opening the doors
to the ascent of evolution beyond the mental to the supramental.
Historically this minority has been influential and enormously
powerful as in Vedic India or in Egypt and determined the civilization of the age by giving it a cultural theme of the spiritual or
the occult. Often they have held high government posts or been
openly influential. At times they have maintained themselves in
their secret schools or orders and did not influence civilizations
sunk in material ignorance, in darkness, chaos or who rejected
knowledge of higher states of consciousness. [17]

At the present time neither suprarational cultures nor any
true rational-intellectual cultures exist. The research data of Integral historiography reveals, however, that in some historical periods rational-intellectual men and some suprarational men have
predominated in certain cultures. Their influence was such that
great periods of cultural florescence took place. Such eras were
those of Italy of the Renaissance, Ancient Athens, Republican
Rome, Sparta and 19th century Europe. [18]

According to the psychocultural evolutionary theory, these
stages do not emerge in a hierarchical order or by necessarily se-

quential steps, and when rational cultures do emerge they are not pure in their nature. Each stage, in fact, reflects the predominant psychological characteristics of the populace. Also infrarational, aesthetics-ethical and even suprarational themes and ethos may coexist.

The anthropologist, Anthony Wallace has demonstrated that contemporary cultures need not be totally integrated around rigid, harmonious and functional themes. [19] Conflicting themes and disharmonies may exist and indeed do exist. From an evolutionary point of view this is because all sides of the; mental life are not simultaneously developed.

Until a culture has a predominant number of the population living in the rational-intellectual or suprarational awareness consciousness, no long term cultural continuity will exist. Since most of the world population is infrarational in substance, no stable psychomental personalities seem able to contribute to world stability. But infrarational man has also a rational and suprarational aspect to his nature. Aurobindo says that this type of man is a thinking animal with a play of reason. At his lucid mental best he is still not a rational intellectual. Even the intellectual is not perfect and must receive touches of suprarational energy, even if the source is not recognized. Man holds in his being these mental abilities in latent form. [20]

Gradually the infrarational population emerges with a rational-intellectual faculty and applies its intelligence to the problems of existence. At first only a few gain this faculty. Eventually the higher classes of society become true mental creatures and then this ability spreads throughout the population, gradually leading whole communities and nations into the mental light. Psychocultural evolutionary theory postuate, however, that even these breakthrough cannot bring in a totally rational age. If the rational age has not arrived then the irrational period of society cannot be left behind. It is not enough that a few sages or a class exercise its intelligence–a multitude must learn to think. Until that time arrives a mixed society, infrarational in the mass must

be saved for civilization by an enlightened class whose business is
to seek after reason and keep the gains of mankind and raise the
life of the culture upward. [21]

The evolutionary process is a complex one and psychosocial
development will vary from culture to culture and from age to
age, according to the dominate and minor themes and the situational life complexities of each region. Broad themes seem clear
from an examination of the research data. The evidence demonstrates that an emergence from an infrarational stage into a rational stage involves either an emphasis on reason or on spirituality
as the dominant power governing society. In ancient Greek civilizations a few philosophers and in a later age the Sophists represented a tendency towards the former. In prehistoric India, however, a few great mystics–the Vedic Rishis, with their small circle
of Initiates–brought in the age of the Upanishads from which
whole classes of society later sought the light and guidance of the
higher reaches of altered states of consciousness. [22] The reason
some individuals and cultures seem to by-pass the rational stage
is that the capacity exists within man to contact deeper areas of
his being and some cultures have emphasized this theme. The
species is not confined within his humanity. It has been less than
human and it has the capacity to become more than human.
Mystically, just as it can find itself in the universe, conversely the
universe finds itself through the species. Mankind is also capable
of becoming more than the universe because he can surpass it
and enter into a dimension of himself and then climb beyond it
to the absolute.[23] This tendency to self-transcendence–the ability
to emerge from an infrarational stage into one in which higher
spheres of supernormal consciousness can occur is a fact, according to Aurobindo. This goal is abnormal for social groups of
infrarational men. It may succeed in specific individuals, however, since by an intensity of the inner life one can out leap the
intellect and seem to dispense with it. Evolutionarily for the species this movement cannot last. The human race cannot raise
securely upward unless the mind and intellect is developed to its

fullest. The lower nature of humanity must be developed and the mind of the species must evolve in consciousness. Even cultures which have emerged into a partially rational-intellectual stage, with their small classes of intellectuals, will collapse after a while. These early dawns cannot endure in their purity, so long as the species is not ready. Society will relapse into infrarational consciousness and an elite group will have to preserve the rational traditions of the culture's past glory. Until the masses themselves emerge into a rational consciousness stage, the rational-intellectual age will not come into being. The infrarational barbarians from without or the ignorant masses from within will destroy culture after culture. No civilization is safe if it confines the cultured mentality to a small minority. The multitude,. the proletariat contains a mass of ignorance and if knowledge does not enlarge itself from above the ignorant night from below will submerge the civilization in time.

The last stage, the suprarational, is postulated as emerging in much the same way as the rational-intellectual. Small groups of suprarational beings, existing in the heights of altered states of consciousness, may create new social forms. Through the insight and development of their transpersonal visions, new and dynamic spatial-logical understandings of the Cosmos, new world views and cultural configurations may emerge into a new age. it may be that such beings will have nothing to fear from lower humanity, just as present humanity has no fear of being overcome by the lower animal kingdom.

At the present time the human species stands at a crucial juncture of the historical process. The emergent evolution of consciousness is causing an emotional and mental anxiety situation throughout the planet. If a new order of transpersonal consciousness does not emerge then the exigencies of human barbarism may result in species extinction through international nuclear destruction, ecological disasters, famines etc.

We have now discussed, in rather technical terms, the concepts of culture and consciousness and evolution and altered states of consciousness. it has been established that man lives within a dynamic process of social and mental evolution. So far we have not discussed the particulars of this process over the last several million years. With an understanding now of the psychocognitive relationship between culture and consciousness we can now examine the interesting way in which the psychocultural evolutionary theory explains how the dynamics of our species works. Mankind is so unique and mental, so dynamic and vast that in order to understand ourselves we must trace our roots.

CHAPTER 8

FAMILY PSYCHO-CULTURAL UNCONSCIOUS

FUTURIST COMMENTARY: There are no families left in the 22nd century except in the free zones of the barbarian mutants and in the Indian Nations guided by Quetzalcoatl, the prophet. All children are cloned by the state and while marriage is permitted both partners must be sterilized before being sanctified by the state; but both are constantly monitored for correct attitudinal behavior by our main computers from data received from the computer chips placed in the heads and hands of the marriage partners.

Perhaps you are shocked by this logical development from 20th century's dissolution of first the extended family, then the nuclear family and finally the single parent family which was found to be injurious generally to the child; so much so that the state began cloning human beings and entirely did away with natural birth.

It has worked out well for the New America empire because with creative genetic engineering we now have a truly stratified society with each class structure engineered to have just the proper amount of intelligence for their life jobs within the corporate state.

One of our more brilliant scientist has aptly characterized this state as, " . . . the perfect beehive mentality which allows unity within diversity yet allows true individualism and freedom within the mentality of each separate but equal class structure."

Since the 22th century no longer has family life you can imagine our joy at finding Dr. Campbell's manuscript on the family unconscious. It has given us an insight into the family unconsciousness process of the 20th century. But it also brilliantly classifies and give insight into the death children phenomenon which ultimate led to the destruction of the United States of America and which eventually allowed us to create our utopian society.

We will examine the overt and covert aspects of family life, that is, the process through which 20th century people connected with each other as a family. Let's discuss Campbell's psychocognitve culture theory and its relationship of human consciousness to the social culture that people live and breath within. Then we will show how the T. P. Titan syndrome operates within the family arena as a psi and telepathic connection on the family unconscious level. Then we will examine case studies of the authoritarian , egalitarian, and permissive families.

The concept of the family and its place in traditional and modern societies has always been of interest to those who study the human condition. The family is now known to be the main battle ground in the dissolution of American society. Within the death families emerges the death children and the future death cadres and it is upon these facts of horror that we must study the nature of the family unit and in particular the family unconsciousness.

In order to understand the family social unit lets briefly examine the psychocognitive culture theory. We must do this because a family is a subculture or a mini-cultural unit. It is a family microcosm of the macrocosm of culture. The family is an integrated unity within the complex whole of sociocultural life.

PSYCHOCOGNITIVE CULTURE THEORY

The psychocognitve culture theory says that language defines the cognitive reality of the sociocultural model. Language structures the human cognitive reality on a conscious and unconscious and transpersonal mind levels as well as on the subconscious mind dimensions. It operates through the personality-mind dynamics on the inner and outer states of consciousness. Science as yet has no clear understanding of this process. Sigmund Freud, in his book Totem and Taboo, suggests that the inner process projects itself and shapes the outer world but that this process is not understood Scientifically. [1] Transintegral Psychology says that consciousness projects itself into the sphere of culture through a telepathic-psi titan factor linage on a conscious, subconscious and transpersonal level. Each child as a member of a family unit is conditioned on all these levels to be a socio-cultural person of a specific culture, thus he becomes part of the cultural process. Culture as a process is thus viewed as a human event—a projection into the world. This projection is a symbolic system–a logico-linguistic matrix. This system is created and maintained, then recreated and transmitted from generation to generation within a complex geophysical system. As a social heritage continuum it has a logico-aesthetic integration on a conscious and unconscious level so that the basic structure and even the subsystems of the culture expresses a common systems model on the ecological, social, psychosomatic and symbolic subsystems dimensions; and they tend to express the same paradigm. Mind states, thus, are modes of being living in time-space but unitive with the biological process. of each member of society. Consciousness, therefore, is a mode of biological man, and psychocognitive mental culture is partially a projection of biophysical consciousness. [2]

This cultural model conceives of social events as wholes which tend to be unitive, complex and multi-valued processes. Social events are not extraneous actions since causality in inherent in the total field of organizational mind, personality, culture and social activities. When a society changes a process of self-formation, reformation and transformation takes place. This process is a fluid, inseparable and interpenetrative field of mind, personality dynamics and sociocultural change activities. Short term social changes are a reshaping of social reality through psychomind projections of the inner state of consciousness of the populous on to the social order. Naturally the usual causal agents of social change, such as the forces of biotic and climatic change, war and conquest, technological change, acculturation and epidemic disease are also operative. Social change on the long term range takes into account all of the above categories but says that social change is the result of a significant number of a population emerging into a higher state of consciousness. This emergent quality of mind then produces secondary results as social change. This change reflects the needs of the new state of mind of the prime social movers of the society. But lets examine some of these concepts in terms of the Psi-Telepathy Titan Factor.

TELEPATHY AND THE FAMILY UNCONSCIOUS

Culture theory and psi phenomena and telepathy manifest within a client-therapist situation yet it exists also within a microscope order called the family.

Experimental and clinical observations demonstrate a telepathic factor is involved in early and late child parent relationships. [3] They suggest also that telepathy plays an important and dynamic part in the early symbiotic stage between a parent and child. [4] Indeed the vast data on psychic research during the past hundred years testifies to the psi elements in interpersonal relationships. [5]

A study by Dr. Ian Stevenson surveys both old and new cases

of spontaneous telepathy, show that 33.8 % of the cases involves child-parent relationships, 15 percentage siblings and 13.7% wives-husbands. [6]

Clinical psychologist, Dr. Taub-Bynum, relates behavioral aspects of the family unconscious through documented case histories of clairvoyance, telepathy and second sight. According to him family communication exists at dimensions beneath conscious awareness yet influences family members in often profound ways. [7] Taub-Bynum speaks of the family unconscious as a field of images, feelings and energy that touches each member each night, each day, as a web of shared feelings and psycho-emotional psi energy. [8]

FAMILY UNCONSCIOUS AS A SUBCULTURE

All human beings live within a web of codified cultural controls that constitutes a world view that contains specific rules concerning human relations.

All human beings of Western civilization are members of a nuclear or extended family or family units that may vary from a one parent family to a variety of cross-cultural family groups. Research had demonstrated that there is a family unconsciousness that is supported by psi and telepathy. Psychologist E. Bruce Taub-Bynum, says that families besides social interactions and genetic similarities also exist within an unconscious sphere of family unconsciousness. He feels that families unconsciously process data together that unites them as a family unit on the unconscious and conscious levels. Families, after all sleep in the same house for years and sometimes generations, thus the family develops not only a social conditioning process but also an unconscious coordinating process. [9]

Psychologist Stanly Krippner says such unconscious behavior rests on hypotheses of extended sensory perceptions and extrasensory perceptions within the family context that emergences subliminally through shifts in posture, through eye movement, intonations of speech and nonverbal communication and body language. [10]

Taub-Bynum points out that the recurrent transactional pattern within the family system influences the family unconscious yet each member throws his influences within this family subculture.

FAMILY SUBCULTURE

The family unconscious exists within family subculture, with its rules and regulations, secrets and world view. The general subcultural dimensions will depend on your social class, ethnic group within the dominant culture and possibly your social subculture. Yet each family will have its secrets, its distinctive manner of relating to each other and overt and covert rules.

This chapter has demonstrated that the concept of culture is a socio-cultural force that partially rests on the psi phenomenon and the concept of telepathy. This process also works within a family microcosm of the overall cultural macrocosm and manifest overtly and covertly as a family unconsciousness.

The family is the conditioning agency for the socialization or acculturation of babies into socially accepted members of society. It is during this acculturation process that the child grows and emerges through his personal maturation process. Obviously a parent-child symbiosis exists on the conscious, unconscious and transpersonal levels.

Dr. Berthald Schwarz, a psychiatrist, speaking of this connection, says "I walked into the kitchen feeling quite exuberant and thought I would clown by showing Lisa a Ninjutsu-like kick and do a little dance. However, before I could demonstrate, she started to kick and do a little dance." [11] Schwarz has compiled 1,520 incidences of parent-child telepathic symbioses. Mrs. R.JP. tell of an incident produced in an anxiety-latent situation connected with her child that occurred while she was folding diapers. She was wondering whether they ought to go away for labor day. Suddenly her daughter Lisbeth, runs into the bathroom and asked, "Pat, we going on a trip?" In another incident, as she changed her diaper, the child rested her hand on her breast and R.P. wondered if she remembered the five weeks she had breast fed her as an infant. Suddenly the child said "I eat your skin all up" and laughed. R.P. asked where and the child answered "your chest," and pointed to her breast. [12]

The psychiatrist Jan Ehrenwald says such incidents demonstrate that the biological matrix of love and social cooperation that is rooted in human existence. [13]

There is also a dark side to such interactions on the telepathic level. Johnson and Szurek, Melitta Sperling and other therapists have described how neurotic children often act out their parent's repressed anti social impulses that may lead to behavioral disturbances and delinquency. Therapist Erik Erikson states this is a process in which children live out their parent's secret dreams.[14]

Ehrenwald writes of one of his cases where a four year old boy acted out his mother's destructive impulses toward Mr. C. The Child attacked Mr. C. with a knife and threw out of the window his mother's gift of jewelry from Mr. C. The child, also repeatedly asked her " . . . is my Daddy my real Daddy? Yes, he is my Daddy, but is he my real Daddy." The child had never been told he was a product of his mother's extramarital affairs. [15]

According to Jung, Aniel Jaffe, etc. the mother-child symbios relationship is an archetypal situation through which telepathy, etc., synchronicity incidents may occur. [16]

Dr. Taub-Bynum says that in family therapy sessions, in which the entire family is present, family secrets often emerge when the timing is right. Each member has a vague image of other family member's unmentioned secrets. He says often these are very intimate fantasies or odd acts. The doctor feels that each member shares a central shared image that seemingly rests on an individual separate perception. [17]

He also found that character problem and drug substance abuse problems that were openly present in one generation and seeming skipped the next generation reappeared in the third generation. Taub-Bynum says that information within a family system is conveyed without overt communication, sometimes through dreams, also across time and space; often across generations, thus, he thinks that each family exists within a family unconscious network. [18] This network is a vortex of shared feelings and family data which contains powerful emotional and symbolic meanings. [19]

Taub-Bynum says the family unconscious is developed empirically through shared family experiences yet inherits aspects of its system from the collective unconsciousness of the Race and from individualized dimensions of the personal unconscious. [20]

Because the family unconscious contains shared images, experiences and role expectations it is a force field of active, immediate and intense images and affects. These shared assumptions and intense affects may be easy aroused and manifest within the family constellation on a negative or positive basis. [21]

A family social unit is a family subcultural unit, existing within the dominant culture. In a sense it is a tribal unit living within the national boundaries of the national state. It is also self-functioning within its collective assumptions and is a matrix of consciousness that has a life of its own and a teleological conscious force in a sense is transgenerational. Thus you find recurrent psychosomatic illnesses or chemical dependence problems from one generation to another or often the problems skip from one generation to the grandchildren.[22] This multigenerational transmission of symptomatology commonly occurs when unresolved struggles with parental figures reemerge within the next generation's nuclear family after the child has children. The grandchild acts out the latent unconscious conflict of his father or mother by taking a role opposite to that of the troubled parent. Psychologist Taub-Bynum says that often this parent influences the child through the projective defense mechanisms so that he or she may relive the unresolved conflict. Thus the emotional fields among and within family members, as well as cross-generational, become active and dynamically powerful psychocultural forces within the family structure. [23]

A family, like a cultural system, exists before the child is born, thus significant conscious and unconscious social interactions exist within the nexus, especially if there are other children. Social patterns and cultural demands and social expectations already exist for the unborn child. These expectations rise out of a shared family consciousness and family collective energy level that is connected through a psi and telepathic factor. Once a person is acculturated by the hypnotic forces of culture and the family unconscious, he lives his life through this dimension of understanding. Even when he is no longer a member of his family of origin his family mythology and its teleological images guide him. Alex Haley's book "Roots" gives a positive image of this fact through the saga of Junta Kinta; whereas a negative example might be a retained image of the jail bird father who gives force and dynamic energy to an adolescent who thus acts out his father's negative image. [24]

We will now examine case studies of the authoritarian family the equalitarian family so we can get a better idea of the varying family structures that exist in America. In the chapter on the Death Children, we will discuss child rearing techniques on the theoretical levels but presently we can observe some real live case studies of these theories in dynamic action

AUTHORITARIAN FAMILY STRUCTURE

Else Frenkel-Brunswik describes a case study of an authoritarian family and child named Karl which brings out some interesting points about the death families. [25] Let examine this family now.

The father comes from an authoritarian family and is a mechanic by trade. His father and paternal grandfather were born in this country but the paternal grandmother was born in Germany. Karl's mother was also born in this country as was her father but her mother was born in Scotland.

0109-CAMP

Karl's grandfather died when his father was four years old and he was raised by Karl's paternal great grandparents who owned a large farm and wholesale store and were quite rich but never too generous with their money. Karl's maternal grandmother divorced her husband after the birth of Karl's mother and married a notary. But Karl's mother had a succession of stepfathers. She finished the eighth grade and Karl's father's education finished even before that level.

The mothers social background is unstable. "I grew up in big cities and in one hotel after another." She and her husband still see themselves in the process of assimilation and thus always stress their "belonging" and social aspiration by rejecting socially inferior factors from their lives.

Their overstuffed living room has lace doilies on their oak furniture which presents an concerted effort by them to stress middle-class identification and to be separated from the underprivileged. Class status is an anxiety factor for them since their socioeconomic history of the family is unstable since their class status has lowed from previous generations. But they own a car and live in a six-room flat.

Strict discipline was practiced in the homes of both of Karl's parents. Karl's father doesn't talk about his own father who he describes as a psychopath and drunkard who deserted his own family but speaks of his grandfather who raised him. He say" "My grandfather was really strict. He had thirteen children, and even when they were grown up, there wasn't one of them that would talk back to him, and he could handle any of them."

Karl's father grew up knowing little but work but his grandfather wanted him to be educated and to have voice training but he didn't live up to any of these goals. But Karl's father now does simple work but he thinks that one day , through his inventions, that he will accomplish a lot, even though there is little evidence of concrete work toward his goal. Karl's mother works in factories and as a waitress but prides herself on her skill as a photographer, composing and writing and has an unrealistic fantasy as to her future accomplishments.

Karl's parents stress strict discipline of their children, for example they must be in bed "sharp at six without fail." They do not have temper tantrums. the mother says" "I should say not. They had better not. If they got mad, I just sat them on a chair and said to stay there until they could behave. I guess they never really had tantrums." Karl, himself, confided to the scientific interviewers that he did have outburst of temper. His mother says that karl is weak but that "has a strength but he hides it."

Both parents use spanking as a disciplinary measure. The mother says "The boys are more afraid of their father than of me; I guess because he is stronger." And the father says "It seems like Karl is afraid of me."

The family supports the rigid dichotomizing of the sex roles. They are also extremely prejudiced and consider the Negroes America's biggest problem because they" want to go everywhere" The mother tells how she personally put Negroes in their place when she was a waitress. She gave them a glass of water but then ignored them. "When they went out, we smashed the glass behind the counter good and hard so they were sure to hear it. The Chinese and Japanese should be separate too." About the Jew, the mother said "The Bible says they will always be persecuted. You know it wasn't a small thing they did-crucifying Christ-God said they would be punished till the end of time."

Karl's social beliefs are interesting. Karl is a passive and unusually fat boy who has had many illnesses.. He is a person who generally mirrors his parents fascistic attitudes. Karl's attitude concerning Negroes are :

> they make trouble, start wars. I wouldn't mind having all the Negroes in Oakland and all the white people in a different state. I would like to have a couple for good fighters. They are when they fight with a knife. Like somebody starts a fight and you have a gang with some Negroes to fight with you on your side with knifes and guns."

Karl wants to segregating all outgroups and he stereotypes Jews also. He says

> "They think they are smart and go anywhere they please. They think they are hot. They dress up in all kinds of jewelry. Some just kidnap girls and boys and use them for slaves."

Karl thinks the Chinese are good fighters and of the Filipinos he says "The are good fighters and definitely good to go through jungles with."Karl thinks there will be many wars in the future. And when he speaks of Hitler he says "He as a little bit OK. sometimes he got a little bit too mean and did dirty stuff like putting lighted matches in the toenails of Americans." But karl thinks "We should have put all the Germans and Japs on an island and put an atom bomb to it." He also feels that "as lot of people are getting mad because everybody is starting war against each other." This themes seems to recur time and time again as an assumption of Karl's that the future hold for us an "almost chaotic war of all against all." Additionally he places an emphasis on regularity on street appearance and on rigid order which contrasts with his advocacy of chaotic aggression and turmoil. In contrast equalitarian children seem to remove themselves from spheres of anxiety and could penetrate to the underlying aspect of human welfare as equality, justice and general moral and ethical value in general.

Karl's brother was interviewed separately, with no opportunity to discuss the questions . Bill, like Karl says that "we should kick out the colored people from San Francisco" because they get drunk and kill people. German war criminals "should all have been hanged and not put in prison" He wants to put "the Japs on an island and throw bombs on them." and like Karl he feels fear of food deprivation as especially important.

Karl and Bills attitudes toward school, family and sex roles are conceived of in through the general stereotypical manner in that it demonstrates their craving for complete surrender to authority. Teachers Karl says "I like everything about teachers," is followed by statements telling of victimization and unjust treatment by these same teachers. Karl says, "A lot of them make you go to the principal's office or out of the room for something you didn't do. I had that happen lots of times."

When asked about what kind of teachers they like Karl says obedience to teachers is necessary but his brother Bill tell of teachers he doesn't like, "Those who tell you in a nice way instead of being strict and then don't make you mind." Bill's ideal teacher is "a man who would be strict," or a woman if "she was very strict." This concept of the ideal teacher surely contrasts the equalitarian child's tolerant concept of a teacher who is helpful, and laughs at jokes and is there to help the child.

Karl and his brother attitude toward teachers demonstrates their hierarchical conception of human relation which stress the weak must exhibit a self-negating surrender to the strong who have the authority. Karl, however doesn't seem to realize that he only partially is a person of submissive obedience because of his destructive forces which are partial directed toward the very authorities he must obey and are also diverted towards people he considers to the society's underdogs.

Karl's attitude toward his fellow students resolves around his fear of being attacked by other boys, whereas his brother Bill stresses conventional values of obedience and politeness. Equalitarian children, on the other hand stress companionship, common interests, fun and mutual understanding of each other as traits one would want in friends or fellow students.

Both Karl and his brother stress that money helps one to have friends but for Bill it possesses magical evil attributes."

"It is the root of all evil. It's bad luck to be born with money. If your parents tell you to put it in the bank and you keep it until your are grown up, it's bad luck."

He tells of how disaster befell some of his acquaintances who had saved money. Great evil forces are at work and one must be ready to anticipate doom and catastrophes in ones life.

Karl would prefer to have a private tutor rather than attend school; whereas his brother Bill rejects this idea. Tutors are "just for rich people, and they are no good." This quotation surely demonstrates how some ethnocentric people have resentment against those who they feel are the oppressors from above but such concepts also exemplifies their fear of the social classes and minority groups below them who may some day take over and exact fearful revenge.

The relationship of boys to girls should be natural they feel but they have rigid conceptions of the sex roles and stress politeness in girls. "If a boy is talking they shouldn't butt in." Girls who are aggressive towards boys or discourteous are rejected."If she pulls a boy by the arm and tells him to take her to a show or some place."

A perfect father to Karl is one who provides material benefits. "He will let you do anything you like and let you get any kind of food you like and let you take a girl out. Will give you about two dollars every day." When asked how he would change his father he says emphatically that "my father is good to me" but said he wished he gave him more money or could go any where he wanted. So we see in every context he uses an explosive manipulative manner toward people. Hostility is more openly expressed toward the mother than the father, probably because he is more powerful and can give them money and goods and can protect them; also this type of dependency and identification reduces any open expressions of hostility to the father. But Karl wants to change his mother , "to make her nice," to have her give him a car.

It is interesting that Karl sees those in authority as giving him goods whereas his brother Bill expects regimentation from them. A perfect father for him is one who "ought not to give it to you right away" when asked for something. The evidence from Karl's interviews and his Thematic Apperception test stories shows that

Karl has an underlying hostility towards his parents. On a "blind" interviewing rating of his attitude toward both parents he earns a "6" which earns the rater's impression that Karl is obsessed by feelings of being threatened and victimized by his parent's hostility. Bill's rating was "5" and one step closer in the opposite direction which indicates a secure, affectionate , compatible relationship toward his parents.

On the externalization of values both boys gained an extreme rating which covers such categories as opportunism, status-concern, conventionality and explicit condemnation of people who do not conform.

Corporal punishment at home is administered by both parents but the boys prefer the father to punish them. Bill says that his mother "is a little too soft-hearted." Both boys feel that severe punishment of children for minor misconduct is correct. Karl says that children ought to be punished for "talking back to grownups" and for breaking windows and that "you should go to Juvenile one year for that."

Karl when he has explosive fits of aggression says "I do anything I can-bite, pull hair, kick, tear into them." Bill says however that he tries to control his anger. Both approaches are typical of ethnocentric children who have explosive outbursts or who try by frantic efforts to control their anger.

Both boys tend to idealize their parents stereotypically while stressing their goodness yet would chose no family member as companions on a desert island. An examination of Karl's dreams and of his Thematic Apperception Test shows he identifies with a girl as being fed by her or of his feeding her and sees her as a safety zone in contrast with connections with boys or men.

Karl has recurrent dreams, "it's about going with a girl for dinner," and also about people being hanged and murdered. He also has childhood memories full of mishaps and catastrophes. He has fears of wild animals, high buildings and drunks and of "death in some dark night." But he says its the girl who is afraid of the dark but he denies he wants to be a girl. He says, "Some guys want to be girls."

Karl's Thematic Apperception Test stories show a rigidification of his personality induced by stress on self-negating submission and on the repression of nonacceptable tendencies which leads him into stereotypical patterns but also to conflicts between his different layers of personality. These tendencies surely contrast to children raised in a more permissive home who has a greater fluidity of transition and is able to communicate between his different personality strata. Karl thus has problems with realistic and spontaneous reaction to social situations because of his rigidity of defense and narrowness of his ego which is tied to an authoritarian personality.

When you examine his dreams you find they are full of murder and gore in which the murder is committed under circumstances that are unusual. One man who won a race is "shot in the back five times" as he lay in bed tired from a long days work. Today you have death children actually killing men from the street in drive by shootings as men die sleeping in their beds as unfortunate victims. In another dream Karl sees a man shot in the back and in another story "a lady is hit in the back with a knife." Usually the women dies for betraying a man, but usually the women find safety with money and food. The passive men generally are attacked in some unusual way and the aggressive men are caught, imprisoned and some are executed in the electric chair. Karl's unconscious wish is that all dangerous men will be caught and he can become passively surrounded by food without fear of aggression. He has insecurity about masculinity and of his feminine identification which finds expression through many phallic symbols and castration threats and his embarrassment about his fat body and his genital organs. Some of his stories has similarities to stories by overt homosexuals. We also see a projection of hostility toward his parents and a feeling that the world is a dangerous place. This coincides with research by Wolfenstein and Leites who found in American movie melodramas there exists a common fantasy which views the powerful father as a imaginary figure but whose force lies in a person's more archaic unconscious levels only.

Karl's brother Bill is more disciplined and would more than likely put his biases into action if the opportunity presented itself but Karl seemingly would actualize them only in a major social upheaval.

It is interesting that if you examine Henrich Himmler's life, a person also from an authoritarian family background you find similarities in his character structure with other people who have experienced an authoritarian family as children.

Through observing his anal-hoarding sadism you find a dehumanized bureaucrat who is a product of an authoritarian upbringing. Himmler was the bloodhound of Europe who was responsible with Hitler of slaughtering between fifteen and twenty million unarmed people; and was a torturer of millions of human beings. He was a person, whom K. J. Burckhardt, who at that time was representative of the League of Nation in Danzig , says that "Himmler impressed one as of uncanny subalternity (subalternitat), narrow-minded conscientiousness, inhuman methodicalness, blended with an element of an automation." [26] He was the essence of a sadistic authoritarian character. A definition of sadism broadly put is a passion for unrestricted and absolute power over another human being. When a sadistic person inflicts physical pain on another it is his wish for omnipotence. Mirra Alfassa also makes the point that cruelty, like sadism is the need to cut through an intensive unconscious layer of insensitive inertia and evolutionary obscurity of the lower subconscious. It is a deformation of intensity of love that is driven to extremely strong sensations for people whose physical sensibility is almost nil. They experience a bliss in their cruelty, that is, an intense joy in their cruelty which is repugnant to the normal person. [27] They are the dark night of human evolution breaking through an unregenerated modern consciousness; they are what all of us must transcend in our march toward self-realization. They are our future Death Masters if we do not stand up as Americans to the true and tried honor of liberty and justice for all!

Another aspect of this trait is that masochistic submissiveness to higher authorities does not oppose sadism but is a part of the symbiotic system through which submission to these controls are a manifestations of the basically same vital impotence. [28]

Dr. Albert Krebs, a leading Nazi who was excluded from the party in 1932, tells of a railroad trip in 1929 in which he was forced to endure Himmler's talk as he sat next to him. He noted Himmler's obvious insecurity and gaucheness and the "stupid and basically meaningless chatter with which he intruded upon me all the time." He said his conversation was a mixture of petit bourgeois small talk, martial braggadocio added with a sectarian preacher's zealous prophecy. Another observer, Emil Helfferich of the German banking elite says that Himmler as "the type of a cruel educator of the old school, strict against himself but stricter against others. . . . The signs of compassion and especially friendly tone of his thank you letters were all fake, as one often finds in clearly cold natures." (E. Helfferich, 19970).

His aide-de-camp. K. Wolff, however speaks of his fanaticism and lack of will, not his sadism. "He could be a tender family father, a correct superior and a good comrade. At the same time he was an obsessed fanatic, an eccentric dreamer and . . . a will-less instrument in Hitler's hands to whom he was tied in an ever increasing love/hate." (K. Wolff, 1961.) [29] His most significant character traits were his lifelessness, his insignificance, his banality and wish to dominate others to his will. But he was submissive to Hitler and his fanaticism. His subalternity of submissiveness seems to have occurred not because he was frightened of authority but because he was frightened of life, thus he had to submit to some authority. And he did, first to his father and later to his superiors in the army and party. He never rebelled and even wrote his diary entry daily following a command of his father or he would feel guilty. He even followed his father's lead by regularly attending church services of the Roman Catholic church three to four times a week during the war.

Himmler was no rebel and followed allegiance from his father to Strasser-Hitler and from Christianity to Aryan paganism; but he never took a step until it was safe to do so. He only betrayed Hitler to submit to the victorious allies in the second world war. It seems Himler needed a powerful and strong guiding figure to compensate for his life weaknesses. If a leader became weak, then in contempt he was rejected.

His submission to Hitler was complete because Hitler was the god-man whose only comparison was Christ or Krishna in the Bhagavadd-Gita. He writes:

"He is destined by the Karma of the universal Germanness {Germanentum}, to lead the fight against the east and to save the Germanness of the world; one of the very great figures of light has found its incarnation to him."(J. Ackerman, 1970)

Himmler thus submitted to the new Christ-Hitler as he had previously submitted to the old Christ/God. Yet it seems that even though previously he had submitted to his father he had a covert deep and intense dependence on his mother. A love which he received from her was an infantile love which all mothers gives to an infant; but in his case even until maturity.

Erich Fromm makes a point that such dependency shows a need for a strong father because the child is weak and helpless which leads the child to remain a little boy who longs always for his mother to protect and comfort him but not to demand anything of him. As an adult he feels like a weak and helpless person without initiative or will and thus he must submit himself to a strong leader to receive his strength from him. But Himmler case it seems he channels the strength he receives into a powerful control and cruelty which he inflicts upon other people; this power being a substitutes for his own lack of strength behind which he temporarily hides his weakness from himself and others so long as he has control over others. [30]

It is interesting that Himmler's pleasure in malignant denunciation of other people first appeared when he was castigating a person who had hoarded some food during the first world war. In another early act of denunciation he ruined his brother's fiance reputation and destroyed their potential union and then warned her and her family not to talk ill of the Himmler family because he said that even though he was a nice fellow "I will be completely different if anyone forces me to it. Then, I will not be stopped by any false sense of pity until the opponent is socially and morally ousted from the ranks of society." [31] Himmler later in his life acted out his sadism on a historical scale through mass executions and tortures of millions of people.

The researcher Else Frenkel-Brunswil says that the authoritarian home seems to foster punitive, intimidating atmosphere that is analogous to policies one finds in totalitarian social and political regimes. The early family conditioning of conventional and rigid rules which are clearly defined as submission roles [32] seems to allow the child later on in life to fit into a death cadre relationship quite easily.

Authoritarian homes force the children into overwhelming, unintelligible and arbitrary demanding need to totally surrender to the parents; seemingly there are apparent parallelism found in submitting to authoritarian social and political organizations and corporational systems. The similarity is obvious if your observe the weakness and dependence of the child to the authority of the parents and in turn notice that these same parents feel threatened in their economic and social status which they counteract by an archaic and unverbalized need for importance. It seems that the stress they experience is not so much their feeling of marginality or their actual status on the socioeconomic ladder but the subjective way they view their situation and how they are controlled by vaguely conceived aspirations. Research data points to the fact that the status concerns of people who are susceptible to authoritarianism rests not on realistic attempts to improve their lot but on rather naive hopes or that help may come from a sudden change in social conditions or through an imaginary strong and powerful person. Karl's father's naive hope of becoming an inventor or his mother's hope of being a photographer, neither ground in overt actions, surely points to vaguely anticipatory but inefficients aspects of social unrest which are passed onto the children through rigid and superficial rules and social taboos that are grounded on their unconscious negative doubts and uncertainties. The parents are impatient for obedience and the children are never able to observe and feel the finer discriminations of their acts; thus their conformity is an nonfunctional caricature of our social institutions based on a misunderstanding of their ultimate intent and these social and intrapsychic activities are in some sense an act of external defiance of culture through their external conformity. The children naturally do not understand these subtle nuances but the very fact that they have not properly internalized the real significance of social rules is one of the major interferences in the development of a clear-cut identity personality. [33]

Discipline in the authoritarian form is 'ego-destructive" because it prevents the development of independence and self-reliance. When you make a person feel worthless you strip him of his individuality and he may even feel depraved. The person must identify with his parents, his corporation, military or other authorities in order to feel safe and secure in the world. When you are fearful and dependent you don't criticize your death masters but praise them through ostentatious glorification and repress your hostility toward them. [34] In the end you becomes a plastic person who lives on the surface of your mentality and suffer all the more because you are only a caricature of a human being and now are a prime candidate for the death generation.

CASE STUDY OF AN EQUALITARIAN FAMILY AND CHILD

Peggy, a twelve-year od girl comes from an equalitarian family and exhibits a democratic outlook on life. [35] She like Karl, exhibits characteristics of the low-scoring group thus highlighting the syndrome under examination.

The socioeconomic backgrounds of both families are similar. Both families have fallen down in social class status from their grandparents time. The two families, however, have reacted quite differently to this fall. Additionally there is appreciable differences in the social situation of the families and a radical difference between the personalities of Peggy's mother and Karl's mother. ""There are also marked difference in their social background, including a much greater stability of Peggy's mother's family."

Peggy's mother is American born as were here parents; her father was born in Italy, the son of a doctor who practiced in a small town. He has worked as a salesman, a clerk, and a waiter and had just sold a small restaurant as a bad investment. He is a college graduate as is Peggy's mother, who is a social worker. Peggy's maternal grandfather was a small town lawyer and "a dictator and patriarch to the population. He entered the army . . . and liked the opportunity which it gave him for expressing authority." Peggy's mother rebelled against her father but received support and warmth from her mother.

The family exists on the edge of socioeconomic marginality but this fact doesn't seem to bother them; in fact most of the time the family members devote themselves to such pursuits as doing community causes and participating in discussions groups, etc. The parents have interests in art, music and reading. The mother has even written poetry. Their economic marginality seems to have given them freedom to follow their pursuits and they even enjoy respect among their friends. Even though the parents are divorced they see each other frequently and are on good terms with each other.

Peggy's parents feel deeply about racial equality and that greater tolerance and more education are the answer to racial prejudice. They are both opposed to any radical movements in the country.

They feel that affection toward their child rather than authority guides them is child rearing. Peggy's mothers perceptiveness and psychological insightfulness is reflected in the ideals she holds for her daughter. She says:

> "I do hope that she will do something that will make her happy and at the same time be constructive. I hope the girl will have experience early enough that she can integrate it and lead an outgoing, constructive life; and she won't have to spend so long working out her aggression that she finds herself no longer young-not that I wish to spare my daughter the suffering and experience necessary for development, but I hope she may get it early and fast. I feel that I can help by giving a lot of trust and confidence in the girl. I do feel that at times in the past I may have expected too high a performance for the sake of my own gratification, and that may have troubled Peggy. The child has always been given more responsibility than the average, but as a rule it hasn't seemed to be a strain." [36]

Peggy's mother has a concern for her inner psychological life and has rejected stereotyped conventionality. She also expressed the hope that her daughter wouldn't take a job for the sake of money or care too much for the acquisition of material objects thus sacrificing her ideals.

Peggy's father also says he wants his daughter "to grow up to have an all-around personality in such a way that she can get the best out of her-self, be happy with herself and with other people. Whatever work she wants to choose—that is her business. If we can bring her up with self-assurance and not to give up at the first obstacles, we will be doing something." [37]

The parents stress that above all they enjoy their child. The mother says that her daughter's greatest trait are "her sensitivity and receptivity to artistic things and to people . . . She has a philosophical interest in people and seems to have a good idea of the interrelationship of people and nations." Peggy's father thinks her strong points are "strength of character and being intelligent and liberal." He also speaks of some of her weakness such as her exhibitionism, insecurity and her interest in boys which he thinks is natural. [38]

Researcher Else Frenkel-Brunswik says that in many educational circles and homes in America the feeling is that to avoid authoritarianism all authority ought to be forsworn; but it must be said that this excessive view leads to total permissiveness and verges on anarchy. For a healthy home and society respect for the authority of outstanding persons and institutions are necessary but this does not lead to a total surrender or the absolute glorification of these authorities. Usually such leadership is limited to specialized fields or specific functions, thus their guidance toward the child linked with acceptance ought to strengthen the moral functions of the child. This will help him overcome the impulses toward aggression and selfishness and help the child to work out his instinctual problems and not repress them so that later in life they may emerge to cause problems. This viewpoint rests on an understanding of the child's particular needs and developmental steps. He is treated as an individual and encouraged to develop self-reliance and independence and above all his weakness is not exploited. He must have the freedom to express his likes and dislikes without being threatened with the loss of his parent's love. [39]

Else frenkel-Brunswil, [40] makes the point that the statistical data on adults and children suggests [41] that disciple in the family is the crucial factor through which an authoritarian, or democratic outlook develops in the child.

In Peggy's case her mother explained to her the family behavioral patterns so that little disciple was necessary. The mother even feels guilty for the few occasions she spanked the child because she now thinks she was angry herself. The fathers independent statement supports the mothers. He says:

> I don't know that we ever tried to discipline her very much. I was guilty of spoiling her when she was a baby

sometimes, but I don't remember ever trying to discipline her. Oh, I have given her a few times a spat on the rear when I was mad. I shouldn't do that, I know. I think the girl is a little obstinate, hot-heated, and not disciplined as much as she should be now, but maybe that's because she is an adolescent." [42]

Peggy's mother says her mother had similar attitudes on child-bearing. But her father was stern and authoritarian and she had to struggle to gain independence from him. She felt she was successful, whereas her brothers were not which she attributed to the fact that she was away from her father the first years of her life. Additionally she attended college and became a social worker who worked with subnormal children and married an utterly unauthoritarian man. Her marriage broke up, a fact she blames partially on her early relationship with her authoritarian father. Additionally she worked long years in psychoanalyst on her feminine identification.

Peggy's social beliefs concerning minority groups emphasizes the equality of the races:

> The Chinese can do really beautiful art work, The Germans have really intelligent and well-known scientists and things like that. Every race has a certain amount of skill. They are pretty well equal. I go to parties at a negro girl's house. I wouldn't mind going out with a Negro boy to a party, but it would probably be better to go with a white one because the other kids would tease me, and the Negro boy and I would both feel funny." [43]

Else Frenkel-Brunswil says that Peggy's attitude toward other races is in sharp contrast with a staggering 96 per cent of children scoring high on the ethnic scale; additionally 83 per cent of the middle scorers and 22 per cent of the low scores all expressed ethnocentric attitudes toward Negroes of a negative manner and stating they favored segregation. Interestingly 60 per cent of the high scorers and middle scorers as well as 18 percent of the low scorers held similar views toward the Chinese. [44]

Peggy thought that America is "really very friendly with many countries," except Russia, which "doesn't understand our ways and she doesn't understand us." Karl in contrast thought most foreign countries are against us and was partially sympathetic toward Hitler. Peggy thought Hitler "was crazy with power." Peggy, incidentally thought of Americans as people who have citizenship papers and said there is some foreign blood in every American.

Peggy, in responding to a question of how she would change America says:

> "Try to have people be more understanding about the Negro problem . . . Another thing is to have better schools and teachers; nice schools that kids would really like. Give them a chance to change the subject often so it wouldn't be so boring. Also a better department for juvenile delinquents. Not treat them as if they did it on purpose; and a better home for these kind. They really don't want to be bad, but they just don't know what else to do." [45]

Additionally Peggy has great admiration for the president of the United States because he is concerned with the welfare of the nation and is a person who "really thinks of others, not of himself; thinks of them as friends; is always kind and works hard for the people."

Peggy does not have any exaggerated submission to authority or demand strictness and supervision from idealized teachers, although she thinks a good teacher is one who can "understand you, be a friend to you, someone you can confide in, someone you like." The teacher she dislikes she calls "dumb, and scream at the kids and tell them to shut up."

She likes girl friends whom she can be a companion with and with whom she has mutual likes.

Peggy's aggression is mild and not repressed like karl who has interspersed violent break-throughs. But Peggy says she tries to like everyone but does have some mild guilt about occasional hostile feelings which alternates with her readiness to accept them as unavoidable facts of life. Peggy occasionally disagrees with her mother's wide-reaching tolerance toward everybody by"when I criticize someone who looks stupid and funny. My Momma and Daddy both think that I shouldn't do this, since people don't know any better, but I think they really do." but Peggy does identify with the underdog and on occasions gets angry "when people pick on someone, even dogs or animals, or when they tease Negroes and call them dirty names." [46]

Peggy feels her father "is a good friend to you and understanding and nice. Just a person." Prejudiced children in contrast think of the ideal father in terms of punishment or not being strict enough, etc., whereas unprejudiced children see companionship as important in a child-father relationship. Peggy sees her father's real personality as that of an idealized parent as she does her mother. she says she has never really been punished by them. "My mother just talks to me. Children should never really be punished, but have things explained to them." [47]

Peggy feels children should behave around boys "Not silly but act like herself .Having a boy friend is just like having a good friend." She also , like most unprejudiced children makes no differentiate between a good profession for a man in contrast to a women. She also seems to have an absence of hierarchical thinking in terms of social status: "What ever he wants to do, whether it is a shoe clerk or a chemist or anything at all. Nobody else should decide for him." she says that the worst procession for a man or women is "To have his life planned, to be what he doesn't want." Peggy wants to be "an artist, a poet, a writer, and a dancer."[48]

Peggy's Thematic apperception Test stories demonstrates a creativeness imagination, in contrast to Karl's primitive, archaic themes of rumination about topics of food and destruction which flooded him from his unconscious. Peggy seems to be at ease with her unconscious trends which find expression in artistic flavor and imagination in a positive manner. She is cognitively disciplined in her free flowing stories whereas Karl's stories were stereotyped and chaotic. Peggy's stories reflect an ease of communication between Peggy's different layers of personality and shows that she has generally an non-repressed approach to life.

The major themes in Peggy's stories are a protective feeling for people who are different or appear weak. Karl, on the other hand is contemptuous of the weak and the "sissy." In Peggy's eyes the sissy is often the real life hero and in one of her stories about a nine year boy she says:

"Whom all the kids in school used to tease and say he was a sissy. Tommy cried when he went home. Next day the boys dared him to fight the biggest bully of the class. The bully hit tommy in the face, and it made him mad. Tommy had to fight , and he licked the bully. after that he was liked. There was one boy that was a leader that hadn't liked him before that invited him to have a soda. And after that all the boys liked Tommy." [49]

This picture of a cruel-looking white boy hitting a Mexican boy was a card selected for the research study. Karl had nothing but derogatory statements about the boy and some equalitarian children expressed pity for the boy but in Peggy's eyes he becomes a hero. Observe also Peggy's response to a picture of a negro boy who is also being maltreated:

> "He {the Negro boy} wondered why people could be do ignorant and not know that everybody is created equal, and that people could believe what people say that isn't true. Someone threw something at him and blinded him. Two kids from the army started beating up on him. Yet in the army you are supposed to learn to stand for what is right . . . He went back to where he came from and

thought that someday he would do something about all this." [50]

Else Fenkel-Brunswik's research study shows that ethnocentric, authoritarian children such as Karl exhibits rigid dichotomizing, aggressive, fear of imaginary social dangers of deprivation and show an exaggerated adherence to conventional values of law and order. They perceive their parents and friend within the same themes; whereas democratic-minded equalitarian children have little dichotomizing or other forms of rigidly and do not have an intolerance of ambiguity like karl exhibits. In prejudiced children there is an inherent conflict and anxiety over sexual, social and personal roles which finds expression in an ensuing desperate avoidance of all ambiguity and its dire consequences for themselves. [51]

The study points to the fact that the rigid authoritarian children represent in some manner an over-all immaturity found in younger children; states which must be overcome if maturity is to be reached. Transintegral psychology, using an evolutionary model would take this conclusion one step further and say that the prejudiced, authoritarian children are infrarational people and on an evolutionary scale must rise upward in their evolution of consciousness. Maturity in this sense is an evolvement in socio-moral consciousness awareness that transforms the lower human nature upward some degrees so there is an unitive communication and empathy with other racial groups that also allows social and psychological ambiguity to functionally exist within each person.

Human beings are evoutionary creatures also on the psychological and social levels . Karl and his parents, as representative examples of the authoritarian personality manifest unusual combination of unrest with a predilection for chaos and total change ;yet has an uncritical, distorted glorification for contemporary institutions and social conditions. They would support a total upheaval with its radical changes within society. [52] These type of people, some would say, are prime candidates for the death cadres and are members of the death generation.

Elsie Frenkel-Brunswik says that "In the contest of American culture, Karl and his family are deviants." They emphasis is on hierarchical rather than equalitarian relations and they have fears about their own abilities to achieve success and social status in society. They have anxiety about the availability of material goods and live within a mystical belief system that supranational forces bring about catastrophes. They can't analysis the social forces occurring within their culture accurately thus makes them susceptible to totalitarian propaganda [53] and prime candidates for the death cadres. They and the million s of families falling apart as they fall down from middle class status to the lower classes and economic destitute will find solace with their death masters ideas of social renewal. But there is still hope for family life and for America's children.

Our children are now marching into the new age of self reliance and an emotional maturity that has not arrived just yet because the battle for America's survival is still on . But this day is almost here and the old outmoded social forms and conventions will be thrown off as our children dance in the street rejoicing; they shall be uplifted into their higher natures and in the future they shall rise up into these peak experiences at will and in an evolutionary short time live within the bussom of a grand gnostic consciousness that will embrace the species consciousness in unison with nature and the cosmos. This is our children's heritage and they shall emerge within it with joy and confidence and fulfill the mandate of their species consciousness. They will no longer creep into life ignorant and oppressed by their parents and destroyed by society and crushed by life and finding in death only release and gratitude that their struggles are all over. Instead our children shall uplift their heads in honor and they shall walk in joy and flow with life with a song on their lips and euphoria in their hearts and all nature shall rejoice and in such living the Cosmos shall flair up from within their very souls and an ethereal course of communion with eternity shall be established through which all life will sing with triumph. God almighty will shine from behind the eyes of our children as they embrace with enthusiasm all nature and species life together in an union that will glow with love and euphoric bliss.

Rise children of America and take your place within the eternity of American life. Lead your death parents into the light of the new tomorrows and lift their tears from the wet ground they stand upon and live the true life that eternity meant for you,. You are our future and if you will not lead we are lost and doomed to species death and none may save us from ourselves; none may uplift our shriveled hands and warped spirits and we shall die in your arms ruined and destroyed by our lack of insight and with our deaths you will know that only one more generation remains as the death children perish one by one, just as a fire fly perishes in the dark of the night.

Children of America look within yourselves and find that light of eternity that sleeps within you. Ignite it with joy and kindle its flame and let it grow spontaneously in the darkness of your dead spirit and be uplifted by those activities. You are the light of the world who shall uplift all humanity into the species light of Gnostic consciousness and by that action transform what was dead into a new light of existence that shall fire up the dying world into a new sphere of activities that will save our age and uplift what was dying into life eternal. Stand up and transform your lower natures into something of glory and hope and stand before all life and pledge your best until death is vanquished . You are our only hope. You are the last of the species and if you do not act then all is lost and our species shall perish quickly and our truth will be no more.

It is written in obscure words that none may predict the human species demise before its appointed time; yet the signs are before us this very day and deceive yourselves not because our time is running out of the hour glasss quickly as the particle of sand flow over our life force and cut us to the quick; and our tears will not wash out its sting and our spirit's waning soon will flow away with the high tide. What remains will be the walking dead looking at eternity from society's living grave as our species is writ-

ten off as a lost cause that perhaps never should have been! Cry
America, laminate, for once America has perished the world goes
next and all nature shall cry in grief; and when it is all over mother
nature will rise up another human species, perhaps better able to
accomplish her goals and aspirations, and Homo sapiens will be
but a dim memory on some future archaeologist lips as he writes
our obituary . Then all the glories that might have been, all the
human aspirations that could have been accomplished; all the
heavenly chorus that we could have sung will never be as America
and the world dwells in death because of the Genocide Phenomenon.

CHAPTER 9

PSYCHOCULTURAL EVOLUTION

FUTURIST COMMENTARY: The 22nd century scholars are now studying the evolutionary process of the human race. Something has seriously gone wrong with this natural process as our race dies to itself and human extinction violently presents itself to us daily. We die a little each day as a human race; and our philosophers tell us that soon our race faces oblivion and no one knows how to side step our apparent destiny.

Oh, to be able to start over again and creatively march with the tide of history and innovatively emerge into our species evoutionary destiny.

But enough of this nonsense. We are the dead lamenting over our obituary and let no man tell you otherwise.

Dr.Campbell's writtings on psychocultural evolution is studied attentively by our scientists and it would benefit the readers to also quietly examine his concepts.

The psychocultural evolutionary theory defines the evolutionary mental process as an emergent evolution of consciousness through three broad cultural states that psycholculturally measures our inner mental evolvement by tentatively measuring our functional cultural position and changes. These cultural stages are not a unilinear or a chronological progression from one cultural stage to another since human mental evolution is not constant.

The human animal does not evolve mentally in a constant chronological progression and specific cultural groups cannot be maintained over long periods of time. Over a broad period of time an infrarational, rational-intellectual and suprarational evolutionary stage may be reached by mankind.

The human race starts with an infrarational stage in which life based its actions on impulses, spontaneous ideas, vital intuitions, desires and need circumstances. Humanity's institutions are based on these dynamics until a rational age became the presiding motive of his rational guidance. The final stage finds the species moving through a subjective era towards a suprarational age where superintellectual and perhaps and intuitive Gnostic consciousness guides the age. [1]

History demonstrates that most of the great civilizations of the past are extinct, and contemporary social orders are constantly changing. Social evolution is cyclic not gradual or progressive in a chronological unilinear line. Social evolution is an upward-moving spiral–a series of ascents and descents. The gains in this process are generally kept, even if eclipsed for a time. Periods of sociocultural decline can be fruitful eras in which elements of perfection laking in an earlier era are worked out and later combined with previously gained aspects, when new curve of progress again occurs. These stages are not universally concurrent. They may be represented in isolated social systems or be culture wide regional happenings. They may even co-exist in different parts of the earth at the same time. we will now examine in more detail the various scientific evidence for psychocultural evolution. Campbell states that:

Hidden within the vastness of primordial time the stream of life emerged on earth eons ago, thus beginning what Loren Eiseley has called the immense journey. [2]

During the late Pliocene or early Pleistocene the emergent evolutionary force brought forth Australopithecus, and "The profound shock of the leap from animal to human status is echoing still in the depth of our subconscious mind." [3] This extraordinary birth that projected the human animal into conscious self-awareness and dimensional time began the startling Psychocognitive emergence of early man and set in motion the psychocultural process.

In order to understand ourselves psychologically and mentality we have to investigate the human species' psychocultural evolution. Humanity is not only an organically evolved species who exists within a primordial species consciousness but also is a species that exists within the womb of learned culture which changes from time to time.

In the last chapter we discussed man's mental-consciousness evolution. Let's examine our history as an evolving self-conscious-cultural species in this chapter so that we can better understand the Genocide Phenomenon and the present Death Generation. It is postulated that the humanity's broad psychocultural stages are culturally reflective of the state of mental consciousness of the species. Presently all members of our species seemingly are equal our scientist tell us but historically this was not the case. Our species has traveled from initially an animal consciousness to a self-transcending state of mind that has left instinctive behavior behind it. Humanity is also a social-culture creature and as such has gone through a process of culture change through out its history. Rapid culture change is now one of the seven postulated causal agents for the present Genocide Phenomenon. But to understand the factors that bring about change within socio-cultural units we must examine two things, that is, the nature of culture and the evolution of culture. In a later chapters we will examine in detail the constituent elements of the nature of contemporary culture, with particular emphasize placed on American's culture of death; but for now we will address the process of cultural history.

PSYCHOCULTURAL EVOLUTION

Man has been a social animal from the dim beginnings of time when a representative sample of protohumans crossed the threshold from instinctive lower animal mentality to cognitive self-awareness. Since that time the human animal, as a social representative, has evolved organically as a physical creature, mentally and psychologically as a self-aware cognitive being and socially as a creature of learned behavior. Without language and a society to socialize and condition him, he is a beast in the field and not a human being. The social aspect of man is the prime mover of present day humanity. This womb of culture is the dynamic stuff of reality to the human species, Homo sapiens, and without it all human life and essence are non-existent and the "human race" is a nothing, ordained to extinction within one generation.

One of the basic reasons for the emergence of the death generation within human society has been the factor of culture change. Culture change can occur within the context of any indigenous culture but also occurs with selective precision; it also emerges through time as a diachronic process.

In this chapter we examine the evolutionary process of culture change and some of the ideas that have developed concerning the crisis that is mankind!

From a historical perspective, humanity's slow climb upwards from non-human existence until now has been a story of social evolution-progressive in many ways and unique in the animal kingdom. This section will examine this social evolution with four basic concepts, that is, with the concepts of unilinear evolution, multilinear evolution, and universal evolution, with comparative comments based on Integralism's multidimensional paradigm concerned with evolutionary consciousness. And we will examine the psychocultural evolutionary theory.

The scientific thought process is not born in a vacuum, i.e., conceptual theories have their antecedents in the speculative arena of the socio-cultural process, thus scientific concerns often follow from directives of theoretical concerns by the intellectual community of any given era.

In the case of social evolutionary concepts, a 19th century phenomenon that died out in the first half of the 20th century with a rebirth in recent years but which we find has antecedents and causal relations in the 18th century through the concept of human and social perfectibility.

The 18th century saw the full flowering of the concept of perfectibility of humanity and society, a humanistic and scientific theme that began in the Renaissance. The idea was that humanity, by his rational faculties, could not only reach perfection himself but could also, through changing the social system rationally, lead mankind to the threshold of a new millennium. This rationale led to the idea that natural law prevailed and that man and all things in the universe–inorganic and organic were subject to the orderly reign of natural law.

The human logic, although subject to natural law, could discover the workings of this law and progress forward to human perfection. As a corollary to this advancement it was realized that all human beings everywhere must have the same potential, regardless of cultural differences, and that human nature is the same everywhere. We find, therefore, that from the period of 1725 to 1890, concepts, data methodology, etc., were developed that studied the human condition, from "savagery" through barbarism to civilization–the ultimate and culminating height of human endeavor.

It was from the 1940's to the 1890's that new concepts of man developed in fields such as geology, paleontology, archaeology, folklore, philology and physical anthropology. These fields converged in ethnological societies, made up of members from not only the above fields but from medicine and anatomy and the concept of really studying man as a physical-psychological being was strong and dynamically in the academic air. To describe and classify actual races, record customs, languages, theorize original ideas about social realities, and develop paradigms concerning the psychophysical and psychocultural development of humanity was the goal of this period.[5]

UNILINEAR CULTURAL EVOLUTION

During the above period a new science of culture was developing. It was exemplified by E. Tylor—a unilinear evolutionist, who conceived that this study should be a science of culture. Tylor states that:

> Culture or civilization, taken in its wide ethnographic sense, is that complex whole which includes knowledge, belief, art, morals, law, customs, and any other capabilities and habits acquired by man as a member of society. [6]

Tylor believed that the findings of ethnography demonstrated an evolutionary process of a unilinear order, that is, that society proceeds to emerge through stages in a set chronological order. Anthony Wallace calls this concept, a partial-ordering evolutionary model that states that for any given society to change from one state to another it must successively pass through a specific sequence of states. [7] Tylor wrote that:

> On the whole it appears that wherever there are found elaborate arts, abstruse knowledge, complex institutions, these are the results of gradual development from an earlier, Simpler, and ruder life. No stage of civilization comes into existence spontaneously, but grows or is developed out of the stage before it. This is the great principle which every scholar must lay firm hold of, if he intends to understand either the world he lives in or the history of the past . . . Human life may be roughly classed into the three great stages, Savage, Barbaric, Civilized . . . So far as the evidence goes, it seems that civilization has actually grown Up in the world in these three stages. [8]

Tylor used the historical social orders, such as Victorian England, ancient Egypt and Babylonia, etc., as specific examples of said states. "Unlike Comte," however, he does not proclaim these stages as a "law of the development of society, but simply maintains the thesis of the progressive development of culture as an inductive, "empirical fact." [9] Tylor felt, in contrast to Comte's concept of static form of nature and human history as progressive within fixed limits, that human history was part of the history of nature and was subject not only to natural laws but to transformation in time. As Tylor puts it, "If law is any where it is every where." [10]

In this position one sees the influence of eighteen century European Enlightenment on Tylor as well as the evolutionary conceptual influence of Comte, Buckle, the kuiturgeschichte of Klemm and Waitz. [11]

Tylor also looked for psychological laws of human nature to explain cultural evolution in contrast to the sociological approach of Comte who looked for historical and sociological laws of human development.[12] To Tylor these psychological causal laws underlying cultural evolution were to be found not in cultural phenomena themselves but in some unchanging laws of human nature.

Tylor states in his text Primitive Culture, that he was concerned with "the study of human thought and action" with "the laws of human nature" and the general laws of intellectual movement." He thus studied cultural history as an evolutionary process to discover the underlying nonhistorical unchanging laws of human nature. The study of this human nature was to be undertaken without regard to biological or racial difference–a factor that modern scientific research upholds and has proved conclusively to be irrelevant to such research. [13]

Unilinear cultural evolution as established by Tylor and Morgan, the American anthropologist, does not maintain that all societies must pass through the three stages of savagery, barbarism into civilization in chronological order, but they state that only those who had reached the civilized state had gone through these stages. Both were well aware of the facts of cultural diffusion and saw no need that all social orders had to become civilized, in contrast to some European Enlightenment philosophers, especially Ficte's concept of a principle of reason and a postulate of divine Providence. A similar concept was presented by Comte in accordance to his three stages of theological, metaphysical, to the positive stage of scientific thought. [14]

Tylor and Morgan had no a priori laws that determined the social steps other than psychological for Tylor and the general law of cultural progress in accordance with geometrical law for Morgan. Morgan especially felt that past people developed along similar lines because of similar human and mental conditions. Morgan states that:

> The accumulating evidence [shows] that the principle institutions of mankind have been developed from a few primary gems of thought; and that the course and manner of their development was predetermined, as well as restricted within narrow limits of divergence, by the natural logic of the human mind and the necessary limitations of its power . . . the argument when extended tends to establish the unity of mankind. [15]

Morgan thus rested his case on biological determinism and a type of universal psychology of the human mind. Human nature was not independent of historical laws. Tylor, however, viewed cultural evolution as independent of biological evolution, in contrast to Morgan. Morgan, it might be added, was influential on Marx and Engels who viewed his concepts as providing proofs to the inevitable progress of the historical-philosophical movement they represented. The present Russian regime,[late Soviet Union] according to Lowie has officially recanalized his work and their spokesman state that his work is "of paramount importance for the materialistic analysis of primitive communism." [16]

An important point that should be noted is that unilinear

evolution ought not to be confused with social Darwinism that viewed social orders as in competition with each other about survival of the fittest–the loser being inferior social orders. This concept of social Darwinism–a concept Darwin did not hold, saw all cultures as having to go through absolute sequential stages and viewed European societies, that is, some European social orders were viewed as being on the top of the ladder, thus giving justification for colonialism and "the white man's burden of uplifting the lower masses of the world to their high apex of civilization."

Unilinear cultural evolution contributed to evolutionary theory as an initial attempt to explain human social evolution: but one can criticize it on several points. Morgan progressive evolution, for example, doesn't provide a mechanism for evolutionary change or account for natural selection. Social development, for him, proceeds in a relatively set track and its driving force is some kind of metaphysical entity.[17] Also both Morgan and Tylor neither differentiate between cultural evolution nor progress.

A priori concepts and logical analysis of judging institutions and cultures with a serial advancement from simple to the complex is an impossible situation–especially with no adequate ethnographic data to base your judgment on. Modern ethnographic research has surely proved that no adequate methodology exists to do this with extant cultures, let alone with extinct ones–especially cultures in which no ethnographic data exists or no historical records exist.

Both Tylor and Morgan's stages were based on technological achievement that can seriously be questioned since evolutionary progress does not necessarily reflect an advanced technology.

A yogi sitting in his cave may manifest supreme high states of consciousness, display unusual states of extra sensory perception and have conscious control over involuntary physiological body process and yet would probably be judged by Morgan and Tylor as a savage. In fact, if one were to use their classification stages, an excellent case could be presented for categorizing all modern

civilization as Barbaric, existing in an era of sophisticated technological Barbarism. Also just because a society has a writing system
does not mean it is civilized; a cynical critic might argue that all
writing has done for modern man is to allow him to record his
atrocities–100+ million dead alone in the 20th century–and lament man's inability to quail the barbarian within himself.

Another point is that to compare cultures' one must have a
more than adequate cultural theory and objective methodologies
to collect the data–no such theory or technique truly exists to this
day. One must also record that no adequate psychological model
of man exists and surely no adequate model of human nature has
been discovered yet. One might state that there probably are no
such things as unchanging laws of human nature and if they do
exist may only reflect specific laws of specific types of historical
and extinct human species. For example, a part of the scientific
community feels that mankind evolved through several species;
there may be psychological laws for each species or specific laws
of the mind that reflect or control only certain mind dimensions;
Transpersonal dimensional research surely points to this conclusion. Also Transintegral Psychology postulates that varying
psychopersonality systems operate under differing mind dynamics–making one law of human nature difficult to support.

It is also difficult to conceive that Morgan's assertion that
American aboriginal culture corresponds to archaic forms of Greek
and Roman Institutions and that all historic cultures passed
through similar technological substages regardless of social circumstances or geography.[18]

Finally, although Tylor cautioned against assuming that contemporary extant native peoples were ethnologically primitive;
but it did not stop his followers from doing so and using such
data as a source of evolutionary speculation. On the lay public
level, to this day, great evils are daily occurring because of such
speculations.

UNIVERSAL EVOLUTION

The concept of universal evolution is a term used by Julian Steward to label the evolution of archaeologist V. Gordon Childe, and anthropologist Leslie A. White. After nearly a half century of rejection of the concept of unilinear cultural evolution, by the dominant relativist school of anthropology–a school that viewed each culture as an autonomous or semi-autonomous, self-contained unit subject only to its own unique value system and sociological reality nature–the universalistic evolutionary school concept as it applies not to particular societies but to cultures as a whole was developed. [19]

Leslie White [20] is a "culturologists" who studies the process of culture. He defines culture as symbolic behavior, a symbol being[21] a "thing the value or meaning of that is bestowed on it by those who use it" Symbol as defined by White is almost identical with the concept of value conceived by Thomas, Sorokin, and Max MacIver and to some extent, Parsons. [22] For White, culture is a reality sui generis–subject only to its own laws and autonomous processes. To understand the laws of cultural evolution look only to the cultural reality structure, not to psychology or human biology.

Cultural evolution is a logical sequence of irreversible stages. Human culture history is merely its manifestion of stages in time. David Bidney, commenting on White's concept says:

> But this does not mean, for White at least, that mankind may be said to have a culture history, as Tylor and the classical evolutionists maintained. By a priori definition he has delimited the sphere of history as comprising the contingent relations of specific, unique temporal events.[23] By similar a priori definitions, evolution is said to deal only with 'temporal-formal processes' which are the thoroughly deterministic and not subject to human controls.[24]

Thus, to White the proper study of evolution is not the temporal, spatial or formal process but in the evolutionary or developmental process. [25] For White this meant studying the dynamic process of cultural evolution as measured by the amount of energy harnessed and put to work per Capita per year. [26] Using a biological thermodynamic analogy White postulated that as energy increased a corresponding development of technology occurred which caused specialization and differentiation within specific cultures—thus evolution and progress took place. [27]

This process took place in three subdivisions: technological, sociological and ideological. Technology is material instrumentation and technique for their use, sociological system is patterns of behavior and the ideological style of beliefs and knowledge as expressed in symbolic form.

Technology as a system is of primary importance as the other two systems are dependent on it. The earliest source of energy is human energy and cultural evolution progressed as animal and agricultural energy was developed.

Progressive evolutionary advancement occurred as new types of energy developed. White felt that particular social systems corresponded to specific energy patterns, i.e., each technological era produces its own social system; therefore social systems and institutions are related to technology.

V. Cordon Childe as an archaeologist and Marxist, holds that Morgan's concept of consecutive stages of savagery, barbarism and civilization is valid in that the technological development that past mankind went through seems to coincide with Morgan's evolutionary process. [28] Childe's evolutionary process is quite close to the Darwinian model since he felt that the carrying capacity of an environmental niche was developed through technology, thus allowing greater numbers of people to exist in said ecological realm. He conceives these changes or technological revolutions in demographic terms. [29] He suggests that cultural adaptation is due to natural selection and insists that Darwin's formula of variation–heredity, adaptation, and selection can be utilized in explaining social evolution, i.e., variation corresponds to invention, social heredity is the transmission of cultural forms from one generation to another and that natural selection is technological inventions as they survive in a competitive business market.

CRITICISMS OF UNIVERSAL EVOLUTION

There are many criticisms of universal evolution; the most prominent probably is Margaret Mead's comment that cultural evolution is directional and polycentric or directed from diverse centers of influence and obviously neither unilinear nor inevitable as White presents it.[30] Julian H. Steward criticizes Childe, because in his search for universal laws of evolution, he discounts cultural differences, and diffusion. He also says both Childe and White's postulated cultural sequence, are too general to be useful and on a developmental scale they present nothing new or controversial and that even White's technological law, expressed in terms of energy, has long been an accepted fact. He also feels that concepts of change in culture which cannot predict specific change sequence in specific cultural cases is worthless; in fact he feels White's energy concept tells nothing about the developmental characteristics of specific cultures.[31] Steward feels that the Universalist side-step important questions that at the very least the unilinear evolutionist attempt to solve. He says:

> The problem and method of universal evolution thus differ from those of unilinear evolution. Right or wrong, the nineteen-century of evolutionists did attempt to explain concretely why a matriarch should precede other social forms, why animism was the precursor of gods and spirits. Why a kin-based society evolved into a territorial-based, state controlled society, and why other specific features of culture appeared.[32]

Kroeber criticizes White for his attempt to separate the concept of cultural evolution from cultural history since modern ethnography research shows otherwise. Bidney feels also, that on this point that this concept is reminiscent of the platonic dualism of ideas and the contingent order of phenomenal nature and that Aristoltle's criticism in his book Metaphysics, that such duplication was not necessary and injurious to the development of a science of nature, was also applicable to White's dualism, i.e., " . . . dualism of normative laws of cultural evolution versus contingent non repetitive culture history". Kroeber also feels that White calls evolution is nothing but a mixture of history and science. White's historical materialism surely leaves out any human volition in the historical process. White even criticized Chile for allowing the subjective human factor in culture change a place in his theories. [35]

Campbell, an Transintegral psychologist, suggests otherwise because he states that the psychological factors of human volition must also be taken into account in the evolutionary process as also the concept of the emergent quality of mind. Recent research of a transpersonal nature on altered states of mind surely demonstrate the evolutionary potential of mind as a process in nature. In point of fact the force of events–the power behind White's cultural determinism, is this emergent quality of mind operating through the psychodynamic nature of the human personality system as emergent cultural dynamics.

This process is not a blind or non-human thing but the dynamic projection onto the sociocultural realm of human aspiration as a relational cultural dynamics. Technological energy is merely the effect of discovered natural energy sources put to the dynamic use of the need structure of the human psyche. One could say that White's energy concept is merely an effect of the causal projection of the psyche in terms of technological effort. Perhaps if one seeks evolutionary understanding, one should measure the energy factor of human nature or even of the primal energy–the kundalini current operative in transpersonal categories of integral being–perhaps energy measured as psychophysical content as reflected in human society will fulfill White's postulates.

Campbell would reject White's contention in his article "Man's control Over Civilization", that "from the cultural determinist's point of view, human being are merely the instruments through which cultures express themselves." [36] White goes on to say that:

> A physician, saving lives each day, is an instrument through which certain cultural forces express themselves; if they were not there or if they were different, the organism in question would not be practicing medicine, or he would Practice it in a different way. The gangster, evangelist, revolutionist, reformer, policemen, impoverished begged, wealthy parasite, teacher, soldier, and shaman are likewise instruments of cultural action and expression, each is a type of primate organism grasped and welded by a certain set of cultural traits. it is only the inveterate habit of thinking anthropocentrically that makes this point of view seem strange or ridiculous.[37]

Transintegral psychologist Campbell questions this position. Surely, he says, man is sub specie temporis as a historical product of cultural experience and is to be viewed sub specie aeternitatis as a part of the order of nature, yet culture cannot be viewed as sociocultural instinct, with human beings as robots fulfilling their assigned functions. Surely there are individuals within societies who are semi-robot in their social activities—recently a young man had an operation to change his sex so "that he could be accepted by society," so White had hold of a half-truth.

White in actuality is speaking of culture and cultural inhabitants of the first stage of infrarational cultures as Aurobindo conceives them. These are individuals who view the structure of cultural activities through mind states which utilize partial rational abilities. These types of persons are rational and utilize conceptual thought but are not deep thinkers or intellectuals and for the most part are controlled by vital and emotional urges and sensate controls.

Because most of today's cultures are infrarational, most of hu-

manity are in varying stages of altered states of consciousness—
many of these would understand social dynamics as White con-
ceptualizes. Rational men and men emerging into higher states of
consciousness would reject White's contention that "we cannot
control its course culture, but we can learn to predict it." [38] On
the other hand, what White says of the cultural process would
refer to a physical or vital-emotional infrarational culture. He
says:

> If the trend of cultural evolution is away from private
> Property and free enterprise, why strive to perpetuate
> them? if it could be shown that international wars will
> continue as long as independent, sovereign nations exist,
> then certain Delusions now popular would find fewer
> nourishment and support. The fact is that culture has
> been evolving as an unconscious blind, blood, brutal,
> tropismatic process so far. It has not yet reached the point
> where intelligence, self consciousness, and understand-
> ings are very conspicuous. Our ignorance is still Deep-
> rooted and widespread. We do not understand even some
> of the most elementary things—the prohibition of po-
> lygamy, for example. In short, we are so ignorant that we
> can still believe that it is we who make our culture and
> control its course. [39]

White feels that our belief in our ability to control culture has
" . . . always been a source of weakness to us" and he says that
" . . . we are now discovering the true nature of culture and we
can in time reconcile ourselves to this extasomatic order as we
have to the astronomic, geologic, and meteorologic orders." [40]
White additionally feels that a growing science of culture will
allow mankind to understand its cultural place in the scheme of
things. In a later chapter a reconciliation of the concept of a
transcendental culture as a superpsychic, autonomous level of
phenomenal reality, independent of the processes of biology and

psychology, as David Bidney defines the objective idealist position held by Kroeber, Sorokin and Spengler and White, will be integrated with concepts of subjective idealism, conceptual idealism, and a type of Berkeleyan subjective idealism. Campbell's psycho-cognitive culture theory as an explanation of evolutionary consciousness can hopefully reconcile and integrate the dimensional realm of psychological and cognitive conscious natures with socio-cultural dimensions. Bidney makes the point that these categories must be observed in a unique manner. He says:

> . . . psychological, sociological, and cultural phenomena do not exist independently, and hence may not be said to constitute distinct ontological levels or be conceived through themselves alone methodologically, it is possible to abstract the latter phenomena and to treat them temporarily 'as if'" they were independent of the organisms upon which they depend. [41]

MULTILINEAR CULTURAL EVOLUTION

The concept of multilinear cultural evolution as conceived by Julian Steward is a search for parallels in specific cases of the evolutionary process. It does not set up a sequence or series of principles to explain cultural evolution from prehistoric times to the present. Its basic goal is to examine specific parallel developmental stages in specific identifiable cultures, in contrasts to White who emphasized specifically the general cultural process.

Steward says in his article Multilinear Evolution: Evolution and Process, that " . . . it is implicit in the evolutionary view that developmental levels are marked by the appearance of qualitatively distinctive patterns or types of organization."[42] Once developmental patterns are discerned they can be compared with other social orders and their cultural patterns and if such similar sequences of culture change have occurred, then the search for like causes can be undertaken. It is assumed as a given that culture change as a process does occur but Steward does not expect to categorize such historical data with universal stages. Steward thus conceives his concept of parallels in culture to the stimulus value of ecological conditions in relationship to the stimulus vale of ecological conditions in relationship to environmental conditions– resources etc. [43]

He does not speak of identical conditions but of similar ones and attempts to pick specific focal points in the ecological system and relate them with the social systems–specifically on social organization and its relationship with environment exploitation and cultural core items, i.e., a concept which ties together sociocultural organizational aspects to technology. Steward's emphasis on the persistence of sociocultural organization as a process allows his methodology to be close to Marx yet his concept of multilinearity placers him close to Darwin with the exception of Childe. His reliance on the superorganic concept of culture, however, isolates him from other ecologists who use a Darwinian frame work. [44] Steward, however, feels that one may find in cultural evolution certain regularities or laws; he thus seeks these laws by searching for cultural parallels of a limited occurrence. He says that:

> The methodology of evolution contains two vitally important assumptions. First, it postulates that genuine parallels of form and function develops in historically independent sequences of cultural traditions. Second, it explains these parallels by independent operation of identical causality in each case, the methodology is therefore avowedly scientific and generalizing rather than historical and particularizing. It is less concerned with unique and divergent (or convergent) patterns and features of culture–although it foes not necessarily deny such divergence– than with parallels and similarities which recur cross culturally. It endeavors to determine recurrent patterns and processes and to formulate the interrelations between phenomena in terms of laws [45]

CRITICISMS OF MULTILINEAR CULTURAL EVOLUTION THEORY

One must be sympathetic with Julian Steward"s approach which attempts to deal with objective cultural data and come up with viable conclusions. On the other hand Robert L. Caneiro–a differential evolutionist, criticism is that Steward limits his goals too narrowly and he confuses the evolutionary process itself with methodology has some merit.[46] The fact that Steward deals with the evolutionary problem from a multidimensional field is excellent; however, his reliance on the superorganic theory bears a similar criticism previously given to White's evolutionary approach. Perhaps one of the chief defects in most evolutionary theories, especially the unilinear and universal approaches, is their lack of explanation on the causal source of variation.[47] Since they reject natural selection and postulate no acceptable mechanism for such cultural variations, their theories reflect catalog lists of parts of the developmental process. Recently, to overcome this problem, Marshal Sahlens and, Service have reexamined evolutionary theory and studies specific developmental forms of historical cultural events. They call their approach specific evolution and their concern is the study of a specific sequence of change within a particular society and their search is for causal reasons for such changes, i.e., they want to know not just the chronicle of events but how the culture changes. They speak of the "law of cultural dominance", i.e., great cultural efficience leads to a greater adaptive response to events, and the law of evolutionary potential, whereas less specialized cultures have a greater capacity for change than highly specialized societies. These laws are inspired by biological concepts but they side step any analogy to Darwinian theory by using White's measure of adaptation.[48]

Other scientists would stress the stimulus value of various relationships people and cultures go through. Laura Thompson describes a generalized cultural evolution in which specific cultures interact on an interactional expansive bases; until a mature sociocultural super system is created. [49] She stresses a biopychic base in comprehension of cultural organization and culture change. She says:

> Every distinctive culture system is created or re-created, maintained, transformed, and transmitted by a group of human organisms who are ultimately biologically oriented [and who] tend naturally, although not always success-fully, to use their built-in culture-creating and culture-maintain propensities to move actively in the direction of goals of maintenance, reproduction, and self-actual-ization of the group, as part of a total communal event. The biological goals are keyed to the long range aim of completing the life cycle of the individual components, generation after generation, and their actualizing and perpetuating the life of the community. [50]

One last basic point is worth consideration and that is that all the literature selected shows that the systems discussed so far have a concept of progress as a forward moving force. This concept is simplistic in many ways and assumes an almost orthogenetic power that the facts don't seem warranted, i.e., the fact is that cultures do die, become extinct or nonexistent and technologies, knowl-edge and language become lost. Where is the force of progress when these thing occur? One could argue that since some of the above things pass on to other cultures through diffusion that the cumulative effect is a progressive one—but that argument seems to beg the question. It is true that technologically the species has seemingly progressed, i.e., some cultures have progressed, but spe-cific societies have not, and surely none of the great civilizations—the ancient "high"cultures have survived socio-culturally, with the exception of India and China, but technologically they are classified as technologically backwards as third world countries.

Perhaps progress is not progressive forward. David Bidney makes the point that if one accepts a cyclic evolutionary theory one can retain a belief of evolutionary progress within fixed limits yet not adhere to the concept of indefinite progress in time. [51] Aurobindo's Psychocultural evolution hypothesis, for example, accepts a cyclic theory since he would reject the linear, orthogenetic conceptions of history. Any good evolutionary theory must come to grips with cultural plurality and cultural relativity and develop a value system which will allow objective comparisons of evolutionary processes. Hopefully this research can provide some ideas toward the discovery of viable methodologies to solve the problem.

THE PSYCHOCULTURAL EVOLUTIONARY THEORY

The psychocultural evolutionary theory conceives of the cultural evolutionary process as an emergent evolution of consciousness through a generally progressive cyclic process of three broad stages.[52] These states are not a unilinear progression from one cultural state to another except on a broad time scale. Social evolution depends on human mental evolution that is not constant: therefore specific cultural groups cannot be maintained over long periods of time. Aurobindo, the creator of this theory, says:

> . . . evolution starts with an infrarational stage in which man has not learned to refer their (sic) life and action in its principles and its form to the judgment of the clarified intelligence; for men still act principally out of their instincts, impulses, spontaneous ideas, vital intuitions or else obey a customary response to desire, need and circumstances-it is the things that are canalized or crystallized in their social institutions. Man proceeds by various stages out of these beginnings toward a rational age in which his intelligent will, or less developed, becomes the judge, arbiter and presiding motive of his thought, feeling and action, the smoulder, destroyer and recreator of his leading ideas, aims and

> intuitions. Finally . . . the human evolution must move
> through a subjective toward a suprarational . . . age in which
> he will develop progressively a greater greater . . .
> supraintellectual and intuitive, perhaps in the end a more
> than intuitive, a Gnostic consciousness. [53]

History demonstrates that most of the great civilizations of the past are extinct, and contemporary social orders are constantly changing. Psychocultural evolutionary theory states that cultural evolution is not uniform, gradual or progressive in a unilinear line. It is cyclic. Progression is in an upward-moving spiral, a series of ascents and descents with the gains of the evolutionary process generally kept, even if eclipsed for a time. [54] Periods of sociocultural decline can be fruitful eras in which elements of perfection lacking in an earlier era are worked out and later combined with previously gained aspects when the new curve of progress again occurs through the emergent mental evolution. These stages are not, however, universally consecutive. They may be specific cultural events, or often regional occurrences on a wide culture area scale. [55] These stages " . . . not only rise out of each other, but may be partially developed in each other and they may come to co-exist, in varying stages, in different parts of the earth at the same time." [56]

The psychocultural evolutionary hypothesis postulates three multidimensional evolutionary stages: the infrarational, rational and suprarational.

INFRARATIONAL EVOLUTIONARY STAGE

The infrarational evolutionary stage begins several million years ago, during the late Pliocence or early Pleistocene. The Psychocognitive emergence of early man through a fortuitous mutation began the psychocultural process. Humanity's mental evolution was an emergence from a lower hominoid with its type of undifferentiated consciousness that evolved by a close cooperative interaction among the variables of mind states and psychosocial situational realities.

We know from documented research that man had upright posture and was a savannah-dwelling creature before the expansion of the brain. There is evidence that this expansion was caused by an interaction between toolmaking activities and symbolic thought process, with the resultant development of the forebrain.

Conceptual thought, the development of the forebrain, and the emergence of the concept of separate individuality probably occurred together. A genetic mutation probably occurring during or before this process, seemingly allowed the expansion of rational consciousness in our ancestral types. The Psychocultural evolutionary theory postulates that this process is still going on today.

With the development of the ego sense humanity becomes a true person and a social being by transcending the bond of nature that welds and holds the animal kingdom within a tight web of instinctive behavioral patterns. Sri Aurobindo says:

> Man the individual has to affirm, to distinguish his personality against Nature, to be powerfully himself, to evolve all his human capacities of force and knowledge and enjoyment so that he may turn them upon her and upon the world and with more and more mastery and force. Man's self-discriminating egoism is given him as a means for this primary purpose. [57]

Once humanity became a thinking being who no longer had to react only to an instinctive code, conceptual thought arose and at that moment, lost in the dimness of prehistoric time, a member of the animal kingdom left behind fixed relationships and bondage to undifferentiated consciousness, as well as an absolute relationship to natural selection.

Learned behavior, objective social relationships or social heritage, created through trial and error methods and transmitted from generation to generation, brought humanity into a new world of time, space and death. Knowledge of the transitory nature of life that ends in death became an objective fact. Language arose, creating learned behavior activities that gradually emerged as codes of law, art and social organization. Culture as a supraorganic structure provided a new dimensional reality that, from the late Pliocence or early Pleistocene to the present, has provided the dynamic psychomental paradigm that embraces all human reality.

SOCIAL DYNAMICS

Although cultural groups now had concrete form, psychosocial group dynamics, according to Aurobindo, would be a spontaneous play of the inherent powers and principles of the infrarational evolutionary stage. [58] The cultural dynamics of this stage would be:

> . . . a natural organic development the motive and constructed power coming mostly from the subconscient principle of the life within it, expressing, but without deliberate intention, the communal psychology, temperament, vital and physical need, and persisting or altering partly under the pressure of an internal impulse, partly under that of the environment acting on the communal mind and temper. In this stage the people are not yet intelligently self-conscious in the way of reason, are not yet a thinking collective being . . . but lives according to its vital intuitions or their (sic) first mental renderings. [59]

To emerge from this type of communal life probably took hundreds of thousands of years because the emergent mental process is a slow one. Slowly small groups of vanguard individuals developed "rational" faculties; political, religious, and economic community evolved. Finally about ten thousand years ago, the hunting and gathering stage of existence was left behind by some groups when animal husbandry and agriculture were developed. A sociocultural revolution took place and settled community patterns developed, finally culminating in the emergence of city states. When writing was invented a greater cultural complexity developed and city states emerged into national states, often followed by empires.

THE RATIONAL EVOLUTIONARY STAGE

According to psychocultural evolutionary theory the total rational state of cultural evolution has not yet arrived. All members of the species Homo sapiens have reached the rational state of consciousness but rational-intellectuals do not exist in sufficient numbers to create a truly rational social order. Humanity, thus, exists still in the upper reaches of the infrarational state of evolution. This is a highly sophisticated level in comparison to australopithecine culture but it is still infrarational in nature and content.

All humans today are rational beings but most are not rational-intellectuals. Most rational people use physical-mental or vital-mental cognitive faculties to conceptualize, according to the Aurobindo personality model. The true mental person is the intellectual giant or genius, whereas the average person is a creature of physical and vital desires who has not learned to use his or her higher states of consciousness. Until individuals emerge into a higher state of mental consciousness most cultures will remain infrarational. The emergent evolutionary consciousness is a slow process and totally dependent upon individual development. Aurobindo says:

> . . . only as the individuals become more and more conscious can the group-being also becomes more and more conscious . . . This indeed is the duly importance of the individual that is through him that . . . it raises Nature from the Inconscient to the superconscience and exalts it to meet the Transcendent. In the mass the collective consciousness is near to the inconscient; it has a subconscious, an obscure and mute movement which needs the individual

to express it, to bring it to light, to organize it and make it effective. [60]

The mass of humanity still has not transcended psychophysical or psychoemotional mentality. Aurobindo goes on to say that " . . . human means a vital animal ego metalized by a little outward thought and knowledge." [61] We are today, thousands of years after the development of city states, little advanced beyond our ancestor's psychologically, morally or mentally. Transintegral Psychology contends that:

> . . . most men live in their physical and vital [emotional consciousness], except a few saints and a rather larger number of intellectuals. That is why, as it is now discovered, humanity has made little progress in the last [few] thousand years, except in information and material [science] equipment. A little less cruelty and brutality perhaps, more plasticity of intellect in the elite, a quicker habit of change in form, that is all. [62]

SUPRARATIONAL EVOLUTIONARY STAGE

While no suprarational cultures exist, most near-rational cultures have been influenced by individuals existing in the suprarational sphere of existence. Even today, revivalistic research studies dynamic mystics or prophets who through the charismatic might of their personality lead whole societies at times of social stress and disorganization into new eras of social rebuilding. Such individuals are supramental humans possessing the emergent evolutionary consciousness at the peak of the evolutionary tide.

According to Aurobindo:

> The mass of humanity evolves slowly, containing in itself all stages of the evolution from the material and vital man to the mental man. A small minority has pushed beyond the

barrier, opening the doors . . . and preparing the ascent of
the evolution beyond mental man into . . . supràmental
beings. Sometimes this minority has exercised an enormous
influence as in Vedic India-[or} Egypt . . . and determined
the civilization of the race, giving it a strong stamp of spiritual or the occult; sometimes they have stood apart in their
secret schools or orders, not directly influencing a civilization which has sunk in material ignorance or in chaos and
darkness or in the hard external enlightenment which rejects knowledge [of higher states of consciousness].[63]

At the present time neither suprarational cultures nor any true
rational cultures exist. The research data of Integral historiography reveal however that in some historical periods rational-intellectual men and some suprarational men have predominated in
certain cultures. Their influence was such that great periods of
cultural florescence took place. Such eras were those of Italy of
the Renaissance, Ancient Athens, Republican Rome, Sparta and
19th century Europe.[64]

According to the psychocultural evolutionary theory, these stages
do not emerge in a hierarchical order or by necessarily sequential
steps, and when rational cultures do emerge they are not pure in
their nature. Each stage, in fact, reflects the predominant psychological characteristics of the populace. also infrarational, aesthetic-
ethical and even suprarational themes and ethos may co-exist.

Anthony Wallace has demonstrated that contemporary cultures need not be totally integrated around rigid, harmonious
and functional themes. Conflicting themes and disharmonies may
exist and indeed do exists. From an evolutionary point of view
this is because all sides of the mental life are not simultaneously
developed. [65] Aurobindo says:

There is too here a greater complexity of unseen or half-seen
subconscient or superconscient tendencies and influences
at work upon the comparatively small part of us which is

conscious of what it is doing. And very often a notion in its
self-expression is both helped and limited by what has been
left behind from the evolution of a past self which, being
dead, yet liveth. [66]

Until a culture has a predominant number of the population
living in the rational-intellectual or suprarational awareness consciousness, no long term cultural continuity will exist. Since most
of the world population is infrarational in substance, no stable
psychomental personalities seem able to contribute to world stability. [67] But infrarational man has also a rational and suprarational
aspect to his nature. Aurobindo says that:

> At his animal worst he is still some kind of thinking and
> reflecting animal: even the infrarational man cannot be
> utterly infrarational, but must have some kind of play
> more or less evolved or involved of the reason and a more
> or less crude suprarational element, a more or less dis-
> guised working of the spirit. At his lucid mental best, he
> is still not a pure intelligence; even the most perfect in-
> tellectual is not and cannot exclude, visits or touches of a
> light from above that are not less suprarational because
> he does not recognize their source. [68]

Gradually the infrarational population emerges with a rational-
intellectual faculty and applies its intelligence to the problems of
existence. At first only a few gain this faculty. Eventually the
higher classes of society become true mental creatures and then
this ability spreads throughout the population, gradually leading
whole communities and nations into the mental light. The
psychocultural evolutionary theory postulates, however, that even
these breakthrough cannot bring in a totally rational age.
Aurobindo, commenting on this concept says:

> So long as the hour of the rational age has not arrived, the
> irrational period of society cannot be left behind; and that

arrival can only be when not a class or a few, but the multitude has learned to think, to exercise its intelligence
actively . . . Until then we have as the highest possible development a mixed society, infrarational in the mass, but
saved for civilization by a higher class whose business it is to
seek after the reason and the spirit, to keep the gains of
mankind in these fields, to add to to them as much as possible the life of the whole.[69]

The evolutionary process is a complex one and psychosocial development will vary from culture to culture and from age to age,
according to the dominant and minor themes and the situational
life complexities of each region. Broad themes seem clear from an
examination of the research data. The evidence demonstrates that
an emergence from an infrarational stage into a rational stage
involves either an emphasis on reason or on spirituality as the
dominant power governing society. In ancient Greek civilization
a few philosophers and in a later age the Sophists represented a
tendency toward the former. In prehistoric India, however, a few
great mystics-the Vedic Rishis, with their small circle of Initiates-
brought in the age of the Upanishads from which whole classes of
society later sought the light and guidance of the higher reaches
of altered states of consciousness. [70] The reason some individuals
and cultures seem to by-pass the rational stage is that the capacity
exists within man to contact deeper areas of his being and some
cultures have emphasized this theme. As Aurobindo says"

> The individual as spirit or being is not confined within
> his humanity, he has been less than human, he can be-
> come more than human. The universe finds itself through
> him even as he finds himself in the universe, but he is
> capable of becoming more than the universe, since he
> can surpass it and enter into something in himself and in
> it that is absolute.[71]

This tendency to self-transcendence-the ability to emerge from an

infrarational stage into one in which higher spheres of supernormal consciousness can occur-is a fact according to Aurobindo. This
goal is abnormal for social groups of infrarational men and especially for those who have the Neanderthal flaw. It may succeed in
specific individuals, however, since by an intensity of the inner life
one can out leap the intellect and seem to dispense with it.[72]

> But for humanity at large this movement cannot last: the
> mind and intellect must develop to their fullness so that
> the . . . race may raise securely upward upon a broad
> basis of the developed lower nature in man, the intelli-
> gent mental being.[73]

Even cultures which have emerged into a partially rational-intellectual stage, with their small classes of intellectuals, will collapse
after a while. These early dawns cannot endure in their purity, so
long as the species is not ready.[74] Society will relapse into
infrarational conscious ness and become a death generation; and
an elite group which often must become a covert-secret society
will have to preserve the rational and esoteric traditions of the
culture's past glory. Until the masses themselves emerge into a
rational consciousness stage, the rational-intellectual age will not
come into being. The infrarational death barbarians and their
death Masters from without or ignorant masses with their death
cadres from within will destroy culture after culture. Aurobindo
point out that:

> Civilizations can never be safe so long as, confining the
> cultured mentality to a small minority, it nourishes in its
> bosom a tremendous mass of ignorance, a multitude, a
> proletariat. Either knowledge must enlarge itself from
> above or be always in danger of submergence by the ig-
> norant night from below.[75]

SUPRARATIONAL STAGE

According to psychocultural evolutionary theory the true rational state of cultural evolution has not yet arrived. All members of the species Homo sapiens have reached the rational state of consciousness but rational-intellectuals do not exist in sufficient numbers to create a truly rational social order. Aurobindo says however, that supramanhood "is not man climbed to his own natural zenith, not a superior degree of human greatness, knowledge, power, intelligence, will, . . . genius, . . . saintliness, love, purity or perfection."[76] "It is something else, another vibration of being, another consciousness"[77]

The human race stands upon a pinnacle of opportunity presently ; yet it must be noted that the evolutionary stress is still with the species. anthropologist Jules Henry says that:

> The ascent of man from the lower animals and the brutality of 'civilized' history show that Nature has destined man to move from one misery to another: but the record proves also that man has sometimes been forced by misery into enlightenment although he has never accepted it without a bitter fight. This, perhaps, is Nature's plan for Homo sapiens, until some time hence, if he has not destroyed himself, he will realize, through misery, that destiny of perfection she holds mysteriously in store for him.[78]

Today humanity exists still in the upper reaches of the infrarational state of.evolution. This is a highly sophisticated level in comparison to Australopithecine culture but it is still infrarational in nature and content. And presently the dark beast of humanity's unregenerated unconscious is emerging as an apocalyptic Genocide Phenomenon that grips the species in it tentacles of death and destruction.

CHAPTER 10

DEATH CHILDREN

FUTURIST COMMENTARY: The 22nd century owes a debt of gratitude to the death generation and its creative destruction of the United States of America. If it were not for their courageous destruction of 20th century American family life our utopian society would have been still born. Our 22nd century readers ought to read Campbell's analysis with care and attentiveness.

Campbell, the cultural Anthropologist, touches on the phenomenon of the death children as a touch-stone to demonstrate that a kinship organization of a people is the core structure through which a culture has life and vitality. For example if you want to learn about the relationship between ideal behavior and the beliefs of a people and their actual behavior, study their kinship system; also through such a study you can make historical reconstructions, or possibly make sense of why people interact in the ways they do. Often through a study of kinship terms a new understanding of how a people view their world and make classification of parts of it are learned. [1] Additionally such studies are of primary importances because of it utilization in scientific theories such as matrix-centered and kinship-centered. Murdock, discovered general postulates of kinship behavior from which specific "theorems" emerge to demonstrate how science can predict or formulate laws of behavior. Of major importance is the fact that functional theory uses kinship studies to show how parts of culture are interrelated and how religion, economics, politics or other facets of culture are related. From such studies it is now clear that different culture complexes are integrated and by studying changing kinship patterns systems you may observe the process of a culture in change. One of the reason for such observations is that kinship may serve as a map or model for human behavior and such studies are vitally important in understanding theories of cognition, not only how kin relations exist but how the world view is conceived.

For example one day two Australian aborigines meet but the first thing they do is determine how they are related. They must know their proper relationship to even exchange greetings. When these two aborigines first met Europeans they killed them because this was the only conceivable behavior to do when facing a nonrelative. Today when one death child faces another he kills him if he is not related to him by gang or corporate relationships.[2]

These types of studies are now popular in the 22nd century because of the Death generations experimentation with Clan Corporations. When the death generation had complete power they divided the United States into regional sections and assigned 700 corporation Clans to absorb and take over the technological population. The rest of the population were labeled underclass filth, and made non-citizens and classified as traitors who ultimately had to undergo ethnic and underclass cleansing through the genocide process.

Corporation clan members lived their entire lives within the confines of their corporate order unless they were sold to another corporation. They were forbidden to have children except through the corporate cloning process which allowed their children to be processed and enculturated into the corporate mentality. In actuality what this means is that they were sold into involuntary servitude, mentally, physically and emotionally. Within this structure were gradations of intellectual abilities. The Death corporation would decide if your child was to be a corporate executive or a factory drone with limited mental facilities or possibly a corporate prostitute. Naturally all clones were sterilized.

Non corporate clan members were at first allowed to reproduce naturally but periodical attempts later were made to sterilize them as a means to fit them within the Death Generations extinction peril concepts.

Campbell discusses the death children below in one of his more popular talks.

THE DEATH CHILDREN

Twentieth Century man has produced a new death peril, an extinction peril that rises up from the loins of America and seals America's destiny. When your children betray you and murder you and malign you and destroy what you hold holy, you have been dealt a death blow from which you will never recover . Life perishes for you and your children when the genocide Phenomenon's culture of death grips you and destroys your sacred relationship to your children.. Nothing shall help you but death itself and from death expect nothing but terror and destruction. Some say that death will eliminate your terror of your children and allow you to escape from the responsibilities of your deeds!

Do you believe that? Do you think you can run away from your destiny. Ah, poor deluded ones that still think that there is hope in your death children's actions and that you can turn the social tide back and that the sun will stop on your command! Fools! Wake up and become alarmed at your situation and stop living like sleeping zombies because your very life and your country's future rests on what you do and become in the next few years.

It is written that our future children shall rise up into the stars and that joy and abundance shall be theirs as they live the abundant life of joy and love; yet the fact is that today 20th century American culture lies dead upon the moral perversity of its children and its old people. Yet some folk critics say the parents brought it upon themselves by treating their own old folks with disdain and moral corruption and they but reap the whirl wind; and that they started the abuse with that common 20th century scenario of kicking mama out of the house so the kids could have a TV room; but some critics say this but begs the question about the overt manifestion of the destruction of the American family while others say that by physically abusing our old in our own homes then putting them in abusive old folks home we but punish ourselves in a masochistic urge of self destruction which comes back to us through our children. For truly we are one, they say and a welt and wolf on one part of the social body finds expression covertly on the seemingly healthy part of the social fabric.

No modern 20th century family takes care of their parents, therefore no modern family truly takes care of their children; no modern 20th century family truly knows or embraces its children; no close family truly exists in this century; but family death waits on no man but proceeds forward as its destroys the very fabric of American social life.

Where there is no family continuity you may find the death of the culture just around the historical corner.

Only in American culture do you find the youth randomly shooting down fellow youths, babes in arms and old people down in the street through drive by shootings. Only in America do you find teenagers kicking down the doors of 95 year woman to rape her while beating her to death! Only in America does the perversity of death take on the face of a teenager.

These acts are harbingers of the death of American Culture. The American cult of youth has finally arrived at its ultimate destination in the symbolic cannibalistic act of species suicide!

These dead zombies of the youth culture, through drugs and

dysfunctional cultural living are the signs of the times and mark well America that your time has come! You have been found wanting and death awaits you at the next corner!

But Beware children of America that mama and papa bear does not first attempt to devour you also and cast you out as an exile forevermore! For your corrupt parents will not die graciously and will rise up and devoir their own; their only flesh and blood children. Remember this is the generation that is sexually and emotionally abusing you and killing you on the killing fields of war and have corruption for their middle name and expediency is their guide and if their children can not be utilized as canon fodder to their perverse needs and urges they will destroy them.

They will place curfews upon you and put you in concentration or retraining camps, drug you and put you in mental warehouse hospitals , they will perform psychic-surgery on you and give you electroshock treatments; they will take away your designer clothes and make you wear uniforms to school, and hang you and kill you and destroy you if need be and if that doesn't work they will cease having children.

Yes, children of the death generation remember America's 75 million guns ride in the hands of your victims and there will come a time when the stalker will become the prey and death will be the mode of the day as the average American joins the crowd of Mad dog killers and by that very action they will becomes bonfire, card carrying members of the death generation!

Remember death children that in a materialistic culture throwaway children are but commodities to either be destroyed or replaced if they don't conform to the system. Already 700,000 + children disappear yearly, seemingly from the face of the earth in America, but does any one care. Why should anyone care-these are throwaway kids; the only concern people have about them is their displeasure at having to hear about them on television occasionally. " God" they think "what a bore, what dribble', what nonsense. Damn kids deserve whatever they get!"

Modern America does not fair well with its children and rejects them in ways unimaginable to past generations. It is a known fact that children compete with the purchase of material goods and no family in America can do without its glittering toys of joy.

So is it any surprise that the breakdown of American culture should first come from the younger generating? Is it any surprise that the death of American culture shall be spoken of from the mouth of a child.

From the mouths of children, these prophets of doom speak the truth to us if we would but listen and if we do not listen then like Cassandra's audience of old we stand condemned to die the slow death of agony.

Our anxiety will be our daily joy and our despair will be our guide and our truth shall be doom and gloom. For by that time life will be but a series of disbelieveable categories of nothingness and our only refuge will be oblivion as a people and a culture.

If you would know the reality of America's situation realize that your children are rejecting their parents as superfluous because the crude and terrible blackness of despair that faces each American in the face daily now takes Mama's and Daddy's name.

What you are America reflects in the face and actions of your drive by shooting children. They are you in your most despicable forms and as children of their parents their youth betrays them as they must be what they are and hide nothing from us. For they are our death staring us in the face and we stare back in disbelief and shutter in fear at our worst fears standing before us as we melt a little and die to ourselves all the more; for we know the end has finally arrived and there is nothing we can do to stop our destiny.

We are the death generation and soon the copses of our people will be rotting on our streets as our children laugh with glee and rejoice at our bewilderment and fear. For our children are the cutting edge of the death generation and nobody can stop them and death holds no fear to them; in fact it is graciously embraced by them. For death is their mother and perversion is their father and their prey are their parents and all life that surrounds them.

They are America's fifth column and they gleefully go about

their job of death and destruction as the average American tittles his thumbs in despair as he operates his television monitor changer.

These children know they are inwardly dead and it is but a matter of time before their corpse lies dead and broken on some city street; for these children are the visual representatives of what America is inside and their stoic faces reflect the soul-quality of the American spirit.

Death is upon the waters of life and the forces of destruction rejoice for mankind is down for the final count and oblivion faces the species and there is no one to cry out to for help !

Death seemingly will devour our race and what remains will be but broken artifacts that convey nothing of our greatness but reveal only the sorrowful plait of our death.

There will come a time when parent and child will grasp in terror their relationship to each other. Then there will even be a period of peace before the final death agony when child and mother, father and daughter will clasp each other in desperation, yet dying together in their final death of separations as their redemption flows forth between child, parent, children and their parents.

But do you think this process is easy or even productive? Do you think it comes about by idle wishes or sick desires that carries hate as its guide and desperation as its goal. No I say, throw yourselves into the life of the spirit and embrace life as your guide. Let truth and honor grasp you by the hand so that integrity might guide your relationships.

Right relationship to yourself and to others require a balanced personality and a sense of purpose in life. It requires you to be at peace with yourself and that you view your fellow mankind as social parts of yourself.

American society are you ready to face yourself? Are you willing to examine your ill personality parts? Will you walk that extra mile toward your inner self?

All these things face you America as the blood of your children drips drop by drop before your very eyes!

Is this the blood of the redemption of the race or the death blood of the race? Will drops of death be our future or will we climb up the drops of death to this source and find redemption through the sacrificial blood of the lamb of the American spirit.

Cry America for you are bleeding to death drop by drop and let it be said that many will rejoice at your demise as eternity checks off another failed social experimentation!

The modern age is the abode of the death children who have emerged from out of the chaos of this century. They are America's future and destiny. They are what America desires and will get; they are America's chickens coming home to roost.

Now the child with his semiautomatic gun can gun down the old and decrepit grandmother and feel no pangs of regrets or sense of having done anything wrong. It is as if they are saying, "The old hag shouldn't have been in my way, that child crying is better off dead, and that man sleeping in his bedroom got his just deserts during our random drive by shooting. What the hell; you only live once; so shoot and stomp whom ever is in your way. Why worry about such small matters when such great concerns of whether the pizza is ready to eat or is our beer cold or is there some bitches available for sex or do we have enough gas to keep the car running tonight, are ever before us to solve."

The death children are you and I and we are 'America's destiny of death. We are the rot and destruction and desolation that modern man deserves. We are the just deserts of an America dying to itself as it slowly hemorrhage to death as she smiles the sweet smile of death. We are the ultimate culmination of a people so corrupt that their own children slay them in cold blood as they smile with joy at the sweet facts of America 's death. We are a generation of perverts and degenerates; a Godless people who rejoice in that fact as we suffer in quiet desperation each minute of our miserable existence even as we pray in every church in America. We are the loyal churchgoers who have rejected the forces of God as we clasp our Bibles to our bussom in our holy than thou smirks of satisfaction.

We are the parents of the death generation. We are the perverts who bore the life germs that will devour us and we are as covertly guilty as if we were pulling the trigger or the lever to the gas ovens or guillotine that will massacre millions of us in the future as we cry out for salvation from ourselves. We are the perversion that is a blight upon the land and we shall fulfill our mandate to be the last generation of free Americans

There will come a day when harmonious parent children relationship occur–that day has yet to arrived! Know this America that the fate of the world lies upon your shoulders and the destiny of the human species lays before you. This is a fact of life and ye may not escape from these conclusions. Oh ye of faint heart stand up and become a man of destiny and the world shall become clear to your inner sight and ye shall rise to the occasion. Can you succeed or must you fail as ye weep and wail and cry in bereavement at your inadequacies?

Well what can we do about this situation? Is there any hope left? Perhaps we can attack the problem by first examining American child rearing concepts; perhaps there is still time left for us to do the right thing!

MAKING THE AMERICAN CHILD

Underlying American child rearing techniques is the monstrous concept of the primordial fear syndrome because no American child is ever truly reared as a person of absolute certitude who has internal strength of fortitude and can say in his heart that come what may I will be supported and loved. No, each child is a provisional child fighter who must prove himself to his parents and the world. He is a child under siege who must accomplish Herculean feats of heroism in the light of the parents eyes and stand up against the hostile world as a savior of his own integrity and sense of being. He can not fail or he is a "nobody" and cast into the piles of desolate no-bodies which litter the land of opportunity. He cannot fail because his very sense of ego and self and personhood and his very being of existence rest on success in life and on his sense of being loved for what he accomplishes. He will never be loved for himself. Love is given him for his accomplishments after it is done.

The child and the man must savor his successes because there will come a time when what he has achieved in life will be tattered and possibly forgotten or at the very best idolized by the statement-"but what have you done lately." Later in life when he is a" has been", his previous accomplishments may give him some status or people may be look down upon because he may have been partially perceived to have received some unusual luck, or have unduly influenced someone, or perhaps out right cheated or have been thought of only as a person who temporarily arrived, had his 15 minutes of glory, and can now be kicked out of the way.

Oh, nobodies on the way up the ladder of success will perhaps idealize him partially and give him some honor but those now on the top or rising contenders will have at best only grudging respect for him; but more than likely will have covert contempt for this has-been who is now only a litter-obstacle barring their own way upward to the highway to success. President Truman couldn't even get one network to record his memoirs as he ended his last presidential term; why? He was now a nobody and every one knows that nobodies have not only nothing to say but are socially putrid and may cast bad luck upon a person, and to be seen with one or worse yet to be seen talking with one is almost as if you were interacting with some type of pervert., And worse still you may be judged by the concept of guilt by association; one never wants to die a quiet social death by association with a social outcast person of defeat.

So we have a small child born into a family who is being conditioned to become a man in a world of rivals who desire nothing more than to step on him and humiliate him and to cast him down as a defeated person or to score an educational coup against him by grabbing that Sunday school honor, or running over him on the football field so that they might themselves achieve status and success. This is the American way, so the child must not stumble in his march for success and if he does he must get up and walk that extra mile until he triumphs over all obstacles and difficulties and proves to himself and the world that he is a success and worthy of acclaim. If he cannot rise up from his failures he is just so much cannon fodder; he is now the example of what not to be and the despicable icon that the all Americans must shun and walk away from and even fear that his failures might rub a little off on him; because to receive his taint of cowardliness would reveal to yourself and the world that you might not have the real stuff either.. Don't catch that fear; don't fall into the cavernous canyon of defeat or you will become the leper of failure and be despised the rest of your days.

The child enters a world of social competition in which his sense of being and life purpose revolve around his varible ego personality which rest socially on what other people think about him. His intrapsychic conflicts lie hidden and he will only be judged on his outward social success. He will never be loved for himself alone but always be judged in terms of his achievements. The child's social and psychological life force will always rest on the intangible spectrum of success and failure in life and always he is just barely above falling into the dark depths of the abyss of failure and nonbeing. This primordial fear-anxiety syndrome of fear of failure is the cornerstone of American life. It is the underlying principle of American life, it is the fear that probes everyone one forward in his life achievements. But the most insidious aspect of the success syndrome is that success equals out to mean love or at the very least being worthy of being love. To be loved by one and all means to be successful in life. But to achieve this love-success, often in the inner cities, means that it is achieved negatively in opposition to the traditional ways to achieve success, such as when a gang makes a kid's successful through allowing him to sell drugs; yet he is also a success in the eyes of his peers and that is all that matters. If he has to put his very life on the line for this success-no matter. He must be somebody and a person of economic substance, if only for a day, a week, a month or a year. Then he can die content on some lonely street, his blood running into the gutter of failure before he is cast upon the large pile of" has beens," and thus he become a nobody who deserved all he got in society's eyes! But in one respect he falls into one category all Americas know they will occupy upon death which is that he will be completely forgotten. Each person's achievement in life, all the good or bad he did now falls into insignificance as he is finally a dead nobody; and although he may have been a somebody in life he is now by his death only an insignificant other whose memory is cast into the pit of social forgetfulness.

The primordial fear-anxiety syndrome, the covert side of personal and worldly success and honor and self-esteem, rules America from the time a child is born until he dies. It is the force that drive the nation and is the fear of failure that dogs every word of praise a child receives and every honor he acquires and every success he garners in life. Without this fear-anxiety syndrome he would not even try to outdistance his peers or strive for greatness or make his stand for or against the world. Mighty is the teleological call to fame and fortune in America but mightier indeed is its opposite, the primordial fear-anxiety syndrome which rests on piles of victims and it shall be mighty and fearsome all the days of your life.

Death and violence are covert themes throughout the social order and our formal and informal institutions and death children reject these themes as powerful cultural forces shape and manipulate the American people. But the forces of death and alienation are also strong cultural forces of indoctrinate which the culture also uses to socialize our children formally.

We indoctrinate children early with tales of fairy tale violence of death and cannibalism and terror of almost unimaginable fiercely. Then we place our impressionable children of light and goodness in front of a television set, usually used as a surrogate baby-sitter in modern life, where our children watch the most unimaginable violence in the cartoons and regular television adult programs they watch. Recently they have accepted a children's program x rangers in which a corps of karata and supernaturalism combine to bring violence into the hearts and minds of our dear children. The program shown in such a context without the constraining influence of a master teacher to instill ethics and control the violence as dance exercises of shadow boxing; thus the program pollutes the children by overwhelming them by the violence and they emulate it in everyday life. Recently three young boys kicked a young girl to death. Now several countries around the world refuse to let the program be aired to impressible children.

Then we push the youth into organized sports such as football with its controlled violence that leaves broken bodies and death zombies with repeated head conclusions and back and knee injuries throughout our culture. Football for modern Americans is the equivalent of watching the Roman gladiators tear each other apart as we get that adrenalin thrill at raw primitive savagery. Boxing is another sport in which modern man must feel the sheer terror of brute force cursing through his veins ands vicariously picture himself as the rugged individual facing a fearsome opponent in a life and death situation where one could be maimed or seriously injured or killed. But at least in boxing when one of the combatants receives a head concussion he cannot box until he is well, but in football you are a commodity of controlled violence and you will get up and play again, immediately if possible, next week if necessary and when they wheel your crippled body eventually away, they think not of your almost dead and useless body but of your replacement. Everybody is a replaceable and interchangeable gear in sports as in industry; but the game of life must march on at a fast pace and none may stand in progresses way because that would be unAmerican and uncivilized. Besides if America didn't vicariously experience their controlled violence weekly their emotional stress and depression would not be temporarily relieved, thus not allowing them to endure another meaningless week of work terror. Americans are so dead inside that mass observation sports are an addiction and they must have this thrill of the sports battle or they cannot rise above their inner discontents and vent their frustrations during the game.

America's death children go one step further than their parents, that is, they actually vent their frustration through death rituals in which they temporarily rise above their death personalities. In 'England our American cousins go one step further by having murderous riots with other spectators at the games, in which death and maiming have become part of the social ritual. In America, isolated from each other through the television or even in the stadiums violence is still vicarious but each spectator of the game must feel the thrill of the adrenalin and the thrill of the battle. If this does not happen then American's inner consciousness gradually reveals to each and everyone his chains and shackles and he will no longer think of himself as free and independent and autonomous, that is, in his off work hours. No longer will he be able to keep up the charade and depression and cultural malaise will manifest more rapidly than it is doing presently and then he will cry louder and louder until his screams of terror will ring throughout the land.

CHILD REARING

In order to understand our death children we must examine child rearing concepts utilized during our nation's history, up to the present, so that we may better understand how we got to the point where our death children can kill their parents and other children with joy in their hearts and a smile of triumph on their faces and truly feel that what they are doing is morally correct and proper!. Even though modern child rearing ideas differ from many we will discuss they may retain a greater hold upon our values and actual thought processes and influence us unconsciously to a degree which we may not like to acknowledge.

We will first examine child-rearing literature between 1820 and 1960 and gradually arrive at the present American child rearing ideas.

The concept of rearing a child in America was considered a rational process if certain procedures were followed. Child-rearing theory was based on Calvinism techniques which attempted to rationally mold the child in the directions of a moral, independent individual who was an honest and religious person who would make a fine citizen. It was felt that the child was an extension of parental ambitions and a representative of his parents social status.

During this time period established patterns of social living were being disturbed by the rapid development of industrialization and urbanization but along with these changes came the growing belief in man's power to control the environment and direct the future including the power to mold children to their parents desires.[3]

The mother's role was felt to be the prime person who molded the child's character during his first six years of life.[4] It was felt that any thing she did with the child shaped it future existence.[5] The mother had to keep her heart and innocence pure and govern her feelings at all time according to Lydia Child in the 1830's.[6] Lydia Sigourney, a writer of advanced views also spoke of the "immensity of the mother's trust in raising a child" and of how this period was the mothers arena of perfect enjoyment. She writes she is "to nurture the infant . . . as a germ quickened by Spring, it opens the folding doors of its little heart . . . like timid tendril, seeking where to twine."[7] Hall in 1849 emphasizes that "yes mothers, in a certain sense, the destiny of a redeemed world is put into your hands; it is for you to say, whether your children shall be respectable and happy here and prepared for a glorious immortality, or whether they shall dishonor you, and perhaps bring your grey hairs in sorrow to the grave, and sink down themselves at last to eternal despair."[8]

It was felt that the mothers eternal voice would act as a conscience throughout the child's life but that the mother must also exercise discipline as well as love in bringing up the child. And gradually she took over much of the disciplining of the children in the home as urbanization and industrialization occurred as the father became more occupied with work. Some writers emphasize, however that often the mother devoted herself to the infant and neglected the older children because the mother was failing to receive the love and gratification in her marriage. [9]

Writers tell us that gradually during this period fathers spent most of their time away from home and had little to do with their children.[10] The mother, therefore daily taught the children but handled the daily disciplinary problems rather than waiting for the father to come home. Daily religious observances, previously done by the father were less and less practiced with the mother gradually taking over this function.[11]

Corporal punishment of children was widespread throughout the country with the father usually administering it in the home and teachers in the school room. It was widely practiced within the school system until a campaign headed by Lyman Cobble lessened it use but also by the 1860's women had basically replaced male teachers.[12] At this time a similar shift occurred inside and outside of the home with the wife taking over the physical punishment which seemed to have gradually been replaced with other forms of discipline. But even the laws emphasized that disobedience to parents or authorities by children, as well as older children, not only carried significant fines but could lead to the death penalty. A 1954 Massachusetts law stated:

> If any children above sixteen years old and of sufficient understanding shall curse or smite their natural father or mother shall be put to death, unless it can be sufficiently testified that the parents have been unchristianly negligent in the education of such children or so provoked them by extreme and cruel correction that they have been force there unto to preserve themselves from death or maiming (Bremmer 1970, P. 68)[13]

FEEDING AND THE DANGERS
OF STUFFING AND DRUGGING

Breast feeding was urged by most experts during this period but the use of the milk bottle was wide spread among the middle and upper economic groups with wide spread use of the wet nurse whom were recruited from the lower classes, usually unwed mothers. Although it was felt that their were dangers in this policy since it was felt that the poor were fretful because of the influences of "the mother's ill-governed passions transmitted through the milk." [14]

The use of artificial feeding became popular and by 1860 the first good formula, "Liebig's" came into use as the rubber nibble was patented in 1845.

The children were weaned between eight to twelve months with the deed done over one or two week period. Most mothers weaned their children in cold weather to avoid the dangers of exposing the child to cholera infantum and other intestinal diseases. [15]

Travelers from abroad observed during this period that bottle fed babies were overfed with supplementary feelings of cake, candy, pap, which consisted of moistened bread or meal, as it was widely felt by mothers that food was mother's love. [16] Observers noted, however that the primary reason for overfeeding was to quiet the baby. There were no regular feeding hour as the feeding schedule was instituted for the mothers convenience. [17]

Drugs were widely given to infants to keep them from crying and to put them to sleep and used also in patent medicines to remedy a variety of sickness. One contemporary writer describes this drug use as "the bane of infants and young children is laudanum [a form of opium] . . . which is the basis of all quack medicine and given almost indiscriminately in this country to infants, from the moment they are born–till–I may say –the day of their death." [18] Another writer talking about laudanum says, "If improper food has slain its hundreds, Godfrey's Cordial has slain it thousands." [19]

Alcohol was also used to keep children quiet, that is, home-made alcohol as well as patent medicine alcohol formulas were used as was Laudanum by working mothers to keep their children sleeping while they were working. Apparently this practice was so widespread that many infant deaths were officially attributed to opium. An inquest in 1837-38 showed that fifty-two infants out of one hundred and eighty-six deaths were due to opium.[20]

MOTOR DEVELOPMENT
AND INDEPENDENCE

During this period swaddling and modified swaddling was practiced. This consisted of using layers of flannel and wool in addition to bands and the use of heavy clothing. The ends of the garments were tied to prevent movement of hands and feet so the baby was shaped properly and kept warm "like in the womb. [21] Most child-rearing literature of this period suggested that the child have free movement and loose light clothing.[22]

Most babies slept in cradles and were additionally rocked a great deal; so much so that one British observer speculated Americans restlessness as adults was due to the violent rocking he experienced in infancy.[23]

Parents often forced their children to perform beyond their physical and mental levels and wouldn't allow the children to crawl. Walkers and leading strings were used to get them to walk.[24] Mental precociousness was also valued so they could be exhibited before company.

A child was encouraged to be independent and allowed to feed themselves from a cup from a very early age and by ten to fifteen months they already sat at the family dinner tables in their high chairs; a fact that foreign travelers from abroad found repellent because of the baby's noise and his constant grabbing for food as the rest of the family were eating.[25]

A parents perennial problem has always been a crying baby;

who it was felt best to let it cry itself out rather than rush and pick it up because this way you broke the child's will. [26] But one school of thought advised parents to let the child cry but eventually go to it because it was felt a certain amount of crying was good exercise for the baby., that is, it strengthened the lungs.[27] The use of drugs and other Calvinist moral development techniques were also used. And as the child grew he was encouraged to develop his independence by arousing his curiosity. Up to school age it was advised to interest him in nature studies and nature collections and to urge it to examine his environment. [28]

Early toilet training was urged and it was generally felt that early success was a credit to the child and to the parents. It was felt that extreme neatness and cleanliness and orderliness in a child was for the best.

Masturbation was felt to be a serious problem which would lead to disease, insanity, and even death in boys and in girls it was felt to promote promiscuity, precocious sexual development and nymphomania. Extreme attempts to curb this practice included slitting the penis, clitoris removal, or cutting the genitalia nerves in both sexes.[29] This danger was applied to young as well as older children. The parents feared the semi-illicit juvenile books which were thought to excite children sexually. It was felt that genitals should only be touched for strictly hygienic purposes.[30] But generally it was felt that children learned how to masturbate through spontaneous sexual play with other children or by being inducted or seduced into such activities by servant, slaves or depraved school children of the lower classes. A comment by one writer says:

> The coarse hugging, kissing, etc. which the children are sure to receive in great abundance from ignorant and low-minded domestics are certain to develop a blind precocious sexualism of feeling andaction, which tends directly to all the evils I have mentioned on the maturity of those offspring, and sometimes in sudden disease and death to little ones. [31]

Catherine Beecher, in 1846 explains that in bringing up children certain difficulties present themselves such as " . . . the low and depraved character of a great portion of those who act as nurses for young people. One single vulgar, or deceitful, or licentious domestic may in a single month mar the careful and anxious training of years."[32]

The rationale for such ideas was the Calvinist doctrine of "infant depravity," which says an infant was surely destined to sin unless guidance by parents took place. External corruption could also influence children; so solitary prayer and Bible reading by young children was encouraged. Hopefully these activities would counteract a child's desire to masturbate but a parent was never sure. One day a parent entered her child's room precipitately and saw the child change her position rapidly. And when the child wouldn't tell mother what she had been doing. The mother said, "But little children who do not like to tell what they are doing are in great danger of doing something they are ashamed of." But the now wounded child answered Mother thus, "Oh no, mother, I was only going to pray a little while." [33] This problem is with us today as President Clifton has recently fired the United States surgeon-general for frankly answering a question on masturbation.

INFANT DEPRAVITY

Moral training of children rested on the Calvinist theory of infant depravity which other Protestant sects, such as the Methodist, congregationalist, Presbyterians and others also believed in and adhered to during this era. This concept stated that the child was born "totally depraved" and would experience depravity throughout his life unless his parents gave careful and strict guidance which ultimately would lead to being saved through Grace. [34] One New Englander pointed out that "No child has ever been known since the earliest period of the world, destitute of an evil disposition–however sweet it appears. [35]

Parents must at all times have complete obedience and submission of their children if they are to be kept from sin. The parents have a sacred duty toward the child, that is, the safety and health of the child depends on the child's complete submission to the parents. Additionally such submission is necessary so the child's submission will allow it to accept unquestioningly the positive virtues of religion until his reasoning faculties are developed.

Parents get the complete submission of their children by breaking their will; and will is any defiance of parents wishes, at any age or time. "The very infant in your arms will sometimes redden and strike, and throw back its head, and stiffen its little rebellious will." [36] At all times the child must be denied his wishes because his desires are sinful and depraved. It was thus the duty of parents to learn techniques for breaking the will.

Numerous Protestant-Calvinist sects developed support groups of mothers who explored child-rearing problems. Throughout the United States, on the frontier and in foreign lands though the wives of missionaries, these groups defined the rules of breaking children's wills for the glory of God. Groups of "Maternal Associations spontaneously developed over the country, generally in the middle-income class, as magazines published by these organizations had wide circulation. [37]

The principle concerns of these organizations was in developing concepts of breaking the will of the child and in infant conversion. When a child professed adherence to God as an adult would it was felt that progress was being achieved. Generally it was felt that the child should be cared for tenderly for the first three months of life and possibly up to a year before his will was to be broken. But then, "Establish your will, as the law". And when the child refuses to obey a command the parent must win out! It was a fatal flaw in childhood training to let any child win over his parents. In 1834, in the Mother's Magazine, the proper procedure to breaking a child's will was illustrated. One day a sixteen month old child was ordered to say "dear Mama" by her father. When she refuse she was led into room where she screamed wildly for ten minutes. When she again refuse to say "dear Mama" she was whipped and given another chance to properly respond to her father. She refused and was subsequently whipped for several hours until she obeyed. [38] Margaret Mead has made the point that in the Western world children are traumatized in childhood in way for which we have no ritual healing to undo the damage; even though psychiatric techniques are often applied to undo the damage. Generally a trauma in childhood is perceived as causing mental damage or intolerable yearnings which must be solved at a later time or solved within the loneliness that all traumatized victims suffer. [39]

Most parent report that after such trials the child becomes permanently submissive. But not all parents used beating to gain submission as gentle drills were used which consisted of refusing to give a child what he wanted or by keeping a child's desired object just out of his reach, no matter how much he cried. [40] It is reported that some mothers didn't do their duty and were exhorted to become proper mothers.

Behind these child rearing procedures always loomed the desire for infant conversion which demonstrated a child's acceptance of the truths of religion that he was well on his way toward being "saved". But parents did not consider quick conversions as sound; a more gradual process was thought proper. But when the child began to practice solitary prayer and read the Bible it was felt that the conversion was more authentic. [41] And when those rare few became devoutly religious they were held up as models even when all their vitality and desires were drained and they met early death, usually by age ten.

Indulgence had to be shunned since it was equivalent to spoiling but religiously it was related to depravity. It was felt that "Men are made monsters in life by indulgence in infancy." [42] If you gave into child's indulgence you helped natural depravity and jeopardized the future of the child who more than likely would end up tyrannizing the family.

Another theory was also present in child raising and that was the theories of Locke who was widely influential. The theory of "hardening" of child , also was influenced by Rousseau and not rooted in religion but accepted as a proper procedure of fostering "naturalness" of childhood behavior. [43] A child must become vigorous and strong and unspoiled. Cold baths and cold plunges were necessary so the child would become strong like the settlers in the early days of the country. [44]

A third minority theory of child raising existed that advocated gentle treatment of the child which derived from English and European movements. A child was to be led and counseled to do the right thing and not commanded but persuaded through understanding and justice. Rewards and encouragements, not beatings, slaps , shaming or reproaches were to be used always. The parents must always understand the motive behind a child's behavior. Corporal punishment didn't bring about desired results, thus, was discouraged; also a child was felt to be too tender for such punishment. The child was to be looked at as if he were "an immortal bud just commencing to unfold its spotless leaves . . . a beautiful flower opening to the sunshine."[45] This approach thus didn't try to break the child's will as he was only ignorant of right behavior . If the parents were firm it eliminated obedience problems. They thus modified the Calvinist attitude by denying infant depravity but urged to keep a good environment for the child since "bad propensities and evil within and without were still present in the world. Corporal punishment was undesirable but a shift in attitude was gradually taking place so that by 1844 even "Mother's Magazine talks about modifying the strict obedience training by telling parents to mingle more with their children and to enter into and understand their feeling. They felt though that such actions would not lessen parental authority. [46]

One of the most basic trends found throughout these three theories is that the mother was expected to take over almost entirely the upbringing of the child as the role of the father declined. Mother's love was no longer unconditional but conditioned upon the child's obedience to mothers standards. Mother became the Mama-boss and instilled her feminine conscience into each child she conditioned in life.

FUN MORALITY

From 1910 to 1951 child rearing concepts changed because of the changing ideas about human impulses and the transformation of American moral outlook and these concepts were reflected in the concept of fun morality. Fun no longer is suspect but obligatory and instead of feeling guilty for having too much fun one feels ashamed if one does not have enough fun. The formerly strict separation between work and play also breaks down as amusements infiltrate into the spheres of work and play. But the Primordial fear-anxiety factor now enters play as it had previously entered work, so that self-estimates of achievement become prominent in one play activities. Even though this concept appears to be in conflict with the older puritan ethic they are related even though fun morality exemplifies a significant moral change in child rearing ideas as presented by the United States Department of Labor Children's Bureau. An examination of the 1914, 1921, 1929, 1938 and 1942 , and 1951 issues of "Infant Care bulletins of the Children's Bureau demonstrates the changing concept of how to raise a child. We will basically highlight the changes between 1914 and 1942 presently. [47]

The "Infant Care Bulletin of 1914 emphasizes that the infant has strong and dangerous impulses; specifically autoerotic, thumb-sucking and masturbate. [48] It is predicted that if the parents interferes with the child's dangerous impulses he will be "rebelling fiercely." [49] Impulses it is warned will grow beyond the parent's control.[50] And then the child may be" wrecked for life." [51] The parents are also counseled that the baby may be controlled by his dangerous impulses or seduced into them through given pacifiers to suck or by having his genitals stroked by that" infamous nurse."[52] The mother, therefore, is advised to be ceaselessly vigilant in her battle against the child's sinful nature. Masturbation "must be eradicated,..treatment consists in mechanical restraints." The child's legs must be tied to each side of the crib so he cannot rub his thighs together and his nightgown sleeves must also be pinned to the bed so he can't touch himself in any manner.[53] To prevent thumb-sucking, "the sleeve may be pinned or sewed down over the fingers of the offending hand for several days and nights," or a patent cuff to hold the elbow stiff utilized. [54] When the child is put to bed his sleeping hand must be covered. [55]

The United Government bulletin of 1942-45, in contrast to the above approach to child rearing has the concept of the child transformed into an almost complete harmlessness. The old ideas of child destructive impulses have disappeared and the drives toward erotic pleasure and domination which were stressed until 1929-38 are now weak and incidental. Even these impulses are diffuse and moderate and it is felt that if a child puts his thumb in his mouth or touches his genitals these are merely in incidents in the child's exploratory progress. The erogenous zones are no longer focused upon as in 1914 and the baby is felt easily beyond them to other interests and will not handle his genitals if he has other interests.[56] The child is now centrifugal as the earlier erotic infant was centripetal, thus, everything now amuses him and nothing is excessively exciting to him.

The mother is now told to disregard autoerotic incidents since the baby will touch and handle and investigate everything it can see and touch and obviously he will touch his genitals. The mother is advised that ' . . . A wise mother will not be concerned about this." [57] A baby merely finds the genitals as a playthings and if he has a toy his concentration will be else where. The mother likewise must not be too concerned with thumb sucking since he will stop as he gets older.[58] Yet this ideas was still very new since the 1938 edition still has an illustration of a stiff cuff that mothers utilized nightly to prevent the child bending his elbow so he could get his finger to his mouth. But the mechanical restraints against masturbation had been substituted for diversion of play by 1929.

An effort was being made to overcome the dichotomy between enjoyment that is wicked or deleterious and enjoyment that is wholesome, that is that does not conflict with American's ascetic moral codes. Now some writers want to say that what is pleasant is also good for the baby. A distinction is made between a baby's legitimate needs, such as hunger , thirst, illness or pain and a baby's illegitimate pleasure strivings. In 1914 it was essential to distinguish between this dichotomy. Crying is considered a bad habit, especially if he has learned from experience that crying brings his what he desires. So if a child cries and the mother determines he has no real needs, let him cry! [59] This concept remains un-changed until 1942. [60]

A mother's role is also changing from one of a strong moral devotion with its self-control, wisdom and strength and persis-tence to that merely of a parent with know-how. The father now comes back into the picture of child raising because now chil-dren are pictured as keeping the couple together by keeping them young as happiness and fun accrue to them both. Mom now is encouraged to breast feed-a factor that will bring her happiness and joy; bath time for the parents is now a time the baby delights his parents.

A new imperative thus comes into being, that is, that parents ought to enjoy their children. If a mother doesn't enjoy nursing she now wonders what is wrong with herself. A shift of reality now enters within the mother-child equation, that is, mother can overtly be doing the right thing but is she subjectively feeling the proper love nuances which are not under her voluntary control. The primordial fear-anxiety syndrome now enters the picture and mama is now haunted by her proper lack of love and emotional connection to her child which exists on such a high idealistic level which only the gifted few will ever obtain. But at the same time mother is now required to have fun with her child which is qualitatively different from the obligations of the older morality and mama is now permanently caught within the primordial fear-anxiety syndrome forevermore.

To put this problem into perspective we must now observe Mama having to love playing with the baby whereas in 1914 it was regarded as dangerous; as unwholesome pleasure which ruined the child's nerves since playful handling of the baby was titillating because it carried the overtones of erotic excitement. Even "playthings . . . such as rocking horses, swings, teeter boards, and the like" is connected with masturbation through which "this habit is learned." [61] Now amusement, fun and play are divested of puritanical associations of wickedness but Mama may now have the fear that she may not be having enough fun! She can't go far enough into the play and may be falling short of being a proper mother. We now find our mother dear facing the serious problem of fun conscience which is now a nuisance since she is freed from worrying about all those previously dreaded impulses. But now she must worry about her personal sense of loss of self-esteem and constantly worry about what is wrong with "me" because I am not having fun!

When you admit to yourself that you are not having fun, when you are supposed too, you experience feelings of shame. The new ethic is "Damn have fun or you will be condemned to feel inadequate, or impotent or worse unwanted and unloved, meaning unworthy as a parent. Previously a young women who went out too often was considered wrong but now if she doesn't go out something is wrong with her. Above all a mother or young women cannot stand the pity of her contemporaries if she does not date or have fun. [62]

This theme is now carried over into father and mother's work place and has become fused in business and professional life. Formerly play was isolated from work but now entertainment is part of business relations. Business life now looks at such factors as fathers or Mama's personality such as pleasingness or likability which formerly was irrelevant to work efficiency; thus we now have mutual penetration of work and play. But play now must be judged by standards of achievement previously applicable only to work and now Papa and Mama must constantly ask themselves am I a successful person? Did I make a good impression or did they like me or am I making the grade or doing as well as I should?[63]

The primordial fear-anxiety syndrome has entered the life of Mama and papa now and they are running scared. Martha Wolfenstein says that possibly a new type of self defense has entered into the situation without conscious calculation, that is, against impulses. This defense is a diffusion which ceases to keep our gratification deep or intense. It is a kind of isolation that allows our fun activities to remain shallow and to thinly permeate all play activities so that this mixture causes a further mitigation; thus enters unacknowledged and unrecognized the tradition of puritanism [64] now allied with the primordial fear-anxiety syndrome which is a prime supporter of the Genocide Phenomenon.

The problem now is that we no longer think we are good but, ye gods, must now secretly worry about how much fun we are having! Wholfenstein makes the point that the submerged superego now intersperses play in small doses with work and applies achievement norms to that play. Now we have a child who doesn't have fierce pleasures of autoeroticism but who must explore his world with some harmless play thrown into his daily routine.

But, observe the daily world of the child's parents, and you will find that now Papa and Mama must now earn their living in a work atmosphere that is permeated with personal relations and entertainment requirements, factors that are not intensely pleasurable, but which are haunted by self-doubts about his capacity to have subsequent fun. So we find the nonsense starts in the cradle and never lets up until the grave.

The United States "Infant Care" bulletin of the fall of 1951 shows some backsliding on the ideas of childcare. Yes "Fun Morality is still in and you must love your baby and enjoy it and the child must learn that Mama and Papa are "two people who enjoy each other." [65] Yes you must enjoy introducing your child to eating solid foods and mama must have a pleasant time giving Baby dear his bath; a time which is a peek experience to all of them. "the pleasant time it should be . . . if you feel hurried bath time won't be fun for either of you and it should be." [66]

A shift of emphasize now takes place because formerly the adult had only to worry if he or she was doing the right thing, but now the infant as well must have fun which equates to him a type of success in life. From this time on, until death, this child must socially perform and succeed in life or he will suffer untold agonies and defeats and be engulfed in deep depressions and despair will be his constant companion; or he may die lonely and forgotten by all, even his parents, who will wash their hands of him in disgust for his life failures. This child must now internally be responsible for his own success in life.

Also the baby must not be allowed to suffer boredom." [67] Now when the baby sucks his thumb he is bored and he may bang his head because of his intense boredom with life. [68] Also the poor frightful mother must now watch the child's toilet training to see it does not become a "hateful bore' for him. Now the child's autoerotic activities , no longer derived from fierce impulses or intense exploratory tendencies, but rest on his need to escape boredom.

It can be observed now that the puritanical condemnation of impulses has now caught up with this displacement and the parents now must put boundaries on the baby's exploration . The old idea that the baby should not get the upper hand over his parents now reemerges and if he gets the upper hand then the parents may be "at his mercy by unreasonable demand for attention." [69] Presently, we are seeing that this rush to attention as it emerges as the death child who beats, murders and rapes parents and adults indiscriminately throughout our culture.

The conflict about facing human impulses is obviously not solved. Our child raising attempts to dilute and diffuse impulses leads us to doubts concerning adequate impulsive intensity, boredom and of our difficulty to achieve fun. We have not transcended the fear that impulses in one form or another, will intensify beyond our control. [70] We are in the midst of the primordial fear-anxiety syndrome and are running scared and will not understand ourselves until we achieve a balanced personality system.

What is certain about child rearing is that the child must have a loving relationship with his mother. An interesting experiment was conducted by Professor Harry Harlow about affection in monkeys. [71] He conducted an extensive photographic and experimental study in the life of laboratory monkeys by controlling the mother variable. He took newly born monkeys from their biological mothers and put them on wire imitation mothers that were covered with terry cloth and heated. Piped in milk through a rubber nipple fed them and the substitution mother was wired for warmth.. He controlled all of the mother variables and rocked the baby's and positioned the imitation mothers at just the right angle of inclination to make a scared monkey feel safe and comfortable and warm.

Yes, the monkeys prospered and became healthier and were trained quite easily in the technical know-how of the laboratory. They were perfect example of fitting into the machine world of today. Yes the lab technocracy world allowed these artificially raised monkeys to become quite superior to monkeys brought up by their own biological mothers. But in the end the artificially raised monkeys became what Harlow calls "psychotics" They would sit passively and stare vacantly. Some of them did terrifying thing such as when poked they would bit themselves and would even tear their own flesh until the blood flowed out; obviously they had not experienced how to interact with other monkeys, whether as mate, mother, child or enemy; and when mated only a minority of the females produced offspring. Only one monkey even made an attempt to nurse its child. Now we know that we can produce psychotics if the mother-child relations become severely disturbed. [72]

Presently we have children rooming the streets of our land gunning down mothers and other children in drive by shootings.

Even when a child in the cradle dies from a random gun shot from the street we see the literal but also symbolic blood flow caused by disturbed youth who must cry out in terror and disgust at mis-spend childhoods and who must kill in order to find meaning in life.. But realize this fact that our children's violence is only one step higher than the monkeys self violence in that instead of always turning the overt violence upon themselves some of them strike out at society who must pay the price for their sociopathic behavior. But the real fear for America is not in the random sociopathic violence toward society but in the more refined death child who seizes the reins of power as the death cadre's all American Fuhrer; and mark my words for he shall exact his vengeance with a steel hand and millions will perish by his actions and momma and papa will lie in death bleeding because their child somehow turned out to be a psychopathic.

Erich Fromm has developed a concept of necrophilia which partially explains death children and their activities of self destruction and death plays upon society. He feels a very unalive, necrophilous family environment is a contributing factor in the development of necrophilia and also in the formation of schizophrenia. Also the lack of hope and enlivening stimulation within a destructive spirit of society are factors as well as probably a genetic factor also.

Fromm's hypothesis concerning the early roots of necrophilia rests on an understanding of the phenomenon of incest that lies within Freud's concept of Oedipus complex. First we will examine these ideas.

The Freudian classic concept says that a boy of five or six will have desires of a sexual nature (Phallic stage) for his mother. The father becomes the hated rival. "When father dies I will marry mother" some boys had said. Fromm feels this actually means that deep antagonism of the boy toward the father is really a rebellion against patriarchal, oppressive authority, instead of the boy actually wanting the father to die (E. Fromm, 1951). Since the boy cannot get rid of the father and fears he will castrate him, the child must do away with any sexual desires he has toward the mother. [74]

When the child reaches the full sexual-genital developmental state at puberty he directs his attention to other women and overcomes his rivalry with father by identifying with him and his prohibitions and commands. The father's norms now become internalized and in Freudian terms become the son's superego. In pathological cases the son still has a sexual attachment to mother and later in life he will be attracted to women who also fulfill mother's function. The son can't fall in love with other women and remains afraid of father or father substitutes. He expects his mother substitutes to give him unconditional love, admiration, security and protection. Naturally American mothers usually never give unconditional love but operate in terms of conditional love.

Mother fixated men can be quite affectionate and in a qualified sense "loving" but are quite narcissistic and feel that they are wonderfully important to mother because they already are father. They do not need to earn love and respect because as adults they are great as long as mother or mother substitutes love them exclusively and unconditionally. Naturally extreme jealous pervades their natures and they are very insecure when they must perform real tasks in the world. Even when they accomplish their task they are insecure because no success can equal their narcissistic conviction of superiority over other men but deep down they have a nagging unconscious feeling of inferiority to everyone. Naturally some mother-fixated men's tie to mother is blended with realistic achievements. [75]

Freud assumed that the son's tie to mother was sexual and thus the child must hate his rival , his father. But the neofreudian Fromm feels other wise, that is, that the tie to Mom. is not exclusively sexual. Fromm makes the point that at the Phallic phase when the child has erotic and sexual desires for Mom that this attraction is not exclusive, that is, that the boy is equally attracted to girls his own age. The tie to Mom is intense because she was the entree way from a world where existential dichotomies do not exist. She is the answer to the existential situation of man's desire to return to "paradise" where one is in harmony with nature and there is no suffering. This universal relationship to mother brings one closest to "paradise." But it is not only a developmental problem for the child but touches on a powerful desire for unconditional love that can never be lost by sinning. Naturally American Moms usually give only conditional love based on their child being "good." [76] American mothers are the culture's Mamabosses and let no man tell you otherwise.

If the incestuous tie to mother is not resolved by puberty we have a male who is neurotic, who is afraid of women but dependent on mother or her substitute and as a person is more of a child than any adult should be. The mother of the boy may not love her husband or has a type of narcissistic pride in possessing her son, is overly attracted to him by pampering, or over protection or even seduces him to be overly attracted to her in many ways.[77] Naturally there are even rare cases of mother-son incestuous behavior; and a contemporary epidemic of father-daughter incestuous relationships in modern America!

MALIGNANT NECROPHILIA

Fromm's Hypothesis states that a son's incestuous fixation to Mom is the early roots leading to necrophilia. He feels there is a spectrum from the autistic children, who form one pole of the continuum to the other pole in which children form proper forms of affection for mother. He feels that some children on the lower continuum pole are not autistic but close to it and they never develop warm, erotic or later sexual feelings for mother or any mother substitutes. Mother to them is a phantom, not a real person, She is a symbol of home and the race but she is also the symbol of chaos and death. Mom for them is not life but death; she is the death-giving mother. Her womb is not a return to paradise but is a tomb, and her embrace is death and their tie to her is one of malignant magnetism which draws them to her to drown them. In fact, they want to drown in her ocean and to be buried in the ground of her attention. If they cannot be related to Mom then the whole world "becomes one of final union in death." Clinically, Fromm states that children's fear of destruction by Mom is more intense than any fear of a punishing father. Fromm says that "It seems that one can ward off the danger coming from father by obedience; but there is no defense against mother's destructiveness; her love cannot be earned, since it is unconditional; her hate cannot be averted, since there are no "reasons' for it, either. Her love is grace, her hate is curse, and neither is subject to the influence of their recipient." [78]

This passion for death is an unconscious attraction which must fight against the life impulses in man. It comes out in the life activities of the person as sadistic control of others or though the urge to gain boundless admiration from others. If the person is successful in life the inner destructiveness of the person sleeps but if he experiences failures then the malignant tendencies emerge and he has a craving for destruction which finds expression as self destruction or in death and destruction for others. Today we have our children gunning down children and babes in arms indiscriminately. [79] Our children are now coming home to us in a death rage against humanity and themselves. It seems only death and destruction will satisfy them as they worship life through death! The evil that they do stifles life and they are content because they are members of the death generation and on the cutting edge of the Genocide Phenomenon.

But mark this down America, in your book of life, that when these children of destructiveness become political leaders or cohorts for a dictatorial leader they become America's executioners, terrorists, and torturers. And they love Papa and Mama and their little brothers and sisters of America and they will do what they have to do and America will cry in the flames of its own extinction peril destruction.

DEATH AND VIOLENCE DRUG CULTURE

A scourge of death has embraced the nation in the form of the illegal use of major drugs. Some of which turn the users into zombies and criminals as they destroy our country through robberies burglaries, killings as they fight to maintain their death habit and become urban guerillas fighting to maintain their drug turf so they can sell the death drugs to middle class America who inhale and inject them into themselves or die of boredom and depress in their unwary round of existence.

Even the legal drugs of alcohol and cigarettes are literally killing its users but the corporation profits must go on, the hospitals and doctors must earn their billions. and the tax payers must use these sin taxes as commodities of death to support government agencies. Death is now a legal commodity that our citizen gain material benefit from which they need as monetary tax funds to uphold the community structures. The Genocide Phenomenon thus finds support by government fiat as our loftiest medical facilities grasp additional billion from their cancer fees; thus this death tax additionally helps to feed and legally support a type of legalized death wish and builds a structure that pathologically feeds America on the one hand and yet destroys it with the other hand. The stench of death flows from our men in white and the drug corporations which covers America the beautiful with its death fragrance. And yet our billions of research dollars can't find the cure for cancer!

The basic question is why are masses of Americas so dead inside of themselves that they must take drugs daily in order to relieve the depression and alienation they feel inside of themselves?

Why, oh America are you dead inside and dying to yourselves that you are a shell of your potential self. You are the walking dead and your putrid countenance infects all you meet and you have death upon your breath and violence in your heart and you are the infection that is killing America. Oh woe is a people who in their weakness cries out for salvation from themselves yet seeks not to look inside their own selves for correction. The breath of death and violence is upon America and She is going down for the count and none may save our country except that we stand up and become men and women of value and integrity once again!

CHAPTER 11

DEATH FAMILY

FUTURIST COMMENTARY: We of the 22nd century have lived through the death pangs and agony of experiencing our way of life disintegrate before our very eyes.

There are few families left in the 22nd century except in the Free zones. Oh, it was not by choice or through the will of the people that the family institution perished. The people desperately clung to their kin throughout America's 2nd and 3rd civil war and even the death squads'massive sterilization program of males in year 2,040 did not wipe out all family bonds. But in the latter part of the 21st century, when the death generation's power reasserted itself again, the sexes were forcibly separated and the cloning of selected personnel commenced in Ernest as the family custom died a tragic death. Later in the century, when the plagues and fiery death fell from the skies, our people became nearly sterile. But family life became active again in the year 2210, when the forces of technocracy darkness became temporarily defeated in Asian military adventurism.

Campbell below speaks of the crucial times just before the second American civil war which commenced in the latter part of the 20th century.

The American family is dying a rapid death along with the weakening of many other American social institutions. Additionally the family has lost its economic, religious, and educational functions. [1] The more rigid forms of family social organization is rapidly changing. All marriages nationally have the fifty percent divorce rate, there is a revolt of youth and almost uncontrolled child delinquency rate and rapidly increasing individualism are found among family members. A family for many people is similar to a gas station in which one periodically comes home to fill up in order to drive on else where again; gone are the love and intimacy that fulfills one and makes each one of us into a human being. So today the American family lies sick and bleeding to death because the most obvious sign of modern America's fatal wound is the mass emergence of the dysfunctional family which is systematic of the destruction of the inner spiritual-cultural mind set of modern man. Additionally witness the dramatic increase in family incest, battered women, alcoholisms and destructive drug use, legal and illegal, within the family are portents of the modern family's demise. The fact of the matter is that many average family member are alienated from their nuclear family and grandparents.

But alienated as each family member is from each other the fact is that each man, woman and child as a family constitutes the foundation stone upon which the entire society rests. In America the family has a particular therapeutic function and personality-stabilizing [2] need that doesn't exist outside of our culture. It is only in America that a person can experience love and security and an honest chance to be a human being within his family. This is because outside the home Americans must work in an industrial systems the generates hostility, insatiability which lives within the primordial fear-anxiety syndrome with its fear of being obsolete and unprotected. America's economic system generates competition and feelings of inadequacy with its hostility, fear and suspicion. So it is only within the family that a person can make up for the anxieties and personality dep-

rivation by working through personality problems that are
subordinated to love. And this love within the family seems
to be almost in direct proportion to the profit, commotion,
destructiveness and de-personalization of the outer world.[3]
If a person cannot be a human being within his family he is
lost!

Destroy the family stone and the rest of our culture
will sink into the quicksand of social destruction; and for
those who have eyes to see let them observe the cries and
lamenting caused by the death pangs of the American's
families.

DEATH FAMILIES

American families are disintegrating because they are dysfunctional
in relationship to the changing cultural norms and the mind sets
which are conditioned by the old ways and norms of society cannot cope with modern exigencies; the family unconscious, which
is the connecting link that bonds a family into a social unit, has
also been broken and often individual family members are antagonistic with one another, if not outright enemies. Additionally individual family members, as members of the species Homo sapiens, are undergoing an evolutionary uplifting on the conscious
level, thus the present emotional, social, and psychological needs
of family members are not being met. The rapid changes in altered
states of consciousness within each family member's personality
becomes a trying time of personal and family ajustment within
the family unit which copes with these exigencies without any real
understanding of what is going on.. If a child already lives within
a dysfunction family and culture then possibly grave psychological traumas occur. Rapid socioeconomic culture change is also destroying any stable family structure in America today. Only fifty
percent of the families are nuclear families, that is, families that
consist of father, mother and children, and if all the data was in
you would find that most of these families are artificial and non-

functional structures that are near collapse. In fact, the majority of children in the country live in one parent home and the near collapse of the entire social system may occur in the next generation some cynic's state.

Is the American family sacrosanct and sacred or is it just another form of family organization. Obviously, it is but one of the multiplicity of family forms found by anthropologist around the world. But it is all we Americans have now yet it seems to be connected together by a death bond. But realize this fact that the present cultural order as we know it rests on the family unit and when it goes the rest of the culture will change also in ways we cannot even imagine now.

THE DEATH BOND

The present generation is held together by a death bond welded together by the exigencies of the 20th century. On the local family level Its legacy is the slowly declining disintegration of the family from an authoritarian extended family made up of several generation and often close relatives, to the industrial age's nuclear family of Papa, Mamma and children to the one parent family, usually of Mama and children but often of Papa and children, to the post single family of grandmother and child and ultimately to an urban tribal family of throw away children who live on the streets prostituting themselves to the depravity of the general public in order to survive. In some parts of south America these children are even preyed on and summarily executed by death squads just because of their existence! In America 700,000 runaway children yearly disappear and never are seen again? A terrible factor that points to a retrogressive family system, that is, historically killing children has been practiced generally in terms of infanticide or the killing of young children or infants but not of adolescents. [4] Infanticide is still practiced world wide on a small scale covertly. Historically Abraham was told by god to sacrifice his son to him, as was the custom in those days. In ancient Sparta deformed children were placed in the mountains for the wolves to kill. In early Rome the father had complete power to abandon, kill or even sell his child. In Hawaii infanticide was a means of controlling the population, as it was in China, especially with girl children and was practiced also in hunting and gathering bands. [5]

In England, as in many other cultures, the unwed mother's solution was to use infanticide to escape from her act of shame. A popular Ballad speaks of Mary Hamilton, lady-in-waiting to the Queen, who becomes pregnant by the Queen's consort. In disgrace, the balladeer sings:

> She tyed it in her apon
> And she's thrown it in the sea.
> Says, "sink ye, swim ye, bonny wee babe
> You'll ne'er get m'air o' me." (Friedmand 1956) [6]

The killing and maltreatment of children seem to us today as horrendous crimes yet remember that in the not too recent past, hidden in the memories of many living persons, was the concept that children were seen as the property of the families and the head of those families determined the manner in which the child was cared for and even if that child was to live. [7] Additionally in ancient time, the female child was especially considered the property of the Papa to do with as he liked and his permission was required in all her dealings. She could be bartered for money or land or betrothal agreement entered into which was sealed by sexual intercourse with underaged (under twelve) daughters. Men Marrying extremely young girls was not uncommon and if the father had no dowries to provide for his daughters he often put them into convents by age nine and they would take their religious vows at age thirteen. [8] Rush states how a prioress's confessed that young nuns were sexual objects to the monks of the convents and were threatened with excommunication if they spoke of their sexual exploitation. [9]

Boys were also objects of sexual exploitation. Perderasty practices of using boys for sexual relationships was common in Greece; and many boys of noble family were actually compelled to take adult lovers who protected and plied them with gifts. It was not until 1548 that legal protection was offered children from sexual abuse. England passed a law in that year against the forced sodomy of boys and in 1576 another law prohibited the forcible rape of girls under ten years old. [10] Recently a gang of death children invaded a home in Covis, California, and held the family in bondage as they gang raped the ten year daughter in front of the family. [11]

FAMILY DESTRUCTION

"Why has the family bond been destroyed? Can it be repaired? First let us examine the family and we will see that the connecting psyche link or psycho social connecting linkage between the generations has been destroyed. On its gross level any family is held together by shared experiences. Traditionally in farm families the sons worked with their fathers and the daughters with their mothers in agrarian society days, thus building up a bond of shared experiences while progressively being socialized into the family and social order. The nuclear family, at first continued some of these functions but because of the nature of living in an industrial society the women had to take a job, often when the child was a few months old. Thus the grosss shared experience of the family became compartmentalized and often the father rarely saw his children. Often the husband and wife worked different factory shifts or one worked nights, swing or grave yard shifts and even then they rarely met. Naturally the child was constantly shifted from one unknown baby sitter to another and unknown to the parents they were occasionally sexually molested by them.

Beyond the gross factor of shared experiences a family must have a psychological connecting linkage which I call the psycho-generational bond which connects each member of the family on the conscious and unconscious levels and even on a dream tele-pathic level.

If the children have interacted with their parents closely during the first two years of life then a socio-hypnotic coding occurs as they learn the overt and covert fact of socialization. If no closeness exists then no true bond exists and the social unit becomes one in name only. There must also be a close bonding during the next four years between both parents or their child will not be their parent's child. Contemporary times find many of these children running away from home at an early puberty ages and becoming street children in our urban ghettoes throughout the country.

This fact is recognized by some of the death squads in some Latin countries who indiscriminately kill the street children as a mean of protecting the public order and the sanctity of the fam-ily. They in their perversion destroy all that is holy and add to their country's corruption thus ultimately creating a rain of terror that signals the end of their culture's life surge.

Presently children are in revolt against their parents and soci-ety in general, often before they reach adolescence. Our social and generational continuity with the past is broken and our fu-ture rests on an ever changing cultural and psychological founda-tion of quicksand that changes direction and meaning even be-fore we can understand and accept the new cultural ways.

Some of our children are turning into predatory animals who consciously chose no specific prey but willingly slay victims at random. If a stranger does not give them a free cigarette they shoot him, if you are walking on the street at the wrong time you are slain, if you look at someone the wrong way you are a dead man!

Our culture has finally so dehumanized our children that some of them are mad dog killers who thrill at the fall of their prey and revel in that peek experience to guide their life course. Death, thus, is an icon to them and a guide. They are so emo-tionally dead inside that they can only feel life by facing death and taking life.

But death is also a comfort to them. In some gangs, girl members are initiated into the gang life by having sex with a person infected with aids; the girls thus aline themselves with a close affinity with the death theme and naturally they will most likely become victims of aids. But no matter, because they are representative of the death generation and they revel in death and embrace it and find joy in it because it allows them to transcend their inner death by embracing the outer forms of biological death.

Some youth have chosen ritual death patterns in which they ritually kill other human beings for the personal thrill satisfaction. Recently three teenagers were convicted in Arkansas for killing three 8 year old boys and for cutting off their testicles and sucking the blood out of their victim's penises. This is reminiscent of savages killing enemies so they can drink their blood or eat their brains. This death theme recently culminated through the mass serial killer Darimons, who starting as a teenager killed ultimately 17 boys to cannibalize them and store their body parts in the refrigerator. Have our young become death savages?

The death theme is a dynamic truth to the barbarian children; it so permiates their personality that Papa becomes to them all men as they shout in glee—death to Papa, and they feel an exhilarated high as they strike down Mama, the giver of life; then they shoot her babe in arms so no future generation can give life; thus they "shit" on life and are fulfilled.

Death and punishment mean nothing to them. " Put that notch on the gun handle Pete. Stomp that two month old baby Jake; rape that 85 year old grandmother Sam and then beat her to death because of the nasty and despicable curses she screams at us."

The death children revel in grandmother's death because she is the symbol of the generation that begat their parent's generation; Grandma's death is a triumph over life and their parents. Through her death they are uplifted into the glory of the death temple itself and they are elated through their bloody deed. They are the avenging angles of the death generation. They are America's death chickens coming home to roost.

In their crazed mind's eye they say,"how dare she criticize us, demean us, ask us for mercy. We are the new death force, the new strength of the future that shall stomp on America as we cleanse her of life, liberty and freedom!"

"We represent the world gone mad. We are your mirror image America–we are your buried subconscious parts and we roar the scream of an age gone Mad. For we are America's failure's rising to haunt you because death is our truth and we will devour you, maim you, degrade you and make you become as we are as you try to defend yourself against us by destroying us!"

Death is upon the winds of America and its stench surrounds us all and its strength shapes our death morals. " America quiver in fright, " your death children tell us, "because we are your future and realize this we shall not be merciful to you; nor will we forgive you; and above all we will not tolerant you."

The death children of America speak in clear and unequivocal terms," Stand up America; get off your knees and face your death as we cut you down, one by one. Beg for mercy Papa and Mama, because we will degrade you, as we eliminate your degenerate stink and its sacred feelings of liberty and justice for all, from the face of America."

"America," our death children say," if you will not get on your feet then grovel in the filth of your ways Mam And Papa as we cut from America what's left of its integrity. Then we will emasculate you so that you can be a mindless death slave to the new world order. Rise America or you shall surely die to yourselves as you drownd in your own filth and naivete."

Is there any hope for us to avert the crisis in modern society or must America walk that slow agonizing walk into social disorganization as our mad-dog teenage killers weave their way through our society?

America's death peril may become an extinction peril because humanity seemingly has deliberately chosen to live out what

Campbell calls the primordial fear-anxiety syndrome within American family society leading into the Genocide Phenomenon. The American family seemingly have stepped outside of nature because they have covertly chosen death willingly, thus putting themselves apart from the rest of the animal kingdom. No other animal species chooses death so absurdly by choosing to die by killing its own kind!

There is no dignity to our deaths for we die with agony in our hearts and our death cry is merely a release for us from our putrid emotional life, our death children are telling us by their acts of death!

But our death generation knows deep down that death holds no redemption for them. Death is their enemy but also the fiend that drive them into insanity and desperation; for humanity has hit rock bottom and neither life nor death can sustain its empty hearts.

Today the death chant calls America's families to the grave yet life holds it back from the abyss of oblivion. Can it be that some hint of life holds the secret that will propel us from a meaningless life and senseless death into an eternity of life? Yet time marches on and death has us by the hand and life barely sustain us while our biological clocks ticks second by second as we approach the road of no-return.

In the meantime our children march before us with the death rattle bursting forth from their mouths as they gleefully slay their fellow human beings in drive by shootings! By those overt and symbolic act they speak to America about things and events of subconscious fury that America will not hear otherwise.

They are the first of our children to celebrate life through death, celebrate death by taking life as a sacrament from their fellow mankind. For in death they celebrate life as a trophy which they flaunt before us as they trample on our most cherished joys—freedom from death and oppression.

Our children are the first to tell us that cultural death faces us and that all of us will soon suffer the death throes of our culture's death. All of us will soon cry out for salvation from ourselves and none may say that we were not warned of our coming demise!

It is written that mankind must face himself and fulfill his innate potential. The human species has risen historically above its instinctive nature it must now transform individually and collectively its lower natures while balancing its warring ego system into something greater than it is now. Only by so doing will the present individual and social, and family crisis be transcended. But to do that we must examine where we began as a family people and how our society developed into American social order we have today.

PARENT-CHILD UNITY BOND

All social organizations are united together in a bond of unity that rests on shared experiences and a psychic unity on the subconscious and conscious levels. On the covert family dimension it is the family unconscious that binds all the members together along with shared experiences and overt family rules and hopefully love. The family is a subculture within the culture in which he inhabits. Within that sociocultural context it is also a member of a social class, possibly a social subculture or may be a member of a subculture ethnic group. Remember also that most American cities contain from five to nine social classes, although most of America consider themselves Middle class, a myth which they find comforting.

The parent-children bonding must take place during the first six years of life. There must be a psychic unity binding all members together or they will be merely coexisting together. There must be love and empathy and unity and respect and above all a subliminal bonding that unites all member together into a family unit.

Family secrets and ways of living and doing things creates a bond which excludes people outside the family unity. A subconscious but fluid merging of fears and doubts and love and compassion and tragedy and triumph flows uninterrupted between and among family members. This is called the family unconscious which is connected to the telepathic-Psi Titan factor. It connects family members together on the dream level and the conscious and unconscious intuitive dimensions. A sincere family is a small social organization that connects to the outside world by certain traditional manners of overt cultural behaviors.

Historically American families were traditionally patriarchal with the father at the head or the grandfather at the head of the extended family, etc. This would vary depending upon the socio-economic circumstances. Non-English immigrant fathers usually lost their power gradually because as their foreign and native born children became integrated and enculturated into this American foreign society they became their parents' cultural parents. [12] They became the model upon which Papa and Mama and the other siblings must imitate to become full Americans. They were the sources that Papa-Mama had to ask about what was culturally appropriate in any given circumstance. But poor Papa could never become a full American–never. If successful at all Papa became only half-an American man. He no longer was a person to look up too but a half-babbling creature with odd social ways who was like the bull in the China closet, that is, what he didn't break he defecates upon. This was the beginning of the loss of the father-force in American society that finds expression as the life of the Papa-Drones of today. Another factor enters into this situation also which is the fact that English and non-English immigrants came here because they didn't want to be fenced in and when they arrived in America had a fear of acquiescing to an inner autocracy or an outer one, thus they kept their cultural identity tentative. The wife had to become autocratic in her demands for family order. [13] Monism thus became nothing more than misplace paternalism as the Mama-bosses of America took over the roles of the grandfathers as the fathers abdicated their family dominance in education and cultural life. The Mama-bosses were force to be both father and mother as they trained their children in the ways of survival in American life. The mother also gradually took over as the husband had to concentrate on his family's survival by working fourteen hour days in the mines and factories of America. This fact also initiated the emergences of the Mama-Boss in American life.

Today psychiatrist tend to blame Mom" as a cold mother, a dominant mother, a rejecting mother or sometimes as a hyperpossesive and overprotective Mama-Boss. In therapy today you will find the patient blaming his mother for having let him down whereas Papa-drone, unless he was unusually stern or an old fashioned individualist or a foreign paternalist is looked upon as not having much to do with the patient. [14] Other Mama-Boss critics refer to "Moms" as " a generation of viper." [15]

Historically in the patriarchal family structure the mother would be second in command with the first son being the surrogate parents and in control when his parents were else where. In the old days girls were subordinate to their brothers unless the first child was a girl, but then generally the first son was gradually put in control and the older sister was a type of surrogate for the mother with a status all her own. In recent years there has been in American society an ongoing war of the sexes between siblings but this factor can be generally attributed to the girls usurping of the power and status of the boys in the family, as well as asserting themselves within the general society as a whole. This general bickering and bantering of competition has been institutionalized so much that it seems natural that brothers and sisters should always be at odds with one another. It is seen almost as a preparatory assertion practice for meeting the turmoil and hazel of everyday market life in which a person must sell himself or perish as a viable American.

MAMA-BOSS RISES

We live in a time in which the rules of parenting are changing. We live in an era that is changing so rapidly that no one really knows the rules any longer. It is also a time when the psychiatric workers talk of "schizoid personality" and maternal rejection," as they speak of the masses of people who do not fulfill the American dream not only from psychotic disengagement from reality but speak of millions who while not overly sick seem to lack ego strengths and mutuality in social intercourse. Critics point out the hundreds of thousands of psychoneurotics that yearly must be rejected from the armed forces. Other critics point out the learned streamlined smile that our trained youth portray within their perfectly tuned countenances and self-controlled behavior patterns hide the true state of American youth's lack of true spontaneity.[16]

Is poor Mama-boss getting the bun rap for this state of affairs. Has she collectively become a generation of vipers? Is she frigid sexually and rejective of her children and is she unduly dominant in her home?[17] Additonally Mama-bosses have outlived their husbands generally and end up owning three-fourths of America's wealth.

Mama-boss is now the unquestioned authority in mores and morals in her home and in clubs throughout America. Yet the strange fact is that she has allowed herself to be vain in her appearances and is egotistical in her demands and infantile in her emotions according to Erikson. If the social situation brings about any discrepancy between the respect she demands from her children and the facts of life she blames her children but never herself. She thus artificially maintains what the anthropologist Ruth Benedict says is a discontinuity between and adults and child's status. Mama-boss doesn't endow this differentiation with any type of exalted meaning through which one could find any superior examples. She also has a determined hostility to any free express of sensual and sensual pleasure on the part of her children. She also makes it clear that their father's sexually demanding is a bore but as she ages she is unwilling to sacrifice any external signs of secular commotion such as cosmetic make-up, frills of exhibitionism or even too youthful dresses. She also is avidly addicted to books, movies, and gossip that addresses itself to sexual displays. So, although Mama-boss teaches self-control and self-restraint she can't keep her weigh down or fit into her youthful dress. But her children must be hard on themselves even though she is hypochondriacally concentrated on herself. So even though she stands for the values of tradition she will not become old and be an honored grandmother but now must have surgical facial make-overs so as to be perpetually young and won't accept the name grandmother or that status.[18] She thinks of herself as young and as a member of the cult of Youth that presides over all American social life of all ages. Erikson stresses that Mom has remnants of infantility which joins with advanced senility in her make-up even as she lives out the middle range of mature womanhood which in most cases has become self-absorbed and stagnant. Self-doubt permeates her personality and she mistrusts her own feelings as a mother and a woman. Her personality demeanor now projects mistrust instead of trust. So now Mama-boss does not like herself and anxiety ridden and she knows that her life is a waste. She knows her children really don't love her and Mama-boss is now a victim of life and she has failed as An American and is worthless and unloved and worse still unsuccessful! [19] Mama-boss has joined the death generation by her self destructive self-image and lives daily through the vissitudes of the primordial fear-anxiety syndrome and will titter-toddles on this factor the rest of her life.

PAPA-DRONE

Culture change has put a quick death to the hierarchical American family. The father is no longer the true head of the family but historically and presently control has given over to Mama-boss. Today Papa-drone is often a sick joke and is portrayed in situations comedies during the life of television as the bumbling Dagwood type idiot who has a mentality of a idiot-drone and the backbone of a scary cat with minimal control of his impulsive emotions. Only the resourcefulness of the wise wife and her astute manners saves the day and family harmony prevails. Dad-drone is now but a caricature of his old self. He is half the breadwinner who is never home and when interacting within the family flows as a stranger among strangers with half the respect of a causal acquaintance.

When American men have undergone psychoanalysis it takes a long time to break through to the fact that there was an early period when Papa-drone seems big and threatening; but even then they don't find that threatening rivalry for the mother that is stereotyped in the Oedipus complex. It seems that Mama-boss ceased being an object of nostalgia and sensual attachments before the child even developed a rivalry with the "old man". It seems as if the child already had a deep seated sense that he had already been abandoned by the mother and this seems to be the silent complaint force behind schizoid withdrawal. The child doesn't regress because there is no one to regress too. He can't catch feelings that are uncertain and so relies upon action until he breaks. When action fails he withdraws. Erikson feels that at the bottom of this situation another factor also presents itself that says the child also abandoned the mother because he was in too great a hurry to become independent.[20]

CHILDREN

The children have been age graded and belong to a subculture, that is, they belong to a school system age grade which has its own culture and rules and no longer does Dad or Mom have the teaching roles and no longer do the children try to emulate them. Often the parents are looked uppon an a nuisance, an awkward relationship that they somehow must endure and tolerate. " Poor deluded parents–noncombatant all; but what can you do. You are stuck with them temporarily and the best thing to do is to ignore them, that is, aside from their custodial duties to be your servants and provide you with their owed niceties. Let them alone and leave them before they are old and nonsensical; but oh they are so loud and narrow minded; yes basically they are dumb and so easily manipulated but all's fair when it comes to parents. Soon

you will be rid of them and halloo lullya, free at last, free at last!"
The death Children alone, among our children, kill their parents
as an act of kindness and place them on the alter of their death
instincts which rises them up into the sphere of death truth itself!

Some Moms are liberated women who see their children as
hindrance to their career or at the very worst stand in their way to
find themselves. Some women desert their children, some leave
their homes and their children to the fathers. some kick the kids
out in the streets at puberty– thinking it best to be rid of those
ungrateful brats! Certainly some mothers belong to a generation
of vipers! Some mothers want the career, the kids, the husband
and the whole brass ring. Most or at the very least a few obtain
while some submerge into prescription drug abuse or alcoholism
or into depression because they are unfulfilled.

Mom when asked by little sissy what to do in a specific situation doesn't know what to tell her little darling; so she says do
what your friends are doing. And papa, poor deluded Papa says
"do what's appropriate for the circumstances." Situational ethic is
his guide and he doesn't have a clue as to what is the right way to
fit in with an aberrational social situation. As far as he is concerned our children learn from their peers as they leave the arena
of family solidarity for they are the death children and if life has
no meaning then they will live out their allotted time facing the
perils of life and society alone and in despair and knowing in
their hearts of hearts that time is not on their side and the grim
reaper is just around the corner and death will come one night in
some drive by shooting or when she is watching television or
sleeping in her bed. She knows she is destined for death and
nothing, nothing will rescue her from her death destiny.

Some families are now falling down from middle class status
to lower class realities. The million and millions of families that
rose from lower class background during world war Two are now
falling back to their origins as the socio-industrial jobs and technology are imported overseas so that a new world order may arise
on the backs of a huge underclass of indentured domesticated

workers. Some social critics would even say by exporting all low paying jobs the underclasses are being set up to rebel, rob and cheat by becoming a huge mass of malcontents. When they rebel they will be put in their place by a new and stronger democracy that is Fascist in content and dictatorial in manner and the lower classes and welfare people will have served their purpose and now can be disposed of in new and unusual manners. Other critics say the lower classes will now be the expendable army needed to occupy the new world order spread over several continents. But this is all nonsense because Americans will rise to the occasion by reforming their families and America the free will march on into a bright future.

So we have the facts of life that the American family unit is disintegrating before our very eyes. Perhaps the new world order no longer needs families. Perhaps covert genetic engineering and scientific cloning experiments have gone further than we know in the secret laboratories of the death masters. Perhaps there will be no families in the future. Does this sound too farfetched. It does, doesn't it; yet the facts are that less than fifty percept of our families are traditional nuclear families. And they are dying off fast.

If future covert science has techniques of cloning perhaps George Orwells speculations in 1984 novel hit the mark exactly. Perhaps through genetic engineering they can breed dumb workers for the mines and steel miles and drudgery work and smarter workers for minor bureaucratics jobs, and more brilliant workers to teach college or to be the future scientists. Perhaps children will live in age grade barracks like the ancient Spartans did or age grade homes like our old people are now forced to do.

Perhaps we don't need families any longer. Perhaps there will be families only in the small elite who will be our death masters and the rest of us will be willing and loving servants of our beloved big brother whom we all will adore and lay down our lives for and will lick his boots and squat when requested too and we will be so fulfilled by so doing.

Perhaps the new age will be one of joy and love for the leaders of a united world order and the rest of the people will live in the depravation and social class of obedience and subservient to those who know and love us and cherish us and know what's good for us. And our daily loving prayer to big brother shall be:

Oh loving father do with us as ye wish for we are your loving children. Kick us or uplift us but don't ignore us for we love thee so dearly. Oh beloved Big Brother use our strong backs to walk upon and punish us if ye will; but realize this fact, we are ever your obedient servants until death do us part. Hail to Big Brother. Hail Caesar! Hail to the eternal families who lead us into the new world order.

CHAPTER 12

TEENAGE DEATH TYRANNY

FUTURIST COMMENTARY: The 22nd century has no
teenagers. What you clasify as teenagers are enculturated
into our adult classes at age 13. Historically, however, the
death generation sprange from Americas teenage class.

Campbell says that," A force of tyranny has descended
upon the present generation from its own children. It is a
scourge of arrogance that find strength within a group of
individuals classified as teenagers in American society. It is a
force of disruption and estrangement from its parent generation that disrupts the peace and serenity of the civilization.

Millions of our teenagers have rejected sensate cultural ideals based
only on sense experience and they are changing the face of American culture positively and negatively. Through the use of LSD
and other drugs millions of Americans know that sensate experience is not the only reality of life. But these children and adults
have also been perverted by the death force of man's lower unconscious because of their still unregenerated evolutionary natures. This change has also its destructive side as the teenagers
join the death generation and indiscriminately shoot down their
parents and other teenagers and children in the street through
drive by shootings, robberies, house invasion and drug trafficking. They are the overt terror that has its source in Papa and
Mama and a dying sensate culture which has lost its cultural soul

and it generational-psychological continuity with it social members.. They are a culture of death who will either kill wantonly for a pair of shoes or a coat or a pair of skates or through organized gang warfare; they are ourselves, our precious children, peering back at us through cool, steel eyes of sociopathic killers who have been institutionalized by their peer group to take what they want from the general population and as a members of the death cadre they have a license to kill indiscriminately without remorse or guilt.

This death force is a revolution from dead and dying social norms and a warning of coming events. It is the rebellion of the youth of American culture against the madness and alienation of the age and it will not cease until it has destroyed America's continuity with the past. It will not cease until it has won the day or our culture goes in a different direction. This death force will succeed because what it attacks is a dying and barely standing corpse of America's cultural integrity which is waiting for someone or a group to push it down, crush it or revive it in a positive and dynamic manner.

America has traditionally and historically been a nation of youth, that is, in the past the life expectancy were low and the girls married in early teen years and by the time they were thirty they were middle aged and by forty they were ready for the grave. Mortality was high and life expectancy was low to moderate. A man would be widowed many times in his lifetime and women died frequently in childbirth and if you were not self-reliant, and a rugged individualist you perished by your own ineptitude and through the visissitudes of life.

Like most of the nonindustrial world cultures today there was no teenage years. You became a man at thirteen and a woman at puberty. We still have a few mountain states even today which allow girls to marry at age 12 + . By age twenty the girls, now the mothers of several children, were getting mighty old and the man himself was approaching middle age. The life expectance was

32+ and you had better get on with life as soon as possible and really start living.

The children had children you might say but remember most people lived off the land and if they received any schooling it was for two or three years and possibly to grade six if your parents had money. Only the elite went to high school and college. Only in the aristocracy was there what we would call a teenage life that might extended adolescence into a person's early twenty's.

When industry developed within America's life its children were put into the mines at age nine or ten and the girls were put into sewing mills and other factories at about the same ages and they generally worked from seven in the morning to nine at night.[2] Indentured child labor also came to America quite early. Children were brought into the colonies to work as indentured labor at young ages to work in indentured slavery until they were twenty-four. Child deaths in the factories were common and generally little was done to prevent future injuries or death because child labor was an inexpensive boon to the labor market and the parents usually signed pathetic documents which would not allow them to make any claims for damages or deaths of their children.[3]

The rest of the children worked on the farms from the time they could walk and the girls worked with their mothers or both worked in the fields if necessary thus the family farms was a collective labor situation and no teenagers existed because you were a man and a women at puberty and you emulated your elder's social norms and mores and you knew you did right when you became an image of your elders and you were glad of it and rejoiced in that fact because you had arrived and were a man or women among your peers and respected elders.

When the American labor laws were passed prohibiting Child labor the teenage class of children was created, that is an elite adolescent grade class of social individuals, an adolescent subculture, came into being, who could not work and were forced into prison like schools to keep them off the streets but ostensibly for

their betterment and upgrading.. It didn't matter if you didn't
want to go to school. They had police officers called truancy
officers to hunt you down and forcibly make you go to the free
schools of social learning. If you absolutely refused that privilege
the authorities sent you to reform schools or children's prisons to
encode you into the right and proper behavioral patterns until
you became an adult or until you escaped[4]

Today there is almost outright rebellion in America's school
system as teenagers bring guns to school; there are even cases of
kindergarden children firing guns in class. The violence against
other children and teachers have reached epidemic proportions.
Regular police officers have to patrol the school halls and metal
detectors are at all the entrances to the schools and the students
are locked into the school until school is let out. And still the
killings and violence goes on because you can't imprison the human spirit in outmoded social forms. A corrupt school system is
finally collapsing and America can't understand what is going on.
In the near future the school system , as we know it, will be
abolished in America; and America will be blessed!

The children's parents, however, just don't understand and
they are angry at the ungrateful brats and want them put in their
place. They demand that they be put in their place immediately!
America's children are protected and are given the best medical
care and fed according to the latest nutritional data with perhaps
overabundance. Obesity has overcome malnutrition as a serious
problem . The children are protected by law from being made to
work until their middle teens and they are offered universal education. [5] Our children, however, are rebelling against life, their
schools and their parents and society. America is it too late to save
our children from themselves?

America perhaps they are telling us something about ourselves. Do you think they are acting out their parent's social and
inner psychological discontent in the market place of school and
society. Perhaps the present generation cannot be enslaved by a
degenerate technocracy and a soulless culture. Perhaps our chil-

dren are our redemption from ourselves. They may be the strength we lack and the force of change we need and the power they hold may lead us from death into life. But above all our children are the signs of the times and be warned degenerate America your time has come!

Yes America, it may be too late because many teenagers have joined the death generation and nothing will ever be the same again. Never!

It is a fact that the death cadres gangs are recruiting teenagers today for their death squads. Our children are our executioners and delight in that fact. They joyously kill Mama and Papa in glee and ascend to the height of immature joy as they look death in the face and laugh! They are the death children and they will eventually rule the day because corrupt America shall willingly lies down in collusion with their death masters rather than face themselves; and they shall willing do this because the strength, self-power and will of the nation lies broken on the steps of expediencies and ignorance.

Americans are degenerate children at heart and know not what they do in life and are easily led by their hidden death master who stand behind their churches and governments and corporation structures. The are self drugged by their allegiance to the senses and their need to experience life only through the senses. They are degenerate Children at heart because their evolutionary state of consciousness is low and undeveloped. They shall perish in the midst of their ignorance murmuring stupidities as they cry out in pain and wonder where they are and how they got there but intuitively knowing that death has finally ringed them in and in agony and quiet desperation they will give up the ghost with a quiet whimper.

Death is upon the winds of time and none shall still its hand. But if the positive teenagers and the nation has strength of purpose and integrity of self all things are possible and if they stand up to the forces of the death darkness they shall triumph and the forces of darkness shall recede from the land and the species Homo sapiens shall rise above themselves by transcending their lower natures as they emerge into a higher state of self-conscious awareness of themselves and of the universe. If the millions of teenagers and their parents will stand up as a progressive movement and tap into their innate goodness they shall triumph over their lower nature; but if they descend into their darkest lower natures this very fact shall signal their defeat under the banner of the Death cadres and they shall fulfill the mandates of the Genocide Phenomenon. What shall it be America? Do you vote for life or death?

Children are our life force and upon them rests the future of unborn generations. Upon their shoulders lies the hope of the world . Know this American that in the near future all things will be clear and true and justice will prevail and all thing shall unfold according to the genies of the species.

We live within an era of permissiveness and our children are confused and unable to steer a course through the malaise of doubt and truth that lies before them. They wish to do what is right but can not find a handle to grasp or a compass to guide them and they flounder in panic and cry out for guidance and wish for perceptions of the moral and correct thing to do in each situation.

But who can guide them when their parents are lost, their teachers confused, and the philosophy of the age lies broken upon the visissitudes of life. There is no sincerity in life any longer and our children and their parents have lost their rational capacity to think clearly and have succumbed to the age's skepticism of doubt and despair. They now cannot even envision that they have the capacity to be able to perceive truth if they saw it or to stand up as a man among men or a woman among women. They are lost ones and lost they shall remain until the innate spark of originality that lies asleep within them becomes awake and they emerge from out the fog of ineptitude that now envelopes them.

It is an age of doubt and confusion and the death generation is the dominant factor that is beginning to lead us to our destruction. When the dark night of despair and doubt takes the name of a teenager the signs of America's doom stands before us.

Is their hope America for our teenagers? Can our teenagers find themselves ? Yes, but only if they can find themselves by standing outside the cultural propaganda and touching their own uniqueness within their own natures. They must find themselves within themselves. They must plunge within their personality structure to that hidden spark of species consciousness hidden behind the heart. Once it is ignited it will direct their mixed up ego powers to revolve around their inner flame of integrity and thus they shall arise into eternity with joy and firmness and all shall rejoice. but in the mean time let's examine the nature of adolescence more closely.

ADOLESCENCE

Adolescence is a time of doubt and confusion. It is a time when the child within us emerges into that twilight zone between childhood and adulthood. It is a time of terror and joy, of confusion and trust. And above all it is a time of growth from within the fragile child-man and child-women who walks into the light of a new adult maturity, into a new country that is new and fresh and unknown; and above all he or she now walks into his very selfhood, that cocoon of integrity that we call adult identity.

The child must let go of his childhood to firmly grasp adulthood. It is a breathless interval between his past and future. What was true and reliable to his childhood must flow into his future and receive the new ways and modes of speaking and thinking and becoming. All that he has learned in childhood must make sense in relationship to his new opportunities in work and love and what he perceives deep down within himself must now join with his new expectations which others bestow on him. His values must also now march in unison with some universal significance.[6]

Traditionally Americans have placed great value on the period between the age twelve and twenty-five. Everyone considers this youth period as the peak of life, the chief raison d' etre of living. It is the solemn duty of those who have successfully passed through this period of life to make certain their successors can enjoy and fulfill themselves as much as they did. Great guilt was experienced by the older people during the economic depression which started in 1929, because it marred the youth of a whole generation. The chief reason for great masses of Americans opposition against sending our boys overseas to fight the war was that the irreplaceable years of their youth "would be frittered away." [7]

In America the "Cult of Youth" represents the entire population. All Americans think of themselves as if they were living at the peak of the life. No American identifies with the older generation; but they identify with their children. Americans even refer to their nation as a "young nation." This is because Youth is so pre-eminently desirable that it must be ascribed as a whole to the nations National identity. [8]

A child's identity rests now on a heightened cognitive and emotional capacity as an adult person in a predictable universe. His new identity transcends his childhood images of himself as it relates to others and he realizes that he is not the sum of his childhood identification but his self identity now rests on a combination of old and new identification fragments.

All societies and culture recognize this period as a time of passage from childhood and put it into an ideological frameworks which requires assigned roles and tasks so that the exchild can recognize himself as a new adult and equally feel recognized by society. Healthy society utilize initiations, ritual confirmations and indoctrination which bestows traditional strength on each child as he emerges into adulthood. The older generations thus bind themselves to the strength of youth and are blessed. The child, now a man or a women, in turn contributes his conflict-free energy to the societies best interests.[9] But America these ceremonies must come from the heart and be culturally viable and not rest on dead and dying social and religious institutional rites and rituals that hold the stench of death within them and clutch firmly the death masters zeal.

The significance of these ceremonies now lie dead in America for many people. Many a child, a near man, at his high school or university graduations, doesn't attend the death ceremony because it signifies nothing to him except that he has escaped from a 12 or 16+ year prison sentence and feels free at last, free at last, which he celebrates in a drunken stupor that represents his zeal and enthusiasm for the future.

When the dead hand of the past imposes extinct rites of passage on children and adolescence they rebel and eventually will destroy what has no meaning to them any longer. Realize this America that the new ways of life must come from the heart of our youth and connect with the inner life of the race and cultural needs of the times. It must be a spontaneous emergence of a truth that has meaning and significance which grasps the inner unconscious potential of the species consciousness. Its transpersonal element must excite and uplift and transform its participants and bring joy and a sense of belonging. It must bring comfort and satisfaction to the individual and the group and have lasting meaning to the cultural and psychological life of the nation.

New forms of identity must be forged when the collective sense of identity which traditional groups bestows on the young person as he emerges into manhood begins breaking down.

When the agrarian, feudal, patrician, or any social-cultural system begins collapsing or rapidly changing the old social identities of the participants of those societies, which are linked to its role and material structure, suffer massive inner and outer psychological traumas of self identity. Now for the child or adolescent entering into those cultural systems, with its social roles changing, you find youth who feel endangered, individually and collectively and not only are they confused but are angry and rebellious and often are ready to fight! Some youth enter gangs and are institutionalized into new modes of self identity that encourages righteousness toward each other and criminality toward others; and often they turn into death squads who kill either for profit or gang turf or just to vent their frustration on society by indiscriminately shooting down other children, adults and babes in arms. They are the death generation and they are proud of it and mark my word America they are you in the youthful garb of death!

When a youth's fear of his loss of identity becomes too great for him he becomes ripe for indoctrination by others into totalitarian organizations and he is available for organized terror and becomes a willing participant in the establishment of major industries of extermination [10] and thus is a willing member of the death cadres. Perhaps the next logical step is their organization under covert and overt governmental agencies set up for the betterment of all mankind.

Whenever you have large scale uprooting found within culture change or migrations of people from one country to another or the migration of 33 million plus citizens yearly within America, the continuity between the generation is broken; the build in corrective factors in the hierarchy of developmental crisis factors is upset and the person is cut lose from his generational membership. [11] Other factors such as America's exclusive concentration on the outer sensate culture of the senses and thusly killing the inner man is presently bringing about a sense of loss and alienation into our culture. Additionally the evolutionary factor found within the species with its gradual rising of consciousness to higher and higher states of altered states of species awareness, is causing a social malaise and general loss of self-identity world-wide. The reason for this is that when you find resistance to internal consciousness change within the species, individually and collectively it results in a crisis of consciousness and this identity crisis manifests first in our children and then in our adolescent children and ultimately within the general population.

The emergence from childhood to adolescence can bring about certain developmental crisis that lie within maladaptive peer solidarity problems. There is the example of a four-year old negro standing in front of a mirror and scrubbing her skin with soap; or a similar research example of a young four year old Mexican-American boy trying to wash off the epithet of "dirty Mexican." [12] When the negro girl was diverted to painting , after trying to wash her black face white, she at first used brown and black colors in an angry fit of rage. But later she brought another picture to the teacher, that is, what she referred to as "a really good Picture", which only consisted of a white sheet of paper covered over with white paint. Ironically this child was not in an segregated school but was studying in an integrated one. But America's crime of racial segregation and its far reaching effects of harm which rises in the identity disturbance of our children and causes them to suffer a life time of painful inner re-identification process that they may never overcome [13] is but part of the problem of self-identity. The consciousness of nation is one and dark and light are but two sides of the same coin and never forget the T.P titan factor which is ever communicating with both sides on an unconscious level.

The self-images which each of us cultivate in childhood stages surely prepare us to develop a sense of identity by recognizing our face among other faces. The life giving power of the eyes and the face expose us to the dreaded estrangement, the "loss of face." To become a person of stature requires a self identification that rest on the basic trust in ones origins. So when that child of pain reaches adolescence his infantile beginnings of recognition may emerge again and we find individuals who will have a partial regression back to their childhood hopes for recognition which may touch on their basic horror of their past failures to receive that recognition. When moments of disapproval and shaming come into his life and they will, he stands exposed to the laughter and frowns of his peers of adults and he can only blush in anger. But that anger is two edged, that is ,there is the anger he has toward his oppressors but also the anger against himself because of his exposed self. Erikson says this is the second uprootedness that a growing person experiences because from now on his exposed self now becomes an outsider to himself. From this point on he will never be himself or can he identify fully with "them." He will try to be himself by identifying with his rebellious impulses or possibly attempt to become identified with the larger social group by obeying their laws and regulation. Usually he will try to do both and end up doubting himself as well as his peers and superiors. [14] It must always be remembered that human beings who operate from their lower vital-emotional personality natures tend to persecute themselves and also to identify with their persecutors. [15] If the teenager can develop his self awareness and ground himself in his inner conscience his growth of character will flow and he will find a clarity and trust in himself. If, however, his conscience becomes exclusively outwardly orientated toward those social rules and peer ideals and adult concepts then the hate and shame and hostile condemnation of himself by others becomes part of his inner judge. This often unconscious judge takes control against the adolescents own innate nature and feelings and the resulting inhibitions and repression allows the person to become alienated from himself and now all that is good and purely himself is alien territory. He thus becomes his own worst enemy. Erikson makes and excellent point when he says that much of what is described as neurotic anxiety or as existential dread is really only a form of primordial fear which the adolescent experiences when he scans both his inner and outer dimensions for indication of permissible social activity which he clings to with the most ferverent hope to find his outer self-identity. [16]

Transintegral psychology's concept of the Primordial fear-anxiety syndrome is operative in this area of personality and social conflict. It is natural for the teenager to have unconscious fears and anxieties as part of his individual maturation process but in America a person is never loved for himself but only for what he achieves socially. This success-failure knife is stuck all so slowly into him as he emerges into adulthood and has to be measured by the peer's accomplishments or by school scholastic standards and he know in his hear of hearts that he must measure up or perish as a has been or worse still as "a never been." American culture shows no mercy and his parents will only tolerate unsuccess so long because their own success in life partially depends on their children"s success. To be a bad parent or worse a delinquent parent is to be labeled with the worst tar brush and come hell and high water they will impose their standards on the young minds and souls of their offspring. How that child is integrated and raised has far reaching effects on his life.

If that adolescent does not find a balanced identity then even in his old age he will live in despair and begrudge the worthwhileness or his life and cry to high heaven for the answer of his meaningless existence. It is a fact that if a person is hindered from a worthwhile mode of living he is thereby deprived of the right to die as a man or women of substance. They become part of the hordes of lifeless men and women who do not expect a meaningful end because they have never developed their proper self-identity. But if a person goes through a relatively successful youth then as an adult he finds his final integrity and lives on certain principles that guide him though life as he becomes a whole person. With such integral personality development a person has the capacity to sustain sameness and continuity against rapid culture changes and the visissitudes of life.. His inner conditions can integrate the outer social situations and conflicts found in his culture milieu by that inner resiliency of personality that maintains itself through the culture change process and developmental stages of life. So in the midst of rapid culture change it is the personality that has a well established identity that can tolerate radical change because it resolves around basic species function that transcends cultural difference yet embrace social values which many cultures have in common. [17] A Mexican peasant's family values of family, work, and religion can be transferred to an industrial center intact or even the "primitive' and isolated Yemenites whose adherence to The Book can fit into modern Israeli society because they bring with them a well-integrated self-image and group identity. Because well integrated persons can function in a chaotic world doesn't mean that they have a closed personality systems impervious to change. What it signifies is that they have a psychosocial process which always preserves some basic but essential features in himself and his social affairs.[18]

The American teenager lives in a culture that stands on the quicksand of social movements. Certainty is nonexistent and massive changes within ones lifetime is built into the cultural life of the nation and personal lives of Americans. Our teenagers are not born into a society linked together by tradition or held together with a group of intimates for life. Their marriage partners are not chosen for them and they are not bound to a caste or social class or enslaved to a specific profession.

Each teenager must become his own social engineer by utilizing his skill at social maneuvering and through his personal appeal develop a personal community for himself. And he must start his run on the treadmill of American life as soon as he leaves his mother's apron by attracting new friends into his personal community. Other children will in turn attempt to lure him into their personal communities, while still others will attempt to win his friends away from him. In other cultures a child or teenager is not surrounded by his friends one day and deserted by them the next day but in America this fact is a constant possibility. Emotional evolvement and intense rivalry for friendship is an integral part of American life and a child and teenager is watched carefully for his wins and failures. The parents are ever watchful and their child's relative success will give them the answer to their perennial question. Have I been a good Parent and does my child have what it takes? Can he hold his own. Can he be more successful than I have been and rise to heights that I can't even imagine? Success for the child and adolescent and his parents now means "Am I loved?" To be loved lies at the bottom of every American's heart and guides his actions daily. The most significant factor is about this love is the fact it is based on a person's childhood success at receiving unqualified love and approval from his mother. But does he or she receive unqualified love and approval from Mama-boss? Never! This love is only given to an American child or teenager in proportion to his success. So by the time a child is an adolescence most "Americans confuse these two ideas together so that to be a success is to be loved and to be loved is to be an successful American. This principle has even a quasi-theological sanction which all American derived from puritanism which states that worldly success is the visible and outward sign of God's love and if you are a failure you are unloved even by God himself and you are a sinner or have not tried hard enough to succeed in life. [20]

In American life an interesting factor enters here and that is that to gain Mama's love, the prototype of all future love, the child and adolescent does not have to show love in return. This is because he gets Mom's love for his accomplishments vis-a-vis one's age-mates; this love is not because of the child's attitude and behavior toward Mama. American love thus is based on a non-reciprocal quality: when you are loved you do not necessarily have to return that love, but rather you must be worthy of that love! Naturally mutual love may also be present but added to the concept of mutual love is the factor of a nonsymmetical component which says love becomes symmetrical by identification and by feeling the loved one to be a part of oneself but that person must also be as worthy of love as oneself, thus he or she has also to be a successful person. [21]

The teenager and child is always pushed to the limits of his capacity since the condition of success are always so vague and out of his personal control. And even as an adult when he must compete with other adults for jobs and friends and social position, just as industry competes for natural resources and manufactured goods for sale to consumers; he must face the facts of life that everyone can be chosen or rejected by others for jobs or friendship, etc., and he will never know for certain why he was rejected or how or why his membership in his personal community of business or friends failed and he knows they may leave him at any time. He has to constantly observe and analyze with great sensitivity the looks, smiles, stares and criticisms that comes constantly from his inner ego, "Am I liked?" [22]

The child and teenager develops an insatiable craving for love and constantly searches for the signs of love, so that he may know he is a successful person. The very least of these signs of love is how much attention does he get from other people or are they even present in his life sphere. If nobody is there then the gnawing doubts are apparent, I may not be a success and worst of all I am not worthy of love. [23] Being worthy of love, however begins from within the family sibling rivalry.

The anthropologist, Margaret Mead, makes the point that we learn within our family the ground plan on personal relations and its themes and plots and that competition for success begins in American life with sibling rivalry. She points out that each child competes for the approval of mom's love by his or her achievements. They do not compete for mother's person , or her breast or soft arms but have rivalry for recognition that they are a person, that is, are they are successful in life. It begins with the fact that an older sibling is scolded for the things he does and his younger baby is not. The two and-a-half-year-old must be dry, feed himself, go to sleep alone or mom's loving approval is gone. The child observes that the younger child is loved and petted even though he can't do any of the hard things for which the older child is praised. He feels betrayal because he observes that Mom's love is given in one case and not in another and he develops a bitterness toward all those who "have it soft" and "get away with murder" in life and he is envious and will hold this attitude throughout his life. The growing child will feel that he has worked hard for his achievements but that young "brat" had it easy from the start. When the child grows into adolescence and adulthood he will feel the hard way is the American way and feel and speak his piece with self-righteousness and know in his heart that whose who have it easy are to be not only despised but envied. This is what conditional love does to you America! It is based on Mom's simplest kiss of conditional love which says I will love you only if you achieve as much as other people's babies and I won't or can't love you, " brat", until you are a success in life! [24]

Mead feels that American family's are no longer the true patriarchal family in which the child's attention is toward his parents and focused toward a loving relationship with them. The Oedipus conflict is not truly operative where one's brother is an ally against the child's deep repressed hatred to his father or a surrogate of the Papa, thus a brother is hated. But in America a child lives in a filling station family and his eyes are focused on the outside world. He will win praise and approval from a loving Mom, not by loving her, but through his achievements; by eating his carrots and becoming the tallest boy in the class. Mom does not measure Papa and son against each other on her personal love scale because they are not in the same class. Papa, as we have pointed out previously in other chapters is a shadow of a person who has little to no power in the family that mom runs. Oh, Mead has pointed out that some American fathers have regressed so badly that they even compete with their small sons for mother's love, thus putting their wives into their biological mother's role. But even here Papa and son are not rivals as in a typical patriarchal society. Mama does not compare Tommy with Papa but with Tommy's elder brother and Tommy's younger brother, with the neighbors But rivalry within the family can be transitory and depends upon the varying achievements of each child or adolescent and rises by the fact that "Gee! Wasn't Mom proud." Usually it is rare to find a teenager or adolescent brothers, who in order to get love, enters Papa's profession and emulates him and others during their lifetime to gain success through sibling rivalry. Generally American teenagers want to bypass papa and choose another skill or profession to their roads toward success. [25]

It must always be noted that in industrialized America men must move from job to job, and from neighborhood to neighborhood from the city to the suburbs or from there to the country and always they will be moving up and down the social ladder. It is thus difficult for the child or adolescent to establish enduring and secure interpersonal relations. The teenager will feel the pain of lost friends every time he moves and must meet new ones yet his previous suffering and withdrawn emotions now doesn't allow him to commit his personality resources too far and wide for fear of waste. But the teenager must go forward and collect his friends and be a part of this new group and the next new group in his perpetual search for recognition and love and success. The teenager must seek popularity as an insurance against the uncertainty in his interpersonal relations. This is covert search to eliminate uncertainty in his life. He must at all costs stabilize his perpetually precarious social situation and he must store up friends against that rainy day in his person-bank when he must take some losses. When you are popular and have many friends you can afford to lose some of them to the vicissitudes of the social-friend market. But you must always watch carefully your person-stock, not to rate it but to see how it rates you! [26]

Your personal community will always be unstable and you must constantly prop it up so the first American rule is conformity to general social norms. You cannot allow your individual idiosyncrasies to show you are not an 100% American. This is your contribution to the cohesiveness of American culture. But teenagers are often also ahead of critics and the intellgentsia at home and abroad because they intuitively feel the changing American spirit as it moves into the 21 st. century. [27]

Social acceptance for our teenager is the price he must pay for popularity, whether he is a gang member or a member of the church choir. He must mortgage his individuality even if he must become a member of the death generation or as an operative death cadre killer!

An American teenager can not tolerate loneliness and must be a member of some social group and in this sense he emulates his parents and all "normal" Americans. This fact of life is built into our social conscious so much that it is reflected in our material culture. Note that in most homes there is a lack of doors except in the most private parts of the house, or the wedged-open doors of studies or office or the shared bedrooms in boarding houses and colleges. On the social front the numerous clubs and fraternal and professional organization and conventions , etc., also keep American together. There is radio music piped into hotel rooms, many railroad cars, or it is left on in the home or the television is left on so that no American can feel as if he is alone with himself.

Observe teenagers walking or riding bycles with a portable radio to their ear. "I should go mad if I had to spend a week {or a shorter period} alone" is constantly heard everywhere." Even American psychiatrists as well as laymen look askance at any one who deliberately eschew company and wants to be alone. You cannot choose privacy in America and be a normal American person. Why? [28] Americans need the admiration of other people constantly or their self-esteem falls and then they know they are not only not loved but in their hearts of hearts they are not worthy of love or success. And then they cry inwardly at any thought about their failure in life.

Our teenage will thus remain doubtful until he becomes a part of the meaningful world and takes his place in it because irrational doubts can never be overcome by rational answers to life's questions. [29] Only faith in yourself overcomes doubt of yourself.

But remember that doubt is the cornerstone of modern philosophy and when you doubt yourself you doubt the world and your place in it. This psychological process has a two edged sword to it though because faith has two different meanings. It can signify an inner relatedness to your fellow humans and an affirmation of life that links you positively to your life goals; or it can be a formation which is a reaction against doubt and its human isolation of the individual and his negative attitude toward his life process. [30] Each American's answer to this dilemma is to strive for success in all things; by so doing doubt becomes temporarily buried by his overcoming of personal isolation and his connection to his particular world process, that is, until in a rapidly changing America he is displaced and must face doubt again and climb the treadmill of success and failure once again, or die trying!

Our teenager who is rapidly approaching adulthood is still tied to childhood fears and anxieties that in American culture is reflected in the Primordial Fear-anxiety syndrome. In childhood naturally fear and anxiety are so close to each other that they are indistinguishable, therefore the child has difficultly knowing the difference between the outer and inner, the imagined and real, dangers. Adult teaching will show him the way of their culture. If he doesn't perceive the correct and moral ways then what he experiences is the adult's latent horror and bewilderment and inside himself the child can sense a vague catastrophe that may strike at any time. When the child becomes an adult many of these fears become irrational anxieties such the urge for protection of territories and individual identities.[31] Our death cadres now project these concerns into extending their territories world wide and embrace world order identities, whereas our death children only want to belong to a gang family but will kill for their territory whom they confuse also with their individual and collective gang identification. Our general teenager identifies with the ever changing fads and their often outrageous clothings and territorially they embrace the culture of rebellious disunity which has no location yet is everywhere they roam.

FEAR OF CHANGE

In American culture, fear of change has it causal factors in childhood fears and anxieties. Babies are startled by sudden intense noise or loss of support or a beam of light. Normally he adjusts to such accidents but if he has learned to fear suddenness in the changes around him he begins to react with anxiety of this recurring suddenness and it becomes social anxiety connected with sudden loss of attentive care.[32] Later in life he will have an insatiable fear of social rejection and know he is not only not loved but a failure in life.

Within the child and teenager, when there is a conflict between his inner control and outer controls, is produced a cycle of anger and anxiety and residue of intolerance at being manipulated develops and often the teenager's outer social control fails. In American culture which isolates its children in age-grade schools away from the adult world this tension begins to flair up intensively when the teenager is taken from his self-contained world and forced into the different adult world of conformity. It is a type of culture shock and the teenager is bewildered and stunned at the prospect of being compelled to conform to norms and mores that may have little meaning to him. He also must give up his autonomy as an individualistic human being and he may not want to do so. This anxiety leads to impulsive self-will and he will not bend and in this we find the origins of compulsion and obsession and ultimately of the concomitant urge for vengeful manipulation and coercion of others [33] and possibly to membership in the death generation.

Social critics naturally see in teenagers only their reluctance to work hard and make something out of themselves. But naturally they forget our age-grade isolated school kids have not been trained for hard work, only trained in impulse release and surely not in impulse restraint. American children are Id-Creatures who live within the euphoria of consumption ecstasy. But don't expect them to work hard; and why should they kill themselves and degrade themselves to be happy as a middle class consumers. They have seen their hard-working daddies are hardly ever at home and are constantly burdened with irritations, coronaries and ulcers because of their hard work. [34] Is there happiness and creative self-fulfillment in enslaving yourself to a process of life that doesn't fulfill you? In the sixties the answer was to drop out and create alternate social organizations. And now the children of those experiments coming home to grandmother's home and her indoor toilet blame their parents for their materialist depredation! But our death children have also rejected modern society but not the consumer ecstasy and they fulfill themselves by robbing and murdering those who have the coveted material goods. After all they want is to be good Americans also and consume the good life. Since they belong to the culture of crime what they do is natural to them. Their behavior becomes thus institutionalized much the same way the cult of thugs did in precolonial India when after joining a traveling caravan and being friendly for several weeks, the disguised thugs killed all their fellow travelers by strangulation for their wealth, in the name of Kali as a religious devotion. Death was their friend and companion much as it is with a drive by teenage shooter who sees nothing wrong, absolutely nothing immoral, in killing innocent people or children walking along the streets. Why, because they are death generation children and the feel of strength and power they find in death is a solace to them and a surge of piety flows to them from their devotion to death which boost their self-esteem and meaning in life. Yes, death is their friend and guide and in death they find life and with each act of death devotion they are sanctified before the Lord of death and destruction and they find joy in that fact! But inside they are dead to themselves and it only through the violence that they become alive so that death to them becomes an aphrodisiac so they can feel life itself and that surge of life energy pushes them forward until they must kill again, and again and again! Our death teenagers are the cutting edge of Americas discontent and they are us in our most despicable form and they project our inner feelings of self-destruction into the market place of life as America begins dying to itself. America if you cut off your death children's hands to spite your heart will you cure the malady of alienation from within your heart? Our children are our hands and to cut them off from us is but a temporary solution because America will soon grow new and more destructive hands which shall strangle America on the expediency of self protection as the professional death cadre members take over America because of your discontent. Remember that your teenagers are yourself and but reflect your anguish and sorrow and they will die alone or with you. If America has the mercy of the heart necessary it will extend its hand in friendship and repentance and remorse and both its children and themselves shall be uplifted into life once again.

Without a self humanity is nothing. Our species is an evolving evolutionary species and it must ever expand and rise to it highest level possibility. Now is the time that Americans must stand up and be counted! Now is the time when the great crisis of humanity is appearing and nature is speaking to us in no uncertain terms. Our evoutionary natures cannot live in outmoded social forms which are controlled by the death masters. A psychological internal revolution is going on which finds reflection in the outer social disturbance of our teenagers. The outer ego systems resident in man feel the humiliation of the age as the inner self surges outward and up into higher ranges of altered states of consciousness. A psychosocial disequilibrium has been created within the inner nature of each one of us and our cultural self and each of us is crying inside and our discontent is flowing throughout the species continuum and our teenagers are acting out our discontent; a fact that is unknown consciously to the majority of Americans.

Social revolutions throughout history generally do not arise from starvation and misery alone but from humiliation. Historically the poor in country after country and ethnic group and diverse cultures show they can endure misery because they are used to it and it is institutionalized in their culture but humiliate them and take away from them what status and material goods they have then they revolt. People don't revolt to get more of what they don't have but because you are taking away from them what they already own in their hearts or personally. If a teenager robs another teenager of his expensive shoes he does so because he has been conditioned from childhood by television to know in his heart that it is his right and duty to have those pair of shoes. The fact that he does not presently own a pair is irrelevant because he knows he ought to be wearing those shoes; and by God he will have them, even if he must kill to achieve his aim. If the social order doesn't provide jobs so he can buy those shoes and if he lives in a criminal gang or culture of crime he takes what is rightly his by conquest. If on the other hand if he lives in a self contained culture with no television or radio and no such material expectations exist then he would be happy to go barefoot as all the other children have done from time immemorial.

But in America our self is our material self and if you do not have the shoes and the designer clothes then you are a teenager nobody. Your real inner self is constantly dying a little bit at a time in America and you suffer in quiet desperation. If you can surround yourself by a rising standard of living or a good status position so that you can forget temporarily that you are alienated from your self, then our teenager is content; but if this is not the case then our death teenager explodes in violence and robberies and in death rages. If he can acquire material good then he is like every other American, that is, until the slowly immolated Self that is buried and while content gives no conscious trouble awakes temporarily again. [35]

THE CHIP ON THE SHOULDER

Violence has always been a part of American life and is a covert part of American national character and an overt fact of life within the culture of our death children. Our death teenagers are following true American form when they kill and maim because they are acting out Americas primordial genocide phenomenon as any American would historically do, that is, they are following tried and true American historical genocide policy.

America's genocide phenomenon rose in the killing fields of American life as the country grew and expanded on the genocide of the native population. Our country and later our west was won by death and violence and every American today identifies covertly with this ideal in its language and thought process. Death by violence has always had an overt but usually covert honor within our society and even the vilest criminal historically has been romanticized and covertly been given honor as an infamous character that usually has supporters and detractors, yet they are constantly spoken about in our stories and movies and television programs.

Why? They were men of action who had the power to make right their wants and desires viable. If they won they were honorable and just; survival being a justifiable criterion for the righteousness of their actions. After all the winners of any war always rewrites history to their advantage and thus did the winners of the range wars and the Indian wars and the wars of conquest when we stole most of Mexico.

We are the ancestors of people who always exterminated most of their enemies and unconditional surrender was required of the remnants of the defeated as part of our national honor. The next step was always to further degrade the defeated indigenous enemy by putting them in concentration camps (reservations), then trying to take away their culture, economic viability, language, religion, and natural dignity as a human beings and in modern times to assimilate them into the Ghettos of America. When historically after conquest cultural depravation didn't work entirely more troops would enter the arena of honor and massacre what remaining integrity was left of the defeated population.

America thus developed a death thrill, a sense of power arrogance that rested on violence and massacres and the genocide phenomenon. Americans, individually and as a nation, cannot stand defeat because if it comes it signifies that we are weak failures and not worthy of love and respect individually or nationally. In this sense the nation is an adolescent teenager who has failed at his task of self-affirmation. When mother nature takes away her conditional love from the nation then nationally America is a nobody in defeat and cries inwardly because its national self identity is lost and lies tattered on the grounds of defeat and dishonor and no true American can face that fact. Even today no true American can stand the dishonor of America's defeat in Vietnam.

Violence is part of our national character and vies with restraint and a common sense urge for justice to quiet the beast within us. All of our major urban center have 400+ homicides yearly and now our teenager youth kill indiscriminately like mad-doggy killers. Guns are sold by the millions yearly in this country. Between 70 million and 200 million Americans own guns and they will not give them up even if the death masters want them too. They are not fools because even they know that power ulti-mately rests in the cradle of the gun arm!

America look also into your childhood for the genesis of your violence that our teenagers are raining upon us daily. No true American will stand silently by while he is being humiliated by the death boss's importation of their jobs and subsequent falling into the slavery of economic depredation once again.

They will fight first by drive by shootings and later will take up arms and then America may experience their second civil war. The time has come and passed when the covert death masters could take over the hearts and minds of America. The heart of America says that if you persist death masters then your treason will bounce back upon you and America will rejoice! Ask any American and he will tell you that Americans are free and shall remain free and let no man say otherwise.

PLAYGROUND OF AGGRESSION

The teenager's feelings of aggression and fair play are developed in his childhood and find expression in interpersonal play as a child. It is on the playground of life that self-reliance and fair play and aggression develops and are nurtured. Observe any play-ground in America and you will see children playing together with their mothers sitting around observing their precious bundle of male and female potential. Yes, in America your children are potentials and no parent knows beforehand whether his or her child has what it takes to be a man or a women of substance.

When little Johnny comes crying to Mama because he has lost his sand shovel to another kid's aggressive behavior the mother with an indignant look of scorn tells the "brat", because all kids are "brats" if they are not self-reliant ." Don't cry to me . Stand up for your self. Take it back kid! Kid you are big enough to take care of yourself!" Later another mother tells her Tommy."Don't hit that little kid. Well, hit him if he hits you." While a third mothers tells little Sammy, "Don't be a sissy. Can't you take it? Show that kid he can't hit you and get away with it Sammy. Meanwhile a fourth mother admonishes her son for pulling another child's hair, "He is smaller than you are Pete. He doesn't know any better. Pete, if you want to fight pick on someone your own size. And Pete don't tear that little girl's dress. Big boys must never hit little girls. And no I won't ask his mother to make Johnny give you back your toy. Get it yourself. He isn't any bigger than you are. Take it away from him and show him you got what it takes kid." As the battle of life goes on in the child's playground of life the children's mothers think to themselves and whether their dirt-smeared champion can take it and dish it out or whether he has what it takes to be a man; or perhaps she laments that Little Johnny ought to stand up for himself more as she wonders why is he so brave when he teases smaller kids or when he pulls the girl's hair but won't stand up to any one his size. [36]

When the kids graduate into the playgrounds of the school system fair play will be stressed and might makes right is looked down upon as the concept of fair play and regulations enters our teenagers life. The teenager begins to get contradictory messages, such as winning is everything, signifying that covert cheating within the rules or outright cheating may be all right if you don't get caught. One soccer coach's lament was that the contemporary kids rejected his cheating ways and won't hurt the opponent un-lawfully or break his leg if necessary as he shakes his head in dismay! But above all the rules teach our teenagers to be tough and stand up for themselves yet at the same time teach them that aggression is wrong. If you look carefully you will find a pattern that underlies these contradictory orders. Aggression is a fact of life but in a civilized society it must be constrained within certain social rules that takes into account the myth of human equality. All men are equal under the law applies also on the battlefield of life because honor and justice and are linked together as a moral imperative that says all acts of aggression must take into account the other person's weakness so that the relative strength of an opponent is a crucial factor in the aggression equation. It is unfair to beat a weaker opponent. So the playground director must factor the weakness of a teenager into his concept of just who shall be that teenager's game opponent. The weak must become stronger and so to do that perhaps a slightly stronger opponent should test out the weak teenager or there is no fairness or honor in winning. The strong must not just win by a triumph of strength over weakness but win only with an equal player. If he fights a stronger player than maxim effort is put forth but if his opponent is weaker, any maximum effort in not compatible with fair play.[37]

The rationale behind this factor is the Anglo-Saxon fear that says while we don't want the teenager to be a coward we also don't want him to be a bully. A bully responds to the same stimulus but the difference is the strength factor and also the bully is responding to his lower animal nature and when he expresses his frustration in the act of bullying he is a coward and is not playing by the rules. If the teenager is a coward but has no strength of action then he cringes and become the victim of another coward who does the bullying. It is a fact that a True American hates a coward. But to a true player the rules of fair play say that the greater strength of an opponent is a stimulus for putting forth the greater effort to win by the rules. An example of playing by the rules is to observe a boxing match and generally you ought see two evenly matched opponents boxing with one or the other occasionally scoring hitting points but generally neither one hurts each other too much and often the match is a tie or one opponent wins by just a few judge's point over the one fighter. They are playing by the rules.

But put one of those same fighters in an ally where he is being attacked by ten teenagers and he takes each opponent out, one by one with clockwork precision. But his fight is an equal one because he is fighting ten to one and fighting them all at once. But put even one of those teenager attacker in the ring or even all ten in the ring with the boxer and the fight is unfair. Aggression of one type is appropriate in one contest and not in another. Another example that took place in a far away land also makes the point . A man is attacked by 15 rufferians and the young karate master, a recent champion, puts all of them in the hospital but he is wounded in the arm and his arm's ligament is cut by a sword as he blocks its blow with his arm as he simultaneously kicks the man once in the stomach. The master-teacher of the karata teenager kicks his out of the gym for two years for using excessive force and killing the sword man. Why? The fight was unequal, whereas another karate teenager faces an equal amount of teenager ruffians and fights them to a standstill over a two hour period using no offensive blows at all is the winner because the fight was equal, that is, that fight was more equal than the former. You see this principle practiced in Goju karate gyms when some students develop a bullying attitude as they progress in their art. In free play fight in which there is no physical contact and you are judged on theoretically points scored, a bully is put up against a more experienced and higher ranked opponent who uses no offensive actions against his opponent although the bully can do his best. After a short while the bully finds his opponent is blocking all his blows and kicks and there is nothing in the world he can do. He is at the mercy of a more superior man who does not hit him or hurt him but backs him in a corner constantly and smiles at him not in triumph but in compassion for the young bully has learned the fairness doctrine.

Americans place less emphasis on rules than the English version of the fair play doctrine. In England boys are looked upon as tough little devils who will kick, bite and hit below the belt until they are taught proper civilized set of rules which are designed to make men behave decently to each other within the arena of life.

In America we give a new twist to the rule in that we say the teenager must think about each situation in terms of its unigue nuances because no set of rule can be used to fit the situation in all instances. In America the opponent may be Asian, negro, Porto Rican, Mexican and a variety of varying ethnic groups who may have other rules of combat than Johnny's. Possibly Johnny may encounters the death children who have no compassion except the death joy!

In England the mother will want to boy to shape up and become polished and become a man but in American Mama observes all the external dangers Little Johnny must face and she doesn't know if they will be too much for him. He must physically stand up for himself, then in business, in politics and he must learn to dish it out and he needs practice in standing up for himself or other people naturally will walk all over him.

In England the mother knows the schoolmasters and policemen umpiring the roughest games will make certain that 99 percent of the games will be played by the same rules. But our American Mom thinks of Americas past and present with its frontier battles, tong wars, feuds gangsters and death children and drive by shootings and she wonders just what battles Johnny must fight in a society that one gains merit and success by competition and when you lose you are nothing.

Our American mother knows, as she looks at her husband viewing the television football game, that her son must be stronger than his father. Papa hardly ever gets angry and rarely stands up for his rights because he has been tamed and dominated by the technocracy and she knows in her heart of hearts that her son must be more successful than his father. He must be more aggressive than his Dad or he won't be strong enough to be a real American!

To not be a real American is the worst fate any child can have; and Johnny's failures will demonstrate to Papa and Mama that they also are parental failures and must bare responsibility before society for that fact! It is also a fact that it is the women and Mama in particular who push little Johnny into being tough and assertive as every American worth his salt ought to be! [38]

Johnny's father may teach him how to double up his fist and how to punch as a skill; but Johnny is also being taught how to be aggressive and defend himself once he is attacked. And no man knows, in today's world, when he personally must defend himself.

Recently a young deaf man's sign language in a restaurant was misunderstood by a gang of teenagers who mistook his gestures for obscene gestures. He was hit over the head with a beer bottle and then the broken and jagged edges of the bottle was used to put his eyes out.

Where was America's fairness doctrine? When death stocks you in the afternoon where can you hide when there are no longer rules. Perhaps this is why Karate and judo are so popular in America now. Now hitting below the belt and breaking a man's leg is proper and you never pick up your opponent from the floor but kick him when he is down. Presently if you do not kick your opponent in the groin or stomach he will kill you for the sheer joy of it as his comrades cheer him on as they circle the victim; and they will have no guilt or remorse because they are teenage death children and have entered the organized death cadres and their death activities are justified principles of death morality and justice.

So what is a Mama to do? She has ambivalence toward fighting and must teach her children that it is wrong but also necessary, yet the child must have practice. But the child and teenager must remember always that what fighting he does must be done in self defense. Even then he must always remember that aggression and fighting will arouse Mother's wrath and fathers disapproval; but as an American he knows that aggression and fighting are necessary whether in the street defending yourselves or in the corporate allies of America. Johnny cannot let any one pick on him or show weakness or take away his job or invade his sacred house. He must be tough in this world and he must be tough to even get along with other obnoxious Americans who will stomp on his rights and privileges and steal from him and even take his life.

Yes our teenager or even when he is a young adult and perhaps even in his middle life career must always face the cold steel eyes of Mama-Boss and explain why he failed or didn't fight hard enough and why he didn't have the right stuff. Then he sinks down to midget size in Mama's eyes as she smiles gently the smile of death, "Well Johnny you aren't quite tough enough. Eh? But your Dad isn't either! [39] IIn that moment of ultimate and figurative male castration, Johnny the child, youth or even as an old man becomes a member of the death generation as the primordial fear-anxiety syndrome pushes him down into despair and he cries inside and knows he is doomed and worthless and a failure and these scars will never go away. But he remembers that as a child when he walked among his contemporaries that he used to put the chip on his shoulder and as he waited for another boy to knock it off his shoulder that he had to oppress his fears and anxieties that he might be beaten up and he must always have an appearance of bravery always. He knew that he had to get practice in fighting and that it was wrong to pick on other people and he realized in his gut that he had to be strong and aggressive to survive in the world and let no man tell him otherwise. And when Mama looks at him askance he will say" Honest Mom he was asking for it; beside you don't want every one to think I am a sissy or pretend I wasn't there." [40]

So when Mama-boss cast her steel blue eyes upon Johnny and says to her self, "Poor fool, he just can't measure up". Then Johnny the teenager or John the old man must get up off the ground or climb out of Mama's scornful deep pit of disapproval and get back into the arena of life and win; because he knows that Mom's love is conditional and when he later wins he and Mama and the world will know he is a successful American that all can be proud to say there goes John triumph, that successful ideal of American society and with those accolades Mother's fears of little Johnny's failures will be forgotten, temporarily.

If you think otherwise America remember that mother's influence is strong and pervasive. Historically it has had the strength to mold minds and spirits.

In ancient Greece the Spartan mothers looked with steel cold eyes into their solder's son's eyes when they sent their young to war! In those days if you found yourselves facing an overwhelming enemy you threw you spear and shield down and ran like hell to safety. But not the Spartan warrior youth because Mama looked long and deep into their eyes before they left for battle and said, "Come back with your shield or on it.! And the Spartans didn't lose a battle for seven hundred years because they ran from no man.

Three hundred and fifty Spartan soldiers held a narrow pass at the battle of Theomopoly and faced off five million troops of the Persian King Darious and only died fighting when betrayed and attacked from behind. But even then the cowardly Persians killed them by surrounding them and from a distance killed them with arrows because not one of them had the courage to face a true man, face to face, man to man, sword to sword, hand to hand.

When a Spartan general succumbed to bribers and was bricked up alive within a house of bricks to slowly starve to death, the first brick mortared was put up by his mother!

So let no man tell you that when Mama-Boss tells Johnny to get off his ass and become a man, that she doesn't mean it, or that Johnny doesn't know that she means it.

But America are you like the ancient Spartan warriors or the cowardly Persians warriors. You don't know that answer do you America? Perhaps only time will tell America; perhaps . . . !

Today no Spartan heros roam among us yet death surrounds us daily through our cowardly teenage death children who cannot face their inner psychological depredation except by killing innocent children and emasculated adults.

Remember that old adage that one American was equal to ten foreigners but the modern rendering of this idiocy is that ten Americans are now equal to one half of one foreigner! Perhaps we should reframe that statement to say ten Americans are equal to one American teenager Death Master!

CHAPTER 13

PANDORA BOX-MENTAL EVOLUTION: THE FOURTH CAUSAL AGENT OF THE GLOBAL CRISIS

FUTURIST COMMENTARY: It is recognized that Western science, since the time of the Renaissance, have failed to understand the nature of the evolution of consciousness and this fatal flaw has destroyed the species Homo sapiens. Today in the 22nd century we are finally grasping the why's and wherefores of our specie's mission and destiny yet we are already dying as a human race. There is no longer any hope for us and we cry out in sorrow and terror yet our cries are in vain and our efforts at our own salvation from ourselves meaningless.

The human race will soon be nothing but a memory reflected only in our archaeological remains.

Psychologist and transpersonal anthropologist **Campbell comments below on this problem of the evolution of human consciousness.**

The first sign of the development of an integral paradigm for 20th century man is that we are again viewing man as an evolutionary mental creature. This concept, a 19th century phenomenon, that died out in the first half of the 20th century, is now being revived as it is recognized that humanity is an evolutionary creature with not only organic, but also social and mental dimensions.

When unilineal cultural evolution or evolution in progressive hierarchical stages was rejected by most 20th century scientists the concept of mental-social evolution died a quick death in the scientific community. The rationale for this rejection was that it was accepted that social change was not primarily connected to an evolution of mentality. Not only did anthropologists reject such ideas but biologists reject the theory of recapitulation as linked with mental evolution, and psychological concepts of evolution fell on "evil days" within the psychological discipline. Animal psychologist ceased to be evolutionary-minded and physical anthropologists became unconcerned with behavioral evolution because of their concentration on evolutionary morphological problems. [1] Even psychologists concerned with studying personality between 1910-1940 preferred not to mention ego or self in their writings, thus effectively doing away with any entity that could psychologically and mentally evolve in time and space. [2]

Today, because of expanded scientific research in the fields of parapsychology, biofeedback research and transpersonal psychology, it is realized by a vanguard group of scientists that man is a self-transcending, evolutionary creature. New concepts and new paradigms now call for new explanations of man. Psychological man is now understood to be a psychohistorical creature, as well as a socio-metaphysical being. Human nature, to be fully understood, must be examined in integral terms that views Homo sapiens as a creature of a long evolutionary process–organic, psychomental and psychocultural. Transintegral Psychology presents the hypothesis that the key to the new structural paradigm is the concept of evolution as a self-transcending process.

PANDORA'S BOX

This concept of mental evolution may open a "Pandora's box" and let loose the past evils and abuses of social Darwinism and the unilinear cultural theory. This is a great danger, especially if future scientific technology develops definitive techniques to prove this hypothesis. The present evolutionary status of the species, therefore, needs to be clarified.

SPECIES CONSCIOUSNESS

Mankind, in the present era, exists within one species, Homo sapiens, divided into racial types that appear to be intellectually, linguistically and physically equal. All are potentially equal in the stream of consciousness evolutional. Transintegral psychology agrees with scientific findings that amply demonstrate that no racial or national community is superior to any other group mentally, psychologically, physically or linguistically. All human kind exists within the higher dimensions of the infrarational stage. All populations exist within a range of altered states of consciousness and are probably statistically equal with the range of mind states. They probably exhibit altered states of consciousness in their population much as I. Q. Variations exist. Now historically this equality of consciousness among groups may not have existed and may not prove to be a fact in the future. Right now, however all social societies seem to be equal in species consciousness in all of **its potential. Within the recent historic past while certain cultural and technological differences exist among and between** groups, these are the result of historic occurrences, borrowing, and cultural diffusion, that allowed certain peoples at the cross-roads of world interaction to gain certain technical and literary sophistications over other groups. History amply demonstrates that even these "high" cultures become extinct, or wane in their power and influence, and often descend into dark ages and even may completely lose their language, technology and cultural sophistication. At any one time one group, nationality, country or radical group may appear superior in some manner or form, but in reality it is riding the tide of the cultural dynamics of the age and will, in due course, face the exigencies of the historical process. From a psychological point of view, however, all people are racially, linguistically, and mentally equal. There is no one group that is inferior as a group. It is possible to take appropriate persons from any group and train them properly in a specific science and it can be demonstrated that the species consciousness is equal in all groups. This applies to culture as a whole when they decide to enter the modern world or gain a certain technological sophistication. All members of the human species belong to the stream of evolutionary consciousness and within all groups exist the total range of psychological types and potentials to enter into the varying dimensions of altered states of consciousness. Within each society an individual may exist in varying dimensions of altered states of consciousness. Some people may even live in very extremely high states of mind. Such geniuses may make dynamic cultural contributions that may transcend the usual cultural diffusion and historical occurrences and borrowing that allow certain cultures to capture technical and literary sophistication over other societies. If large numbers of such individuals exist within one specific society then great social gains and mental leaps can be made for humanity. No scientific evidence now exists that proves that any one culture has a monopoly of large masses of people living in higher states of consciousness. All societies are probably statistically equal within the range of mind states, much an I. Q. Variations exist within specific groups. Scientifically we can verify these states when our technology becomes more technical and sophisticate. Elmer green of the Menninger Foundation says that direct verification of higher mind energy states and their structural arrangements must now be inferred from parapsychological data and from reports of mystic and occultists from various cultures. This is because our electronic instruments are constructed of minerals and cannot quantify the higher ranges of altered states of consciousness because the transducer components are inadequate. Because humans, according to Green, have all the necessary parts and can detect a greater spectrum of energies we must rely on the descriptive analysis of men who have lived in such state of mind.[3] It would be advantageous for science to make a thorough analysis of the literature, both East and West, on the ranges of consciousness described by men who have existed in the higher dimensions of mind. It would even be better to examine living sages who can demonstrate such states of mind. Some scientists, such as Anthropologist Philip S. Staniford, are attempting this type of research and are utilizing empirical subjectivism techniques to duplicate the higher states of mind. This attempt supplements the empirical findings of biofeedback research, through which we have found that in some way the research subject can control this internal b body and mind states. Biofeedback research utilizes electronic instruments to monitor and feed back information to the scientist and the research subject on the minute internal happenings of the subject's body and mind. This transpersonal technique to monitor "inner space" is a development stemming from the research and experiences of psychologist, meditators, engineers, physicists, and physiologists, and draws on electronics and psycho-physiological operant conditioning procedures. Examples of recent research using these techniques are the various projects of Elmer and Lyce Green of the Menninger foundation. In their laboratory in the United States, they have conducted research on autogenic training and biofeedback focusing on alpha and theta brain-wave states, reverie and imagery. Also, with their portable laboratory, they have carried out cross-cultural research on altered states of consciousness and have made physiological studies of yogis in India and in the United States. Luids West, University of California at Los Angeles anthropologist, has also used electronic equipment to study the transpersonal abilities of the Tarahumar Indians of central Mexico.[4]

Through such scientific research social psychology and physiology, will hopefully gain and understanding of social phenomena's and man's altered states of internal awareness. Better still they will understand the relationship between consciousness and culture and how the integration of mind, culture and personality are related. We must know these answers if we are to construct a new theory of man for the 20th century. It is not enough that we think we know the above categories are integrally related. We must understand and examine the actual process in detail. This is why when we talk about the new development of a viable model of humanity we must have an interdisciplinary approach to the problem. We must set up research projects that can quantify ego states in a meaningful manner with specific psychocultural processes. Already you have researcher, such as Paul Bakan, with his controversial hemisphere study correlating certain behavioral activities to the left or right hemisphere of the brain. He believes that through the measurement of eye movements called "clems," or conjugate lateral eye movements, that he can judge whether one is an analytical person or a vital-emotional person. He also types people according to alpha waves. [5] Other researchers are using behavioral therapy techniques to replace anxiety states by relaxation responses. A specific example is the systematic desensitization technique. This concept says that muscles become tense during anxiety situations, therefore, if the muscle is relaxed one is not tensive. The approach conditions muscular relaxation through an abbreviated Jacobean progressive relaxation technique and the subject remains calm under testing. This type of testing uses a graded series of anxiety sciences called a hierarchy to test the subject. The researcher Wolpe reports that the learning transference from the lab to life situation reveals a success rate of 80% to 90% on anxiety phobias. [6]

This type of research can show us the way to control our runaway vital nature and at the same time map the plural personality system's life process. Some biofeedback research demonstrates that alpha brain waves can overcome anxiety. [7] Additional research shows that meditation changes the activity of the electrical waves in the brain. 8 It is interesting that some studies have shown that alpha waves are in some brain cells and not in other parts of the brain. Research by Akiva Kusamasui on skilled Zen monks showed, however, that strong alpha waves existed in all the lobes of the brain. Obviously meditative training increases the brains' abilities over visual attention, body senses, memory and verbalization. Meditative transformation techniques used by Transintegral Psychology and other traditions should go a long way in helping humanity to control his nature and then transcend it.

It is also interesting that observing man from an evolutionary viewpoint we see that individuals differ in their mixture of beta and alpha brain rhythms. Some people generate no alpha, some mostly alpha. Seemingly biofeedback and transpersonal meditative techniques can help man in his emergence toward a more balanced and harmonious existence. Kamiya and Faulk's observations definitely show that personality change does take palace after a person experiences much alpha waves over time. A person becomes more aware, sensitive, and relaxed after taking the training. [9] It is in this realm of personality change and mapping the inner dimensions of the human race's ego system that the greatest promises lie in biofeedback research. A start has been make at scientifically recording in a systematic manner some of the inner states of man's subconscious. Inner dream states, for example, can now be correlated with eye movements so that a person can be awakened and a recording made of hypnagogic images. Interpretations made from a person's subconscious now can give important information on the inner being of humanity.

The Russians are also making some fantastic discoveries concerning the nature of man. They have scientifically verifies what Transintegral Psychology calls the subtle physical consciousness or aura. It is an environmental consciousness or nervous envelope that surrounds the physical body. This circumconscient protecting envelope is a type of environmental atmosphere that protects the body from foreign thought forms that are sent or wander in from other peoples subconscious mind, passions, suggestions or forces of illness. [10]This physical consciousness is part of humanity's plural personality structures and is everywhere in one form or another in the consciousness. [11] One cannot localize it in the other personality divisions unless one's awareness becomes sufficiently subtle.[12] The Russians state that all living things, plants, humans, and animals have a physical body made of atoms and molecules, but have also a counterpart body of energy. Russian biologists, biochemists and biophysicists are using new instruments that are connected to an electron microscope to investigate this living double of organisms that previously only clairvoyants could observe. They have also developed a Kirlian camera that uses high frequency electrical energy to photograph what the Russians call electronic bioplasmic energy. This camera works by itself independently or can also be connected to the electronic microscope. Another instrument, called a Sergeyer detector, developed by Dr. Sergeyev, a neurophysiologist, apparently measures the human force field at a distance of four yards from the body–this research is classified by the Russian military, however. Similar works on human force fields are being conducted at the university of Saskatchewan, Canada by Dr. Abram Hoffer and Dr. Harold Kelm. Dr. Gulyaiev, of the Biological Cybernetic laboratory in the University of Lenigrad, is also said to be working on an "electro-aurora" device that is so sensitive that it can measure the electrical field of a nerve. This device is reportedly able to detect even the muscular reactions that accompany thoughts. It measures these reactions and reveals factors about the organism from the electrical signals of the aura. [13] The Russians don't understand the nature of this bioplasmic energy yet, but they do know it isn't electromagnetic or electrical and it somehow has energy focal points that coincide with the 700 plus needle point positions on the human body which the Chinese system of acupuncture had documented. Czechoslovakia scientists, with the backing of the Central committee of the Czechoslovakian Communist Party and the Czechoslovakian Academy of Science, are developing psychotronic generator which somehow taps this human energy potential. They have also applied information theory to telepathy in an unusually successful manner. A field of research that scientists at the Westinghouse Electrical Corporation, at its Astronautic Institute in Baltimore, began studying to see if it could be utilized in communications technology.

From a psychological point of view, the above discoveries, are now just being appreciated, although as long ago as 1921 Sigmund Freud wrote that he would devote his life to psychical research rather than to psychoanalysis, if he had his life to live over. [14]

Transintegral Psychology feels that to understand man we must map man's parapsychological potential. These seemingly supernormal powers, such as telepathy, clairvoyance, second sight, and certain psychological phenomena are quite normal to man's subliminal mind. [15] The problem, of course, is to scientifically map these normal powers of man's subliminal mind. In most cases we have not the scientific technology to measure these psychological phenomena. This is why breakthroughs such as Kirlian photography, with its use of a high frequency spark generator that generates up to 200,000 electrical oscillation per second, is so important to true scientific research. Because this device can be connected to clamps, optical instruments, plates, microscopes or electron microscopes its wide utilization is ensured. It is rather remarkable that the Russians' discovery of the bioplasmic body causes some sort of bioluminescence onto photo paper. What is even more startling is that the bioplasmic body or secondary "energy body," somehow projects states of mind and illness onto the physical body. The energy flow of the bioplasmic body, reflecting states of mind, thoughts, emotions, illness, and fatigue as energy flows described as flares of varying colors. This energy field seems to be a unified system. Scientists at the State University of Kazkhstan, say that the aura causes the bioluminescence to be visible in Kirlian pictures and not any electrical state of the organism. Interestingly this energy body has its own labyrinthine motion quite unlike the energy pattern of the physical body. [16] All living things seem to have this double energy body. When researchers cut parts of a leaf or a salamander limb off, this double energy body is still visible on the Kirlian photograph. [17] Because the focal point of the human energy field seems to be the 700 + points of the acupuncture system it is said that these energy points are in communications with organs deep within the physical body. This research seems to prove the contention that every organ has an energy connection with the skin. It also seems to prove that mind, body and the cultural environment does affect the individual and his energy body. Kirlian photography research shows that thoughts, moods and emotions does have enormous effects on a person's energy field. Psychosomatic illness and depressed states of mind seemingly do cause illness that incidentally shows up on Kirlian film even before they manifest in the physical body. It seems the acupuncturist may be correct when he asserts that the energy body within man links man with the Cosmos. Grihchenko and inyushin say that because man's vital energy links humanity with the cosmos that any change in the environment or the universe causes a resonance in the vital energy field that in turn affects the physical body. This is how the body adjusts to its surroundings. Research by the University of Kazakhstan shows that the bioplasmic body is affected by changes in the atmosphere. [18] This energy body is also affected by telepathy. A young physicist, victor Adamenko has invented a new apparatus called the CCAP-Conductivity that locates the acupuncture points and measures any changes of energy flow in the bioplasmic body. He demonstrates that these variations in energy flow can be graphed and its intensity shown on a numerical scale. [19]

This instrument when used in a telepathy experiment in Moscow, had its needles flicker back and forth as the subject telepathically sent messages when they are picked up by the bioplasmic body. [20] There is also a response or change in blood volume in one's body when telepathic messages are received. In the United States, Douglas Dean's research at the Newark college of Engineering, shows that while a person is not aware of a change in the blood volume such changes can be measured with a plethysmograph attached to the thumb.[21] Researcher, sister Dr. Justa has even found that psi affects enzymes.[22] Research also show that seemingly changes in brain waves coincide with telepathy being received by subjects. The polygraph (lie detector) also is felt by some scientists to indicate when ESP reaches the body. [23] Other scientists think that the sender and recipient of telepathic messages attune unconsciously their brain waves together when communicating telepathically. Dr. Sergeyev says that when their heart beats, synchronization takes place that is attested to by the electrocardiographs attached to both sender and receiver. There is also simultaneous increase in arrhythnia, greater cardiac noise and a quicker heartbeat. There is also simultaneous changes in the frequency range and spectral structure of the tremor registration curve when telepathic contact occurs. [24]

There is great significance in the results of all of these experiments. A significance that goes far beyond what is seemingly apparent. This factor is that a single human being is not alone in the universe. He is connected to other members of his species and to the animal kingdom in general. Humanity cannot escape from itself. The species is connected together on the conscious, unconscious and transpersonal levels of consciousness. This connection with cognitive reality is a linguistic process that unites the species together through a telepathic lineage on the conscious, subconscious and transpersonal dimensions. It is a consciousness projection on to the sphere of culture as an anthropologist understands sociocultural reality. Culture in this sense is a human event that is projected into the world as a symbolic system—an integrated logico-linguistic matrix. This creation is not just an abstract social heritage continuum but a live force that operates somewhat similar to a bouncing ball in a pin ball machine.

Mind states in this sense are states of being, living is time-space but unitive with the biological process. Consciousness and cognitive culture, thus are partially a projection of biophysical consciousness. Sigmund Freud, in his book Totem and taboo, suggests that man somehow projects from within himself the force to shape the outer world. [25] Transintegral Psychology calls this process the Psychocognitive culture theory.

THE CONCEPT OF CULTURE

To understand the psychological meaning of our modern day pre-dicaments we must understand that culture is a sphere of linguistic reality that codes the people of any society in such a way that one may say they are human beings. Edward Tyler says that "Culture or civilization, taken in its wide ethnographic sense, is that complex whole which includes knowledge, belief, art, morals, law, custom and any other capabilities and habits acquired by man as a member of society:" [26] Man acquires human culture as a participating member of society. It is transmitted though psycholinguistic symbolism. There is a sharp disagreement as to its definition, scope and functional relation to individual man and society. The realist, for example would say that culture is learned behavior, institutions and customs. It has no life independent of society. The individual, on the other hand, is looked upon as one who is affected by the customs of society. The idealist school of culture conceives of culture differently. For them culture is a stream of ideas or patterns of behavior or designs for living. Culture is something perceived by mind.

Both schools of thought conceive of culture as objective and impersonal social heritage or as the sum of socially inherited tradi-tions. The realists say cultural heritage is material objects, customs and ideals. The idealist, following in the tradition of Plato and Hegel say cultural heritage is a supraorganic stream of ideas. The objective idealist would even say that culture as a heritage of ideas has a tran-scendent reality all its own. This is a super-psychic reality indepen-dent of human beings. The Psychocognitive school of thought says that a new perspective must be developed that view the problem from inside and outside, from above and below the culture.

MIND STATES AND
SOCIOCULTURAL DYNAMICS

The missing ingredient in the definition of culture is the ideas of consciousness in interaction with society. Mind states are not passive and static but dynamic linguistic processes. They are psycholinguistic forces projected into the cultural process. They are also linked with the psycho-personality systems on the conscious, unconscious and the personal dimensions. But the idealism of a culture is structured in linguistic parameters, its ultimate expression is psychological and mental. The connecting link among these three phases is a telepathic lineage. This telepathic linkage is what constantly reinforces the implicit and explicit cultural ideals in each society; this factor is what Transintegral Psychology calls the concept of transcultural synthesis.

Anthropologist Laura Thompson says that each society's rules and regulations are even conditioned into the very neuromotor structure of the human body. When one is doing the right thing in society one feels it in one's bones. This right mode of thought is projected out from a society's population daily as an unconscious telepathy. It is interesting that Margaret Mead has said that the prevailing understanding of culture borders on that of a "group atmosphere." [27] Mind, language and culture are circular agents acting on each other. Each in its turn is a causal force that acts on each other and feeds on each other in a circular manner. Anthropologist Paul Bohannan says that language is the medium that encodes culture into a viable system. Language is culture he says. [28] The psycholinguist Sapir and Whorf go one step further and make the assertion that the language one speaks somehow structures the way one perceives reality. Sapir says that our thought groves and our language are inextricably interrelated and integrally the same. [29] Language and culture are one. Language and its structure is thus a cognitive map of social reality. Language in this sense does not merely inventory experience but is self-contained. It is a creative symbolic organization that defines experience because of its formal completeness but also because of the manifolds unconscious projection of its implicit expectations onto the arena of experience. [30]

Benjamin Lee Whorf, the co-founder of the Sapir-Whorf hypothesis, stresses that language is a type of logic and frame of reference that conditions and molds the thought processes of its habitual users. When a language and a particular culture develop together, important relationships exist among aspects of the grammar and the structure of the culture as a whole. 31 Kluckhohn and Leighton, for example, say that the Navaho tongue is so radically different from English that it exists almost practically in a different world. [32] It is rather obvious that language and vocabularies reflect a culture's world view. Kluckhohn says that different languages reflect distinct ways of defining thoughts and experience. [33] Whorf even says that the process of thinking itself has to be understood by looking at the relationship among the dynamics of language, mind and culture. Whorf says that a person's thought patterns are controlled by inexorable linguistic laws that are unconscious. Every language has its own vast pattern-system that the personality communicates through and builds the house of his consciousness. [34] This house of consciousness is the syntheses of mind, personality dynamics and the logico-aesthetics of the sociocultural process. Language is the key factor in this mix.

THE NOTION OF THE UNCONSCIOUSNESS

Campbell's Psychocognitive culture hypothesis says the dynamics of culture lie in the domain of the unconscious. Claude Levi Strauss says that most linguistic behavior is on the unconscious level. The rules of our language structure unconsciously how we will speak to an issue. Language is not only structured unconsciously at the phonological level but also at the grammatical and lexical level and even structures our discourse. To Levi Strauss, linguistics reveals the phenomenal reality of mental life that is to be found at the unconscious level of the human dimension. [35] Boas also makes the point that because language is the product of basic psychological processes that are unconscious their origin lies in the unconscious mind. [36] Modern depth psychology has shown the unconscious to be the primordial foundation of reality. Philosophers like Von Hartmanns say this unconsciousness is the mysterious and hidden power that guides the real world and the subjective ideal mind. [37] Edward Sapir makes the point that language habits demonstrate unconscious indicators that constantly reveal to society the psychological status held by its members. [38] This concept agrees with Levi Strauss's contention that linguistic and social phenomena are projections onto the social and conscious level of universal laws that regulate the unconscious mind activities. [39] Laura Thompson says that this complex projection expresses the hidden wisdom of the unconscious when it is revealed in dreams, myths, poetry, dances, music, ceremonies, architecture and literature. These projections also include unconscious symbolisms of space and time relationships. [40]

THE TRANSPERSONAL DIMENSION OF THE UNCONSCIOUSNESS

An adequate concept of culture requires that we bridge the idealist and realist cultural themes. Campbell's Psychocognitive culture hypothesis does this by recognizing the truth of both positions and by adding the transpersonal concept of consciousness.

The realists are correct in emphasizing culture as an attribute of social life and learned behavior. The idealists are right in their emphasize on culture as a stream of ideas, an aggregate of ideas in the minds of people. Surely culture is patterns of behavior or designs for living. Our investigation of the conscious and unconscious nature of language surely gives support to the idealist position that culture has a transcendent reality structure. This is a superpsychic reality structure that has a type of autonomous reality independent of human beings. This position has validity in the sense that most human beings do not have control over their unconscious moreover because of the unconscious telepathic projections that occur daily. The realists, on the other hand, have a point when they say social heritage is ideas, ideals, customs and institutions. They are both wrong when they don't recognize the creativity, self-actuality and self-transcendence of humanity. The psychodynamics of the inner self and the transpersonal nature of man is the hidden ingredient that ties the realist and idealist positions together. The inner dynamics of the psyche and the emergent quality of mind operating on a conscious level as higher mind dimensions and unconsciously in the subliminal mind as extrasensory perceptions are the key factors in the integration of consciousness and culture. In some cultures, such as Buddhist communities in Tibet, the Papago, and the Dakota, these Psychocognitive abilities are integrated on the sociocultural level. Not only do these groups strive to consciously actualize themselves but this striving consists of directive movements at the unconscious level. Among the Dakota, the Lauans, and the Papago, these include activities such as dreams, visions, and hallucinations. This integration process of consciousness and culture is a normal and developmental thing, although at the unconscious level. It is what Laura Thompson calls the wisdom of the unconsciousness within the cultural process.

This takes place with three levels, that is, on the implicit linguistic level, on the transpersonal level and on the subliminal unconscious dimension. On the implicit linguistic level it is a mechanism that allows specific metaphysical models to operate almost invisibly to the conscious mind. Whorf for example says," Thus, the Hopi language and culture conceal a Metaphysics, such as our so-called naive view of space and time does, or as the relativity theory does; yet it is a different metaphysic from either." [41]

Whorf in giving us a specific example stresses that these abstractions are either explicitly in words that are metaphysical or psychological terms or are implicit in the structure and grammar of a language and in Hopi language accounts for all phenomena and their interrelations and functions as an integrator of Hopi culture in its varying phases.[42] For example Whorf states that on the linguistic level:

> In the Hopi view, time disappears and space is altered, so '
> that it is no longer the homogeneous and instantaneous

timeless space of our supposed intuition or of classical
Newtonian mechanics. At the same time, new concepts and
abstractions flow into the picture, taking up the task of
describing the universe without reference to such time or
space–abstractions, by approximations of which we attempto
reconstruct for ourselves the metaphysics of the Hopi, will
undoubtedly appear to us as psychological or mystic in character. [43]

Whorf also speaks of covert class within languages which is a
classification of whole worlds of objects such as the Navaho concepts of round objects and long objects which attempts to depict
the subtle in terms of the gross. He says that such covert concepts
like covert gender is definable but partakes of a sense or feeling of
a rapport-system that fall on an intuitive quality that is sensed
rather than comprehend and is similar to the Hindu concept of
arupa, the formless. [44] He says:

> A covert linguistic class may not deal with any grand
> dichotomyof objects, it may have a very subtle meaning
> and it may have no overt mark other than certain dis-
> tinctive 'reactances' with certain overtly marked forms.
> It is what I call a cryptotype. It is a submerged, subtle,
> and elusive meaning, corresponding to no actual word,
> yet shows by linguistic analysis to be functionally impor-
> tant in the grammar. [45]

Transintegral Psychology stresses the fact this unconscious process
is a continuous telepathic event. Mirra Alfassa says that the aura
or bioplasmic body since it extends beyond the visible limits of
the physical body is in constant contact with the subtle physical
consciousness of other people. This reciprocal contact is
influencial–the most powerful thought patterns gain control. A
thought becomes an entity almost seeking to realize itself in the
cultural dimension of man. [46] The individual is, according to Mirra

Alfassa, constantly being imbrued with telepathic suggestions of this kind on psychomental levels. These telepathic messages at contact enter into the vital-emotional physical consciousness of man. This process is generally unconscious and ordinarily a person feels that these thought are his own. This process, surely supports the idealist position that culture is a stream of transcendental ideas. Telepathic communication is quite similar to Bagley's contention that culture is often thought of as a set of platonic ideas which floats over the heads of the culture bearer. [47] Anthropologist Margaret Mead also says that the common idea of culture is near the concept of a group atmosphere. [48]

What we find within the social life of a culture is a continuous conscious, unconscious and transpersonal communication by the people of that social order with each other. Transintegral psychology states that mankind lives surrounded by people who are constantly communicating on an unconscious level with each other. Mirra alfassa says that in a social situation certain obligations and expectations are required of everyone. Often these cultural rules are not vocal but nevertheless are expected to be fulfilled. These social rules and aspirations become formations which telepathically enter the other person as suggestions which are absorbed without resisting and awakens within one a similar impulse. These telepathic suggestions enter people from morning to evening and often are accentuated during the sleep process since a person's consciousness is not awake, watching and giving some type of protection. There are ways to strengthen the aura so that such suggestions can be stopped. There are techniques to balance the personality systems and to transform the vital barbarian that is man of the 20th century.

Generally this type of cultural reinforcement is unconscious. And the overt cultural situation is influenced through their linguistic metaphysical terminology belongs to the subjective realm. Every language contains certain concepts and terms of a cosmic nature in which is couched the themes and thought of a people and civilization. In American culture such words are substance, reality, matter, cause or past, present, future , space, time. In hopi, for example, they think in terms of tunatya or of hope or of in the action of hoping. Most of their metaphysical words are verbs which contains the concept of hope or in our words thought, desire and cause. Whorf says the Hopi term crystallizes their philosophy of the universe in which the objective and subjective dualism comes together. And refers to the subjective, unmanifest, vital and causal aspects of the Cosmos or that action or fermentation that works toward manifestation in the world. It is a mental-causal activity that presses upon and into the realm of the manifested cultural stream of life.

This overt and covert system finds expression in Hopi culture in their burgeoning activity in growing plants, or in the forming of clouds and their condensation in rain, etc., and in any activity in which hoping , wishing and striving thought is developed. You find they have concentrated prayers, and a hopeful praying of the general community which finds expression through exoteric communal ceremonies as well as certain esoteric rituals in the underground kivas. All these activities bear the pressure of the collective Hopi-thought and will from the subjective to the objective world.[50] So in this sense the metaphysical term tunatya transcends, begins to hope, and comes true. Whorf says that " . . . tunatya 'coming true' is the Hopi term for objective, as contrasted with subjective, the two terms being simply two different inflectional nuances of the same verbal root, as the two cosmic forms are the two aspects of one reality." [51]

SCIENTIFIC PROOF FOR THE MIND CULTURE CONNECTION

We have discussed a few of the scientific proofs to the psychocognitive culture theory at the beginning of this chapter. We will now explore additional insights on the mind-cultural linkage. The conection is rather obvious on the conscious linguistic level but the dynamics of the process lies on the unconscious dimension. Mind to mind communication, whether on a conscious or unconscious level, is always in cultural and linguistic terms. On the transpersonal dimension the communication may be symbolic but representative of psychocultural categories of reality. Through such communications social ideals are upheld and cultural themes and ethos ideas which represent the psychological needs and health of the population are projected into the social order. The question now arises as to what type of scientific proof exists to demonstrate that a mind to mind telepathic connection exists within the cultural order. Research up to the present seems to point to the fact that such a connection does in point of fact exist. For example, Dr. Pavel Nasumov in his paper, "Scientific Problems of Telepathy", demonstrates that a telepathic connection exists between a mother and her child. In an experimental situation mothers were separated from their children in another part of the clinic where neither the children nor the mothers could hear each other. When a baby cried, the mother became nervous, when a child was in pain because a doctor took a blood specimen, the mother showed anxiety signs. None of the mothers in the experiment knew when the doctors were interacting with their children. [52] According to Jung and his followers this parent-child symbiosis is an archetypal situation par excellence in which telepathy demonstrates synchronicity. [53] Iran Stevenson has made as survey of spontaneous conditions of telepathic impressions which supports this premise. It seems that 33.8 percent of his cases within the family involved telepathic interchanges. There was a 13.7 percent intercommunication between husbands and gives and a 15 percent sibling telepathic connection rate. [54] This interchange can be negative as well as positive. Berthold E. Schwarz in some of his studies surely has shown the close interrelationship between a patient's psychopathology with telepathy. In one case study he show how telepathy unconsciously can be an emotionally destructive force in the parent-child relationship. [55] The studies by Johnson and Szurek, [56] Melittta Sperling, [57] and Ja Ehrenwald also point out the negative aspects of telepathy by showing how neurotic children act out the antisocial impulses which their parents have repressed. [58] The psychoanalyst Erik Erikson refers to this same principle as the tendencies of children to live out the secret dreams of their parents. [59]

Possibly the mother child connection is a holdover from our animal past. Russian research with rabbits show a similar telepathic connection between mother and off-spring. Scientists placed baby rabbits aboard a submarine while the mother rabbit stayed in the laboratory on shore with implanted electrodes deep in her brain. Below the surface of the water each baby was killed one by one. At each synchronized instant of death the brain of the mother rabbit reacted. Naumov emphasizes that communication took place and the Russian's instruments registered these moments of ESP. [60]

Mind communication with plant kingdoms seems also to occur. Research in New York by Cleve Backster with tiny shrip show that when they are killed a reaction occurs with plants in the surrounding area. Backer makes the point that nothing seems to impair this communication. Even lead shields did not stop it. [61]

Perhaps on the human dimension communication on the unconscious level cannot be stopped also. Dr. Gardner Murphy, President of the American Society for Psychical Research, for example, often compares individuals to volcanic islands which project above the sea yet beneath the slope they all connect together at ground level. [62] At the unconscious ground level mind to mind communication seemingly can be spontaneous. Professor C.D. Broad, in his book, Religion, Philosophy and Psychical Research, says that telepathic interaction may be taking place, even continuously, without the receiver being aware of such messages. [63] The receiver in these cases may feel only a mood or sensations. Russian research seemingly collaborates this point. Naumov-sergeyev-pavlov teaming together demonstrated that feelings of anger, fear and violence not only could be telepathically sent from room to room but also from Moscow to Lenigrad. They also found that the EEG records changed dramatically when telepathy was emotionally grounded. When negative emotions were transmitted a cross-excitation of the brain took place. The spontaneous EEG character changed to the tired brain state which was dominated by a slow, hypersynchronized delta and theta type brain waves. Receivers experienced very unpleasant head pains and bodily sensations.[64] Similar research findings have appeared in the United States according to Dr. Berthod Schwarz, a renowned and highly honored New Jersey neurologist, psychiatrists and writer. He has collected over five hundred cases of telepathic transmissions of bodily ills between parents and children. He feels that telesomatic and motor-acting thought patterns of a child or parent cause physical reaction in the other.[65] On a more overt level Dr. Leonid L. Vasiliev, in his book, Experiements in Mental Suggestion, reports how he conducted hundreds of experiments in trying to think people into action. The subjects responded to telepathic commands to cross your legs, raise your right hand, walk forward. Dr. vasiliev even found that the impact of his thought could influence the body sway in some people.[66]

Research even more bizarre than simple telepathic commands to get people to respond bodily is now taking place. The objectives of this research is to control a person's consciousness with telepathy–the telepathic knockout! Research on this aspect of telepathy has progressed from 1924 to the present in Russia.[67] Subjects are initially hypnotized and then days, weeks, months later are telepathically knocked out at will from a distance. It has been found out that one can even talk and question people in such states. The telepathic force that knocks subjects out is created by holding strong visual images of the subject.[68] Subjects not only can be put to sleep telepathically from room to room, from building to building but from more than a thousand miles away.[69]

At the present time, such research is going ahead rapidly in Russia. Parapsychologists in Lenigrad and Moscow are using telepathic manipulation of consciousness while recording each success with the EEG. Both receivers and senders are attached to this machine. The sender at random moments was able to wake up the subjects six out of eleven times. At another time the subject was woke up six out of eight times. As soon as the message is sent the subject wakes up within twenty to thirty seconds. At the Lenigrad laboratory subjects have also been put to sleep telepathically.[70]

The Russians have apparently discovered aspects of the sub-liminal force which "Aurobindo says are inherent in the transpersonal nature of our species. He says that there is such a thing as a willed use of any subtle force, whether it is transpersonal, mental or vital-emotional which can be used to secure particular results from any point in the world. Just as there are unseen elec-trical waves so there are also mind waves, and waves of emotion, anger, sorrow, etc., which can affect people without them know-ing it–they only feel the results.[71]

The Russians have added a further development to telepathic knockout research. One parapsychologist put an entranced sub-ject in an isolated room and watches on close-circuit TV, while they telepathically guided the subject dimensionally to physically fall forwards, backwards, etc. In one test the subject fell ten times out of ten commsands and fell in the correct direction commanded eight times out of ten. According to Naumov, over one thousand people have been tested in this way. [72] In the light of such research the contention of philosopher Henri Bergson that the nervous sys-tems' function is really to blot out irrelevant material may have some validity.[73]

Mind dynamics and the power of consciousness within the social context is seemingly more complex than heretofore was conceived. Aurobindo makes the point that the mind is a potent agency which can make formations which effectuate themselves in our own and others' consciousness. It can even have an effect on matter.[74]

Campbell's psychocognitive culture theory contends that this mind flow is the connecting link between consciousness and cul-ture and when it occurs it is the transcultural synthesis linkage. As scientist Naumov says telepathy is probably always flowing among people. We probably are always telepathically aware of the feelings and thoughts of peoples in groups. This is probably why some people get along well with each other and some instantly dislike one another. Some Russian scientists believe that ESP is enmeshed in the daily social life and affects any group situation. [75] Transintegral psychology says that individuals are affected in a group situation because each individual is connected together in a group by a force field of energy–subtle physical or aura as Mirra Alfassa and Aurobindo contend.

This electronic sphere was established to exist in 1935 by Dr. Harold Burr, professor of neuroanatomy at Yale University, around all living matter as a electromagnetic field. [76] Later research by Yale neuropsychiatrist, Dr. Leonard Ravitz, led to the discovery that not only could the mind influence this field around the body but that by measuring this electromagnetic field the researcher could determine a person's state of mind and depth of hypnosis.[77] Another instrument, invented by Russian scientist Sergeyev, can now pick up this electrostatic field around humans. This detector picks up this field up to 12 feet from the body without any direct contact and records the data as a graph on a film. Dr. Ravita stated in the 1951 Yale Journal of biology and medicine that research demonstrates that this body field is affected by the sun and moon. [78] The Russians contend that three things affect this field. They are energy fields produced by machines, natural forces produced by the moon and sun and possible planets and energy fields produced by human emotions, individually and in groups. [79] It seems as though mind, energy, consciousness, culture and existence are all connected together in some inexplicable manner. Perhaps it is as Aurobindo says that force which is inherent in existence may be at rest or in motion but it is there and cannot be abolished, diminished or essentially altered in any way.[80]

Dr. Naumov says that the discovery of magnetic and electrostatic field energy as well as the recent discovery that currents of energy flow in the body are neither blood nor electrical, may hold the key to a new concept of the personality structure.[81] One Russian experiment showed how telepathy influences a group. Dr. Naumov would get a total electromagnetic impression of a group and then records how the introduction of a new member changed this electromagnetic pattern. They feel that present day psychology in the future will revolve around parapsychology. Psi will surely be the dominant concept of the subconsious, the emotions and the personality. [82] Physicist George Anderson, at a convention for the Association for Transpersonal psychology at Stanford University, makes a similar statement concerning group energy. He feels that the universe, from a physicist's point of view, seems more like thought patterns–very similar to that found in human beings. This thought is energy and energy constitutes the makeup of all things.[83]

CHAPTER 14

PARADIGM CRISIS

FUTURIST COMMENTARY: Twentieth century is a time of scientific Crisis in various fields of science and new ideas and concepts have yet to be discovered which will allow a dynamic paradigm to come into being. It is also the end period of the industrial revolution and mankind and his societies lie wallowing in the quicksand of scientific and social despair.

This despair is still facing us today in the 22nd century and there is almost no time left before our social order collapses into extinction.

Campbell, the social scientist, comments on this situation in the latter part of the 20th century.

The first causal agent of the global crisis of consciousness is the lack of an adequate paradigm or super theory for man of the 20th century. Our age needs a new world vision or paradigm view. A paradigm is a scientific model that includes theory, law, application and instrumentation. It provides theoretical formulae from which spring particular coherent traditions of scientific research.

It is realized by a vanguard group of scientists that science needs to develop new concepts and paradigms that can give new explanations about man in the world. This has to be done because the old conceptual framework or paradigm, through which the scientific community design's hypothesis models, has developed massive anomalies that can only be corrected when the scientific community accepts a new conceptual structure, allowing a return to normal, scientific endeavors.

Today the scientific world exists in a period that Thomas S. Kuhn calls "the emergence of the crisis in the scientific community."[1] It is realized by a vanguard group of scientists that science needs to develop new concepts and paradigms that can give us a new and expanded understanding of humanity. It is a point of fact that in an age of technology that relies on science for innovations and new concepts and for discovering the law of nature that if the old rules and scientific hypotheses are disintegrating the age begins to stand on quicksand and the entire foundation of the modern age order begins to crack and fall apart. When the scientific world begins to fall apart new ideas and paradigm models of science must be created or scientific progress stops. But you ask, just what is a paradigm or scientific model?

A paradigm is a scientific model that includes theory, law, application and instrumentation. It provides theoretical formulae from which spring particular coherent traditions of scientific research.

A scientific crisis exists today. The old hypotheses about science and humanity are no longer giving us the right answers and within the physical sciences itself, the revolution against traditionally accepted ideas have almost undermined old scientific realities.

It is the lack of a viable Weltanschauung—a vast world-view, which gives existential design to humanity's reason for existence, that is one of the causal reasons for the crisis of the 20th century. Particularly the lack of such a paradigm is affecting us on a scientific paradigm level, on the sociocultural dimension and on the personal psychological functional level.

The critical times of the 20th century present the need for the development of an authentic concept of man, a new scientific model of culture and consciousness with scientific models that relates humanity to the world he lives within. The commencement of the dawn of a new era demands an indepth inquiry into the significance of humanity's psychosocial nature. The human race needs a dynamic new world vision–a comprehensive paradigm that can give our age meaning and significance.

This chapter will examine the paradigm crisis as it affects, American culture, modern science, and the social evolution of humanity. We will start with an examination of the changing scientific paradigm models which are affecting America's concept of reality.

It is essential to reexamine the human evolutionary process, especially because most of the major philosophies of history now reject the concept of the progressively linear historical process and accept either a cyclical, eschatological, creatively rhythmical, or Messianic form process. Also the social sciences have shifted their scientific orientation also by rejecting the hitherto dominant "positivistic and empiricists techniques of investigating and understanding of social phenomena; thus they state as inadequate old empiricist theories of cognition and truth. Now we find the hitherto scientific investigation techniques of sociocultural phenomena and concepts such as naturalistic, scientific, operational, mechanistic, instrumental or quantitative are suspect and at best can give us data on only one aspect of sociocultural phenomena. A sharp rupture, thus, has arisen in the scientific community as the dominantly progressive, positivistic, empiricist theories die as science gasps and can no longer utilize its techniques as a predictive tool.[2]

BASIC SCIENTIFIC RESEARCH CONCEPTS

Science is a technique that relies on objective sense experience. Human perception is the foundation of scientific exploration which is expressed in the collection of data facts. If any discrepancy exists between data and concepts there must be a defect in the concepts, thus science always invites attention to corrections and improvements of theoretical formulations.[3] Scientific truth rests on the workability of its theory in practice and its ability to predict accurately in terms of its interests. When a theory is confirmed its truth is revealed as scientific fact since the unity of scientific concepts rests on their verifications.[4]

There are three major characteristics found in the scientific cultivation of objective consciousness. Roszak calls them (1) the alienative dichotomy; (2) the invidious hierarchy; (3) the mechanistic imperative. [5]

Objective consciousness, on the scientific level divides reality into a dualism of two spheres which we can describe as "In-Here" and "Out-there." "In-Here", is a style or state of conscious awareness which stands apart from our subjective emotional nature and utilizes what Integral Psychology calls the higher rational mind. The scientist removes himself subjectively from that which he is observing by not identifying or being involved with the data he is studying.. He becomes isolated from the facts as an impartial observer of the process he is studying. In the national sciences such activiities are observing, measuring, experimenting, classifying and dealing with the basic quantitative relationships. In the humanities and behavioral sciences, the scientists are varied but usually seek to imitate the natural sciences by tabulating and using game stategies or information theory, or numerious social theories that deal with people who generally are not in a laboratory situation, and generally cannot be manipulated in a certain limited ways in some social labs. Generally the subject matter is groups of people who exist as social entities in the field and the oberver is limited to observation of his observed human data. Examples of this approach is the anthropologist or a cross cultureal psychologist living in his living lab for long or short periods of time to collect data for an ethnography or if possible to test a hypothiesis. The scientist will also use the "In-there" mode of objective consciousness when he observes documents, a book or an artifact, as if his feelings and emotions were not aroused or being touched by the psychological ego.

The scientist distances himself by his "In-Here" attitude from "Out-There reality by using various mechanical gadgets between the observed and observer; or through using chilly jargon and technical terms; or though the invention of strange methodologies which connect to the subject matter like mechanical hands; by subordinating experience to statistical generalition; or through appealing to professional stands which forces the scientist to separate himself because of his pursuit for truth or because of pure research standards. [6]

Many scientists affirm that in the search for knowledge we must provide the facts and nothing but the facts but other equally bright scientists ask just what are the facts? They point out that the facts of science imply that empirical facts lie on theoretical elements and that the composing of theories rests on symbol-making activity. The results of such inquiries are symbols of nature and that scientists are the prime architects.[7]

Einstein states that there are two aspects of scientific knowledge, that is, what the scientist can empirically observe and what he can mentally imagine or theoretically conceive. The scientist joins these two thing together by correlation with the theoretical structure; but these are not tied together by logical relation or extensive abstraction. For example the observed color blue is correlated blue as wave length. So according to Einstein the axiomatic basis of science is a tentative deduction which must be invented. [8]

Northrop states that the implications of this type of scientific thinking is that "we cannot validly derive theoretical descriptions from empirical assertions." Thus, it may be said that knowledge gained from a priori theoretical constructs will provide different data from experimental observations but possibly give us tentative deduction of reality itself.[9]

Most scientists have retreated from the above implications by modifying their theories in the light of more accurate observations. Their hope is that by successively refining measurements it will lead to more precise predictions of events, thus, there can be no limits to scientific progress. Yet the facts are that "there are situations in mathematics, for example, in which the approximation to the solution becomes worse as computation is labored beyond a certain point." When there are experiments involving minute increment of matter, you cannot refine the data unless different rules are used. Bridgman states "Events are not predicable in the realm of small things" It is now known that the difficulties found in the old Newtonian concepts cannot be dissolved by successively refined measurements but by using radically new relativity concepts. Siu says that" We cannot extrapolate from thin statistical slices into the remote reaches of space and time." [10]

The implications of this situation is that relativity theory points out that many former scientific statements that were susceptible of demonstrable truth are now only mere definitions such as 5,280 feet are a mile. Croce states that "Science itself is nothing but a set of definitions, unified in a supreme definition; a system of concepts, or highest concept."[11]

RATIONAL KNOWLEDGE CAN BE SOMEWHAT SHAKY

The scientific method rest on the concept of cause and effect! Scientists are causationists. If a cause is unknown then it is felt that the causal factors are temporarily beyond their grasp.

A cause is thus a relation between phenomena in which one event gives rise to another event and brings out definite changes in the process.

Another viewpoint, however, is the Hindu one which simply abolishes the concept of cause and effect by stating that both are actually the same thing observed from different vantage points. The effect is thus latent in the cause and only when a cause exists can you observe an effect.

An example is that if you were to observe a piece of fabric, which is an aggregate of threads, you would note not the cloth but threads along the filings and the warp. Observe that the threads are made up of finer threads, then still finer threads, etc. Ultimatetly the causal factor can be said to be the finest threads.

Other critics say that often the cause cannot be observed in the effect, that is, observe an acorn from which a great tree will emerge. The causal factor of the seed gives birth in an overt tree but the cause surely moves beyond the sphere of visibility, in this case. The concept of Sat-caryatid presents the idea that every effect pre-exists.[12]

The mathematical economist, Vilfredo Pareto, gives us a contemporary analogy to the Hindu fusion of cause and effect. He states that though most people would consider the independent variable in an algebraic equation as a cause, that actually this may not be the case or"an admissible translation.' for example he points out that the market price of a hammer can be looked on as an effect of the cause which is the cost of production. But this viewpoint can be turned around if you regard that the cost of the hammer becomes the effect of the sales price that now becomes its cause. You can also look on the mutual dependence of supply and demand as something that can be interpreted in either direction, that is, a manufacturure may put a product on the market prior to its demand and vice versa. So in effect, all we can say about such mutually dependent terms is that there is an equation relating them together. Pareto concludes that we must restrict the colloquial description of cause and effects to special cases and be quite circumspect in our operations.[13]

HUME'S CRITICISM OF CAUSE & EFFECT

Scientists prefer to perceive cause and effect as separate entities which are connected by their relationships to each other. Science, however, has not refuted Humes's contention, made two hundred years ago, that any knowledge about causal relation is quite uncertain and probable at best. Science finds this concept difficult to accept but equally difficult to refute.

Hume says that all our facts regarding knowledge is based on the postulated relation of cause and effect and that only through causation can one event be inferred from another event. He makes

the point that we must examine the grounds on which these relations exist

Remember that Descarte and the Scholastics consider that
cause A and effect B are necessary connections. The basis of science and the social order as well as humanity's grasp of reality
rests on our sense's experience of causal reality, according to them.

Hume's point is that only through sense experience can you
observe knowledge of cause and effect; but this knowledge is not
one of logical or intuitive certainty. If you observe event A, it may
not lead to B event. If through constant sequential conjunction
of A with B you may conclude a causal function between A and
B. But in actuality all you have found is that A and B are found
conjoined. The reason for this connection is unknown and even
after having observed this same squence of one event following
another all we are doing is conjuring up the idea of B as an effect;
A, as an object is now thusly connected in our mind with B as an
object. Hume says that objects have no discoverable cause and
effect relations between them because causation is merely a sequential derivation and has no independent relational existence.
He makes the point that even though experience shows a fre-
quent conjunction of A and B it may not have the same conjunction in the future.[14]

Marcus Long tells a story about a chicken with scientific pro-
clivities which illustrates Hume's thinking. It seems this chicken
one day saw a man near the hen house who had left some corn.
The chicken being wary decided to conduct a scientific examination of the causal relations between the causal man A and the
Corn B, which is the effect. After observing for 999 times he
concluded that when the man appeared the corn was found, thus
there was a necessary causal connection between the man and
the corn. On the thousandth time the chicken went forward to
thank the man and had his neck wrung. [15]

Bertrand Russell agrees with Hume but states that the form A
causes B are generally admitted only in the early stages of the
experiment as crude points of departure. As the experiment be-

comes refined these simple statements are replaced by complex pictures that extend far beyond our perception limits. A and B now are mere elaborate inferences.

Whitehead, however, says that to solve this problem we must search for the intrinsic character of each instance and not in its numerous occurrences.

The noted physicist Planck, suggests a compromise by stating that "Causality is neither true nor false It is a most valuable heuristic principle to guide science in the direction of promising returns in an ever progressive development." [16]

The statistical conclusions of Bolzmann and Gibbs, a century ago, supports Hume's blow to the certainty of the scientific method. In the Eighteen and Nineteen century Newtonian laws were applied to all types of systems even though such system had different position and moments. They, however, were suppose to obey the same laws which were considered quite rigid and unchangeable. Bolzman and gibbs demonstrated that, in point of fact, this was not so; and that even systems with similar amounts of energy were not forever fixed in the same patterns. Nature, thus, exists with a tenuous hedge of contingency and its secrets are basically ones of probability. [17]

When attempts were made to reconcile the principle of causality with probability nothing is arrived at conclusively. Some feel that discrepancies occur because of our inability to measure the data to a necessary degree of refinement; while others feel that probability is merely a temporary haze of ignorance within the scientific process. Bridgman, for example, says that our observation of the scientific events interfere in an unpredictable and incalculable amount. But he emphasizes that this unpredictability is due to nature herself and not sciences ability to make precise measurements. Modern statistic theory now makes a list of different sources of error, etc. So that in atomic physics some errors are due to "uncontrolled errors whereas others are "errors due to technique. Surely Heisenberg's uncertainty relations principle reinforces any concepts of scientific probability .

But old ideas must die as new concepts develop. Science is more aware now that the universe seemingly is an interconnection of events. Events are inextricable forces found within the totality. Causality may be but an incident within the overall system, and then only a facet of its myriad components. For example, Sui points out that, if you add water to sodium, is water the reason or cause of the hydrogen liberation or is it the sodium? Or Both? He asks, Can there be gaseous liberation without time? Or Space?" He states can time flow without substance? Can space expand without content?' [18]

MODERN SCIENTIFIC CRISIS

The modern scientific crisis has occurred because theory or the super paradigm has developed massive inconsistencies which can not be corrected because in the physical sciences statistics have replaced necessity by probability and chance and the concept of relativity, the elimination of absolute time and space, the acceptance of the atom as a complex universe of intra-atomic forces, and the use of the principle of indeterminacy, especially ideas about entropy, etc., are bringing about the dissolution of physics and Nature-Knowledge. New concepts of physics and mechanics now contradict "the Galilean-Newtonian" physics and mechanics. Presently, becoming and become and causality and destiny, as well as historical and natural science elements are beginning to be confused. The old formulae of age, growth, life, direction and death are crowding up. [19]

Modern science now realizes the limitations of any knowledge obtained by present day scientific techniques, particularly in modern physics. It is obvious that the classical concept of scientific objectivity can no longer be upheld. Modern physics challenges this myth of a value free science because in sub-atom research it has been found that the observer influences the observed, thus as Capra [20] says," The patterns' scientists observe in nature are intimately connected with the patterns of their minds-with their concepts, thoughts, thoughts and values." Physicists' Werner Heisnberg also says "that every word or concept clear as it may seem to be, has only a limited range of applicability."[21]

Added to these facts is the concept that the division between organic and inorganic matter has become blurred, that is, the definition of organic matter is that it responds to processed information. Quantum mechanics demonstrate the astounding discovery that subatomic particles constantly seem to be making decisions! These decisions rest on movements of other particles; amazingly they seem to know instantaneously what the other particle's decisions are elsewhere, even if it is a universe away.

So what does all this mean? Well, it seems that these particles are related in some dynamic and intimate way that coincides with the scientific definition of organic life. The philosophic implication of this quantum mechanic's discovery seems to infer that everything in the universe are parts of some all-encompassing organic pattern and that none of these parts are ever really separate from each other. [22]

Are these particles some type of primordial consciousness? Strictly speaking, however, these particles are not things or objects. [23] They are a quantum or a quantity of something, that is, they are mass and energy that changes unceasingly into each other yet they communicate with each other. [24]

What does this mean? One hypothesis, Charles Muses's CM Quantum model, for example, states that all matter is alive in a protobiological sense and that ultimately we will discover that subtle forms of living substance exist beyond our concepts of electron-proton theory.[25] On a more human level I.I. Rabi P. KIusch and S. Millman of Columbia University have demonstrated that each living cell, living or inert, is a radio transmitter and receives and sends a continuous broadcast of waves that cover the whole electromagnetic spectrum.[26]

THE TRANSPERSONAL
SCIENTIFIC SOLUTION

An integral theory of science requirs an open mind and an ability to transcend past bias and scientific techniques. It requires that truth and integrity be the guide lines in the search for an authentic paradigm model that sincere scientists can utilize in the course of their scientific work.

No longer can science accept the concept of cognition of the world based on John Locke's classical formula: "Nihil esse in intellect quod non fuerit prius in sense" Nothing is in our intellect that has not previously been in our sense.[27]

The idea that sensory perception and observation are the only ways to do the scientific method has become obsolete and has been replaced by more adequate theory's of reality.

Sorokin makes the point that an Integral Theory of Knowledge has not one but three different channel of cognition, that is, sensory, rational, and super-sensory-superrational.

The sensory organs and their extensions: microscopes, telescopes, etc., constitutes Locke's clasical approach to scientific exploration. The rational aspect is comprehended by us through reason, mathematical and logical thought. The third form of integral cognition is superrational supersensory forms of reality that comes to us through intuition, or transpersonal inspirations or "flashes of enlightenment". Creative geniuses, great scientists, artist, moral leaders and founders of great religions, sages, seers and prophets speak of the superconsciousness or super-rational cognition as the source of their discoveries and creation of their masterpieces. This type of cognitive knowledge is different from sensory perception or logico-mathematical reasoning but works hand in hand with the superconscious intuition as tests through which scientific knowledge can be tested and developed. [28] In fact, Dr. Siu says that even though logician deprecate intuition fuzziness, and intuitionist decry logic strictures he states "Discursive reasoning is not possible without intuition." Langer's syllogisms are merely devices to lead the scientist from one intuition to the next step. The scientist's ability to react with intuitive understanding at each step in the process is a prerequisite to rational analysis. She feels the emergence of meaning is a matter of logical intuition or insight. Sui, maintains though, that in real life this intuitive understanding does not develop step by step but by an immediate total apprehension of the solution to the problem. [29]

R.G.H. Siu, an eminent biochemist and director of organized research in United States governmental and private institutions says that superconscious knowledge is not irrational but extrarational. This source of knowledge is often covertly used in a rational sensate culture but in past cultures and nonwestern contemporary cultures intuition plays its part dynamically and concretely. Intuition, Sui maintains that intuition has particularly been influential with "political decisions in international statesmanship, maneuvers and countermaneuvers in military campaigns, estimates of the surges of people in elections, inspirations of poets, painters, and sculptors, conscience of holy men—all have been repetitiously exhibited through the ages." [30] Sui states that:

> The silent and formless depth of life had passed many
> times before the mind of man in its full sweep. This type
> of knowledge is not enkindled by mathematical formu-
> lae and scientific treatises. To pursue this latter means of
> communication is to remain in the realm of the rational.
> The inspiration can be shared only by those willing to
> accept the extrarational sources of enlightenment and
> keep the flow free from the dam of rational analysis. [31]

There is a source of knowledge so profound that an intuitive grasp of its essence allows the scientists to gain insight into his scientific problems. Albert Eistein, spoke on this subject when he described his scientific abilities said that, "The really valuable thing is intuition." [32] This source is not to be confused with conscious and subconscious aspects of the scientists personality structure. Sorokin makes the point that little is known of the supraconscious, but that it seems to be the fountainhead of creative discoveries and achievements in most fields of human creative activate. He says that without its genius and operation the fields of science, philosophy, technology, religion and ethic, law , economics, politics and the fine arts would have produced only mediocre achievements. He says that even though a professor of English or of musical composition may know all the rules of his arts but if he is devoid of the supraconscious genius he will never produce anything great or remotely near the great works of art.[33]

Sorokin, feels that supraconscious intuition comes as a momentary flash and at times and places that cannot be foreseen, predicted or voluntarily brought about and in actuality usually appears under the most unexpected conditions. He also says that this superconscious lies at the base of sensory and logical knowledge or value experience and has historically been called by many names such as eternal reason, sublime stupidity, nous, no-knowledge, grace of God, divine or mystic revelation, pneuma, "docta ignorantia," inner light, or genius. Sorokin points out that that " . . . the sovereign intelligence which in a twinkle of an eye sees the truth of all things in contrast to vain knowledge, " "celestial inspiration," and "supramental wisdom that goeth beyond all knowledge" are still other names which one could label the supraconscious.[34]

Dr. Sui says that supraconscious knowledge does not involve the selection of specific events as its knowledge objective but concerns what the East calls Wu or nonbeing. Wu has no shape, no time and transcends qualities and events and thus cannot be the object of ordinary knowledge.

Sui makes a distinction between having no-knowledge of a situation with having "no-knowledge" or the ability to tap timeless being for answers to scientific problems. "Creation in research is the fluorescence of no-knowledge" It is the process of reaching into the ineffability and emerging with its rational synonym in human language. Sui goes on to point out that in ordinary scientific research the transformation of one rational cog into another and any adaptation of theory to new process and systems with its conversion of scientific models and hypothesis into pragmatic and practical hardware are not creative research. He says they are merely varieties of tautological research which are naturally worthy pursuits since they forge the linkage between utility and theory and human welfare. But he is emphatic that this type of scientific research is not creative. [35]

MATHEMATICAL PRODIGIES

A perfect example of supraconscious knowledge is that utilized by mathematical prodigies or calculation boys. These persons are often of low intelligence and have not the capacity for elementary mathematical reasoning yet are able to make complex mathematical calculations instantaneously such as determining the logarithm of any number of eight digits. They can find intuitively what factor divide a large number, not a prime. Give them a number of 17,861, they tell you instantly that it is 337x 53.

When in the presence of the French Academy, Arago asked Vito Margiamele, an uneducated ten year old, the cubic root of 3,796,496, he responded "156 in about 30 seconds. When he was asked to determine 'What satisfies the condition that its cube plus five times its square is equal to 42 times itself increased by 40?" Vito responded that 5 satisfies the condition is less than a minute.[36]

SUPERCONSCIOUS INTUITION

Superconscious intuition is an indispensable factor in mathematical discoveries. H. Poincare, G. Birkhoff, Arago, and an entire mathematical School of mathematics stress that faith and intuition are the "foundations for the rational superstructure erected by means of deductive and inductive reasoning". They assert they are "of supreme importance,' and are "heuristically valuable", and "beyond reason."

The well known mathematician Jacques Hadamard's study of the psychology of mathematics reveals how some of the eminent living mathematicians received "sudden and spontaneous," or "without any time for thought, however brief" insights into their mathematical discoveries. Gauss, for example struggled with a mathematical theorem for years but says that:

> I succeeded, not on account of my painful efforts, but by the grace of God. Like a sudden flash of lightning the riddle happened to be solved. I, myself, cannot say what was the conducting thread which connected what I previously knew with what made my success possible. [37]

Dr. Sui says that when we plumb the depth of no-knowledge that the scientist must rely on his own unique ineffable awareness of the ineffable. He feels that during this period rational knowledge is a hindrance and the scientist must make his mind clear of general cognitive-rational thinking. The scientist must use his inner no-knowledge to fuse with the no-knowledge of the comprehended. After the ineffable union takes place, and only then must his insights be transfigured into rational and conscious analogue. The scientist will then test his new insights for adaptability as new conscious techniques and forms develop. Most scientist may not even describe their indescribable experience to the world. [38]

C. Gernard, in a study of 232 natural scientists found that eighty-three per cent, of these scientists studied by the American Chemical Society said that they had an unpredictable flash of insight that solved their scientific problems with adequacy and finality.

Sorokin makes the point that great scientists such as Kepler, Pascal, Galieo, Newton and others used intuition and were mystics in the narrow sense of the term. Sir Isaac Newton's discoveries of the fluxion method of mathematics and the compositon of light and the law of gravitation were started intuitionally as was true of the discovers of other great scientists. [39] Bertram Lewis's essay on Descartes famous dream trilogy[40] stresses the dreams as a force of revelation and as an epileptic experience in sleep from whence came the "origin of the Cartesian idea. Descartes was twenty two and absessed with the idea of discovering the foundations of a science and the dream trilogy seemingly was a type of initiation rite that allowed him to become a discoverer of new horizons in science. In his last dream a figure appears behind him, representing an unseen power which presents books and pictures to him and Descartes knows he is dreaming and thus develops Cartesian ideas.[41]

We have discovered in this chapter that supporting world views and a culture's core values rests great truths discovered by philosophical, scientific or religious intuition. It is recognized that intuition has an honorable past and future in scientific work and individual life processes and through the fine arts.

INTUITIONAL CREATIVITY

The nature of the super sensory consciousness seemingly works through poets and music creators as well as scientists. When Mozart was asked how he wrote his music he answered "I can, in fact, say nothing more about it than this: I do not know myself and can never find out. When I am in particularly good condition . . . then the thoughts come to me in a rush, and best of all. Whence and how, I do not know and cannot learn."[42]

When Beethoven was asked the same question he states: "You will ask me where I get my ideas. I am not able to answer that question positively. . . . What we conquer for ourselves through art is from God, divine inspiration . . . Every genuine creation of art is independent, mightier than the artist himself, and through its manifestation, returns to the Divine. With man it has only this in common; that it bears testimony to the mediation of the Divine in him."[43]

Tchaikovsky, in greater detail describes the intuitive process:

"Usually the seed of a future musical creation germinates instantaneously and most unexpectedly. If the seed appears at a favorable
moment, the main difficulty is passed. The rest grows of
itself . . . [A new idea gives Tchaikovsky aboundless joy . . .] One
forgets everything, one is a mad-man . . . Sometimes inspiration
takes flight, one has to seek it again—often in vain. Frequently one
must rely here upon a quite cold, deliberate technical process of
work. Perhaps such moments are responsible, in the works of the
Great Masters, for those places where the organic coherence fails,
and where one can trace artificial coherence, seams and patches.
But this is unavoidable. If that spiritual condition of the artist
called inspiration . . . should continue uninterrupted, the artist
could not survive a single day.. The strings would snap and the
instrument would fly to pieces. One thing, however, is indispensable; the main idea of the piece, together with a general outline
of the separate parts, must not be found through searching, but
must simply appear as a result of that supernatural, incompre-
hensible and never-analyzed power called inspiration." [44]

When a person is creative he touches on sources of knowledge and wisdom that often seemingly transcends his own unigue
abilities. Scalding makes an appropriate statement in this regard:
"Just as the man of destiny does not execute what he will or
intends, but what he is obliged to execute through an incompre-
hensible fate under whose influence he stands, so the
artist . . . seems to stand under the influence of a power
which . . . compels him to declare or represent things which he
himself does not completely see through, and whose import in
infinite."[45]

SUPERCONSCIOUS IN INVENTIONS

Elias Howe had tried for years to perfect the sewing machine
without success. An ultimatum was given him one night in a
dream, that is, a king of savages gave him twenty-four hours to
produce a sewing machine or he would die by the spear. After the

deadline came Howe faced a group of savages, in his next night's dream, and as they stood over him menacingly with raised spears he observed that all of the decending spears had eye-shaped holes. He immediately awoke and ran to his laboratory and placed the hole in the sewing needle near the point and the problem was solved and the future of the sewing machine was secure.[46]

James Watt was seeking a new process for making lead shot for shotguns. During a dream of several nights he found himself walking in storm of lead rain. Awakening he realized that molten lead as it fell through the air whould harden into small spheres, thus was invented shot gun lead pellets.[47]

Naturalist Louis Agassiz was trying to sketch on canvas the impression of a fossil fish on a stone slab. But since the fossil image was blurred he couldn't decipher it and thus abanded the project. The next night a dream showed him an image of the entire fossil fish, but the image faded upon awakening. The following night, when he had the same dream he woke up and drew a sketch of the fish. The next day he hurried over to the Jardin des Plantes and using the sketch as a guide chiseled on the surface of the stone. Suddenly the layer of stone fell loose revealing a fossil in excellent condition which was identical to the fossil in his dream.[48]

The Denver psychiatrist, Dr. Jule Eisenbud, had a patient who was a bird-watcher. Awaking from a dream he felt if he visited a certain park he would observe a rare bird, the worm-eatin warbler, which generally appeared in that park no more than one day per year. After arriving at the park he spotted the bird within ten minutes. A year earlier he had also observed another rare bire–a kingfishers after another precognitive dream.[49]

INTUITION IN PHILOSOPHY

Intuition is also recognized in philosophy. In the East the Upanishads of India and the Taoism of China as well as the other great philosophical Easterns systems all recognize intuition as their source of origin. In the West the mystic philosophies of Plato,

Aristotle, the Neoplatonist , such as Proclus, Porphyry, Plotinus, the Neo-Pythgorians such as Apollonius of Tyana and Gnostics, all bare testimony to this process of intuition. Within the Western Church, St. Augustine and the Church Fathers: J.S. Erigena, Nicholas of Cusa, Pseudo-Dionysius and most of the Scholastics of the late middle ages, including St. Thomas Aquinas, especially in the latter part of his life, all fall into the intuition's camp.

When you examine the modern philosophers even the rationalist such as Descartes and Spinozo recognize some sort of intuitional axioms or intuitional truths. Philosophers such as Kant and Hume, schopenhauer, Schelling, Fichte, Nietzche, as well as objective idealist such as Hegel, as well as H. Bergson, W. James in his later period , A.N. Whitehead. E. Husserl and other phenomenologist such as N. Berdyaev, S. Kierkegaard, J. Maritain and the Neo-Thomist: M. Scheler, K. Jaspers, M. Heidegers, etc., all accept some sort of "forms of mind" or intuitional truths which lies at the basis of logical, mathematical and sensory-observational verities found with human cognition and creativity and is a natural condition species wide. [50]

Nietzsche, speaking of the creative process and intuition says:

> . . . one becomes nothing but a medium for supermighty in-influences. That which happens can only be termed revelation; that is to say, that suddenly, with unutterable certainty and delicacy, something becomes visible and audible and shakes and rends one to the depth of one's being. One hears, one does not seek; one takes, one does not ask who it is that gives; like lightning a thought flashes out, of necessity, complete in form. . . . It is a rapture . . . a state of being entirely outside oneself. . . . Everything happens in the highest degree involuntarily, as in a storm of feeling, freedom, of power, of divinty. [51]

Dr. Sui makes the point that through rational knowledge the scientist is a spectator of nature but that when he communicates with no-knowledge, he dynamically participants within the sphere of nature. The scientist really does not experience selflessness until he has intimately shared knowledge with nature, according to Sui. But Sui says that, although, No-knowledge is superrational in origin it is found not only in man but also in nature. In fact he feels it is indigenous to all of nature and when the scientist communicates with No-knowledge it is not a projection of his ego into nature but with nature's ego which is also shared by all of humanity.

Dr. Sui states that with rational knowledge a person is in tune with the scientific man, with intuitive knowledge he is in tune with the integral or total man; and with no-knowledge the person is in tune with nature.[53]

Eugene O'Neill speaks on no-knowledge through the words of Edmund Tyrone, in Long Day's Journey Into Night:

> When I was on the Squarehead square rigger bound for Buenos Aires. Full moon in the Trades. The old hooker driving 14 knots. I lay on the bowsprit, facing astern, with the water foaming into spume under me. I became drunk with the beauty and singing rhythm of it and for a moment I lost myself–actually lost my life. I dissolved in the sea, became white ship and the high dim-starred sky. I belonged, without past or future, within peace and unity and a wild joy, within something greater than my own life, or the life of Man, to Life itself! To God, if you want to put it that way.[54]

F.S.C Northrop calls no-knowledge the undifferentiated Aesthetic Continuum. It cannot be analyzed or conceptualized scientifically or described by any concepts or terms because it is ineffable and must be experienced directly as a "pure fact through transpersonal techniques.[55]

Northrop says intuitional cognition or aesthetic knowledge is derived from direct experience of pure fact. The color blue, for example is inaccessible to the blind or music to the deaf and love experiences lacking in the unloved. All sensed experiences make up the aesthetic continuum or nature reality.[56]

The aesthetic continuum has two basic forms. The first aspect is the Differentiated Aesthetic continuum which is an all-embracing form of differentiation, that is, it means that some aspects or parts of the continuum are different from each other; aesthetic signifies that some parts of this continuum are qualitatively ineffable. [57] The scientist, through direct intuition, perceives as "pure fact", the differentiated, "soft", "blue", "lovely, etc., when some of the properties of the second aspect, the Undifferentiated Aesthetic Continuum are specifically distinguished.[58]

The undifferentiated Aesthetic Continuum is the primeval aesthetic continuum from which arises any directly sensed differentiation. This is the continuum component apart from the differentiations.[59] It pervades, according to Northrop, all the differentiated aesthetic phenomena but is neither A nor non-A, neither this nor that but is the coincidentia oppositorum that embraces A as well as non-A.

It is the Divine Nothing of true mystics, the Jen in Confucianism, Tao in Taoism, Brahman, Atman or Chit in Hinduism, Nirvana in Buddhism and the Infinite Manifold, and the Supra-essence of St. Augusine, Pseudo-Dionysius or Nicolas of Cusa, according to R.S.C. Northrop.

COVERT TRANSPERSONAL REALISM

The intuitive aspect of discovery often remains hidden behind a scientific fracade of silence. Scientific discoverie often appear in dreams and visions. It is said that the discovery of the genetic helical structure or double helix emerged out of a vision as the scientist looked at the fire in an open fireplace. "In aflash of insight Watson . . . "(flowers:168:1998) got the answer. Often many scientific discoveries are covered up under a dull factors of expected scientific procedures and methodology that must cover up the true dimensions of the discovery so that the dull and pedantic scientists of little imagination can accept the new and dynamic discoveries as authentic and valid insights of the scientific approach to hypotheses solution.

A perfect example of this fact is the true facts of Descartes Cartesian ideas. Ideas which brought in the rational age and pushed the following ages into the use of scientific methodology as a mode of investigating reality. Some accounts talk about his vision and others such as Bertram Lewin's lucid essay on Descartes famous dream trilogy place the origin of the "Cartesian idea" as dreams.[60] These dreams seem to have been a type of initiation rite which placed this young scientist into the history of revelation thought; culminating in the last dream where suddenly there suddenly appears a man who stands before the unseen powers of the universe with books and pictures which are place in front of Descartes, thus are born the thoughts which brought mankind into the modern age![61]

CHAPTER 15

AMERICAN EDUCATION-SEPULCHERS OF DEATH

FUTURIST COMMENTARY: It was not until the collapse of the New American Empire in the 22nd century that innovative educational systems began to be accepted under the guidance of Quetzalcoatl who formed youth corps that are called, servants of the people, to help his people rebuild their lives and recreate civilization on a sound ecological environment. He has formed new agriculture and industrial schools and reorganized society in new and brilliant ways and preaches the equality of the races of the world and the equality of the sexes.

Wherever he travels he creates universities and schools of creativity for children and also builds what he calls temples of light and their adjacent medical centers of healing; and the youth view him as a dynamic warrior of God almighty and the elite of these youth he puts in schools of eternal learning, as he calls them, and it is reported by our spies that mighty warriors come out of these centers with miraculous powers of psi abilities and healing power, yet are magnificent solders and martial artists who have swore that they shall achieve success at revitalizing society or die trying. Fanatics they are all and the rest of the civilized world quake in fear at this internal enemy.

Campbell speaks below to the problems of traditional
education and it failures.

The American dream of social progress through education has failed
and in its decline has accepted the death pangs of the death generation as its theme and goal! Our schools are a national disgrace
and need to be abolished because they are places of death symbolically and in actuality as students carry guns to school to waste
fellow students and their seemingly oppressor teachers. In 1996
and 1997 alone, 192 students were killed in our schools. In 1998
and 99 the killings continue well into the year 2,000. The violence is so bad that the bureaucrats can no longer cover up the
scandal that we call schools!

It is a time of madness in the educational community and
the cadres of death swirl around the halls of education and embrace our educational code with glee and triumph. For they know
we are on our knees and must bow down in defeat to the inevitable death of America's educational system. For it is a system of
death and defeat, dishonoring it recipients-our children and its
mentors, who in the anguish of the moment dare not admit defeat yet cry out in anguish at a system that is collapsing and disintegrating before their very eyes.

Universal education has failed and the students—zombies
they process, are for the most part detrimental to society or so
confused that we have a generation of graduates who can't read or
write or speak intelligently, for they are the youth of the death
generation. Death is on their lips and from their hearts comes the
scream for vengeance against their oppressor who imprison them
for twelve years as they mold them and make them conform to
idiotic rules and regulations.

They are mad as hell and won't take it any longer. They are
rebelling in great numbers. Even kindergarten children often take
guns to school and the carnage of maiming and deaths of their
oppressor the teachers continue daily as the death generation
changes our institutions of education into the killing fields.

In response the teachers are turning the schools into prisons, with high containing walls and guards and often with regular policemen paroling the grounds. Some schools have even medal detectors at their sacred entrance grounds where guns and knives are confiscated. For the teachers now fear their students, because their students are the death generation and they are mighty and powerful and hardly controllable and all know it is but a matter of time before they openly rebel and put their prisons to the torch. In fact, vandalism of schools and the burning of schools surreptitiously is almost a national pastime these days. For we are the death generation and let none forget that fact!

What is a child but a spark of humanity ready to experience life and his destiny within the sphere of the socio-cultural reality he is born within. Parents and educators are merely the custodians of the child's aspirations and joy at being alive; therefore they must treat this bundle of joy with respect and consideration and with the objective of unfolding his talents in as spontaneous manner as possible and feasibility given the circumstances of the situation. In this type of educational environment possibly education as a system of punishments and rewards may not be appropriate. For in all frankness can you figuratively whip the love of inquiry into the small child's psyche with threats and intimidations of bad grades and parental and teacher disapproval or with small rewards of praise or acceptance. No, these techniques will not work yet we must also recognize that "tough love" may be needed for children already corrupted by the present educational system.

If you cannot instill the love of learning into the child early it may not emerge within his student career except by the accidental touch of an unknown teacher. Additionally it often happens by an intuitive immersion into some beloved subject matter or by the sheer joy of meeting head on a problem of immense interest that may soar you up to the stars.

Yes, there are peek experiences among seekers of knowledge. There is truth hidden among the lilies and joy hidden among the pathways of life and best of all there is individual upliftment through intellectual and emotional unity with life itself in its many guises. Spread out your hand and believe the joys of intellectual discover, grab that bit of social and philosophical knowledge, shift through your hands the social data and become one with your educational task and thus you come full circle back to the joys and accomplishment of education.

It is written that if the joy of inquiry does not lie within your grasp then search for another field of study until the process of creative selffulfillment becomes yours by self development. Remember this, the old system of education is dead and woe to those who hold on to this dead horse thinking that with the resurrection of that horse a new and brighter educational future waits on the wings of time. For now we are in the midst of the destiny of man and none may stay the hands of fate as mankind faces the challenges of his evolutionary future. Move on with the times or be ground under by the dead hand of the past! For death is on the wings of time and our children must grow new wings and breathe new air and fly where we know not if the cadres of our elite children are to escape the influence of the death generations.

Plato many years ago affirmed that children merely learn what is within their natures and the task of the educator is to bring out what ever is there. Can the talents of each child rise up to the occasion and embrace him in his task of self-education and liberate him from his ignorance? Can this child rise on the wings of his inspiration and bring joy and new knowledge into the world of man? Can he? Will he? Well, it all depends on whether society in general and mankind in particular wants to rise above their negativity and vile and lowly natures that enslave them and discourage the antics of the Death generation. Success or failure lies before us and only the future will know where we have trodden and how Earnests were our efforts and whether we justified the innate faith of the human race in itself.

If a child is left alone to unfold his very nature in a spontaneous way he will become his own person; and his inner creed will seemingly say strive on lonely soul for truth and virtues are not easily won and woe to those who shrink from their own destiny, for who but the fate of life itself can guide us and lead us to ourselves.

There was once a boy who one day wandered down the road of life with joy in his heart and a sense of excitement and enthusiasm and he was met with tasks and challenges that met his joy of life and life triumphed, whereas in another part of the country his twin brother, with all the same attributes, also met life with joy and courage but life returned his joy with its hate and disgust upon him Through educational and cultural determinism with such a fearfulness that the boy crumbled and shrink and quivered with fright and gave in by destroying all that was good and pure within his nature; but he made it through that terrible educational system and graduated magma cum latter and received the cheers of grateful parents and the applaud from the community for his achievement.

Yet within the young boy's heart, who is now a man, lies the dead hand of the death generation that grippes his mind and soul and his cry of rebellion and hateful malice roars with strength and purpose; for now he is one of the leaders of the death generation and death is his motto and enslavement of the masses his creed and he will not stop his social malice until the total enslavement of humanity.

We must face this man a thousand times, a thousand times over, until he and his hordes of death whimper and die with a grateful glee within their hearts. His death or anyone is his goal and he will go down fighting, giving no quarter and expecting none, and beneath his feet will lay the multitudes who believe his madness and yet embrace him yet in death for death must embrace death. The dead masses will embrace this cult of death through programs of social reform and cheer within their dead hearts for their truth of death. Oh woes are they who embrace death for by their choice death triumphs and the world is remade in its madness.

NEW EDUCATION

An entirely new system of education must now enter on the American scene, for time is short and if we are to survive into the next century we must cut our losses and move in an entirely new educational direction.

New dynamic institutions of education must be developed that integrates all phases of life experiences together into one harmonious whole. The kindergartner and the high-school graduate must form a continuous line of communication and self-fulfillment.

HIGH SCHOOL EXTERNAL DEGREE PROGRAM

I propose that we start two types of education, that is, complementary systems that will integrate each other. One system will be a nine year high school diploma program which is a modification of our present educational system and the other one will be a creative alternative educational system that only the elite of our children will be interested in utilizing. The first system relies on self reliance and creative and dynamic techniques of educational innovation! Students will attend full time school for only the first three grades and continue their education at home until graduation . The full use of computers, video types , audio material, films and books and home study courses will guide them. Every six weeks they will spend two days with their mentors, and they will have national examination every six months at educational centers. Each student will have open access , through computers , telephone or personal visits with his mentors at all times.

By utilization of this system we allow the creative abilities of the student to come to the fore. He will have access to the most creative teachers in the nation through television programs, and other media resources and can work at his own pace on his particular major interests while maintaining the requirements of his grade. If the student has the ability to finish his schooling in a shorter time than required he can graduate earlier than the rest of his national class through examinations. If he desires to enter college after graduating, regardless of his age, he should be encouraged to do so. If he is old enough to enter the national apprenticeship program at age 14, which we speak about later on in this chapter, then so be it. If he is not old enough to be appendiced but still would like further high school education then he can enter another field of study and becomes an honors student.

All students who prove to be creative and intuitive and possibly of genius status will be placed on national scholarship. Hard work will be required of them, but in an creative manner and the genius of the top brains of the country will set aside part of their time to tutor the fruit of the nation. All avenues of accessibility will be open to these children. They are the glory and honor of our future elite minds and diligence and patience and creativity must be utilized by our greatest minds in order to bring out the creative forces of their genius.

We want a balanced education for the children; ones which will create integrated personality systems. We do not want primadonna students. But if they respect themselves and are at peace with their abilities and potentials our children will be transpersonal gifts to the nation. Each child will be encouraged to master one individual sport, such as track and field events , gymnastics, sports Judo and noncontact sports Karate, wrestling Etc.If they wish to participate in group sports they will be permitted to do so an local sports centers.

NINE YEAR HIGH SCHOOL DIPLOMA PROGRAM

A new system of education, based on 9 years of schooling, within a creative matrix of programs must be created. After graduation, those with trade aspirations will enter governmental-industrial appendices' programs at age 15; those with college aspirations will enter corporate appendices' programs, those with neither goals will enter local core-youth programs that are designed to work with local government and industry to better the community. When each child who reaches 18 years of age the program ends-period for all students. The college bound youth will enter college, the trade oriented youth will formally enter apprentice's programs, and the rest will go on with their life aspirations in whatever direction they wish. Some of the youth-core member will opt to enter Jr. college or enter into formal apprentice's programs, or enter the military or peace corps or to enter the work force.

The nine years educational program would be a gradual progressive upgrading of skills in the traditional subjects but on a pragmatic and practicable level so that each child is fully aware of his abilities and capacities on the practicable level. All courses must be integrated into a complex educational whole that socializes each child into the realms of citizenship with all its obligations. The courses thus will be a flowing together of traditional disciplines on a practical and pragmatic level, so that mathematics and spelling, and civics and social studies and philosophy and anthropology all flow together as one whole life experience.

It will be as though the child is growing up and spontaneously absorbing the flow of life and its experiences naturally and intuitively and creatively as a joy of life. The child will be emerged into the subject matter in depth and not in pieces spread over years. Continuity must flow and history must become real and dynamic and the joys of learning must well up from within as each child finds himself and joyously embraces life as a living experience.

School no longer will be a prison but a field of self expression and a spontaneous joy; thus each child will draw on his inner resources to know himself and the world about him and he will embrace life as something to be lived. In return the schools' counselors will attempt to find each child's natural abilities and creatively design with each child individual program that fit his personality and style. So each child will be competing against him-

self through the development of his individual talents and propensities. When he graduates he will have all the skills necessary
to function in society yet be whole and dynamic and loving toward himself and others and best of all his particular geniuses
will uplift the nation. For this child will be full of love and contentment and take his place as a full member of society and become a wholesome functioning spark of truth and honesty among
America's citizens.

There will be special programs for the gifted, who will be
supported by the government as national treasures. Most of these
children shall finish college before they reach puberty; then become graduate students and finally doctors of whichever field
they enter before they reach the age of twenty. During their entire school careers they will be under the guidance of the most
creative teachers and scientist available and have civil and governmental resources available to them. Some of these children
will wish no extended schooling but will be allowed to develop
spontaneously and follow their intuitive destiny. Our country's
future rests upon such "Aquarian Age Children."

Futurist Commentary: Campbell, the College professor, also
speaks concerning student estrangement and the college educational crisis. In a paper given before the American Anthropology
Association convention in 1970, and later published by the Community College Social Science Association, he says:

A state of crisis exists today in higher education; a crisis so
serious that many traditional educational commitments and pri-
orities are either being altered or reorientation along new guide
lines. The crisis causal nature lies partially in some aspects of the
educational methodology that is presently in vogue, but more
specifically the causal agents exist within the social complexities
of this society's rapid social change. This process of fast social and
cultural change, with its anxieties and stresses, has dramatically
focused attention on the need to reexamine the uniqueness and
relevance of our present philosophy of education. A new philosophy of education is perhaps needed—one that is not only relevant

to the age but also functionally able to operate in a pluralistic industrial society.

The present educational climate of opinion, surely demonstrates that many contemporary college students and teachers often exist in an educational milieu that is antagonistic and even hostile to the learning process, that is, the new value system of many college students is leading to a serious lack of student responsiveness to traditional curriculum subject matter; also, in addition to these passive frustrations, increasing violence of riotous nature is daily occurring on the campus scene. Obviously the causes of this strife, whether from internal strains in the educational process itself or because of student concern with unsolved social problems cannot be discussed in this short paper, therefore, this paper will address itself to an examination of several concepts that may prove useful in creating a new and viable educational philosophy–a philosophy of existential interaction between student and teacher. This approach envisions an altered student-teacher behavioral relationship, the development of new teaching methods and ultimately the utilization of curriculum subject matter that is relevant to the life situations of the contemporary age–an age of inquiry and rapid culture change.

Examining these subject-categories in chronological sequence we find that higher education is today at a crucial juncture in its relations with the student population. Subtle changes in American National Character have made past teaching techniques obsolescent; therefore, new, dynamic, imaginative and non-static teacher-student relationships must be established if the best of past teaching methodology is to b e creatively synthesized with contemporary innovation concepts.

The first step that must occur, to cause this change, is that the teacher must reevaluate his relationship to the student so that creative and democratic change can take place in the educational process; creative steps in attitude and educational methodology can result in a new era of cooperation and educational innovation. Only in this manner can truly creative innovation occur, that is, innova-

tions that will allow us to view the teacher as a human and es-
teemed authority figure who functions not as a taskmaster but as a
guide and helper whose goals it is to suggest, not impose, and
whose task is to show the student how he can perfect and acquire
his knowledge. The day is long past when the teacher is the im-
parts solely of knowledge, the conditioner of student minds, the
programer of student moral character. The teacher must cease being the classroom policeman, the authoritarian taskmaster, the
personification of "the one who knows." He can no longer command the authority that a staff general does in battle. The authoritarian teacher can no longer act as though he were the headmaster
in a boy's dormitory school. He may no longer be the "Man" epito-
mized in Gerald Farber's article "The Student as a Nigger." Farber
states that, "when a teacher says, 'Jump' students jump." Farber
goes on to say:

> They tell him what's true and what isn't. some teachers
> insist that they encourage dissent but they're almost al-
> ways jiving and every student knows it. Tell the man what
> he wants to hear or he'll fail your ass out of the course.
> (1968:1)

The teacher must also cease thinking of the student as a second-class
citizen who must prove his manhood in academic achievement's
before he can have authentic existence as a human being. The times
demand an ideological change away from this boot-camp atmosphere, this academia sink or swim school of negativity.

Show me a dehumanized student brought to this state as the
result of his educational encounters and I'll show you a sick educational system. Education's task is not to program and breaks
down what little humanity the student personifies in his personality make-up but " . . . its central aim is the building of the
powers of the human mind and spirit, it is the formation or, as I
would view it, the evoking of knowledge, character, culture-that
at least if no more." (Aurobindo: 1969)

Student attitudes must also change, that is, the arrogance of youth must be replaced by a more trusting identity with the educational process-individuals over 30 surely must be considered as human beings. A greater commitment to scholarship and more intensive motivational attitude toward research innovation could also result in greater creative self-fulfillment, not only for the anthropological disciplines but for the student community. Above all, however, both student and teacher must develop closer channels of communication and responsiveness to each other-perhaps in some cases noted research scientists should be encouraged to return to teaching.

To grasp the 'crisis' situation in education, symbolically, it must be recognized that the ideological system of teacher-student society is tied explicitly to the educational methodological system, that is, student-teacher behavioral patterns are functionally interrelated with education methodology, therefore, any creative change in the present system cannot occur without an alteration in both phases of the educational process.

We have discussed the first phase of this duality already, the second category concerning educational methodology has been established and its relationship to teacher-student attitudes recognized. The question now presents itself as one of relating the goal of reversing the process of student dehumanization, this process of depersonalizing human beings, to that of the educational process itself. It is surely not enough to state that honesty and ethical responsibility, and that commitment to mutual trust and freedom of expression are the requisite requirements that students and teachers must personify in their relations with each other. No much more is needed if a truly just and democratic educational system is to be created that is not based on fear and the avoidance of academic punishment. Something more is needed to eliminate the impersonality of the present system and the inherent lack of protection and instability that the student must face during his student career. The obvious solution is that the student needs a protector, a guide, a counselor-perhaps even a father image, who can provide the necessary inspiration and guidance to win that formidable battle over the frightful odds' academia presents to the green student.

What must be established then is a proper and formal apprentice system for the neophyte student. This system would embrace the willing student during his second semester of training. Then he could make the necessary decision whether he wished to be a part of this voluntary system and whom he would pick as his guide and counselor. The guide and his group of not more than four other students could refuse permission to the green outsider if they so wished.

Once our neophyte student is a member of the group, he would, of course, be required to keep a weekly or perhaps monthly contact with the professor-guide, as well as attending group encounter or sensitivity training sessions. The student would remain a member of his group throughout his student career, that is, until he became a senior or a candidate for his degree or until he had selected his theses or dissertation committee, then his contractual obligations and apprenticeship would be dissolved.

The student, thus, strengthened and nourished by a fair and just academic system can continue his educational program alone, satisfied that future successes or failures will be based solely on his academic merits. The program must obviously be more than a paper model of teacher-student relations. To be successful the apprenticeship must be a viable and dynamic relationship. The teacher must want to give his time and effort to the student. Naturally, the student must want to receive and change if growth and academic harmony are to exist. When these social conditions exist the professor-guide, confidant, advisor and protector can initiate the green student into the mysterious rites of the anthropological order of social academia. The professor-counselor, on the other hand, can " . . . learn to work 'with' the students, talk to them, listen to them, smile and feel with them, and for them." (Cahn: 1968)

We have discussed, up to this point, the student-teacher behavioral relationship, and the teaching techniques that control this relationship; we must now concern ourselves with curriculum subject matter the essence that supports the entire educational structure. It is by now rather obvious to most members of the academic community that the encyclopedic concept of anthropological education is functionally an impossible task, that is, to program total anthropology into the student, although an admirable goal. It is also rather obvious that most anthropology department attempt to do just such a thing, that is, to program the student to be experts in all the field of anthropology, thus contributing to the general chaos of mental vacuity found in many graduate students.

To counteract this student disease I propose that a new teaching modal be created that will be called the variable-concept Game theory. This theory would be utilized by forming a select group of not less than five but not more than ten students on a grand tour of one culture, that is, a classroom systems model would embrace the student group into an intensified and accelerated culture contact program, right in the classroom.

The variable-concept systems technique, utilizing all the modern film and audiovisual, computor and television resources would immediately incorporate the intellectual and psychological natures of the student group into the play series of the game practice. This would existentially bring satisfaction and integration, on various psychological levels, to the student group while the game taught the nature of culture to them in a realistic but simulated manner. The rationale, obviously, would be to give the student an inner conviction concerning the nature of culture, almost an emotional-existential awareness-generally accrued by seasoned anthropologists only after years of field work.

The rules and structure of the game are as follows. All the players would be bound together academically for one semester, that is, the group players would take all their course together as a group.

The group would either be divided into two teams that would compete with each other in a program of intensive conceptual game playing or the entire group would compete against a computer. These encounters would ideally take place at an isolated retreat during a three day play series through out the duration of the semester.

The objective of the game would be to simulate the multidimensional nature of just one select culture under a multiplicity of circumstances and situations-thus, altering the variables in various manners and forms to suit the games varying conceptual framework. All the subtleties of conceptual paradigms and cultural model systems from diverse schools of thought must structurally be an integral part of the game theory. The players themselves must integrally be assimilated into the heart and fiber of the conceptual machination, in such a manner that predisposes them to think only with how ideologically the culture would act or react under a given situation or circumstances.

The professor-guides will monitored the Variable-Concept Game program, leading the student group through core courses on linguistics, ethnoscience, culture theory-yet creeping ever so slow and imperceptibly into the nature of the chosen reality-culture. When the moment arrives, the time of immersion into the conceptual being of that structure-that culture extraordinary, that now has existential reality as a dominates and forceful thing in itself in the students' minds and existential beings, then and then only does the game truly begin. From this point on the game cannot stop, must not stop; the place of variable force put in motion and supporting the game's internal reality structure must continue until the students have solved their conceptual problems, that is, each student must as a group meet the demands of the game and solve the collective grand problem, and at the same time working on their own creative situational puzzle.

While the student scientists work on the central core problem the game progresses forward into the realm of change relationships where we find that cultural variables introduce into the game the nature of culture-change in all it's varying dimensions and ramifications, thus changing the nature of the game into one of dynamic movement in contrast to the game's past static nature. Only now does the student, accompany by their professor-guides, truly enter into the nature of culture as a diachronic living "creature-almost alive," almost out of control. It is here, at the crucial juncture in their study of the nature of culture that the student-group truly grasps its nature through multi-dimensional systems models of every conceivable theoretical formal and paradigm. At this time and space and only at this point does the Variable-Concept Game fulfill its potential and uniquely solve the teacher-student problem of how to make the requisite subject matter intellectually dynamic.

In summary we find that higher education is today at a crucial juncture in its relations with the student population. Education to many students has become an obsolescent and meaningless exercise. If we are to continue to have a meaningful and relevant educational system then our task as students and educators are to revitalize and reorganize the educational process so that it may again become dynamic, imaginative and relevant to our age.

CHAPTER 16

ARMAGEDDON U.S.A.-
AMERICA'S EXTINCTION PERIL

FUTURIST COMMENTARY: Death is the ultimate end of all social systems. This is a fact and it is folly to believe that American culture shall escape the invariable fate of all cultures–death! The last 500 years has seen the death and destruction of thousands of cultures throughout the world. In many cases the inhabitants of many of these cultures died through either the overt or covert hand of genocide and in cases where some inhabitants survived their cultural organization and languages were lost.

It is a sad fact that humanity has within its personality system a runaway perversion that allows it to kill fellow members of the human race and exterminate them and degrade them and think nothing more of these acts than one would of crushing a bud beneath one's feet.

Campbell, the social scientist, comments on the fact that the 20th century is a time of darkness instead of the light of modern progress it is portrayed to be by the controlled presses the world. He sees this century as one of barbarism and death that rivals the dark days of the church's inquisition and sees the 20th century as a return to the dark ages and one in which the forces of humanity's unregenerated unconscious are setting the mood and creating the death knolls of the human race and its cultures. He says:

It is a sad day when we have to faces facts that regardless of all of our modern technologies that the race of man is still struck in the dark mud of his primordial death consciousness. And the fact of the matter is that the genocide phenomenon is alive and well within the consciousness of the species. The human race now has the capacity to annihilate the human race and it rejoices in this fact.

Individual nations shout with glee that as kings of the mountain none may touch them and that they may dictate policy and truth to the rest of the world of mankind. Yet other segments of mankind, who also have the "Bomb" threaten with equal bravado that none may dictate to them and that history is on their side and that if they are restricted in any manner their bombs will annihilate their enemies. Thus the age of nuclear terror began and another notch is cut on the gun that kills American culture.

When there is no hope for the future and death may face one at any time, the joy and fun and humor goes out of a culture; then the spectacle of death takes over and insidiously destroys whatever fiber of morality and ethic remains. The primordial fear syndrome takes over covertly at first and then it seeps up to conscious awareness and life become a dreary round of insidious anguish. You know deep down you will never face old age and that there is no real hope for the world because the forces of primordial atavism rule the day. Even reason is of no avail because it is allied with the industrial-military complex and if it is used at all is utilized to figure how many millions of expendable lives they can allow to fall as canon fodder.

Corruption surely takes over as small minds and infrarational idiots and incompetent people use top-secret classifications to hide their bungling and idiotic errors as hidden technologies are developed that allow hidden power factions to do what they will under the cloak of covert secrets and national defence.

There comes a time, that no man can predict with sureness, when the spirit of the nation and culture flees to the hills of despair and dies in agony alone and in disgrace and it whimpers are heard by no man, who in the arrogance of his pride has no ears to hear and no comprehension of his coming demise and would reject outright any news of the pending death of American life and spirit.

Woe to a nation who, in the ignorance of the night of their falsehood, rejects the signs of the times and instead rejoices at their freedom of degeneracies and thrills at the touch of aid victims and in his euphoria shits on all that is holy as he laughs of his triumph over superstition and death. What he thinks is life is death and realizes not the fact that he is a dead man walking through life as a zombie who is controlled by the dark forces of his unconscious and by the dead hand of tradition. And when he partially wakes up he is taken by the hand into the camps of the culture's morticians and given uniforms of war and political worth to wear and thus undocumented is embraced within the ranks of the dark ones who preach peace and truth and love and justice. Now as a card carrying member of the death generation he is a purveyor of truth and modern ideals and by upholding the agenda of the dark priests of hell he too contributes to the death generations ultimate goal of truth through death, life through holy dementia.

ARMAGEDON-
AMERICA'S EXTINCTION PERIL

Futurist Commentary: Campbell's editorial on the nuclear madness of the Russian and American terror tactics were in actuality just a prelude to the trying times of the 21st century. When these two great nations joined together to negate an outside threat to the peace of the world certain third world countries became out of control and the world entered an era of nuclear destruction. A third of the world's population was decimated with over three billion deaths and hundred of millions of casualties which made many parts of the world uninhabitable.

Today, in the 22nd century, one of our most pressing problems is to keep the hordes of human mutants from overrunning the remnants of what civilization is left. Strangely some of these inhabitants of the poison zones of the earth has reverted back to ancestral types. Some look like australopithecines and some resemble Homo erectus and there are even black co-magnons, strangely found in Scandinavians and northern Europe. Most are horribly mutated and in their madness keep overrunning our defenses, primarily because our solders cannot enter their territory of radiation and because they live under ground where our bombs are useless against them.

In some sectors of the world's civilizations they have annihilate whole societies, killing the men and raping the women and making them slaves to childbearing so that they can again uplift their race.

We tremble at this dark tide of ignorance and filth that beats at our doors and won't go away as our race dies and our women become more sterile and rarely can we find a man who has the capacity to sire an offspring.

The end is in sight and I cry up to God almighty for help but can he hear our whimpers of death and our cries of lamentation or even wish to help the descendents of the 20th century man. Let us hope that there is still time to save the human race and that the spirit of mankind will rise up to the occasion and that our cries of help will be heard but if we are annihilated let our records show we stood up proud and faced death with honor and let no man say otherwise!

When death roars and the faint hearted quell and shutters and fall down in fright there is still hope in the winds of time. It is a fact that within the race of man lays a spark of divinity that will rise up the fallen and uplift the confused and take the gifted ones by the hand of providence to the glory land. What is needed is a small core of giants who can uplift themselves into eternity and by so doings lead the race of man into the promised land of harmony and stability and truth and justice.

It is written let the weak fall by the roadside for they have voluntarily chosen death, let the confused wallow in their filth of depravation, let the hostile warriors of death fall on their spears of doubt and destruction, but let the chosen ones enter the light of civilized life so that the race may walk into eternal life and preserve the species Homo sapiens.

There is now a mystic warrior called Quetzalcoatl, from the province of darkness who preaches this message of hope and millions now follow him. Wherever he goes society is reformed and revivalistic movements of various kinds spring up.

Our spies tell us that even groups of the barbarians from the radiation zones have bowed down to him by the thousands and are even now entering his centers of healing and are ceasing attacking our outer provinces. It is even reported that whole providences of the polluted areas has partitioned to become states of the American empire.

When the army of the Barbarians Sotoclum was defeated on the plane of Seth and their leader was slain in a personal combat with this mystic leader, whole clans of the polluted ones converted to the one they call "the light of heaven."

He is looked upon as a miracle worker by some and by his enemies as the most dangerous man in the American empire and many wonder how he has survived the numerous assassinations attempts on his life; yet the common folk adore him and applaud his great healing powers and many view him as an incarnated God, especially the barbarians of the polluted zones; yet he is also a mighty warrior and many warriors have been slain in personal combat by his hand and apparently he is a general of magnificent proportions.

One thing is certain he is no pacifist and ten thousand disguised Nija Warriors travel with him wherever he goes and in the provinces revitalized by him, millions obey his every command as if truth and glory flow from his very mouth.

He has formed youth corps that are called, servants of the people, to help his people rebuild their lives and recreate civilization on a sound ecological environment. He has formed new agriculture and industrial schools and reorganized society in new and brilliant ways and preaches the equality of the races of the world and the equality of the sexes.

Wherever he travels he creates universities and schools of creativity for children and also builds what he calls temples of light and their adjacent medical centers of healing; and the youth view him as a dynamic warrior of God almighty and the elite of these youth he puts in schools of eternal learning, as he calls them, and it is reported by our spies that mighty warriors come out of these centers with miraculous powers of psi abilities and healing power yet are magnificent solders and martial artists who have swore that they shall achieve success at revitalizing society or die trying. Fanatics they are all and the rest of the civilized world quake in fear at this internal enemy.

This man surrounds himself with thirty high priests and priestesses of light, who are allegedly almost as knowledgeable and mighty as he is, and these in turn control seven hundred mystic warrior generals who are his officer corps but are also his priests of Eternity. Collectively they are called the immortals.

All the immortals are celibate until aged 27, then if they chose, they can marry another priest or priestess of the opposite sex or a vestal virgin from the Temples of light. The children from these marriages are said to be prime candidates for what the mad scientist calls the supramental force-an energy system that purportedly has the power to transform even cellular matter and create Gnostic beings who have transcended death itself. Naturally this nonsense is a superstitious absurdity but how can you convince true believers of falsehoods?

It is said that all one of the immortals has to do to raise an army is to raise his finger and success will be his yet remarkably these generals are brilliant scientists and mystics with remarkable abilities. And each one of them has sworn an eternal fidelity to their cause that they will take up the mantle of leadership if called by Providence, or if their leader, the mad mystic scientist, falls in battle or is assassinated. For this reason their enemies have attempted time and time again to kill them.

Our forces have attempted to assassinate them also but success was achieved in only two cases but this evoked what they called,

"The wrath of God against the enemies of the people." They searched throughout the American Empire for the killers and one morning in every province their appeared, on their poles of death, the heads of the assassins and the instigators of the assassinations and all their immediate governmental leaders and their eldest sons and also the top fifty leaders of each of our five intelligence organizations. Now we all quake in fear for we know that no place is Safe from these demons.

But the fundamentalist Christian churches still call him anti-Christ and the covert elite of the rest of Christendom's hatred of him is so pronounced that they will not give up trying to kill him.

But even their assassins have had no success because he converts them; and even the American Empire's, Cal Pol's army of 100,000, on the plane of stupor, all to a man, threw down their arms and converted to this mad mystic warrior's cause.

It is certain if the empire does not perish from without it will surely do so from within. No one seems to know how to stop this misguided fiend.

Already this infection has spread to the confederation of Nations as elite members of the Mad mystic's inner core of believers spread their missionary lies throughout the world. And the fools of the world respond and embrace these young men and women of beautiful countenance when they say "Join us and become as we are. Help us create a new earth and uplift the family of man into Eternity itself!"

The elite forces, called the servants of the people, are reputedly almost as miraculous as their Mad Mystic leader and their miracles flow off them into the multitudes and large masses of the world population fall under the sway of these fanatics. It is as if there were multitudes of Appollonious of Tyana and Jesus Christs running around the world rising the dead and healing the multitudes.

Their fifth columns are everywhere and their free healing colleges and universities and wisdom children centers have spread world-wide and their priests of light, as they call themselves, heal our sick and revitalize the world's cities and when danger presents itself they don their warrior armor and become mighty warriors; who seeming know no defeat since most of their enemies become converts to their cause and even the "alien forces" have begged for peace.

The masses adore them but they seemingly have no need of worship or of the applaud of the multitudes because they gently counsel peace and charity to all mankind, even including the obscene mutant barbarians who daily join their ranks.

Their agents are everywhere. You find them working among the field workers and beside the industrial workers and they are found as humble workers in the deep mines. And no scientific profession is without these fifth column madmen. And to make matters worse, our most brilliant scientists are graduates of their universities and their political scientists are everywhere in all political parties.

Yet they are not forceful in proselyting They are not dogmatic, they force no one to believe as they do. They say the light of truth exists in all dogmas and concepts if ye but look for it.

We do not know how to stop these infiltrators who seemingly touch both heaven and earth; and to be touched by one leads one toward the light of truth, their converts say!

What nonsense, what fools, what idiots. It is not yet their time! There is still hope for the world and the American Empire. Pray for our deliverance from such Madness!

This month our philosophers and greatest church leaders and top scientists were forced by public pressure to debate the Madscientist himself, at the center for applied sciences in New York City. All to a man, fell down in defeat to his brilliance and oratory. Even our greatest scientists seem to be babbling idiots in comparison to his brilliant scientific knowledge and mathematical genius. His new paradigm concepts and scientific models baffle our conception of the cosmos and his engineering feats, including the development of new air craft and industrial innovations, astound our scientific experts. His biological breakthroughs on genetic engineering confuses our experts and his knowledge of all of the world's religious scriptures astound the theologians and now even our mystics seek his guidance.

Quetzalcoatl's psi abilities of psychokinesis, clairvoyance, clairaudience abilities, and general transpersonal knowledge makes everyone in comparison to him seem as if they are babbling idiots; and those who do not bow down to him cry out in terror for a world gone mad as fear itself causes them to quake and tremble before this master of life!

Now half the scientific community reads his books and practices his philosophy of eternal renewal and our greatest universities now have over a third of their facility as followers of this mad one.

Our most brilliant youth are sneaking into his territory to study at his Universities, much as the Christian scholars of mediaeval Europe ran eagerly to the Arab universities of Moonish Spain.

Why are they doing this? Primarily, because of the scientific breakthroughs of three of his followers in biology, and especially because of his creativity in the philosophy of science and mathematics and in engineering where his superior weapons and unusual flying machines dominate the empire so that even the "alien force" has made their peace with him. All of our sciences are now obsolete. And our Nobel prize winners stare in disbelief at the irrelevance of their past glories.

But the saddest tragedy of all is that our youth are running toward the new ways at break neck speed and embracing the new biology and now perhaps the race will not become extinct; but those of us who are wiser cry out at the destruction of our civilization and dread the end of the era. Even the average youth in the streets is confused and some cry out and take up the sword in one hand and the mad-mystic's holy scriptures in the other hand and wander around the empire as holy emissaries of his word.

Our churches are empty an what congregations that are functional now are converting to his ideas of mystic revivalism and our most brilliant young ministers are falling down before his feet and asking this Mad one to lead them into the greater light of Eternity as he tells them not to worship any man but instead he counsels each person to concentrate on their inner light so that they may walk into eternity as conscious human beings. They are entering his Mystic fellowships and becoming practioners of direct illuminations from God, instead of following the written word of God!

This mystic leader is a dangerous man; especially since all of Christendom and most of the major world religions are now falling at his feet.

In the month of truth, he made a pilgrimage to sites throughout Greece to revitalizing the ancient oracle sites; ending up at Deli, where the oracle priest of Apollo hailed him as the new philosopher King –the new cosmic world leader.

Next, our spies tell us he went to Lake Moreous in Egypt where he sat in meditation in the darkness before dawn. As the sun rose it showered its golden rays upon him as if he were Aknaton of old; and as this mystic rose and raised his hands all of Egypt bowed down to him in adoration!

On a certain day of destiny Quetzalcoatl, the Chisted one, entered the ancient pyramid at Giza, just as the gentle Essene Jesus and John the Baptist had done 2200 hundred years previously, to be inititiated within the holy of the holiest by the eternal hand of destiny itself.

At the alter of history the holy one presents himself to the tender mercies of the cross of truth as he rides upon the tide of destiny itself.

The hierophant and the ancient Magi of old, circle the holy gift of man to the Cosmos, as he lies upon the cosmic cross of truth; suddenly a force of Cosmic light encircles the holy one. A voice from out of Eternity says, "Go forth, beloved Son of God and rise up my other children into the evolutionary light of Eternity. From this day hence thee are a being of Gnostic light and the pinnacle of species evolution. From thy loins shall emerge a new race of species beings that shall shower their light upon all creation."

From that blaze of light the Christed one rose up seven feet off the cross of truth and entered that blazing light from Eternity. When the holy one emerged out of the mist of destiny his countenance was of glorious light which glowed from the essence of his being.

Our spies found him next on the shores of the Dead Sea where he took on the mantle of the Essene teacher of righteousness. It was on this shore that representative mystic orders of Islamic Sufi and Jewish Cabalists hailed him as their enlightened teacher of wisdom and accepted him as their Grand Master!

In a deep eternity grotto Quetzalcoatl climbed the seven steps to the throne of Seth where the mantle of Melchizedek emerged from his inner being and he personified Melchizedek who was "without father, without mother, without genealogy, having neither beginning of days nor end of life and abideth a priest continually." [1]

Months later we tracked down this mad scientist in India as the parsi Zoroastrians consecrated him as the righteous Zoraster. The Buddhist hailed him as Maitria the coming Buddha. The Hindu rose up in mass by the millions as they bowed down in joy to him as the tenth Kalki avatar of enlightenment.

Wherever he walked new institutions of learning arose which combined the study of ancient knowledge with modern technological know how. He even reestablished the ancient Rishi universities which the children of the elect now attend in forest retreats.

After several weeks stay in the heights of Tibet this mad scientist, under the cover of a rainbow of five colors, walked over the waters of lake Dhanakosha to the isle of destiny and sat upon the lotus throne of Padmaa-Sambhava. When he was asked who his father and mother were and what caste and country he was from, he said "My father is Wisdom and mother is the Voidness. My country is the country of the Dharma. I am of no caste and of no creed. I am sustained by perplexity and I am here to destroy Lust, Anger, and Sloth." [2]

Immediately he becames the reining Dali Lama. He made a vow before Eternity that day that all hidden truths of life would be revealed worldwide to those who were pure enough to handle the esoteric verities of life.

We lost track of him after his instillation as Dali Lama but later caught up to him as he traveled throughout China revitalizing Taoist and Buddhist temples. Many Taoist and Buddhist universities were formed by his priests of Eternity and hundreds of thousands of people were personally initiate by him as they hailed him as an ancient immortal from the past, possibly Lao Tzu, himself.

Quetzalcoatl next went to the island of Besalem where he rested in Solomon's house. It is said that his thirty high priests joined him as he consecrated the world to truth and justice as he uttered NOVUS ORDO SECLORUM. It is reported that as he drank the nectar of life from the chalice of victory, transpersonal doves of peace descended upon as he swore before God almighty that justice and constitutional guarantees would prevail in God's worldly empire.

Within a month he turned up on the isle of Patmos where St. John the Divine wrote Revelations. In a deep grotto, Gnostic Christians in an historic mystic ceremony hailed him as the historical Christ, a Cosmic being who descends as an incarnated force of Divine light, whom they call Appollonious of Tyana.

Quetzalcoatl next makes a triumphant entree into Jerusalem where jointly the Jews proclaimed him as their messiah, and Islam accepts him as their long awaited leader.

Most of the Christian world imbraces him as the risen Christ. All of the major protestant denominations are represented, also the Roman Catholic, Greek and Russian Orthodox and other Christians of various kinds.

Our mad charlatan descends from a cloud in his unusual air ship with his thirty immortals, as the fools of Christianity accepted him as the returning Christ and savior of the world.

As he accepts the mantel of Christ he rose seven feet into the air and from his countenance flowed a massive beam of light that uplifts the masses into a rapturous swoon of love and compassion. It is said that many flew to eternity that day as the great world revitalization of humanity commenced.

Quetzalcoatl, the risen Christ, next enters Rome on a donkey to the cheers of the tumultuous masses as he is crowned as the Roman Catholic pope.

His first command is to retire and pension off all clergy of Christendom. All are now to take their places as lay persons within the church of God. Immediately 700,000 priests of Melchizedek and their 3,000,000 priest of Eternity take over the command structure of all Christendom.

The second command of the risen Christ was that all high initiates of the Cosmic mysteries were henceforth to be honored and respected whether they were Christian, Taoist, Buddhist, Hindu or indigenous native religious personages.

The third command is that all church dogmas and creeds are abolished as the transpersonal light of mystic revelation takes president throughout all world religions.

The fourth command is that Henceforth all people must earn their way into eternity, Christ the risen one states. All concepts of vicarious salvation, based on the name of Christ, are abolished and each person now must walk into eternity on his own merits.

The church's purpose now is to give worthy individuals the methods to transform themselves but that each individual bears personal responsibility before Eternity for his own thoughts, words and deeds.

Membership in the church no longer will guarantee salvation. Each person must now earn his own way into Eternity!

Quetzalcoatl, the risen one, as we laughingly call him, has now returned to his American Indian empire and is posed to take over the New American Empire. And cry as we might we are powerless to stop him.

Presently, even the President of the American empire has this mad man at his right elbow as a consultant and our senators and elected representatives quake in fear at his approach but even here some of our most influential elected officials are his followers and are even now presenting legislation to reform the empire along the lines of his mystic renewal concepts of social reorganization. Has the world gone Insane?

Recently our intelligences tell us that the President is considering making him his vice-president but other sources tell us that this mad man's forces has so infiltrated the three main political parties that next month collectively they will nominate him for President of the American Empire.

If something is not done quickly the empire will collapse from within and we will all be doomed to live in this mad man's shadow.

" Oh, God almighty why do you let our race perish from the face of the earth and allow this mad mystic-scientist to mislead our people into hell?"

It is interesting that Campbell spoke of such people in one of his articles on revivalistic cults. He says in his article ''the Transpersonal in Cultural Revitalization Movements" that:

When a crisis of identity occurs within a culture, on both individual and social levels, often the transpersonal emerges though the revelations of a prophet who has entered into a higher state of consciousness. The emergent quality of mind, as reflected through the charisma of the prophet, then becomes a new and dynamically focused force which reorganizes the society and the conceptual framework of the society's socio-ideological system. New concepts emerge in the moral, economic, political and religious reality systems of the people.

If the state of consciousness of the prophet is high enough, select disciples and at times large masses of people often emerge into higher realms of consciousness and become dynamic examples of the new awareness. Often, however, only the prophet can emerge into the higher reaches of altered states of consciousness and the revitalization message he brings serves its purpose, living for a while and eventually dying—the fate of all social systems. Such systems, however, can provide techniques of mind emergence which select people within the social tradition can utilize on a linguistic consciousness and mind level. These techniques not only help people to emerge into higher ranges of consciousness but also serve as unifying rituals in religion or myth to bridge the contradictions found in all cultural situations.

Benjamin Lee whorf, linguist and scientist, commenting on the relationship of transpersonal dimensions to the world of man and linguistics, says that a noumenal world full of hyperspace–of higher dimensions awaits science to discover it. Science will unite and unify it through the discovery of its patterned relationships and affinity to linguistics, music and au fond mathematics as a systems organizer. [3]

Reality, mind-consciousness and culture are pattered wholes in continuous progression according to Whorf. This view conceives of patterns–form wholes which are connected together in continual progression. Thus a serial or progression of levels of mind dimensions are connected with the human race and reality. Linguistics recognizes this serial dimension, and historically some societies have realized that nature and language are connected and has an inner affinity with the cosmic order. [4]

Language as mantras, or chant formulas as symbolic sound models–correlated to bring responses to the subtle and bioplasmic bodies–through the chakra energy centers are the linguistic connection between consciousness and transcultural spheres of reality. Whorf makes the point mantrams become conscious patterns which assist the consciousness into the noumenal pattern world. It allows the human organism to control, transmit and amplify the internal energy system behind the personality dimensions. [5] This force repatterns nervous systems and glands and in the subtle electronic or etheric forces in the physical body one can amplify and activate latent forces resident in man. Through the amplification of such latent forces in the human consciousness, according to "Whorf, one can transcend the dimensional worlds of form. One can gain entrance to the formless transpersonal state. He says that it is within the possibilities of the culture of consciousness that such states of mind can be contacted as an expansion of consciousness. [6]

Just such contacts are made by leaders of revivalistic movements and suprarational men, and the key to the integration of consciousness and culture lies in just such a union. It is also through such an expansion of consciousness that the malfunctioning–the dysfunctioning within the human personality system can be corrected.

This book has discussed the seven causal reasons for the present global crisis. It has shown that a peoples' socio-cultural environmental system and personality system are symbolically and functionally interdependent. The key to overcoming the causal agents of the Genocide Phenomenon is human self-transcendence.

The hour is late and destiny is calling the human race. Each of us must rise to the challenge by fulfilling his full human psychodynamics. Will the human race achieve species success or racial destruction? Transintegral Psychology says that man's humaneness and speciehood potential can only be fulfilled by self-actualization and the transcendence of man's lower biological nature–an emergence into the further reaches of biological species consciousness!

At the present time no adequate paradigm exists for man of the 21st century. This book has talked about some of the clues and research data which may help us to develop this new theory. Today, however, we are still using personality theories and world views which are based on classical Judeo-Christian or Aristotelian concepts. Learning theory and Freudian ego theory have been added to these concepts but these personality theories still embrace the idea that existence is connected with Euclidean space and follow Newtonian laws of mechanics while operating in pre-Einstenian absolute time.

This concept of a self-contained, closed and isolated personality system, operating in prerelativistic time and subject to Euclidean space laws of cause and effect, has to be rejected by the mod-

ern space age. A new, open transpersonal species model of personality must be developed. It will discard the old Cartesian dualism
of mind and body and replace it by concepts which intersect mental and universal categories of existence–new space-time orienta-
tions consistent with quantum physics, transpersonal psychological data and parapsychological findings.

If five to ten percent of the world population can emerge
into the dimensions of the supramental species consciousness,
the human crisis will be overcome. Destiny calls Homo sapiens!
Will humanity answers the call!

Through the transforming techniques of Transintegral psychology, transpersonal psychology, Eastern and Western esoteric
traditions, hopefully the species crisis can be overcome. Naturally, none of the present transforming techniques are perfect and
new scientific systems must be developed which have an affinity
with life affirmative principles.

Modern man lives in an action world and must change within
the dynamics of the 21st century. Escapism and withdrawal from
the world will only contribute to the problem by taking out of
the battle the gifted and able of the human race–defeat by default must not repeat itself again in this century.

THE END TIMES

America do you care about yourselves and your nation? Are you
so far gone that death is a relief to you and a joy which you
willingly embrace because of your fear of life? Does life scare you
and death depression embrace you? Oh woe America for the primordial fear-anxiety syndrome and its child the Genocide Phenomenon is upon the land and none may say if the victim's of life
will succumb to death or be revived to life. For the truth of the
matter is that you must choose life voluntarily and walk into the
joys of life with your eyes open and emerge into something greater
than yourself. If you do not you are a member of the death cadre
and the Lord of fear is your leader and loud in his voice and clear

his call and deep his influence and deadly his way and all who follow him are doomed to a living death and shall perish in the social fires of fear's hell.

America can transcend and overcome its problems and save themselves; yet I fear time is running out and that our death children will rule the day and that collectively the death generation will march in unison into the pits of hell singing glory to God and Good will to mankind as the skulls of death swing from their belts and as they enthusiastically inhale the stench of death which surrounds them in their glory march.

It is written in the annals of old that 21st century man must face himself in all his naked glory or perish in the wars of terror. The dark ages are emerging again into the life of the species and all the humanity that man has developed up to now is gradually being eroded away by this onslaught. It is a time of species crisis and the call has emerged from the dark recesses of the human race to emerge into a new order of things or perish in the night mare of total annihilation. It is a time when we are being called upon by our innermost self to stand up and graduate into a higher human reality and to create new social orders and international systems of justice and prosperity that will uplift the human race. We are in the midst of this battle and upon its resolve rests either victory or death to our way of life.

America, stand up for life while there is yet time for action and reflection and truth and integrity to win the day. Let not hope die within the members of the elite of life; for it is written that all who chose life are an elite that shall overcome defeat and darkness and triumph over the darkness of the world. Are you of the elite of Light or a card carrying member of doom and defeat. Chose death or life, light or blackness; but chose for the fence sitters shall endure their own grade of hell and woe to they who sit out the end times because the time is now and the call has gone out and the clarion tune floods over the planet and none may sit out this battle and none may reject their birthright; none may cowardly slink away from the battle of life and death.

Stand up America and live the bill of rights and worship the goodness within your own heart and throw your higher countenance upon the troubles of the day with love and trust in your heart. There is yet time America, but the sands of time waits for no man or nation.

There is still some stillness upon the waters of life and some modem of goodwill in the countryside. The populace of darkness still fear the forces of light and there is yet a majority of people who have goodwill and love in their hearts.

Realize this fact humanity that a choice must be made and implemented soon before international ruin descends upon you and the extinction of the human race occurs. It is written that soon the apex of destiny shall reach you and none may escape their destiny in the new age.

Humanity, if you move with all deliberate speed your secure destiny shall emerge and the race shall be illuminated into the new age of fortunate results. If you delay and continue to fight among yourselves then the powers of darkness shall engulf you and none shall escape the wars of terror.

Go forward America and reach for your destiny or else it shall allude thee; go forward humanity and ye shall emerge into a glorious future which shall pull you forward into eternity itself. The choice is yours America.

The 20th century is a time of destiny and humanity is being called upon to stand up and reveal where it stands. Are you for death or life? Are you standing up for your race, and your species or cowardly succumbing to the allure of the Genocide Phenomenon and following the scheduling of the covert death generation. Stand up America and be counted!

FOOTNOTES

CHAPTER ONE:

1. Tillich, Paul. **Existential Philosophy,** Journal of the History of Ideas. 1944, 5:1, p. 67.
2. Jung, Carl G. **Psychology and Religion.** New Haven, Conn., 1938, pp. 14-15.
3. Hutschnecker, Arnold, **The Drive for Power.** M. Evan & Co. Inc., New York, N.Y. 1974 P. 183.
4. The death cadres may not be organized internationally but all share the common characteristics of having the fatal Neaderthal flaw.
5. Kuhn, Thomas. **The Structure of Scientific Revolutions.** University of Chicago Press: Chicago, 1962.
6. Sorokin, Pitrim A. **The Basic Trends of Our Times.** New Haven, Conn., College & University Press. p.17.
7. Ibid. p. 16.
8. Lerner, Michael I. **Heredity, Evolution and Society.** San francisco: W. Freeman & Company, 1968. p.x.
9. Macleish, Archibald. **Our altered Conception of Ourselves, Evolution of Man,** Louise B. Young, editor. New York: Oxford University Press, 1970, pp. 609-610.
10. Aurobindo. **The future Evolution of Man.** east Midland Printing co., Ltd. Bury St. edmunds, England, 1960. p.27.
12. Aurobindo, Sri. **On Yoga 11 tome Two. International University Centre collection Vol. V11.,** 1958. Sri Aurobindo Ashram Press, Pondicherry, India 1958, P. 692.
13. Hesse, Hermann. **Steppenwolf.** New York; Bantan books, 1963. p. 25.

14. Sorokin, Pitrim A. **The Basic Trends of Our Times.** New Haven, conn., college & University Press. p.234.
15. Mumford, Lewis. 1944. **The Condition of Man.** New York: Harcourt, Brace co., Inc. p. 234.
16. Ibid.
17. Fromm, Erick, D.T. Suzuki, and Richard DeMartino. **Zen Buddhism and Psychoanalysis.** New York: Harper & Brothers, 1960. p. 86.
18. Chaudhuri Haridas in a private conversation.
19. Satprem, **Mother's Agenda** 1971 Institute for Evolutionary Research, New York, 1982, p. 328.
20. Fromm, Erich. **The Anatomy of Human Destructiveness.** holt, Rinehart & Winston. New York, 1972. p.255.
21. Gandhi, Kishnor. **Social Philosophy of Sri Aurobindo and the New Age.** Sri Aurobindo Ashram Press, Pondicherry, 1965, P.66.
22. Aurobindo, Sri, **The Human Cycle, The Ideal of Human Unity, War and Self Determination.** Pondicherry: Sri Aurobindo International Centre of Education Collection, vol. IX 1962, P. 314.
23. Aurobindo, Sri. **The Life Divine.** New York India Library Society, 1965. p.934.
24. Ibid.
25. Aurobindo, Sri, **The Human Cycle, The Ideal of Human Unity, War and Self determination.** Pondicherry: Sri Aurobindo International Centre of Education Collection, vol. IX 1962, P. 315
26. Gandhi, Kishnor. **Social Philosophy of Sri Aurobindo and the New Age.** Sri Aurobindo Ashram Press, Pondicherry, 1965, Pp. 228-229.
27. M. scottpect **People of the Lie; The Hope of Healing Human Evil** 'Simon & schuster, New York, 1983, p. 121.
28. Bernard, Raymond. **Apollonius the Nazarene.** Health research. Pomeroy, Washington,. 1956. Bernard, Raymond THE UN-

KNOWN LIFE OF CHRIST, POMEROY, WASHINGTON, 1966. the unknown Life of christ

29. Koestler, Arthur. **The Evolution of Man; What Went Wrong?** Human variation: readings in Physical anthropology, Herman K. Bleibteu and James Down, editors. Beverly Hills: Glencoe Press. 1971, p.76.

30. Lorenz, Konrad. **On aggression.** New York: Bantam Books, 1971 p.228.

31. Ibid. pp. 230-231.

32. Satprem, **Mother's Agenda** 1971 Institute for Evolutionary Research, New York, 1982, p. 193

33.. M. scottpect **People of the Lie.: The Hope of Healing Human Evil** 'Simon & schuster, New York, 1983, p. 47.

34. Ibid. pp. 42-43.

35. M. scottpect **People of the Lie.: The Hope of Healing Human Evil** 'Simon & schuster, New York, 1983, p. 43.

36. Fromm, Erich. **The Anatomy of Human Destructiveness.** holt, Rinehart & Winston. New York, 1972. p. 74.

37. Ibid. P. 328. also in **The Ideal of the Karmayogin**, !11. p. 347.

38. Henry, Jules, **Culture Against Man.** Random House, New York, 1963. p. 474.

CHAPTER TWO:

1. Mead, Margaret. **And Keep Your Powder Dry.** William Morrow & co., New York 1965. pp. 162-163.

2. Hutschenecker, Arnold a. **The drive for Power.** M. Evans & col, Inc. New York, N.Y. 1974. Pp. 176-177.

3. Thompson, William Irwin, **At the Edge of History.** New York: Harper & Row, colophon books, 1971 p..76.

4. Fromn Erich. **The Revolution of Hope: Toward a Humanized Technology.** Bantam Books 1968. p.1.

5. Brzezinski, Abigniew. **The Technetronic Society.** Encountr, Vol. XXX, No I JAN., 1968. P.19.

6. May, Rollo, **The Innocent Murders.** Psychology Today, December 1972.

7. Henry, Julies, **Culture Against Man.** Random house, New York, 1963. p. 476.

8. Ibid.

9. Ibis.

10. Ibid. P. 16.

11.Josphen, Eric & Mary. **Man Alone: Alienation In Modern society.** Del Publishing co. Inc. New York, 1962. p.107.

12.Ibid. p. 25.

13. Ibid. p. 21.

14. Josphen, Eric & Mary. **Man Alone: Alienation in Modern Society.** Dell Publishing co. Inc. New york, 1962. p.56.

15. Ibid.

16. Henry, Julies, **Culture Against Man.** Random House, New York, 1963. p.16.

17.Ibid. p.28.

18. Josphen, Eric & Mary. **Man Alone: Alienation In Modern society.** Dell Publishing co. Inc. New york, 1962. p.56.

19. Henry, Julies, **Culture Against Man.** Random House, New York, 1963. pp. 27-28.

20. Ibid. p.24.

21. ibid. p.26.

22. Ibid. pp. 26-27.

23. ibid. p. 24.

24. Ibid.

25. Toffler, alvin. **Future Shock.** Bantam Books New York 1971. pp. 116-119.

26. Ibid.

27.ibid.

28. Ibid.

29. Whyte Willams Jr. **The Organization Man.** Doubleday Anchor books, New York. P. 1965. p. 191.

30. Ibid.,pp. 192-193.

31. Ibid. pp. 92-93.

32. Ibid. p.3.

33. Hutschnecker, Arnoldd, **The Drive for Power**. M. Evan & co. Inc., New York, N.Y. 1974 P. 180.

34. Ibid. pp. 38-39.

35. M. Scottpect **People of the Lie.: The Hope of Healing Human Evil** 'Simon & Schuster, New York, 1983, p. 47.

36. Ibid. pp. 42-43.

37. Ibid. p. 69.

38. Mead, Margaret. **And Keep Your Powder Dry**. William Morrow & co., New York 1965. p. 202,

39. Hutschnecker, Arnold, **The Drive for Power**. M. Evan & co. Inc., New York, N.Y. 1974 P. 184.

40. Mead, Margaret. **And Keep Your Powder Dry**. William Morrow & co., New York 1965. pp. 201-203.

41.Ibid. pp. 69-70.

42.Ibid. pp. 74-75.

43. Ibid. p. 77.

44. Ibid. pp. 124-125.

45.Ibid. p. 51.

46. Ibid. p. 128.

47. Ibid. p. 129.

CHAPTER THREE:

1. Henry, Julies, **Culture Against Man**. Random House, New York, 1963. p.47.

2. Ibid, p. 86.

3. Ibid. p.92.

4. Ibid. P.60.

5. Fromm, Erich. **The Anatomy of Human Destructiveness**. holt, Rinehart & Winston. New York, 1972. p.350.

6. Ibid. p. 351.

7. ibid.

8. Ibid. p. 272. Original source Davie, M.R. 1929. **The Evolution of War**. N.Y. Kennikat.

9. Ibid.

10. davie, Ibid. 1929.

11. Malinowski, Bronislaw, **Freedom and Civilization**. Roy Publishers, New York 1944. p.336.

12. Sorokin, Pitirim **A Modern Historical and Social Philsophies,** Dover Publications inc. New York. 1963. p.104.

13. Ibid. p.105.

14. Ibid.

15. Ibid. p. 10.

16. Hutschnecker, Arnold, **The Drive for Power**. M. Evan & co. Inc., New York, N.Y. 1974 P. 67. In Lasswell, Harold, **Psychopathology and Politics**. New York:Viking Press, 1960. pp. 67, 71.

17. Ibid. pp. 172-173.

18. Ibid. lp.61.

19. Henry, Julies, **Culture Against Man**. Random House, New York, 1963. p.8.

20. Hutschnecker, Arnold, **The Drive for Power**. M. Evan & co. Inc., New York, N.Y. 1974 P. 67. In Lasswell, Harold, **Psychopathology and Politics**. New York:Viking Press, 1960. p. 60.

21. May, Rollo, **The Meaning of Anxiety**. Pocket Books, N.Y. 1977. Pp. 162-165.

22. Lynd r.s. & Lynd H.M. **Middletown,** New York. 1929. P. 72..

23. May, Rollo, **The Meaning of Anxiety**. Pocket Books, N.Y. 1977. Pp. 162-165.

24. Ibid. p. 3.

25. Lynd r.s. & Lynd H.M. **Middletown,** New York. 1929. P. 87.

26. Ibid. p. 493.

27. Ibid. p. 315.

28. Ibid. P. 177.

29. Lynd r.s. & Lynd H.M. **Middletown in transition**. P. 315.

30. May, Rollo, **The Meaning of Anxiety**. Pocket Books, N.Y. 1977. Pp. 8-9.

31. Roszak, Theodore. **The Making of a Counter Culture.** Anchor books, Garden City, New York 1969. pp. 5-6.

32. Ellul, Jacques, **The Technological Society.** trans. John Wilkinson New York: A.a. Knopf. 1964. P. 138.

33. . Roszak, Theodore. **The Making Of A Counter Culture.** Anchor books, Garden City, New York 1969. p7.

34. Northrup, Bowen, **They Think for Pay,** in the Wall Street Journal, Sept. 20, 1967.

35 Roszak, ibid. pp. 8-9.

36. May, Rollo, **The Meaning of Anxiety.** Pocket Books, N.Y. 1977. P. 163.

37. Tawney, R. H. **The Acquistive Society.** New York, 1920, P. 47.

38. Ibid. [.47.

39. Ibid. p.49.

40. May, Rollo, **The Meaning of Anxiety.** Pocket Books, N.Y. 1977. P. 163

41. Ibid. p.9.

42. Tillich, Paul, **Existential Philosophy.** journal of the History of ideas, 1944, 5:1 p. 67.

43 Ibid. pp. 10-11.

44. Ibid. pp. 10-11.

45.McNamara's Robverts .S. **The Essence of Security.** new york harper & row, 1968. pp 109-110.

46. Roszak, Theodore. **The Making of a Counter Culture.** Anchor books, Garden City, New York 1969. p.18.

47. burke, James. **Something for Nothing.** produced for BBC and shown in London on June 27th, 1968.

48. Rozak Ibid. p. 21, see also Times diary, the Times London, July 5, 1968. P. 10.

49. Aurobindo Sri. **Early Letters** 27:475.

CHAPTER FOUR:

1. 1962 address by President Kennedy on his plans for resuming nuclear testing, March, 2, 1962.
2. Rifkin, Jeremy with Howard Ted. **Entropy: a New World View.** Bantam books, 1981, pp. 5-6.
3. Ibid. p. 15.
4. Randall, Hohn Herman. **The Making of the Modern Mind.** New York: Columbia University Press, 1940. p.224.
5. Ibid. Op. cit., po. 224.
6. Jean Houston, **Prometheus Rebound: An Inquiry into Technological Growth and Psychological change.** in alernative Yo Growth, Dennis Meadows, ed. (Cambridge, Mass: Ballinger, 1977, p. 274.
7. Randall, oop. cit.,p. 241.
8. Ibid., pp. 241-242.
9. Ibid p. 259.
10. Rifkinl, pp. 21-22.
11. Randall, p. 259.
12. Fromn Erick, **The Revolution of Hope: Toward a Humanized Technology,** Bantam Books, New york, 1968. p.140.
13.Rifkin, pp.23-24.
14.Strauss, Leo, **Natural Rights and History,** Chicago: University of chicago Press, 1953. p. 258.
15. Locke, John, Second treatise, in John Locke, **Two Treatises of Govement.** ed. Peter Laslett cambride University Press, 1967. p. 315.
16. Ibid.
17. Ibid.
18. Rifkin, Jeremy with Howard Ted. **Entropy: a New World View.** Bantam books, 1981, p26.
19. Ibid. pp. 26-28.
20. Ibid. pp. 28-29.
21. Sartre, Jean Paul. **Literary and Philosophical Essays,** Collier Books, New York, NY. 1962. p.200.

22. IBID. P. 202.
23. May, Rollo, The Meaning of Anxiety. Pocket Books, N.Y. 1977. PP.20-21.
24. Casssirer, Ernst, An Essay On Man, New Haven Conn: Yale University Press 1944. p.16.
25. May, Rollo, The Meaning of Anxiety. Pocket Books, N.Y. 1977. P. 23.
26. Fromn Erich. The Revolution of Hope: toward a Humanized Technology. Bantam Books 1968. p. 27;
27. Fromn Erick. Escape From Freedom, Avon books, New York. 1965. p. 28. Sorokin, Pitrim A. The Basic Trends of Our Times. New Haven,Conn., College & University Press. pp.125-126.
29. Ibid. pp. 139-141.
30. Weber, Max. The Protestant Ethic and The Spirit of Capitalism, Charles Scribner's sons, New York, 1958l pp. 2-4.
31. May, Rollo, The Meaning of Anxiety. Pocket Books, N.Y. 1977. P. 169.
32. Ibid. p. 53.
33. Ibid. p. 51.
34.Ibid. p. 53.
35.Gorer, Geoffey, The Danger of Equality. Weybright & Talley, New York 1966. p.21.
36. Weber, Max. The Protestant Ethic and The Spirit of Capitalism, charles Scribner's sons, New York, 1958l pp. 149-150.
37. Wolfe, Ldon M. The Image of Man in America. Thomas Y Crowell co. New York 1969. pp. 24-25.
38. Ibid. p. 27.
39.Ibid. P. 29.
40.Ibid. p. 30.
41. May, Rollo, The Meaning of Anxiety. Pocket Books, N.Y. 1977. P. 19.
42.Jefferson, Thomas, Notes on the State of Virginia. Philadelphia, 1788. in Wolfe p. 30.

43. Sorokin, Pitrim A. **The Basic Trends of Our Times.** New Haven, Conn., College & University Press. p. 17.

44. Sorokin, **Modern Historical & Social Philsophies.** pp.7-8.

45. Henry, Julies, **Culture against Man.** Random House, New York, 1963. p.5.

46. Gorer, Geofrey. **The American People: A Study in National Character.** W. W. Norton & Co. Inc. 1964, p. 229.

47. Ibid. p.23.

48. Freud, Totem and Tabu 3rd edition, 1922.

49. Gorer, Geoffrey **The American People.** W. W. Norton & co. 1964, p. 245.

50. Ibid. p.30.

51. Ibid.

52.Ibid. p. 32.

53.Ibid. p. 33.

54. Ibid. p. 254.

55.Ibid. p. 255.

56. Mead, Margaret. **And Keep Your Powder Dry.** William Morrow & co., New York 1965. p. 264.

57. Ibid. p.35.

58.Ibid.

59. Ibid. pp. 38-39.

60. Ibid. P. 40.

61.Tawney, R. H. **The Acquistive Society.** New York, 1920, P. 47.

62. Ibid.

63. Gorer, Ibid.p.40.

64.Ibid.pp. 40-42.

65. Mead, Margaret. **And Keep Your Powder Dry.** William Morrow & co., New York 1965. pp 288-290.

66. Gorer, Geoffrey **The American People.** W. W. Norton & Co. 1964, pp. 44-47.

67. Ibid. p. 55.

68.Ibid.

69. Ibid. pp. 55-59.

70. Ibid. pp.62-64.
71. Whyte Willams Jr. **The Organization Man.** Doubleday Anchor books, New York. P. 1965. p. 16.

CHAPTER FIVE:

1. Aurobindo, Sri. **The Human Cycle the Ideal of Human Unity, War and self-determination.** Sri Aurobindo Ashram Pondicherry, l962. The Human cycle pp. 307-308.
2. Alexander Marshack in his book **The Roots of Civilization,** has demonstrated through research on the artifacts and cave drawings of the ice age and ancient man's use of the symbol notation and of language, that the infrarational stage in its highest reaches is at least 500,000 years old. Naturally man as an austropithecine person is many millions of years old. Emotional-vital man also according to Aurobindo is not much different from that of the animal, i.e., the vital mind is a lower part of the mind and is shot through with feelihgs and emotions of a primoridial order. (1971:21 in Bef. Issue of Mother India, Pondicherry India.
3. Aurobindo, Sri. **The Human cycle the Ideal of Human Unity, War and Self-determination.** Sri Aurobindo Ashram Pondicherry, l962. The Human cycle pp. 208-209.
4.Ibid. pp. 212-213.
5. Ibid p. 213.
6.Ibid. pp 213-214.
7. Ibid. pp. 30-31.
8.Ibid. p. 32.
9.Ibid. pp. 33-34.
10. Ibid. p. 35.
11. Ibid.
12. P.36.
13.Ibid. p. 39.
14.Ibid. p. 55.
15.Ibid. p. 56.
16. Ibid. p.307.

17. Ibid.pp.71-73.
18. Ibid. p. 74.
19. Ibid. p.91.
20. Roszak Theodore, **The Making of a Counter Culture**. Anchor Books, New York, 1969. pp. 208-209.
21. Ibid. p. 214.
22. Ibid. p. 216.
23. Ibid. p. 215 see also Michael Polanyi, **Personal Knowledge: Towards a Post-"Critical Philsophy**. Chicago: The University of Chicago Press, 1959.
24. Roszak Theodore, **The Making of a Counter Culture**. Anchor Books, New York, 1969. p. 216.
25. Ibid. p.205.
26. Ibid. p. 215.
27. Larsen, Stephen. **The Shaman's Doorway**. Harper & Row, New York. 1976. p.1.
28. Rozak Ibid. p. 167. The quotations arc from a 1967 TV program called "The Mind Alchemist", presented on the British Broadcasting company. The evolutionary concepts are presented through Leary's Post Magazine, September 14, 1967. p. 45.
29. Larsen, Stephen. **The Shaman's Doorway**. Harper & Row, New York. 1976. pp. 122-123.
30. Kopytoff, Igor, 1964. "Classifications of religious movementws; analytical and synthetic." Proceedings of the 1964 annual spring Meeting of the American Ethnological society. Seattle: University of Washington press.
31. Gerlach, Luther P. & Virginia H. Hine. **People, Power, Change: Movements of Social Tranformation**. Bobbs-merrill co. Inc. Indianapolis and New York, 1970pp. 1-3.
32. Ravenscrofc Trevor. **The Spear of Destiny**. Samuel Weikser, Inc. York Beach Maine, p. 95.
33. Ibid.
34. Ibid. pp. 95-96.
35. Larsen, Stephen. **The Shaman's Doorway**. Harper & Row,

New York. 1976. p.206.

36. Ravenscrofc Trevor. **The Spear of Destiny.** Samuel Weikser, Inc. York Beach Maine, p. 149.

37. Ibid.

38. Ravenscrofc Trevor. **The Spear of Destiny.** Samuel Weiser, Inc. York Beach Maine, pp. 178-179.

39. Ibid.

40 Aurobindo, Sri. **The Human Cycle the Ideal of Human Unity, War and self-determination.** Sri Aurobindo Ashram Pondicherry, l962. The Human cycle p.56.

41. Ravenscrofc Trevor. **The Spear of Destiny.** Samuel Weiser, Inc. York Beach Maine, p. 244.

42.Ibid. p. 252.

43. Aurobindo, Sri. **The Human cycle the Ideal of Human Unity, War and self-determination.** Sri Aurobindo Ashram Pondicherry, l962. The Human cycle pp. 267.

44.Ibid.

45. Ravenscrofc Trevor. **The Spear of Destiny.** Samuel Weikser, Inc. York Beach Maine, p. 64.

46.m Ibid.

47. Kubizek, August; **Young Hitler-Friend of My Youth.** London, 1950. also on p. 3 of the spear of Destiny.

48. Ravenscrofc Trevor. **The Spear of Destiny.** Samuel Weikser, Inc. York Beach Maine, pp.249-250.

49.Ibid. pp.250-251.

50. Ibid. pp.251-252.

51.Ravenscrofc Trevor. **The Spear of Destiny.** Samuel Weikser, Inc. York Beach Maine, p.38.

52. Aurobindo, Sri. **The Human Cycle The Ideal of Human Unity, War and Self-determination.** Sri Aurobindo Ashram Pondicherry, l962. The Human cycle p. 814.

53. Ibid. pp. 103-104.

54. Ibid. p. 114.

55. Ibid. p. 115.

56. Ibid. p. 116.

57. Ibid. pp. 116-117.

58. Aurobindo, Sri. **The Life Divine.** New York India Library Society, 1965. p.372.

59. Aurobindo, Sri. **On Yoga 11, Tome One, Sri Aurobindo International University Centre Collection Vol. V1.,** 1958. p. 273.

60. Hallowell, Irving. **Behavioral Evolution and the Emergence of the self.** Theory in Anthroplogy. Robert Manners and David Kaplan, editors aldine Publishing Co. Chicago, 1969. p. 343.

61. Ibid.

62. Green, Elmer & Alyce. **Beyond Feedback.** Delta books; New York, 1977. pp. 303-304.

63. **Wild Science: Mind and body.** Encyclopedia Britannica film: 1977.

64. Lawrence, Jopdi. Alpha Brain waves, New York: Avon Book, 1972, pp.32-33.

CHAPTER SIX:

1. Aurobindo. **The Future Evolution Of Man.** East Midland Printing co., Ltd. Bury St. Edmunds, England, 1960. p. 51.

2. Rishabhchad. **In the Mother's Light.** Pondicherry; Sri Aurobindo Press, 1967. p. 386.

3. Ardrey, Robert. **African Genesis.** New York: Dell Plublishing co., Inc. 1967.

4. Lorenz, konrad. **On Agression.** New York: Bantam books, 1971.

5. Bleibrreu, John N. **The Parable of the Beast.** New York: collier books 1969. p. 274.

6. Eliselyh, Loren. **Free Will, Evolution of Man,** Louise B. Young, editor, NewYork: oxford University Press. p. 606.

7., Snow, C.P. **The Two Cultures and the Scientific Revolution.** 'Cambridge University Press, 1959.

8. Satprem, **Mother's Agenda** 1971 Institute for Evolutionary Research, New York, 1982, p. 330.

9. Young, Loluise B. **Evolution of Man.** Louise B. Young, editor, New York: Oxford University Press 1963.p. 560.

10. Eliselyh, Loren. **Free Will, Evolution of Man,** Louise B. Young,

editor, New York: oxford University Press. p. 606.

11. Ibid.

12. Tart, Charles T. **Altered States of Consciousness.** New york: John Wiley & sons, 1969.

13. Tart, Charles. **Scientific foundations for the Study of altered States of consciousness.** Journal of Transpersonal Psychology. no. 2, 1971. p. 115.

14. Ibid.

15. Hallowell, Irving. **Behavioral Evolution and the Emergence of the Self,** in Theory in Anthropology. Robert Manners and David Kaplan, editors. Aldine Publishing co; Chicago, 1969. p. 343.

16. Ibid.

17. Tart, Charles. **Scientific Foundations For the Study of Altered States of Consciousness.** Journal of Transpersonal Psychology. No. 2, 1971. p. 115.

18. Ibid.

19. Ibid.

20. Ibid.

21. Bentov, Itzhak. **Micromotion of the Body as a Factor in the Development of the Nervous system.** In Kundalini, Evolution and enlightenment. Ed. John White. Doubleday: Garden city, New York, 1979. p. 337.

22. Aurobindo. **The Future Evolution of Man.** East Midland Printing co., Ltd. Bury St. Edmunds, England, 1960. p. 51.

23. Ibid.

24. Katz, R. **Education for Transcendence:** Lessons from the Kung zhu twasi. In Jounal of Transpersonal Psychology, November 2, 1973.

25. Sannella, Lee. **Kundalini-Psychosis or transcendence?** Published by Lee Sannella, 3101 Washington St. San Francisco, 1976.

26. The comments above were made by the late Dr. Chaudhuri-Ronald Campbell's mentor for 20 years in the course of conversations and counseling.

27. The Muladhar is the lowest chakra, situated in the area of the sexual organs at the base of the spine.

28. Aurobindo, Sri. **Letters on Yoga.** Part i, vol 22. Sri Aurobindo birth centenary Library, Sri Aurobindo Ashram: Pondicherry, India: 1972. p. 74.

29. Motoyama, Hirosh. **The Motoyama device: Measuring Psychic Energy In Future Science,** eds. John White and Stanly Krippner. Doubleday: Garden City, New York. 1977. p. 217.

30. White, John **Exploration in Kundalini research.** In **Kundalini, Evolution and Enlightenment.** Ed. John White. Doubleday: Garden city city, New York, 1979. p.216.

31. White, John. **Some Possibilies For further Kundalini Research.** In Kundalini, Evolution and enlightenment. ed. John white. Dougleday: Garden city, New york, 1979. p. 352.

32. Fertguson, Mailyn. **Kindling and Kundalini Effects.** In Kundalini Evolution and Enlightenment. Ed. John White. Doubleday: Garden city, New York 1979. pp. 298-300.

33. Ibid.

34. Peck, Robert. **A Research Note on Kundalini energy.** In Kundalini evolution and enlightenment. Ed. John White. Doubleday: Garden City, New York 1979. pp. 301-302.

35. Fertguson, Mailyn. **Kindling and Kundalini Effects.** In kundalini Evolution and Enlightenment. Ed. John White. Doubleday: Garden city, New York 1979. p. 301.

36. Rele, Vasant. **The Mysterious Kundalini.** D.B. Taraporevals Sons & Co. for Bombay, 1967. pp.xxxi-xxvii.

37. Green, Elmer and Alyce. **Beyond Biofeedback.** Delta books: New York, 1977,pp. 198-199.

38. Ibid. p. 263.

39. Goyeche, J .Hohn. **Kundalini As Prevention And Therapy For Drug Abuse.** In Kundalini Evolution and Enlightenment. Ed. John White. Doubleday: Garden City, New York 1979. pp. 303-305.

40. Inyushin, Viktor, **Bioplasma: the fifth State of matter.** In fu-

ture Science Ed. John white and Stanley, Doubleday: Garden city, New York, 1977. pp. 82-83.

41.Ibid. pp. 91-92.

42. Inyushin, Viktor, **Bioplasma: the Fifth State of Matter.** In future Science Ed. John White and Stanley, Doubleday: Garden city, New York. pp, 116-119.

43. Samatanand, Swami. **The Mystery of Kundalini,** A talk given by the Swami at a New York intensive. In Meditate, a newspaper style publication issued by the Oakland, California Siddha Yoga ashram, 1978.

44. White, John. **Kundalini, Evolution and Enlightenment,** paper delivered at the 1978. American Anthroplogical Association meeting in Los Angeles, california. pp. 5-6.

45. Ibid. p.9.

46. Gandhi, Kishnor. **Social Philosophy of Sri Aurobindo and the New Age.** Sri Aurobindo Ashram Press, Pondicherry, 1965, Pp. 261-262.

47. Eiseley, Loren. The Immense Journey. New York: Vomtage books. 1957. p.92.

48.Jung, C.G. **The Undiscovered Self.** New York Mentor book. 1958. p. 123.

49. Aurobindo, Sri. **The Hour of God.** Pondicherry, Sri Aurobindo Ashram Press. 1964. p. 10.

50. Aurobindo, Sri. **The Life Divine.** New York India Library Society, 1965. p.859..

51. Ibid. p. 875.

52. Ibid. p.860.

53.Chaudhuri, Haridas, **Sri Aurobindo: the Prophet of Life Divine.** Sri Aurobindo Ahram, Pondicherry. 1960. pp. 179-180.

54. Huxley, Julian. **Evolution in Action.** New York: Mentor books, 1975. p. 192.

55. Aurobindo, Sri. **The Life Divine.** New York India Library Society, 1965. p.863.

56.Ibid.

57. Ibid. p. 886.

58. Huxley, Julian. **Evolution in Action.** New York: Mentor book, 1957. P.192.
59. Aurobindo, Sri. **The Life Divine.** New York India Library Society, 1965. p.863.
60. Ibid.
61. Ibid. p. 886.
62. Alfassa, Mirra (Mother) in Gandhi, Kishnor. **Social Philosophy of Sri Aurobindo and the New Age.** Sri Aurobindo Ashram Press, Pondicherry, 1965, Pp. 261-262. Also in Bulletin of Sri Aurobindo International Centre ofEeducation, (Feb, 1963).

CHAPTER SEVEN:

1. Gorer, Geoffrey. **The American People.** W.W. Norton & Company, Inc. New York. 1964. pp. 34-35.
2. Fromm, Erich. **The Anatomy of Human Destructiveness.** holt, Rinehart & Winston. New York, 1972. p.350.
3. Ibid. p. 351.
4. Ibid.
5. Malinowski , Bronislaw. **Freedom and Civilization.** Roy Publishers, New York, 1944. p. 336.
6. Ibid. p. 105.
7. Ibid.
8. Ibid. p. 10.
9. Hutschnecker, Arnold. **The Drive for Power.** M. Evans & Company, Incl, New York, p. 67. in Lasswell, Harold. **Psychopathology and Politics.** New York: Viking Pressl 1960. pp.67,71.
10. Ibidl pp. 172-173.
11. Hutschnecker, Arnold a. M. d. **The Drive for Power.** M. Evans & Company, New York.p.61.
12. Henry, Julies, **Culture against Man.** Random house, New York, 1963. p.8.
13. Hutschnecker, Arnold a. M. d. **The Drive for Power.** M. Evans & Company, New York .p.60.

14. Aurobindo, Sri. **The Life Divine.** New York India Library Society, 1965. pp. 616-617.

15. Aurobindo, Sri. **The Human Cycle The Ideal Of Human Unity, War And Self-Determination.** Sri Aurobindo Ashram Pondicherry, 1962. The Human cycle p. 381.

16. Aurobindo, Sri. **On Yoga 11 tome Two. International University Centre collection Vol. V11.,** 1958. Sri Aurobindo Ashram Press, Pondicherry, India 1958, Pp. 395-396.

17. Aurobindo, Sri. **On Yoga 11, Tome One, Sri Aurobindo International University Centre collection Vol. V1.,** 1958. p.3.

18. Gandhi, Kishnor. **Social Philosophy of Sri Aurobindo and the New Age.** Sri Aurobindo Ashram Press, Pondicherry, 1965, P 98.

19. Wallace, Anthony, F.C. **Culture and Personality.** New York: Random House, 1964. p. 98.

20. Aurobindo, Sri. **The Human cycle the Ideal of Human Unity, War and self-determination.** Sri Aurobindo Ashram Pondicherry, 1962. The Human cycle p. 248.

21. Ibid. p. 254.

22. Ibid. p. 252.

23. Aurobindo, Sri. **The Life Divine.** New York India Library Society, 1965. pp.929

CHAPTER EIGHT:

1. Freud, Sigmund. **Totem and Taboo.** Modern Library: New York, 1957, P. 857.

2. Thompson, Laura. **Toward a science of Mankind.** mcGraw Hill: New York, 1961, p. 198.

3 Ehrenwald, Jan, **The ESP Experience,** Basic books, New York 1978, pp. 3-21.

4. Ibid. p.21

5. Ibid p. 26.

6. Ibid.

7.Krippner, Stanley, (forword) in e. Bruce Taub-Bylnum, **The Family Unconscious,** Quest Books, Wheaton, Ill, 1984. P. ix.

8. Ibid. p. xiii.

9

10. Ibid. p. ix.

11. Ehrenwald, Jan, **The ESP Experience**, Basic Books, New York 1978, p. 12. Ibid. p. 16.

13, Ibid.

14. Ibid. pp. 16-17.

15,Ibid. 17.

16. Ibid.

17.Taub-Bylnum e. Bruce,, **The Family Unconscious**, Quest Books, Wheaton, Ill, 1984. P.4.

18.Ibid. p. 6.

19. Ibid. p.7

20. Ibid. p.10.

21. Ibid. p.11.

22. Ibid. p.12

23. Ibid.

24. Ibid. p. 14.

25. Else Frenkel-Brunswik, in **Childhood in Contemporaray Culture**, edited by Margaret Mead & Marth Wolfenstein, University of Chicago Press, 1955, pp. 372-385.

26. Fromm, Erich. **The Anatomy of Human Destructiveness.** Holt, Rinehart & Winston. New York, 1973. p, 299. Original Source Smith, B.F. Heninrich Himmlr: **A Nazi In The Making**, 1900-1926, Stanford: Hoover Inst., Stanford Univ.

27. Satprem, **Mother's Agenda 11 1961** Institute for Evolutionary Research, New York, 1961, pp. 266-267.

28.Ibid.

29. Ibid. p. 300.

30. Ibid. p. 304.

31. Ibid. p. 318.

32. Else frenkel-Brunswik. **Differential Patterns of Social Outlook and Personality in Family and Children** p.383. in **Childhood in Contemporaray Culture**, edited by Margaret Mead & Marth Wolfenstein, University of Chicago Press, 1955.

33.Ibid. pp.383-384.
34. Ibid., P.384.
35. Ibid. pp. 385-394.
36. Ibid. pp.386-387.
37.Ibid.
38.Ibid. p. 387.
39. Ibid.
40. Adorno,T. W. Frenkel-brunswik, E. D. J. and Sanford, R. N. 1950, **The Authoritarian Personality.** New York: Harper & Bros.
41.frenkel-Brunswik, E. 1949a, **A Study of Prejudice in Children, Human Relations,** 1, No.3, p. 295-306. & Frenkel-Brunswik, e. and Havel, JH. 1953. **Prejudice In The Interviews Of Children: Attitudes Toward Minority Groups,** journal of Genetic Psycnology, LXXX11, No. 1, 91-136.
42. Else Frenkel-Brunswil. **Differential Patterns of Social Outlook and Personality iI Family And Children** p. 388. in **Childhood in Contemporay Cultures** . edited by Margaret Mead & Matha Wolfenstein, Univ. of chicago Press, 1955.
43.Ibid. p. 389.
44. Ibid.
45. Ibid. pp. 390-391.
46. Ibid. pp. 3290-391.
47. Ibid. p.391.
48.Ibid.
49. Ibid.p. 392.
50. Ibid. pp. 392-393.
51.Ibid. pp. 396-399.
52. Ibid. p. 397.
53.Ibid. p. 400.

CHAPTER NINE:

1. Aurobindo, Sri. **The Human cycle The Ideal of Human Unity, War and self-Determination.** Sri Aurobindo Ashram Pondicherry, l962. The Human cycle p. 247-248.

2. Eiseley, Loren. **The Immense Journey,** Vintage books: New York, 1957. p.1

3. Ibid. p.92.

4. Honigmann, John J. **Handbook of Social and Cultural Anthropology.**Cchicago: Ran Mcnally & co., 19l73. P. 8.

5.Ibid. p.13.

6. Tylor, Edward. **Primitive culture.** 2 vol., Ist and 5th eds. London 1971-1913. p. 1.

7.Wallace, Anthony. **Culture and Personality.** New York: Random House, 1964. p. 128.

8. Tylor. 1900. p. 20, 23-25.

9.Bidney, David. **Theoretical Anthropology.** New York: Schocken Books. 1967. P. 185.

10.Ibid.

11.Ibid. p.202.

12. Ibid. pp. 192-193.

13. Bidney, David. **Theoretical Anthropology.** New York: Schocken Books. 1967. P. 192.

14,Ibid. p.212.

15. Mogan, Lewis H. **Ancient Society Or Researches In The Lines of Human Progress From Savagery Through Barbarism To Civilization.** Chicago, Charles H. Kerr & Co., 1908 pp. 18 & 562.

16. Lowie, Robert. **The History of Ethnological theory.** New York: Holt, Rinehart & Winston, 1937.p. 54.

17 .Honigmann: 1973: p. 158.

18. Bidney, David. **Theoretical Anthropology.** New York: Schocken Books. 1967. P. 219.

19. Steward,Julian: 1955. p.316.

20. The writer wishes to thank Leslie White for the personal meeting we had and for the stimulating exchange of views.

21.White, Leslie A. **The Science of Culture: a Study of Man's Civilization.** New York; "fal, straus & co., 1949. P. 25.

22. Timadheff, Nocholas s. **Sociological Theory: Its Nature and Growth.** New York Random House. 1968. p. 284.

23.White. 1949. p.8.

24. Bidney, David. **Theoretical Anthropology.** New York: Schocken Books. 1967. P. 270.

25. White, Leslie A. **The Science of Culture: A Study of Man's Civilization.** New York; "fal, straus & co., 1949. P. 11.

26. Ibid. p. 281.

27. White, Leslie A. **The Evoution of Culture.** New York; Mcgraw Hill, 1959. p.157.

28. Timadheff, Nocholas s. **Sociological Theory: Its Nature and Growth.** New York Random House. 1968. p. 285.

29. Honigmann, John J. **Handbook of Social and Cultural Anthropology.** Chicago: Ran Mcnally & co., 19l73. P. 158.

30. Timadheff, Nocholas s. **Sociological Theory: Its Nature and Growth.** New York Random House. 1968. p. 286.

31. Kaplan, David & Robert Manner, editors. **Theory in Anthropology.** Aldine Publishing co., 1969. p.245.

32. Ibid.

33. Bidney: 1967. p. 298.

34. Ibid. p.293.

35. Ibid.p. 112.

36. Fried, Morton H. **Readings In Anthropology,** vol 11 New York: Thomas & Crowell Co. 1979. p. 59.

37. White in Fried: vol 11. 1970, p.58.

38. Ibid.

39. Ibid. p. 59

40. Ibid. p. 61.

41. Kaplan in fried: Vol11: 1970. p.68.

42. Kaplan, David & Robert Manner, editors. **Theory in Anthropology.** Aldine Publishing co., 1969. p.242.

43. Voget in Honigmann, John J. **Handbook of Social and Cultural Anthropology.** Chicago: Ran Mcnally & co., 19l73. P. 61.

44. Alland & McCay in Honigmann, John J. **Handbook of Social and Cultural Anthropology.** Chicago: Ran Mcnally & co., l973. P. 159.

45. Steward in Kaplan, David & Robert Manner, editors. **Theory In Anthropology.** Aldine Publishing co., 1969. p.2423.

46. Carneiro in Honigmann, John J. **Handbook of Social and Cultural Anthropology.** chicago: Ran Mcnally & co., 1973. P. 101.
47. Ibid. pp. 112 & 161.
48. Alland & McCay in Honigmann, John J. **Handbook of Social and Cultural Anthropology.** chicago: Ran Mcnally & co., 19173. P. 161.
49. Vegeot in Honigmann, John J. **Handbook of Social and Cultural Anthropology.** chicago: Ran Mcnally & co., 19173. P. 62.
50. Thompson, Laura. **Toward A Science of Mankind.** New aYork: Mcgraw-Hill, 1961. pp. 171-173.
51. Bidney, David. **Theoretical Anthropology.** New York: Schocken Books. 1967. P. 220.
52. This theory was developed by Sri Aurobindo Ghose.
53. Aurobindo. **The Future Evolution of Man.** East Midland Printing co., Ltd. Bury St. Edmunds, England, 1960. pp. 346-347.
54. Aurobindo, Sri. **On Yoga 11, Tome One, Sri Aurobindo International University Centre** collection Vol. V1., 1958. pp. 3-4.
55. Gandhi, Kishnor. **Social Philosophy of Sri Aurobindo and the New Age.** Sri Aurobindo Ashram Press, Pondicherry, 1965, P 70.
56. Aurobindo, Sri. **The Human cycle the Ideal of Human Unity, War and self-determination.** Sri Aurobindo Ashram Pondicherry, 1962. The Human cycle p. 248.
57. Aurobindo, Sri. **The Life Divine.** New York India Library society, 1961. pp. 616-617.
58. Aurobindo, Sri. **The Life Divine.** New York India Library society, 1961. pp. 228-229.
59. Aurobindo, Sri. **The Human cycle the Ideal of Human Unity, War and self-determination.** Sri Aurobindo Ashram Pondicherry, 1962. The Human Cycle p. 381.
60. Ibid. pp. 611-619.
Ibid. 365.

62. Aurobindo, Sri. **On Yoga 11 Tome Two.** International University Centre collection Vol. V11., 1958. Sri Aurobindo Ashram Press, Pondicherry, India 1958, Pp. 395-396.

63. Aurobindo, Sri. **On Yoga 11, Tome One,** Sri Aurobindo International University Centre collection Vol. V1., 1958. p. 3.

64. Gandhi, Kishnor. **Social Philosophy of Sri Aurobindo and the New Age.** Sri Aurobindo Ashram Press, Pondicherry, 1965, P 98.

65. Wallace, Anthony, **Culture & Personality.** Random House: New York, 1964.

66. Gandhi, Kishnor. **Social Philosophy of Sri Aurobindo and the New Age.** Sri Aurobindo Ashram Press, Pondicherry, 1965, P 98.

67. Aurobindo, Sri. **The Human Cycle The Ideal of Human Unity, War And Self-Determination.** Sri Aurobindo Ashram Pondicherry, 1962. The Human Cycle.

68. Ibid. pp. 229-230.

69. Ibid. pp. 253-354.

70. Ibid. p. 233.

71. Aurobindo, Sri. **The Life Divine.** New York India Library society, 1961. p. 929,

72. Aurobindo, Sri. **The Human Cycle The Ideal of Human Unity, War and Self-determination.** Sri Aurobindo Ashram Pondicherry, 1962. The Human Cycle. pp.233-234.

73. Ibid.

74. Ibid. pp. 233-234.

75. Ibid.p.98.

76. Aurovindo, **The Hour of God,** XVilll 1971. also in **Mother's Agenda 1971,** Pl 329.

77. Satprem, **Mother's Agenda 1971** Institute for Evolutionary Research, New York, 1961, p. 329.

78. Henry, Jules. **Culture Against Man.** Vintgage books, 1963. p. 477.

CHAPTER TEN:

1. Schusky, Ernest L. **Manual for Kinship**. Holt, Rinehart & Winston. New York, 1965. p. 1.

2. Ibid. p.2.

3. Sunley, Robert, **Early Nineteenth-Century American Literature on Child Rearing**, in **Childhood in Contemporary Cultures**. Edited by Margaret Mead & Martha Whofenstein. 1955. p. 151.

4. Ibid. also in fowler, Orson .s.. 1847 **Self Culture And Perfection of Character**, Including **Management Of Youth**. New York: Fowler & Wells.

5. Sunley in Mead ibid. also in allen, rev. Ralph w. 1848. **A Mother's Influence, Mother's Assistant**. X111, No. 5, 97-100.

6. Sunley in Mead Ibid. Original source, **Child, Lydia. 1831. the Mother's Book**, 2nd ed. Boston: Carter & Hendee.

7. Ibid, Sunley in Mead Original source Sigourney, Lydia H. 1838. **Letters to Mothers**. Harford: Hudson & Skinner.

8. Ibid. Sunley in Mead P. 152. Original source Hall, Mrs. Elizaabeth. 1849. **A Mother's Influence**. Mothers Assistant. XIV, No. 2 25-29.

9. Ibid. Sunley in **Childhood in Contemporary Cultures**. Edited by Margaret Mead & Martha Whofenstein. 1955. p. 152. Original source is Calhoun, Arthur. 1917-9. **A Social History of the American Family from colonial Times to the Present**. 3 Vols. Cleveland: Clark.

10. Ibid. Sunley in Mead. Original source is Beste, Jh. Richard. 1855. The Wabash. 2 Vol. London: Hurst & Blackett.

11. Ibid. Sunley in Mead Original source Kuhn , Anne L. 1947. **Mother's Role** in Childhood Education: New England Concepts. 1830-60. (Yale Studies in Religious Education, vol. XiX.) New haven: Yale University Press.

12. Ibid. Sunley in Mead. Original source is cobb, Lyman. 1847. **Tendencies of Corporal Punishment as a Means of Moral**

Discipline in Families and Schools. New York: Newman & Co.

13. Towr, Cynthia Crosson. **Understanding Child abuse & Neglect.** allyn & Bacon, Boston. 1886. P.3. also in Bremmer, R., ed. **Children and Youth in America: A Documentary History.** vol. Cambridge, M..A. Harvard University Press, 1970.

14. Ibid. sunley in Mead. p. 153.

15. Ibid. Sunley in Mead. pp. 153-154. Origianal source is Combe, Andre. 1840. **Treatise On Physiological And Moral Management Of Infancy.** Philadelphia: Carey & Hart. 'Dewees, William P. 1826. **Treatise On The Physical And Medical Treatment Of Children.** Philadelphia: carey & Lea, PP. 187-188. Donne, Alfred. 1859. **Mothers And Infants, Nurses And Nurseing.** boston: Phillips, Sampson & co. p. 154.

16. Ibid. Sunley in Mead p. 154. Original source is graves, Mrs. A. J. 1844. **Girlhood And Womanhood.** boston: Carter & Mussey.

17. Ibid. pp. 154-155. Original source is drwight, theordore. 1834. **The Father's Book,** Springfield, Mass: G. & c. Merrian.

18. Ibid. P. 155. Original source is ireland, W.M. 1820. **Advice To Mothers On The Management Of Infants and Young Children.** New York: B. Young.

19. Ibid. Original source is Searl Rev. Thomas. 1834. **Companion to Seasons of Maternal Solicitude.** New York: Moore & Payne, Clinton Hall. p. 212. American ed., 1862. London: Balliere. P. 46.

20. Ibid. Chavasse, 1832. p.124.

21. Ibid. Sunley in Mead. Original source is Alcott, William a. 1836. **The Young Mother.** Boston: Light & strarns. P. 49. & dewees, William p.1826. **Treatise On The Physical And Medical Treatment Of Children.** Philadelphia: Carev & Lea. P. 65.

22. Ibid. Dewees 1826. p.65 & barwell, Mres. 1844. Infant treat-

ment, Ist American ed. with supplement for the U.S .Boston: James Mowatt. P. 40.

23. Ibid. Sunley in Mead p. 156. Original source is Bishop Isabella L. 1856. **English Woman In America**. London: John Murry. p. 122.

24. Ibid. Origianal source is Wilson, Eliabeth A. 1940. **Hygenic Care and Management of The Child In American Family Prior To 1860**. unpublished Master's Thesis, duke university, durham, Nc. pp. 105-6.

25. Ibid. Sunley in Mead. Pl 156. Gallaudet, t. H. 1838. **On The Evidence of Early Piety**. Mother's Magazine, V!, No 11, 241-45., also Duncan, Mary, 1852. **America As I Found it**. New York: Robert Carter & Bros. p. 78. also Thomson, Willian. 1842. **A Tradesman's Travels In The United States**. Edinburgh: Olvr & Boyd. P. 31.

26. Ibid. Sunley in Mead. Original source is Warren, Eliza. !865. **How I Managed My Children** . . . Boston: Loring. **What Manner Of Child Shall** This Be?1843. Mother's Magazine, X! No. 3, P. 52-54.

27. Sunley in Mead in **Childhood in Contemporary Cultures**. Edited by Margaret Mead & Martha Whofenstein. Original source is Dewees, William P. 1826. **Treatise on the Physical and Medical Treatment of Children**. Philadelphia: Carey & Lea. p. 115.

28. Sunley in Mead, Original source is Abbott, Hohn LS.C. 1842. **Paternal Neglect**. Parents Magazine, 111, No. 3148. and Holebrook, Josiah. 1838. **Domestic Education**. Mother's Magazine. V!, No. 8, 188-92.

29. Tower, Cynthia Crosson. **Understanding child Abuse and Neglect**. Allyn & Bacon, Boston 1986 p.5. Also in Conte, J., and Shore, D. **Social Work and Sexual Abuse**. Journal of Social Work and Human Sexuality. Vol. 1, No. 1-2 New York: Haworth Press, 1982.

30. Sunley in Mead. Original source is Ray, Isaac. 1863. **Mental Hygiene**. Boston: Tichnor & Fields. p. 280.

31. Sunley in Mead, original source is Hough, Lewis S. 1849. **The Science Of Man.** p. 160.

32. sunley in Mead. The original source is Beecher, C.E. 1846. **The Evils Suffered By American Women And Children,** New York: Harper & Bros..

33. Sunley in Mead. P. 158. original source **Little Ellen,** 1840.

34. Sunley in Mead, original source is Hyde, Rev. Alvan. 1830. **Essay on the State of Infants.** New York: C. Davis.

35. Sunley in Mead. Original source is dwight, Theodore, 1834. **The Father's Book.** Springfield, Mass. G & C. Merriam. p.31.

36. Sunley in Mead. Original source is Humphrey, Herman. 1840. **Restraining And Governing Children's Appetites And Passions.** Mother's Magazine, V111, No. 6, 124-30. P. 127.

37. Sunley in Mead Ibid. p. 159. Original source is Mother;s Assistant. 1841-63, Mother's Magazine, 1832-76; Parents Magazine, 18404-50.

38. Sunley in Mead Ibid. P. 160. Original source is, **To Mother's Of Young Families,** 1834.

39. Mean Margaret. **Children And Ritual In Bali** in **Childhood In Contemporary Cultures.** Edited by Margaret Mead & Martha Whofenstein. 1955. p. 44.

40. Sunley in Mead. Original source is Warren, Elia. 1965. **How I managed My Children.** Boston: Loring. **What Manner of Child Shall this Be?** 1843. Mother's Magazine. X!, No. 3, 52-54. P. 39.41.

41. Sunley in Mead. Original source is Gallaudet, T.H. 1838. **On the Evidence Of Early Piety.** Mother's Magazine, V!. No. 11, pp241-145.

42. Sunley in Mead, p.161. Original source is **Hints for Maternal education.** 1834. Mother's Magazine, !1, No. 8. pp. 113-115.

43. Sunley in Mead. Original source is Dewees, Willian p. 1826. **Treatise On The Physical And Medical Treatment Of Children.** Philadelphia: Carey & Lea & edgeworth, Maria and Richar. 1815. **On Practical Education.** 2nd American ed.

Boston: Wait. & Humphrey, Herman. 1940. **Restraining And Governing Children's Appetites And Passions,** Mother's Magazine, V111, No. 6-124-130. & Wilson, Elizabeth a. 1940. **Hygienic Care And Management Of The Child In The American Family Prior To 1860.** Unpublished Master's thesis Duke University, Durhamm, NC. Pp. 71 & 132. & Kuhn, Ann L. 1947. **Mother's Role in Childhood Education:** New England concepts, 1930-60. Yale Studies In Religious Education Vol X1X. New Haven: Yale University Press, Pp. 54 & 162.

44. Obid, Sunley in Mead. Original source is Hoare, Mrs. Loussa. 1829. **Hints For The Improvement Of Early Education And Nusery Discipline.** Reprinted from the 5th London ed. salem: Buffum. p.86.

45 Ibid. Sunley in Mead. Original sources are L. Taylor, Catherine L. 1849. **Education,** Mother's Assistant, XV, No 4, 73-80. P.24. & Briggs, Caroline A 1849. **Intellect Of Children.** Mother's assistant, X!V, No. 5,97–101. p.97.

46.Ibid. Sunley in Mead P.162. original source is Abbott, J .Hacob, 1844. **The Importance Of Sympathy Between The Mother And Child.** Mothers magazine, X11, No. 4-111-19 p.119.

47. The information on fun morality is taken from Wolfenstein, Masrtha;s article Journal of social Issues, V11, No. 4 (1951) 15-25 and her article **Fun Morality: An Analysis Of Recent American Child-Training Literature** Pp. 1688-179. in **Childhood In Contemporary Cultures.** Edited by Margaret Mead & Martha Whofenstein. 1964.

48.Children's bureau, department of Labor. **Infant Care.** 1914-51. Washinton, D.C; Government Printing Office.

49. Infant Care (1914), p. 58.

50. Ibid. P. 62.

51. Ibid.

52. Ibid

53 Ibid

54. Ibid P.61.

55. Ibid

56. Ibid. (1942), p.60.

57 Ibid .

58. Ibid Pp. 59-60.

59. Ibid Pp. 60-61.

60. Wolfenstein, Martha, **Fun Morality: An Analysis Of Recent American Child-Training Literature.** in **Childhood in Contemporary Cultures.** Edited by Margaret Mead & Martha Whofenstein. 1964. pp. 170-171.

61. Wolfenstein in Mead p. 172.

62. Ibid. p. 174.

63. Riesman, David. 1950. **The Lonely Crowd.** New Haven: Yale University Press.

64. Ibid. p. 175.

65. Children's Bureau, Department of Labor, **Infant Care** 1951. p.1.

66. Ibid. p. 64.

67. Ibid. p. 87.

68. Ibid. p. 56.

69. Ibid. p. 55.

70. Wolfenstein in Mead. P. 177.

71. H.f. Harlow & M. K. Harlow, **A Study of Animal Affections,** The Journal of the American Museum of Natural History. Vol. 70. No. 11, 1961.

72. Erikson, Erik H. Insight and Responsibility. W.W. norton & co. Inc., New York, 1964. Pp. 228-229.

73. Fromm, Erich. **The Anatomy of Human Destructiveness.** Holt, Rinehart & Winston, New York; 1973. Pp. 35l8-365.

74. Ibid. p. 359.

75. Ibid. , P. 360.

76. Ibid., Pp. 360-361.

77. Ibid., P. 362.

78. Ibid., Pp. 363-364.

79. Ibid., P. 364.

CHAPTER ELEVEN:

1. Ogburn, W. f. 1953. **The Changing Functions Of The family In Marriage And The Family**, ed. R.F. Winch and R. Mcginnis, New York: Henry Holt & co.

2. Henry, Jules. **Culture Against Man**. Vintage books, Random Houe, New York. 1963, p. 128.

3. Ibid. Pp. 127-128.

4. I am not saying that these children are being systematically killed. They have merely disappeared.

5. Tower, cynthia Crosson. **Understanding Child Abuse And Neglect**. allyn & Bacon Boston, 1989. p.1.

6. Ibid., Pp.1&2. also in Friedman. A.B. **the Viking book of folk Ballads of the English speaking world**. New York: Viking. 1956.

7. Ibid., Tower p.1.

8. Ibid., p.5.

9. Rush, f. **The Best Kept Secret: Sexual Abuse Of Children**. New York: McGraw-hill, 1980. p. 37.

10. Conte, J. and shore. D. Social Work and Sexual Abuse. Journal of social Work and Human Sexuality. Vol. 1, No. 1-2. New york; Haworth Press, 1982. p.22.

11. May 7th, 1995. Channel 9 fox) news, Fresno, California.

12. Erikson, Erik. H. **Childhood And Society**. W.W. Norton 7 co, inc., New York 1963. P. 294.

13. Ibid. p. 291.

14. Ibid. Pp.195-196.

15. Erikson, Erik. H. **Childhood And Society**. W.W. Norton 7 co, inc., New York 1963. P. 288.

16. Ibid.

17. ibid. p. 2911

18. Ibid. p. 290.

19. ibid. Pp. 290-1911

20. Ibid. P. 296.

CHAPTER TWELVE:

1. Campbell relates an instance of doing ethnographic research in 1967 in Indian Mexico and speaking to a 26 year old women, mother of 11 children, who considered herself quite old, even though she was attractive.

2. Adams, J. **Twenty Years At Hull-house.** New York: Signet. 1910. P. 148.

3. Adams, J. **Twenty Years At Hull-house.** New York: Signet. 1910. P. 148.

4. The author remembers vividly a conversation in his youth with an old man who had escaped from father Flanigan's boy's town.

5. Hechinger Grace & fred M. **Teen-Age Tyranny.** Fawcett Publications, Greenwich, conn. 1963. p. 13.

6. Erikson, Erik H. **Insight and Responsibility.** W. W. Norton & company. Inc. New York. 1964. p.90.

7.Gorer Geoffrey. **The American People.** p. 122.

8. Gorer Geoffrey. **The American People: A Study in National Character.** W..w.Norton & co. Inc. New York 1964. p. 122.

9. Erikson, Erik H. **Insight and Responsibility.** W. W. Norton & company. Inc. New York. 1964. pp. 90-91.

10. Ibid. p. 93.

11.Ibid. P. 96.

12.Personal research data, unpublished by the author.

13. Erikson, Erik H. **Insight and Responsibility.** W. W. Norton & company. Inc. New York. 1964. p. 96.

14 .Ibid.Pp. 102-103.

15. Ibid. p. 102.

16. Ibid. p. 103.

17. .Ibid. Pp. 94-96.

18. Ibid. P. 16.

19. Henry, Jules. **Culture Against Man.** Vintage books, Random Houe, New York. 1963, p.147-148.

20. Gorer Geoffrey. **The American People: A Study In National**

0109-CAMP

Character. W..w.Norton & co. Inc. New York 1964. p. 106.

21. Ibid. p. 107.

22. Henry, Jules. **Culture Against Man**. Vintage books, Random Houe, New York. 1963, p.148.

23.Gorer Geoffrey. **The American People: a study in National Character**. W..w.Norton & co. Inc. New York 1964. p. 107.

24. Mead, Margaret. **And Keep Your Powder Dry**. William Morrow & co., New York 1965. pp 106-108.

25.dIbid. Pp. 110-111.

26. Ibid. Henry, Jules.,p. 148.

27. Ibid.

28. Gorer Pp. 101-108.

29.Fromm, Erich. **Escape From Freedom** . Avon books, New York 1965. P. 96.

30 Ibid. P. 97.

31. Erikson, erik H. **Childhood and Society**. W.W. Norton & co. Inc. New York: 1963.P. 408.

32.Ibid. P. 409.

33. Ibid.

34.. Henry, Jules. **Culture Against Man**. Vintage books, Random Houe, New York. 1963, p.172..

35. Ibid. P. 379.

36. Mead, Margaret. **And Keep Your Powder Dry**. William Morrow & co., New York 1965. pp 141-142.

37. Ibid. Pp. 142-144.

38. Ibid. Pp. 144-148.

39. ibid. p. 151.

40. Ibid.

CHAPTER 13:

1. Hallowell, Irving. **Behavioral Evolution and The Emergence Of The Self**, Theory In Anthropology. Robert Manners and David Kaplan, editors. aldine Publishing co. chicago, 1969. p. 343.

2. Ibid.
3. Green, elmer & Alyce. Beyond Feedback. Delta Books: New York, 1977. pp. 303-304.
4. Wild Science: Mind And Body. Encyclopedia Britannical Film: 1977.
5. Lawrence, Jodi. Alpha Brain Waves. New York: Avon books, 1972. pp. 32-33.
6. Ibid.
7. Karlins Marvin & Lewis M. Andrews. Biofeedback. New York: "Warner Books, 1973.p. 39.
8. Ibid.
9. Lawrence, Jodi. Alpha Brain Waves. New York: Avon Books, 1972. p. 210.
10. Achasrya, K. d. Guide to Sri Aurbindo's Philosophy. Pondicherry: Divyha Jivan Ahitya Prakashan, 1968.p. 28.
11. Aurobindo, Sri. On Yoga 11, Tome One, Sri Aurobindo International University Centre Collection Vol. V1., 1958. p.356.
12. Ostrander, sheila and Lynn schroeder. Psychic Discoveries Behind The Iron Curtain. New York: Prentice-Hall, 1968. P. 202.
13.Ibid. p. 392.
14.Jones, Ernest. The Life and Works of Sigmund Freud. Vol 111. New York: Basic books, 1957. p. 392.
15. Chaudhuri, Haridas. The Philosophy of Integralism. Pondicherry: Sri Aurobindo Pathamandir, 1954. P. 274.
16. Ostrander, Sheila and Lynn schroeder. Psychic Discoveries Behind The Iron Curtain. New York: Prentice-Hall, 1968. P. 202.
17.Ibid. p. 203.
18. Ibid. p. 214.
19.Ibid. p.216.
20. Ibid.
21. Ibid., p.215.
22. Ibid.

23.Ibid.

24. Ibid.p.117.

25. Freud, Sigmund. **Totem and Taboo.** Modern Library: New York, 1957. p.857.

26. Tylor, Edward. **Primitive Culture.** 2 vol., !st & 5th eds. London: 1971-1913. p.1.

27.Mead, Margarete. **The Study Of Culture At A Distance.** Study of culture at a distance. Mead & Rhoda Metraux. editors, chicago: University of Chicago Press, 1953. p.22.

28. Bohannon, Paul. **Rethinking Culture: A Project For Current Anthropologtist,** Current Anthroplogy. (oct., 1973) P. 359.

29. Ibid.

30. Henle Paul, **Language, Though and Culture,** Cultural And Social Anthropology. London: The Macmillian Company, 1964, p. 379.

31 Ibid.

32 Whorf, Benjamin Lee. **Language, Thought, and Reality.** Cambride, Massachusetts: The MI.T. Press, 1964. p. 28.

33. Kluchkhohn, C. **Culture & Behavior,** Handbook of Social Psychology. editor. Cambridge: Addison Wesley, vol 11, 1954, pp. 921-938.

34. whorf. p. 28.

35.Mauss, Marce. **Sociologie LEt. Anthropologie,** Paris : Presesses, Univesitaeres de France, 1966. p. 31.

36.Boas, f. **Introduction to Handbook of American Indian Languages,** Lincoln, Nebraska: Univeristy of Nebraska Press, 1968. pp. 63-67.

37.Darnnoi, Keneday D.n. **The Unconscious and Edward Von hartman.** The Haque: Martinus nijhoff, 1967. p. 50.

38. Sapir, Edward. **Culture, Language and Personality.** Berkeley: University of California Press, 1961. p. 20.

39.Strauss, Levi, Claus **Totemism.** Boston: Bacon Press, 1963. P. 59.

40. Thompson, Laura. **The Secret of Culture.** New York: Random House, 1969. p.331.

41. Whorf, Benjamin Lee. **Language, Thought, and Reality.** Cambride, Massachusetts: The MI.T. Press, 1964. p. 58.

42. Ibid. p.59.

43. Ibid. p.58.

44. Ibid. pp. 69-70.

45. Ibid. p. 70.

46. The Mother, **Questions & Answers,** Mother india . Sri Aurobindo Ashram Press, Pondicherry, India. 1974, p. 342.

47.Bagby, Philip H. **Culture And The Causes Of Culture.** American Anthropologist. 91953) p. 543.

48.Mead & Metrauz.p. 22.

49. The Mother, **Questions & Answers,** Mother India . Sri Aurobindo Ashram Press, Pondicherry, India. 1974, p. 343-344.

50Whofr, pp. 61-62.

51. Ibid. p. 62.

52. Ostrander & Schroeder. p. 30.

53. Aniela Jaffe. **From the life and Works of c.G. Jung.** Jung. New York: Harper Colophon Books, 1971.

54. I. Stevenson. **Telepathic Impressions.** Charlottesville University of Virgina Press.

55.Schwarz, Berthold, **A Psychiatrist Looks At Esp.** New York: New American Library, 1965. PP. 75-96.

56. Johnson & Szurek, **The Genesis Of Antisocial Acting And Out In Children and Adults.** 1952. Psychoalysis Quartely. p.21.

57.Sperling, Melitta, **The Neurotic & His mother: A Psychoanalytic Study,** American Orthoopsychiatry Quartely, 1954. pp. 351-364.

58. Ehrenwald, Jan. **The ESP Experience: A Psychiatric Validation.** New York: Basic Books, 1978.

59. Erikson, L. Erik H. **Childhood And Society.** New york: W.W. Norton & co. 1963.

60. Ostrander & Schroeder. p. 31.

61. Ibid. p. 32.

62. Heywood, Rosalind. **ESP: A Personal Memoir.** New York: E.P. Dutton& co. 1964. p. 42.

63. Ibid. Broad, c.d. **Religion, Philsophy and Psychical Research.** Routledge kegan Paul, 1953.

64. Ostrander Schroeder. p. 34.

65. Ibid.

66. Ibid., p. 35.

67. Ibid.

68. Ibid., p.97.

69. Ibid. p. 101.

70. Ibid.

71. Aurobindo, Sri. **On Yoga 11 Tome Two. International University Centre Collection Vol. V11.,** 1958. sri Aurobindo Ashram Press, Pondicherry, India 1958, Pp. 239-240.

72. Ostrander & Schroeder. p. 105.

73. West, d. J. **Psychical research today.** London" Penguin books, 1962. P. 206.

74. Aurobindo, Sri. **The Life Divine.** New York India Library society, 1961. p. 693.

75. ostrander & Schroeder. p.8.

76. Ibid. p. 69.

77. Ibid.

78. Ibid. p.72.

79. Ibid.

80. Aurobindo, Sri. **The Life Divine.** New York India Library society, 1965. p. 70.

81. Ostrander & Schroeder. p. 134.

82. Ibid. p. 135.

83. Anderson, Geoge, **Energy & Consciousness** (Sundays, July 20, 1975 Stanford University convention of the Association For Transpersonal Psychology.

CHAPTER 14:

1. Kuhn, thomas. **The Structure Of Scientific Revolutionl** University of Chicago Press: Chicago, 1962.

2. Sorokin. pp. 8-9.

3 Siui. G. H. **The Tao of Science: An Essay On Western Knowledge and Eastern Wisdom.** MI.T. Press, Massachusetts Institute of Technology, Cambridge, Massachesetts. 1957, pp. 17-18.

4. Ibid. pp. 22-23.

5. Roszak, Theodore, **The Making of a Counter Culture.** Anchor books Doubleday Co., Inc. Garden Ciity, New York, 1969. p.217.

6. Ibid. pp. 217-219.

7. Ibid p. 46

8. Ibid p. 18.

9. Ibid

10. Ibidpp. 18-19.

11.Ibid p.20.

12.Ibid p.27.

13.Ibid p.28.

14. Ibid pp.28-29.

15.Ibidp. 29.

16.Ibid p. 30.

17. Ibid

18.Ibid p.31.

19. Sorokin, Piirim a. **Modern Historical And Social Philosophies.** Dver Publications, Inc. New York 1963. p. 88.

20 .Capra, fritjof. **The Tao of Physics.** Bantan books, 1983. New York. P. xvii.

21. Ibid. p. 125.

22. Zukav, Gary. **The Dancing Wu Li Masters: An Overview Of The New Physics.** Bantam Books, New York, 1980, pp. 47-48.

23. Ibid. p. 32.

24. Ibid.

25. Inyushin, Victor m. **Bioplasma: The Fifth State Of Matter.** In Future Science: Life Energies And The Physics Of Paranorma

Phenomena. edited by White, John & Krippner, Stanley, Anchor books, Garden City , New York 1977. pp. 125-126.

26. Ibid., Day, Langston. **Radiations Known And Unknown.** p.73.

27. Sorokin, Pitirim a . **The Basic Trends of Our Times.** College University Press, New Haven, Conn. 1964. P. 28.

28. Ibid. pp. 28-29.

29. sui. p.75.

30. Siu r. G. H. **The Tao Of Science: An Essay On Western Knowledge And Eastern Wisdom.** MI.T. Press, Massachusetts Institute of Technology, Cambridge, Massachesetts. 1957, p. 74,

31. Ibid. pp; 74-75.

32. Ornstein, Robert, e. **The Mind field,** Pocket Books, New York, 1978. 1978, P. 53.

33. Sorokin, Pitirim a. **A The Basic Trends Of Our Times.** College University Press, New Haven, Conn. 1964. P. 29.

34. Ibid. pp.29-30.

35. wsui. pp. 75-78.

36. Sorokin, Pitirim a . **The Basic Trends Of Our Times.** College University Press, New Haven, Conn. 1964. Pp.30-32.

37. Ibid.

38. Siu r. G. H. **The Tao of Science: An Essay On Western Knowledge And Eastern Wisdom.** MI.T. Press, Massachusetts Institute of Technology, Cambridge, Massachesetts. 1957, p. 78.

39. Sorokin, Pitirim A . **The Basic Trends Of Our Times.** College University Press, New Haven, Conn. 1964. P/ 32.

40. Bertram Lewin, **Dreams And The Uses of Regression.** New York: International Universities Press, 1958.

41. Erikson, Erik H. **Insight and Responsibility.** W.W. Norton & co. Inc. New York. 1964, pp. 198-199.

42. Ibid.

43. Ibid.

44. Ibid.

45. Ibid.

46. Greenhousek Herbvert b. **Premonitions: A Leap Into The Future.** Bernard Geis Associates, 1971. p. 210.

47. Ibid.

48. Ibid.

49. p.187.

50. Ibid. pp. 32-33.

51. Ibid. p. 343.

52. Sui. pp. 76-77.

53. Ibid. pp.76-79.

54. Sui. p. 80.

55. Sorokin, Piirim a. **Modern Historical and Social Philosophies.** Dover Publications, Inc. New York 1963. p. 153.

56. Ibid. P. 152.

57. Sui. P. 81.

58. Sorokin, Piirim a. **Modern Historical and Social Philosophies.** Dver Publications, Inc. New York 1963. p. 153

59. Sui. p. 81.

60. Lewin, Bertram, **Dreams and the Uses of Regression.** New York: International Universities Press, 1958.

61. Erikson, Erik H. **Insight and Responsibility.** W.W. Norton & co. Inc. New York. 1964, pp. 198-199.

CHAPTER 16:

1. **Hebrews** vii. pp. 2-3.

2. Wentz Evans editor. **The Tibetan Book of the Great Liberation.** Oxford. university Press, London, 1968. P. 109.

3, Whorf, Benjamin Lee. **Language, Thought, and Reality.** M.I.T. Press: Cambridge, Mass., 1964. pp. 247-248.

4. Ibid., p. 249.

5. Ibid. pp. 253-254.

6. Whorf, Benjamin Lee. **Language, Thought, and Reality.** M.I.T. Press: Cambridge, Mass., 1964.

GLOSSARY

AUROBINDO GHOSH: Transpersonal psychological researcher and creator of Integral Psychology. Aurobindo Ghosh was President of Aurobindo International University. He was born in Calcutta, on August 15, 1872 and died December 5, 1950. His vast researches into human consciousness and social psychology rest on personal research experiences that explains the evolution of the species on organic, mental and social grounds. Upon his research findings a new and dynamic concept of man is emerging within the scientific community. Many of the concepts of Transintegral psychology rests on his dynamic research insights.

ALFASSA MIRRA: Transpersonal researcher, founder of the International center of Education, and the city of Auroville. She was born in Paris on February 21, 1878, the daughter of an Egyptian mother and Turkish father and died 1973. It is upon her research into body consciousness and her discovery of a "cellular mind" capable of restructuring the nature of the body that the emerging scientific paradigm on the human species will rest. It is upon many of her psychological research findings that Transintegral Psychology rests.

ATAVISTIC ANIMAL UNCONSCIOUSNESS: Human beings have evolved from the lower animal evolution and are still connected to this evolution. Man's unconsciousness and lower vital personality still dwell in this consciousness. When a person rises to a higher level of consciousness and replaces the animal unconsciousness by a transpersonal super-consciousness then a person sees the goal of his existence and also gains a clear-sight and trust in the higher transpersonal powers.

AVERAGE PERSON: The average human being is an emotional-physical person with a subordinate mental nature. A few men have a strong mental natures but even these intellectual giants have generally unregenerated emotional and subconscious natures that occasionally overwhelm them and usurp the mental controls from the mental personality from time to time.

CULTURE: Edward Tyler says that "Culture or civilization, taken in its wide ethnographic sense, is that complex whole which includes knowledge, belief, art, morals, law, custom and any other capabilities and habits acquired by man as a member of society." Man acquires human culture as a participating member of society. It is transmitted though psycholinguistic symbolism. There is a sharp disagreement as to its definition, scope and functional relation to individual man and society. There is surely evidence that the acculturation process or the social conditioning of a child in the ways of society is a conscious and unconscious type of hypnotizism.

Culture is a sphere of linguistic reality which codes the people of any society to think and behave and live in such a way that classifies them as human beings with self-awareness. Through such cultural perceptions they become socialized within a social reality and thus transcend their animal origins.

CULTURAL REVIVALISTIC MOVEMENTS: When a crisis of identity occurs within a culture, on both individual and social levels, often the transpersonal emerges through the revelations of a prophet who has entered into a higher state of consciousness. The emergent quality of mind, as reflected through the charisma of the prophet, then becomes a new and dynamically focused force which reorganizes the society and the conceptual framework of the socio-ideological system. New concepts emerge in the moral, economic, political and religious reality systems of the people. If the state of consciousness of the prophet is high enough, select disciples and at times large masses of people often emerge into higher realms of consciousness and become dynamic examples of the new awareness.

INFRARATIONAL EVOLUTIONARY STAGE: The infrarational evolutionary stage commenced several million years ago, during the late Pliocence or early Pleistocene. The psychocognitive emergence of early man through a fortuitous mutation began the psychocultural process. Man's mental evolution was an emergence from a lower hominoid with its type of undifferentiated consciousness which evolved by a close cooperative interaction between the variables of mind states and psychosocial situational realities.

DEPRESSION: From a clinical point of view it is a syndrome consisting of lowering of mood-tone ,i.e., a person has feelings of painful dejection and difficulty in thinking and possibly psychomotor retardation. Generally depression is masked by anxiety, agitation and obsessive thinking and in certain depressions involutional melancholia.

DEPRESSION-TRANSPERSONAL: This type of depression is called a personality systems dysfunction.

DEPRESSION-EMOTIONAL: Depression is a vital-emotional contagion. It rises up from the lower unconscious and causes uncontrollable fits of anxiety and frustrations. Its dimensions can be measured by a paralyze of will and an inability to perform social actions.

EGO SYSTEMS: Each person has an outer ego system which contains an autonomous cognitive, emotional and physical will consciousness.

Behind these ego systems each person has a permanent self which is asleep most of the time and an inner mental, emotional and physical ego system and a subconscious below each of the ego systems. An unconscious but transpersonal subliminal consciousness connects the person to higher dimension of consciousness. Each person has the capacity to rise up into higher ranges of consciousness and connects with illuminating experiences to transpersonal forces of the universe.

EMOTIONAL PERSONALITY TYPE: The emotional person's dominant personality drive is that of the kinetic individual of force and action. He is concerned with the satisfaction of ambitions, desires, excitements, emotional impulses, domination, the will to power and outer adventures. His life experiences may be full of sensational life dramas because his nature is turbulent, chaotic, and often unregulated. Often he is preoccupied with the acquisition of material objects and possessions. The vital mentality deals with possibilities. It has a passion for novelty and seeks to extend its experience through an enlarged self-affirmation program. It deals with self-aggrandizement actualities while extending its areas of power and profit. It also seeks after unrealized possibilities which it desires to materials, possess and enjoy. The subjective and the imaginative and purely emotive satisfaction and pleasure is a requirement of the vital-emotional nature also

EMOTIONAL-VITAL: The vital-emotional in man is the seat of desire and passions, of revolts and depressions of violent impulses and equally violent reactions. These emotions have a force and power pressure independent of mental will and choice. They are so ingrained that a great deal of time and effort are necessary to root them out.

EMOTIONAL-VITAL LOVE: Conventional love is vital-emotions love. It is actually a type of egoistic vital love. But this is romantic love and it makes life worth living for the masses. When it is not experienced at least once in life many consider existence a dismal failure. Actually there are two types of vital love-a lower emotional and a higher vital love. The first type is a love which is full of ego cravings and demands. This love phase and its continuance depends upon the satisfaction of its love demands. When it doesn't receive its desires or imagines it is not being treated correctly, it becomes sorrowful with emotionally wounded feelings of anger. This type of vital love is full of imaginations, jealousies, misunderstandings and misinterpretations. By its very love nature it is unreliable and ephemeral. Some people of such persuasions fall out of love easily since this type of lower vital live is a source of trouble, suffering, disillusions and full of disappointment.

Couples who are in the throes of lower vital-love are often at odds but still half in love with each other. They are not in harmony with each other yet are joined together of vital necessity on an unhappy leach until they are divorced or separated by death.

EMOTIONAL-NEGATIVE VITAL: When a negative vital emotions is in control of a person it continuously repeats itself in the same manner and form, no matter how often the mind counsels it or gives logical proofs against its emotional irrationality. These movements seem to be an almost invincible, recurring movement of blind obstinate habit.

EVOLUTION OF CONSCIOUSNESS: Transintegral psychology postulates that humanity is genetically coded-through a fortuitous mutation which allowed our ancestors to become mental creatures several million years ago—to progressively emerge into higher and vaster altered states of consciousness. The selective advantage given by that mutation is still with us today, but this potential is still latent in most of humanity.

EGO SYSTEMS: Each person has an outer ego system which contains an autonomous cognitive, emotional and physical will consciousness.

Behind these ego systems each person has a permanent self which is asleep most of the time and an inner mental, emotional and physical ego system and a subconscious below each of the ego systems. An unconscious but transpersonal subliminal consciousness connects the person to higher dimension of consciousness. Each person has the capacity to rise up into higher ranges of consciousness and connects with illuminating experiences to transpersonal forces of the universe.

EXTERNALIZING MIND: The externalizing or physical mind is concerned with physical objects and actions. It is a recording faculty basically. It infers knowledge from its observations and relies on the higher minds for its guidance. Its basic orientation is with external mind observations and conclusions based upon such even. In a sense it is a mechanical thing which continually turns around in a circle upon its thoughts of observation. It is not a true thinking mind but concerns itself with physical things and events. It is a "sense" mind that observes objects and the interaction of objects, and then infers from such relationships. Its basic goal, however, is to give expression to the thinking minds ideas in speech and in any form it can achieve its end results

The externalizing mind, however, is usually narrow and limited and often stupid, especially when it is disturbed by the emotions. Often the emotions supply its desires and justifications of its wants to this mind and gain control of it. Unless the inner self or a clarity from the thinking mind comes to the rescue, the externalizing mind will do the emotion's bidding. This mind also regards the material world as an objective factual thing and views what is not material or physical as unreal.

GNOSTIC CONSCIOUSNESS: The gnostic consciousness is a mind through which all contradictions are cancelled or fused into each other by a higher dimension of being and seeing that unites world knowledge with self-knowledge.

GNOSTIC MAN: A gnostic man is the consummation of the Transpersonal Man; and he emerges through the transpersonal man's soul consciousness and turns it into a dynamic luminous becoming of knowledge and a power of being. His way of life, living, thinking is governed by the power of a vast universal transpersonal consciousness.

HIGHER MIND: When you step out of your normal intelligence your ascent is into the higher mind which is a luminous thought-mind; which has the power to formulate a multitude of aspect of knowledge and concepts and of their significance as a process. It has a clarity of judgment that transcends the necessity of logically examining a process of actions step by step by implied deductions and inferences toward a conclusion.

This will of the higher mind works on the rest of the person through the lower mind, heart and its feelings, the life, body, through its power of thought and idea-force. Its task is to purify through knowledge by putting ideas into the heart and life to be worked out so that one's feelings and action start to become vibrations of higher wisdom which are powered by the urge of self-effectuation.

INCONSCIOUS MIND: The inconscient comprises the material basis of our life and body. It is the foundation of our inferior parts of being and their activities. It reinforces our emotional fixation and mechanical obstinacies of character. It is the source of all consciousness. It is somewhat similar to Julian Huxley's concept of life stuff in matter.

Aurobindo says that all life is based upon the inconscious but that in actuality this inconscient is really a complete subconscience which is a suppressed or involved consciousness. It is everything but is not expressed or formulated. Originally all life and mind and immanent being evolved out of this inconscient.[1] In terms of individuality this inconscient provides the material for the physical body. One can readily see that matter is consciousness fallen asleep. Finally the inconscious is also an aspect of man's subtle nature. And for sake of clarification we should understand that the subconscious lies between the inconscious and the conscious mind. It is the inconscious in its process of emerging into consciousness

INTEGRALIZATION: The process of self maturation that takes place when the inner self emerges and eventually integrates the mental, emotional and physical egos around itself and self-realization occurs. Eventually the egos dissolve as independent autonomous forces and become functional arms of the one self.

It is a process of psychicisation in which the self changes the lower nature and brings about right vision into the mind and right feeling into the emotional nature and correct habits into a person's physical nature. Only then can the true self take up the reins and govern the mental, emotional and physical natures of man.

KUNDALINI: Transintegral psychology asserts that the kundalini energy is the basic energy system behind the evolution of the human species and is the link to the human race's transpersonal natures. And that even in its seemingly latent or asleep form it provides the energy that drives and supports each person's individual existence. Future research will hopefully provide us with hard data to support this hypothesis.

SOCIAL IDENTITY: An American's sense of identity is tied up with our country's social concepts of rugged individualism and self-reliance, which in turn is connected to the American concept of job and social class mobility. Our personality concept of self and sense of identity and self-esteem are intimately tied to our achievement of success in our culture.

Our sense of who we are is tied to what we achieve and what we materially acquire in life. And naturally to be successful and achieve social mobility in jobs and social climbing is intimately connected with our sense of self and our personality strengths.

To succeed in our culture is to move up to a higher social class position or acquire a lot of money or have a job which gives one a lot of money and prestige.

SPECIES CONSCIOUSNESS (COGNITIVE): All members of the human species belong to the stream of cognitive evolutionary consciousness and within all groups exists the total range of psychological types and potentials to enter into the varying dimensions of altered states of consciousness.

Mankind, in the present era, exists within one species, Homo sapiens, divided into racial types which appear to be intellectually, linguistically and physically equal. All are potentially equal in the stream of consciousness evolution.

SUBCONSCIOUS: The subconscious is the primordial species consciousness which lies below the threshold of consciousness. This region of darkness and obscurity, with its incoherent and ill organize elements sustains all our impulses and uncontrolled fixities of character.

The subconscious is the submental base of man. It is a submerged aspect of being. There is no waking awareness at this level beneath the conscious mind. This mind does, however, receive impressions and responds with habitual and instinctive forces which come to the surface of the mental, emotional and physical minds. The forces of obstinate experiences from past existence are also active here.

The negative attitudes which often cause psychosomatic illnesses are active in this state of consciousness since ideas and forces after being rejected by the waking mind return inward or sink into the subconscious. They later emerge, even after lying quiescent for long periods of time. Also when ideas are thrown out of the emotional or physical minds they usually go down into the subconscious as a seed form and emerge again when the opportunity presents itself.

It is a fact that the ordinary person lives in the subconscious physical. All the habitual movements of the mental, emotional and physical minds are stored and emerge eventually into the waking mind. If they are not able to emerge freely, then they come up in dreams. This is why it is so difficult to change a person's character or to get rid of habitual emotional movements since even when suppressed they surge up again and again.

SUBLIMINAL SUBCONSCIOUSNESS: The transpersonal subliminal is a region of luminous consciousness behind the surface mentality of man. It is a dimension of supernormal consciousness where much of the aspirants inner experiences will occur.

Its characteristics are qualities of luminosity and freedom which find expression as modes of the higher forces of consciousness. Individually the subliminal self supplies the base and dynamism to man's nature. It supports the whole superficial man. It also opens up into the higher superconscious dimensions of mind levels which must be brought down into man's lower nature to purify and transform him.

The subliminal contains the inner subtle physical consciousness, the inner luminous vital evolutional and luminous inner mental and the authentic self, the soul personality. This mind is in direct contact with the forces of the universal mind of the cosmos. The emotional subliminal is open to the currents of universal life, while the subliminal physical in us is in direct contact with the universal energy of cosmic matter.

The real inner self or soul personality is a representative of the overself which presides from above over the evolutionary process of the empirical self. The subliminal dimension is a consciousness that connects the lower evolving consciousness from below with the descent of the higher consciousness from above.

SUPERMIND: This consciousness exists beyond ordinary comprehension. Its vastness is an all comprehensive unity with knowledge and the rhythm of the will of the transpersonal Absolute. It is a "truth-consciousness" which is free from ignorance, mistakes and misuse of beauty and delight or error from divine rectitude. It is said that even an incomplete statement made in this type of consciousness will lead one toward a further truth completeness. It is an integral consciousness with an all-comprehensive world-knowledge. It is the perfect identity of knowledge and will.

SUPRARATIONAL EVOLUTIONARY STAGE: According to psychocultural evolutionary theory the rational state of cultural evolution has not yet arrived. All members of the species Homo sapiens have reached the rational state of consciousness but rational-intellectuals do not exist in sufficient numbers to create a truly rational social order. Humanity thus exists still in the upper reaches of the infrarational state of evolution. This is a highly sophisticated level in comparison to australopithecine culture but it is still infrarational in nature and content.

THINKING MIND: The thinking mind concerns itself with abstract ideas and knowledge. It deals with rational and logical categories of thought such as world views and scientific models as thought processes out of which systems of certitude are created and tested by the evidence of the senses.

Its basic function is to think, reason and give value judgments. In most men the intellect is imperfect and ill trained. The logical conclusions of such thinking is generally half developed and ill founded, if nor erroneous. Even when they are right it is more by chance than merit or correct thinking. Even when the intellect is fully trained and developed we must realize that it cannot arrive at absolute certitude or complete truth. self-realized.

TRANSPERSONAL ANTHROPOLOGY: Transpersonal Anthropology is a science which investigates the relationship between consciousness and culture, altered states of mind research, and the integration of mind, culture and personality. As a science it incorporates, transcends, and contributes to the traditional discipline of Anthropology, and its various sub areas. (Ronald Campbell)

Transpersonal Anthropology considers the evolving (open-ended, cumulative) processes of human physical, conceptual and cooperative realms of reality. We consider species-wide, cultural and individual levels of existence including states of ordinary observed behavior, paranormal abilities and creative consciousness as they exist in fact and as a further potential of human development. (Philip Staniford

TRANSPERSONAL MAN: A transpersonal man has discovered his soul and lives within this Self consciously. He lives in this joy and requires nothing external to be a complete human being.

TRANSPERSONALIZATION: Transpersonalization is uniting of the liberated evolutionary soul-personality with the higher and vaster states of consciousness which transcend the inner self. It is a movement into the greater self, into the central being or oversoul or overself which may extent into ranges of Cosmic Consciousness

TRANSPSYCHOMENTAL CONTINUUM MODEL: Transintegral psychology contends that a transpsychomental continuum exists from the depths of the psychological systems to the mental heights of human nature and the cosmos. Human nature being but an extension on the finite level of the transcendent dimension, that is, a linkage exists within the human dimension which correspondence with the cosmos. If this fact were not so, no communication, no dimensional connection with other human beings and the universe would take place; no mystical connections with ultimate reality, no transpersonal experiences would take place.

TRANSPERSONAL PSYCHOLOGY: Transintegral Psychology is an Integral or Transpersonal psychology developed from concepts of Psychology East-West. It presents several theoretical models to explain the human condition, reconciling and integrating the concepts of mind, culture and personality.

TRANSCULTURAL SYNTHESIS: The missing ingredient in the definition of culture is the ideas of consciousness in interaction with society. Mind states are not passive and static but dynamic linguistic processes. They are psycholinguistic forces projected into the cultural process. They are also linked with the psycho-personality systems on the conscious, unconscious and the personal dimensions. But the idealism of a culture is structured in linguistic parameters, its ultimate expression is psychological and mental. The connecting link among these three phases is a telepathic lineage. This telepathic linkage is what constantly reinforces the implicit and explicit cultural ideals in each society; this factor is what Transintegral Psychology calls the concept of transcultural synthesis.

TRANSINTEGRAL PSYCHOLOGY: Transintegral psychology is an integral or transpersonal psychology which is the product of psychology East-West. It has a clinical, a counseling, a transpersonal, and a social science dimension to its practice.
transintegral therapy:
    Transintegral therapy consist of four therapeutic systems. Integral Analysis concerns itself with the analysis and treatment of sick, psychologically disturbed patients. Transintegral Brief therapy deals with problems that require short term solutions. Transintegral therapy is the upper arm or head of the first two systems since it deals with the transpersonal dimensions of altered states of consciousness. Transintegral Interpersonal social therapy deals with the therapeutic aspect of neuroses caused by behavioral and social causes.

TRANSINTEGRAL BRIEF THERAPY: Transintegral brief therapy's goals are to correct minor dysfunctional problems by changing negative conscious, subconscious and behavioral states. This therapy, thus, deals only with specific problems on a short term basis; its expertise is designed to help the marginally dysfunctional person or the person who has a working compromise with life but who has one aspect of his world view or functional relationship with himself out of synch with his personality or life style.

TRANSPERSONAL PROCESS: The transpersonal process allows people to gradually emerge into the higher reaches of altered states of consciousness. Some transpersonal men may even descend into the dynamic unconscious and ultimately emerge with a transformed lower nature. Through such a venture, the terrifying depths of the unconscious is cleansed and balanced. A harmonizing of the plural ego systems around the inner self occurs through such a process. Such transformed persons are able to exist in the world yet somehow transcend the world. The call both heaven and earth home.

TRANSITIONAL BEING: Man is an unfinished product of the evolutionary process; unfinished by nature because mankind must go through a conscious evolutionary process to finish what nature has started and emerge into a Gnostic being manhood.

The human species, however, has an inherent potential to overcome its limited human nature. This is because humanity still has within its nature the results of that ancient mutation which caused the emergence of mental awareness from the previous instinctive anthropoid mentality. Once individualized consciousness was achieved and mental man emerged from the subconscious abyss of primordial darkness, human beings became consciously responsible for their further mental and emotional growth.

TRANSPERSONALIZATION: When the higher energy of the overself or oversoul force descends and transforms a person or when the inner self's ascent into the higher oversoul takes place.

TRANSFORMATION: "transformation means that the higher consciousness and nature is brought down into the mind, vital and body and takes the place of the lower."

UNCONSCIOUS: The unconscious layers of being exists beneath the ordinary consciousness. The subconscious, inconscious and transpersonal subliminal subconsciousness, will be discussed in relationship to the physical, emotional, and mental modes of the personality. This relationship is basic to the whole concept of immanent being. The inconscious is the evolutionary basis in us, while two of the hidden sources of our actions, the transpersonal subliminal subconscious, and the subconscious are individualized in each person.

PARADIGM CRISIS

Hypothesis 1. Today the scientific world exists in a period that Thomas S. Kuhn calls "the emergence of the crisis in the scientific community." It is realized by a vanguard group of scientists that science needs to develop new concepts and paradigms that can give new explanations about man in the world.

Theory in its basic concept is a series of two schematic labels that have been demonstrated to show a meaningful relationship with each other by factual evidence or hypothesized constructs. And when we speak of the human condition and sociocultural reality and rapid socio-cultural change we must examine all these factors together in order to understand the Genocide Phenomenon. The rationale for this point of view is that human experience is psychocultural, involving a creative synthesis of cultural achievement and psychobiological activity in relationship to the social and physical environment. The human organism, cultural concepts, and material objects, all belong to the cultural dynamic realm and must be integrally understood; and not to do so risks the destruction of life as we know it as the extinction peril consumes America!

RAPID CULTURE CHANGE-

Hypothesis 2. The second causal reason for the Genocide Phenomenon's emergence into modern life are the facts of rapid culture changes of social norms and family structures, massive industrial changes and developments, and drastic changes within the social organization and institutions.

SUBJECTIVE ERA

Hypothesis 3. The rationalistic-individualistic age of the past several centuries is coming to an end and a subjective era of individual and social subjectivism is emerging, as the third causal factor for the emergence of the Genocide Phenomenon. This is indicated by the trends in art, poetry, political and economic changes taking place on a wide world scale. This subjectivism, however has temporarily been side tracked by a false subjectivism, a Genocide Phenomenon, that has been captured by the vitalistic life surge of the covert primordial fear-anxiety syndrome which embraces unregenerated humanity— an extinction peril of primordial proportions which is causing the world wide tension, wars and Nuclear confrontation crisis. Man's Unregenerated vital-emotional forces, linked up with technological industrialism, has given vital life to this subjective aberration of human nature. This false vital subjectivism, allied with gross materialism and technological innovation, as causal agents of vast sociocultural change, has caused a malfunctioning—a psychological dysfunctioning within the human personality system as a modern death generation emerges into modern society. The proper balance between the outer objective consciousness and the inner psyche and the dimensional-social personality systems no longer exists and it is not functioning properly. As a result a deep anxiety, a primordial fear-anxiety syndrome has developed within the human race—a crisis of self-esteem and a lack of a proper individual and social identity consciousness has occurred in the species Homo sapiens. Humanity cannot shake off the grip of this false subjectivism and its insistent demands yet it finds no satisfaction in fulfilling its concepts.

PSYCHOLOGICAL DYSFUNCTIONING

Hypothesis 4. A psychological dysfunctioning of the human race is the fourth causal factor in the present world crisis. The proper balance between the outer objective consciousness and the inner psyche and the dimensional personality systems no longer exists and it is not functioning properly. As a result a deep species anxiety develops within the human race—a crisis of self-esteem and a lack of a proper individual and social identity consciousness occurs in the species Homo sapiens.

Symbolically and existentially individual man and women are thrust into a time of disquiet because their outer natures are so out of tune with their inner essence that social violence and an inner quiet desperation yield up such a sense of despair that life holds no meaning and death no allure! It is a time when mankind cries out in bewilderment at his lack of authentic living and he wonders what curse is he born under.

PRIMORDIAL FEAR-ANXIETY SYNDROME-

Hypothesis 5. This study postulates that man, culture and consciousness are united together into a continuum of interacting movement. This is a process in which man cannot act without producing movement in the natural world or in the cultural realm or within the personality of man. This interaction goes on within the spectrum of animal existence, culture and the environmental womb of nature. All combine together in the drama of the emergent evolution of consciousness. The psychosocial nature of consciousness has beneath the surface of its interacting a primordial fear-anxiety syndrome that is activates within normal social life but rapidly accelerates when vast changes occur with in the socio-cultural arena.

EVOLUTION OF CONSCIOUSNESS

Hypothesis 6. The sixth causal factor is the biological human evolutionary process of consciousness which is constantly occurring within the nature of human consciousness. It is the biological emergent evolution of human consciousness which has presently reached a crisis stage and is causing a tension of mental and emotional anxiety as infrarational man seemingly evolves into a higher stage of rational consciousness.

FATAL NEANDERTHAL FLAW

Hypothesis 7. The most important causal reason for the emergence of the Genocide Phenomenon is the inherent fatal flaw within some members of the species called the Neanderthal flaw. Individuals who have this fatal flaw often become death masters or become members of the death generation people. They exist in the lower reaches of human infrarational consciousness and have impulsive urges to enslave their fellow mankind, thus enters the death generation. Individuals who have this Neanderthal flaw exist in all stations of life, social classes and cultures. They have an excessive compulsive need to control other people and to set up totalitarian dictatorships, government bureaucracies and corporate structures if the opportunities presents itself. They are the insidious force that threatens America's destiny

BIBLIOGRAPHICAL ENTRIES

Acharya, K.D. *Guide to Sri Aurobindo's Philosophy*. Pondicherry: Divya Jivan Sahitya Prakashan, 1968.

Adams, J. **Twenty Years At Hull-House.** New York: Signet, 1910.

Adorno, T. W. Frenkel-Brunswik. E.D.J. and Sanford, R.N. 1950, **The Authoritarian Personality.** New York: Harper & Bros.

Anthony, James E. Benedek, Therese, **"Depression & Human Existence,"** Little Brown & Company, Boston, 1975.

Aniela Jaffe. *From the Life and Works of C. G. Jung.* Jung. New York: Harper Colophon Books, 1971.

Aurobindo, Sri. **"Letters on Yoga". Part i, Vol. 22.** Sri Aurobindo Birth Centenary Library, Sri Aurobindo Ashram: Pondicherry, **India: 1972.**

Aurobindo, Sri. **"The Mind of Light"**, E. P. Dutton & Co., Inc. New York, 1953.

Aurobindo, Sri. *On Yoga II Tome Two.* Sri Aurobindo Ashram, Pondicherry, Sri Aurobindo International University Centre Collection Vol. VIIi,1958.

Aurobindo, Sri. "The Human Cycle: The Ideal of Human Unity, War and Self Determination. Sri Aurobindo International Centre of Education Collection, Vol. IX, Pondicherry, 1962. p.248.

Aurobindo, Sri. *The Life Divine. Pondichery*: Sri Aurobindo International Centre of Education, 1960.

Aurobindo, Sri. *The Life Divine*. Pondicherry: Sri Aurobindo International Center of Education, 1960.

_____. *The Life Divine*. New York: India Library Society, 1965.

Aurobindo. " The Future Evolution of Man". Sri Aurobindo Ashram, Pondicherry, 1963.

Aurobindo, Sri. "The Future Evolution of Man". East Midland Printing Col. Ltd.: Bury St. Edmunds, England, 1960.

_____. *On Yoga II Tome One*. Sri Aurobindo Inter-National University Centre, Vol. VI., 1958.

_____. *The Mother*. Pondicherry: Sri Aurobindo Ashram Press, 1965.

Bernard, Raymond. Apollonius the Nazarene. Health Research, Pomeroy, Washington, 1956.

Bernard Raymond W. The Unknown Life of Christ. Health Research, Pomeroy, Washington. 1966.

Bernard, Raymond. The Hollow Earth. Carol Publishing Group. New York, N.Y. 1991.

Boas, F. **Introduction to Handbook of American Indian Languages.** Lincoln, Nebraska: University of Nebraska Press, 1968.

Bagby, Philip H. **"Culture and the Causes of Culture"**, American Anthropologist. (1953).

Bagby, Philip. **Culture and History.** University of California Press, Berkely & Los Angeles, 1963. p. 88.

Bateson, G. **"Steps to an Ecology of Mind.** New York : Ballantine, 1972.

Bellak, L., and Small, L. **"Emergency Therapy and Brief Psychotherapyl"** 1965. New York: brune & Statton.

Bendit, L. J. : **Paranormal Cognition.** London, Faber and Baber, 1944.

Bentov, Itzhak. **"Micromotion of the Body as a Factor in the Development of the Nervous** System". In "Kundalini, Evolution and Enlightenment. Ed. John White. Doubleday: Garden City, New York, 1979.

Berdyaeo, Nicolas. **The Beginning and the End.** Harper Torchbooks, New York, 1957.

Bhagwan Shree Rajneesh. "The book of Secrets" New York: Harper & Row, 1974. pp.. 352-353.

Bidney, David. **Theoretical Anthropology.** Schocken Books, New York.

Bleibreu, John N. **The Parable of the Beast.** New York: Collier Books 1969.

Bohannan, Paul. "Rethinking Culture: A Project for Current Anthropologists", Current Anthropology (Oct., 1973).

Bowlby, J. " Attachment and Loss." London: Hogarth, 1969.

Bowlby, J. " The Making and Creating of Affertional Bonds: II "Some Principles of Psychotherapy." British Journalof Psychiatry, 1977.

Broad, C.D. Religion, Philosophy and Psychical Research. Routledge Kegan Paul, 1953.

Brother Lawrence. The Practice of the Presence of God. New York: Spire Books, 1969

Brzezinski, Abigniew. The Technetronic Society. Encounter, Vol. XXX, No 1 Jan., 1068..

Bucke, Richard, Maurice. "Cosmic Consciousness" E.P. Dutton & Company, Inc. New York, 1962.

Butler, W.E. "The Energy Behind True Magic", in Future Science. White, John, & Krippner, Stanley. Anchor Books, Doubleday & Co. Inc. Garden Cityt, New York.

CASSIRER, ERNST, AN ESSAY ON MAN, NEW HAVEN CONN: YALE UNIVERSITY PRESS 1944.

Cohen, S. "The Beyond Within: The LSD Story." New York: Athenaeum, 1964.

Campbell, Ronald. Concept of Man in Integral Psychology. University Microfilms International , Ann Arbor, Michigan, U.S.A. London, England 1976..

Campbell, Ronald L. "Emergent Cultural Systems: ThePsychocultural Evolution of Man." *Phoenix, New Directions in the Study of Man.* Vol. I, No. I., 1977. Standford, Cal.

Campbell, Ronald L. & Philip S. Staniford. "Transpersonal Anthropology". *Phoenix: New Directions in the Study of Man.* Vol.II No. I, 1978.Standford, Cal.

Campbell, Ronald L., "The Nature of Transpersonal Anthropology, Vol.V., No. 1, 1981, pp. 119-131. Phoenix: Journal of Transpersonal Anthropology.

Campbell, Ronald, "Journal of Transpersonal Anthropology, Volume VI. Nos. 1 & 2,1982. Phoenis; Journal of Transpersonal anthropology

. & Shirley Lee. "Notes and Comments on the Kundalini Phenomena". Standford, Cal. *Phoenix: New directions in the Study of Man, volume II, No. II. 1978.*

. *Soul Journey Into Eternity: A transpersonal fable on self transcendence. 1998.* Xlibris Corp. Princeton, N.J.

Campbell Ronald L. "The Photosymbolistic Technique: Photograph As A Projective method in Organizational Research." 1978. Unpublished MPA thesis.

Campbell, Ronald. Transpersonal Psychology: An Integral Encounter with Self-Awareness, Xlibris Corp. Princeton M.J. 1999.

Capra, Fritnof. *The Tao of Physics.* Bantam Books, New York, 1988.

Chaudhuri, Haridas. " Sri Aurobindo: The Phophet of Life Divine" Sri Aurobindo Ashram, Pondicherry. 1960.

Chaudhuri, Haridas. *The Philosophy of Integralism.* Pondicherry Sri Aurobindo Pathamandir, 1954.

. *Mastering the Problems of Living.* New York: The Citadel Press, 1968.

. *Integral Yoga.* London: George Allen & Unwin Ltd, 1965.

. *Philosophy of Meditation.* Philosophical Library, New York. 1965.

. *The Integral Philosophy of Sri Aurobindo* Edited by Chaudhuri & Frederic Spiegelberg. Ruskin House, George Allen & Unwin Ltd. London, 1960.

Coleman, Daniel. **Varieties of Religious Meditations.** Irvington Publishers, Inc., New York, 1977.

Cooper, William, **Behold the Pale Horse.**

Corso, Philip, J. **The Day After Roswell**, Pocket Books, Simon & Schuster Inc. New York, 1997.

Day, Langston, **"Radiation Known and Unknown"** excerted from *New Worlds Beyond the Atom.* Devin-Adair co. 1963, the article is also published in *Future Science. Edited by John White & Stanlye Krippner, Anchor Books, Doubleday & Co., Garden City, New Your 1977.*

Darnoi, Kennedy D.N. *The Unconscious and Edward Von Hartmann.* The Hague: Martinus Nijhoff, 1967.

David-Neel, Alexander Lama, *Magic and Mystery in Tibet.* University Books, New York, 1958.

David-Neel, Alexandra, *Initiations & Initiates in Tibet.* University Books, New York, 1959.

Devereux, George, "The Technique of Analyzing "Occult" Occurrence in Analysis", in *Psychoanalysis and the Occult.* edited by George Devereux, International Universities Press, Inc. New York. 1970

Douglas Dean E. "Precognition and Retrocognition". in *Psychic Exploration, Edgar D. Mitchell editor.G.P. Putnam's sons, New York. 1974.*

Dubrov, Alexander P. "Biogravitation and Psychotronics". in *Future Science.*

Edinger, E.F. "An Outline of Analytical Psychology. Quadrant Reprint. no. 1. San Francisco: C.G. Jung Institute, 1968.

Ehrenwald, Jan. The ESP Experience: As Psychiatric Validation. Basic Books, New York. 1978.

Ehrenwald, Jan. *The ESP Experience. Basic books, Inc.* 1967. Basic Books, New York.

Ehrenwald Hans [Jan] "Telepathy in Dreams". *British Journal of Medicxal Psychology,* 19:313-323, 1942. also "Telepathy and Medical Psychology". New York, *Norton,*1948 (London , Allen and Unwin, 1947).

Eiseley, Loren. "The immense Journey". Vintage Books: New York, 1957.

Eisenbud Jule. "Psychiatric Contributions to Parapsychology: A Review". p. 7. in *Psychoanalysis and the Occult.* International Universities Press, Inc. New York 1970.

Eliselyh, Loren. **Free Will.** Evolution of Man. Louise B. Young, Editor, New York: Oxford University Press.

Else frenkel-Brunswil. **Differential Patterns Of Social Outlook and Personality In Family and Children.** in Childhood in Contemporary cultures, ed. by Margaret Mead & Marth Wolfenstein, Univ. of Chicago Press, 1955.

Erikson, Erik H. *Childhood and Society.* New York: W.W. Norton & Co. 1963.

Flach, Frederic, F., " **The Secret Strength of Depression,** " 1974, Bantan Books, p.1.

Frankle Vicktor E. **"Man's Search For Meaning."** Washington Square Press, Inc. New York . 1966.

Frankle Victor E. " **The Unconscious God"** Simon & Schuster, New York1975

Ferguson, Mailyn. **"Kindling and Kundalini Effects".** In "Kundalini, Evolution and Enlightenment". Ed. John White. Doubleday: Garden City, New York. 1979.

Flowers, Charles. T **Science Odyssey: 100 Years of Discovery.** william Morrow & Company, Inc. New York,1998.

Fodor Nandor: **"Telepathic Dreams.** *American Inago,* 3:61-85, 1942 (also in 63) also "Encyclopedia of Psychic Science." London Aurthus Press, 1933.

Fortune, Dion. *Esoteric Philosophy of Love and Marriage.* SamuelWiser Inc. New York, 1974.

Freud, Sigmund. **"Totem and Taboo".** Modern Library: New York, 1938.

Freud, Sigmund: "Remarks upon the Theory and Practice of Dream-Interpretation". *Collected Papers,* 5:136-149. London, Hogarth, 1950 (1923).

Fromm, Erich. *The Art of Loving.* Bantam Books, New York, 1963.

Fromn, Erich. "Man for Himself"An inquiry into the Psychology of Ethics." New York, Toronto: Rinehart & Co., Inc., 1947.

Fromm, Erich. **The Anatomy of Human Destructiveness.** Holt, Rinehart & Winston. New York, 1972.

Fromn Erich. **The Revolution of Hope: Toward a Humanized Technology.** Bantam Books 1968.

Fromm, Erick, D.T. Suzuki, and Richard DeMartino. **Zen Buddhismaand Psychoanalysis.** new York: Harper & brothers, 1960

Gandhi, Kikshor. :Social Philosophy of Sri Aurobindo and the New Age". Sri Aurobindo Ashram Press: Pondicherry, 1965.

Gerlach, Luther P. & Virginia H. Hine. **People Power, Change: Movements of Social Tranformation.** Bobbs-Merrill Co. Indianpolis & new york, 1970.

Goodman, Jeffery. *We Are the Earthquake Generation: Where and When the Catastrophes Will Strike. Seaview* Books, New York, 1978.

Gorer, Geoffey, **The Danger of Equality.** Weybright & Talley, New York, 1966.

Gorer, Geoffrey, **The American People.** W.W. Norton & Co. 1964.

Goyeche, John. "**Kundalini as Prevention and Therapy for Drug Abuse**". In Kundalini, Evolution and Enlightenment, Ed. John White, Doubleday: Garden City, New York, 1979.

Green, Elmer and Alyce. " **Beyond Biofeedback.** " Delta books: New York, 1977.

Grof, Stanislav. "**Theoretical and Empirical Basis of Transpersonal Psychology and Psychotherapy: Observations from LSD Research.**" "Journal of Transpersonal Psychology, No. 1, 1973.

Hallowell, Irving. "**Behavioral Evolution and the Emergence of the Self**" in Theory in Anthropology. Robert Manners and David Kaplan, editors. Aldine Publishing Co.; Chicago, 1969.

Hallowell, Irving. "**Culture , Personality and Society**" in Cultural and Social Anthropology, Peter B. Hammond, editor, Macmillan Co: London, 1964.

Hoover, Eleanor, "**Alpha, the First Step to a New Level of Reality**", Human Behavior, Vol 1, No. 3.

Harman Willis W.. "**The Societal Implications and Social Impact of Paranormal Phenomena**", In *Future Science.*

Harris, Obadiah. *Unitive spirituality.* Santa Barbara, J.F.. Rowny Press, 1966

Hechinger Grace & Fred M. **Teen-Age Tyranny.** Fawcett Publications, Greenwich, Conn. 1963.

Henderson, S., Byrne, D.G. Duncan-Jones, P., Adcock, S, Scott, R, & Steel,G.P.."**Social Bonds in the Epidemiology of Neurosis**". " British journal of Psychiatry, 1978, 132, 463-466.'& Henerson, S. Duncan-Jones, P., Byrne,D.G., Scott, R., &

Adock, S. "Social Bonds, Adversity And Neurosos." Paper Louisk October, 1978.

Henderson, S., Duncan-Jones, P.,McAuley, H., & Richie, K. "The patient's primary Group." "British journal of Psychiatry," 1978, 132, 74-86.

Henle, Paul. "Language, Thought, and Culture," *Cultural and Social Anthropology.* London: The Macmillan company, 1964.

Henry, Julies, **Culture Against Man.** Random House, New York, N.Y. 1963.

Hesse, Hermann. **Steppenwolf.** New York: Bantam Books 1963.

Heywood, Rosalind. *ESP: A Personal Memoir.* New York: E.P.. Dutton & Co., 1964.

Hinsie, Leland, Campbell, Robert, **Psychiatric Dictionary,** Oxford University Press, 1974.

Hollos, Istvan: **Psychopathologie alltaglicher telepathischer Erscheinungen.** Igagoo 19:529-546, 1933.

Honigmann, John J. **Handbook of Social and cultural Anthropolog,** Chicago: Ran Mcnally & Co. 1973.

Horney, Karen, *Self-Analysis.* W.W. Norton & Company, New York, London. 1942.

Horney, Karen, ' **Neurosis and Human Growth,** " W.W. Norton & Co., New York, 1950.

Hutschnecker, Arnold, **The Drive for Power.** M. Evan & Co. New York, N.Y. 1974.

Houston, Jean, **Prometheus Rebound: An Inquiry into Techno-logical Growth and Psychological Change in Alternative to Growth1**, Dennis Meadows, ed. (cambidege, Mass; Ballinger, 1977.

Hutschnecker, Arnold. **The Drive for Power.** Evan & Co. New York, N.Y. 1974.

Inyushin, Viktor, **"Bioplasma: The Fifth State of Matter".** In Future Science, Ed, John White and Stanley Krippner, doubleday: Garden City, New York,1977.

Jaspers, K. **"The Way to Wisdom."** Translated by R. Mannheim. New Haven: Yale University Press. 1951.

Jones, Ernest. *The life and works of sigmund freud.* Vol. III. New York: Basic Books. 1957.

Josephen, Crid & Mary. **"Man alone:Alienation in Modern Soci-ety."** Dell Publication Co. New York, 1962

Jung, Carl G. **Psychology and Religion.** New Haven, Conn., 1938.

Kardiner, Abram, **"The Psychological Frontiers of society,"** New York, 1945

Katz, R. **"Education for Transcendence: Lessons from the !Kung Zhu Twasi".** In Journal of Transpersonal Psychology, November 2, 1973.

Kaufman, w. (Ed.) **"Existentialism from Dostoevsky to Sartre."** Translated by W. Kaufman. new York: Meridian. 1956.

Kaufman, M.R. **"Discussant on brief Psychotherapy."** in Pro-ceedings of the 4th world congress of Psychiatry, Madrid, 1966,

Part i (Ed., J.J. Lopex ibor). amsterdam: Excerpta Medica foundation. l967.

Kiev, Ari. *Curanderismo: Mexican-American Folk Psychiatry.l972*. The Free Press, New York, Collier-Macmillan Limited, London.

Klein, G. "Is Psychoanalysis Relevant?" In B. rubenstein (Ed.), "Psychhanalysis and contemporary science," New York: Macmilan, 1973.

Klerman, Gerald, Weissman, Myrna M. "Interpersonal Psychotherapy: Theory and Research," in "Short-Term Psychotherapies for Depression." Editor: A. John Rush. Guilfor Press, New York, l982.

Koestler, Arthur. The Evolution of Man: What went Wrong? Human Variation: Readings in Physical Anthropology. Hermajn K. Bleibteuand James Down, editors. Beverly Hills glencoe Pres, 1971.

Krishna Gopi. "Prana: The Traditional and the Modern View.",in White, John & Krippner, Stanley. *Future Science*. Anchor Books, Doubleday & Co., Garden City, New York.

Krippner, Stanley, (forword) in Bruce Taub-bylnum, " The Family Unconscious," Quest Books, Wheaton, Ill. 1984.

Kubizek, August. Young Hitler-Friend of My youth. London, 1950.

Kuhn, Thomas. The Structure of Scientific Revolutions. University of Chicago Press: Chicago, 1062.

Johnson & Szurek, "The Genesis of Antisocial Acting and out in Children and Adults". l952. *Psychoanalysis Quarterly.*

Jones, Gadys." Reincarnation: Sex and Love." New Age Press, La Canada, Calif. 1971.

Kaplan, B. and D. Johnson. "The Social Meaning of Navaho Psychopathology and Psychotherapy". In *Magic, Faith and Healing.* edited by A. Kiev. New

Karlins Marvin & Lewis M. Andrews. *Biofeedback.* New York: Warner Books, 1973. p. 39.York: the Free Press, 1964.

Kiev, Ari. "Curanderismo: Mexican-American Folk Psychiatry." The free Press, New York, collier-Macmillan Limited, London. 1972.

Klerman, Gerald L.,Weissman, Myrna, M. "Interpersonal Psychotherapy:theory and Research, pp. 88-106. In "Short-Term Psychotherapies for Depression. Editor, a. john Rush. The Quilford Press, New york, 1982.

Kluckhohn, C. "Culture & Behavior", *Handbook of Social Psychology.* editor, Cambridge: Addison Wesley, Vol. ll, 1954.

Krippner, Stanley, (foreword) in E. Bruce Taub-Bylnum, *The Family Unconscious.* quest Books, Wheaten, Ill. 1984.

Kuhn, Thomas. "The Structure of Scientific Revolutions". University of Chicago Press: Chicago, 1962.

Landmann, Michael. translated by David J. Parent. *Philosophical Anthropology.* The Westminster Press, Philadelphia, 1974.

Laning, R. D. "The Divided Self". Baltimore, Md: Penguin, 1965..

Laren, Stephen. The Shaman's Doorway. Harper & Row, New york, 1976.

Lawrence, Jopdi. *Alpha Brain Waves.* New York: Avon Books, 1972.

Lerner, Michael I. **Heredity, Evolution and Society.** San Francisco Freeman & Company, 1958.

Lewin, Bertram, **Dreams and the Uses of Regression.** New York: International Universities Press, 1958.

Lorenz, Konrsd. **On Aggression.** New York: Bantam Bookds, 1971.

Lowie, Robert. **The History of Ethnological Theory.** New york, N.Y. Holt, Rinehart & Winston, 1937.

Macleish, Archibald. **Our Altered Conception Of Ourselves,** Evolution of Man. Louise B. Young, Editor. New York: Oxford Univrsity Press, 1970.

Maloney, Charles. **"Evolutionary Psychology"**, *Mother India. Pondicherry, Sri "Aurobindo Ashram Trust. Jan-March. 1975.*

Malinowski, Bronisaw. "**A Scientific Theory of Culture".** Galaxy Books: New York, 1961.

Maslow, Abraham. *Toward a Psychology of Being.* London: D. Van Nostrand Company, 1962.

. *The Farther Reaches of Human Nature.* New York, Penguin Books. 1978.

Masumi Tssurouka, May, 1966, "**The Samori"s Method of Wxpression,**" Black Belt Magazine.

Mauss, Marce. *Sociologie Et Anthropologie.* Paris: Presses, Univesitaeres DE France, 1966.

May, Rollo, **The Innocent Murders.** Psychology Today, December, 1972.

may, Rollo, **The Meaning of Anxiety.** Pocket Books, N.Y. 1977.

Mead, Margaret. "**the Study of Culture At a Distance**", *Study of Culture at a* Margaret Mead & Rhoda Metraux. editors, Chicago:

Mead, Margaret. **And Keep Your Powder Dry.** William AMorrow & Co, New York, 1965.

Meyer, A. A Psychobiology: A science of Man." Springfield, Ill. Charles C. Thomas, 1957.Distance.

Miller, Robert, "**Methods of Detecting and Measuring Healing Energies**", in *Future Science:Life Energies & the Physics of Paranormal Phenomena.* Anchor Books, Doubleday & Company, Inc. Garden City, New York. 1977.

Mother's Agenda, Institute for Evolutionary Research 200 Park Avenue, New York.

Mother. *Questions & Answers 19l50-5l.* Pondicherry: Sri Aurobindo Ashram Press, 1972.

. *Questions & Answers 1957-58.* Pondicherry: Sri. Aurobindo Ashram Press, 1973.

. *Questions & Answers 1956.* Pondicherry: Sri. Aurobindo Ashram Press, 1973.

. *Health and Healing in Yoga.* Pondicherry: Sri. Aurobindo Ashram Press, 1979.

. & *Sri Aurobindo. Mother & Aurobindo on Education .Pondicherry:* Sri Aurobindo Ashram Press.

. *Mother's Agenda* . 13 volume set. Ed. by Satprem.Institute for Evolutionary Research, Mr. Vernon, Wa. U.S.A. Published in France, L'Agenda DE Mere—1951-1960.

Mother (Mirra Alfassa). "**Questions and answers**". *Mother India.* Pondicherry: Sri Aurobindo Ashram Trust, May, 1974.

Morgan, Lewis H. **Ancient Society or Researches in the Lines of Human Progress from Savagery through Barbarism to civilization.** Chicago, Charles h. Kerr & Co. 1908.

Motoyama, Hiroshi. "**The Motoyama Device: Measuring Psychic Energy**". In "Future Science, Eds. John White and Stanley Krippner. Doubleday: Garden City, New York. 1977.

Mumford, Lewis. **The Condition of Man.** New York: Harcourt, Brace co. 1944.

Nagin doshi. *Guidance From Sri Aurobindo: Letters to a Young disciple.* Pondicherry: Sri Aurobindo society, 1974.

Nishimaru, S "**Mental Climate & Eastern Psychotherapy**" *Transcultural Psychiatric Research 2.*(April 1965).

Nydes, Jule: "**The Magical Experience of the Masturbation Fantasy**". *American Journal of Psychotherapy,* 4:303-310, 1950.

Ostrander, Sheila and Lynn Schroeder. *Psychic Discoveries Behind the Iron Curtain.* New York: Prentice-Hall, 1968.

Ogburn, W. F. **The Changing Functions of the Family in Marriage and the Family.** ed. R.F. Winch & R. Mcginnis, New York: Henry Holt & Co. 1953.

Peck, Robert. "A Research Note on Kundalini Energy". In "Kundalini, Evolution and Enlightenment", John White and Stanley Krippner. Doubleday: Garden City. New York, 1977.

Pelletier, Kenneth &Garfield, Charles, "Consciousness East West." Harper-Colophon Books. .

Plato, "epistle VII, 341 C. in Steiner, Rudolf, "Occult Mysteries of Antiquity & Christianity as Mystical fact". Rudolf Steiner Publications Blauvelt, New York: 1961.

Prince, R. "Indigenous Yoruba Psychiatry". In *Magic, Faith and Healing.* edited by a. Kiev. New York: the Free Press, 1964.

Rabel, A. J. "The Epidemiology of a Folk Illness: Susto in Hispanic America", " Ethnology 3 , 1961.

Ravenscrofc Trevor. The Spear of Destiny. Samuel Weikser, York Beach Manine.

Rele, Vasant. "The Mysterious Kundalini. D. B.. Taraporevals Sons & Co.: Fort, Bombay, 1967.

Rishabhchad. In the Mother's Light. Pondicherry: Sri Aurobindo press, 1967.

Roszak, Theodore, The Making of a Counter Culture. Anchor Books Doubleday Garden City, New York, 1969.

Rush, F. The Best Kept Secret: Sexual Abuse of Children. New York: McGraw Hill, 1980.

Sapir, Edward. *Language.* Harvest Books, Harcourt, Brace & World, Inc. New York.

Sannella, Lee. "**Kundalini-Psychosis or Transcendence?** Publ. by Lee Sannella, 3101 Washington St. San Francisco, 1976.

Samatanand, Swami. "**The Mystery of Kundalini**", **a talk given by the Swami at a New York Intensive.** In Meditate, a newspaper-style publication issued by the Oakland, California Siddha Yoga Ashram, 1978.

Satprem. "**Sri Aurobindo: or The Adventure of Consciousness:** India Library
Society: New York, 1964.

Schuskky, Ernest L. **Manual for Kinship.** Holt, Rinehart & Winston, New york, 1965

Schwarz, Berthold. *A Psychiatrist looks at Esp.* New York: New American Library, 1965.

Servadio, Emilio: **Otto sedute col. medium Erto. La Ricerrca Psycnica,** 32:231-2344-235, 1932. also "**The Psychic Mechanism of Telepathic Hallucinations.** Journal of the American Society for Psychical Research, 28:149-159, 1934 (1933).

Shubhanarayanan, N. "**Occult Psychology of the Hindus**". Pondicherry: Dipti Publications, India. 1975.

Sitchin, Zecharia, **Genesis Revisited.** Avon Books, New York 1990.

Snow, C.P. **The Two Cultures and the Scientific Revolution.** Cambridge University Press, 1959.

Speers, F. W. "**Brief Psychotherapy with College Women.**" American K. orthopsychiatrist.

Sperling, Melittta, "**The Neurotic & His Mother: A Psychoanalytic Study**", *American* Orthopsychiatry Quarterly, 1954.

Sorokin, Pitrim A. **The Basic Trends of Our Times.** New Haven, Conn., College University Press, New HAven, Con. 1964.

Sorokin, Pitrim A. **Modern Historical and Social Philosophies,** Dover Publications,Inc. new york 1963.

Staker, M. **"Brief Psychotherapy In An Outpatient Clinic: Evolution and Evaluation",** . *American Journal of Psychiatristry.* 1968.

Stevenson I.. *Telepathic Impressions.* Charlottesville University of Virginia Press.

Stekel, Wilhelm, *The interpretation of Dreams.* 2 vol. N.Y. Liverright 1943., also in Die Sprache Des Traimer, Munchen, Bergman Hill.

Strauss,Levi, Claud. *Totemism.* Boston: Bacon Press, 1963.

Siu G.H. **The Tao of Science: An Essay on Western Knowledge and Eastern Wisdom.** M.I.T. Press, Massachusetts Institute of Technology, Cambridge, Massachesetts, 1957.

Sullivan, H.s. **"The Interpersonal Theory of Psychiatry."** New York: Norton, 1953. & "conceptions of Modern Psychiatry." New York: Norton. 1953

Szurek & Johnson. **The Genesis of Antisocial Acting out In children and Adults.** Psychoalysis Quartely, 1952.

Tart, C. t., Ed. **Altered States of Consciousness: A Book of Readings.** New York: Wiley, 1969.

Tart, Charles. **"Scientific Foundations for the Study of Altered States of Consciousness,** "Journal of Transpersonal Psychology. No. 2, 1971.

Taub-Bynum, E. Bruce, *The Family Unconscious.* Quest Books, Wheaton, Ill. 1984.

Thompson, Laura. *The Secret of culture.* New York: Random House, 1969.

Thompson, Laura. "**Toward a Science of Mankind**". McGraw Hill: New York, 1961.

Tillich, Paul. "**Existential Philosophy**, "Journal of the History of Ideas." 1944.

Tiller, Willian A. "**New Fields, New Laws**", *Future Science.* Edited by John White & Stanlyey Krippner. 1977., Anchor Books, Doubleday , Garden City, New York.

Timadheff, Nocholas S. **Sociological Theory: Its Nature and Growth.** New York, Random house 1960.

Tower, Cynthia Crosson. **Understanding Child Abuse and Neglect.** Allyn & Bacon B ostaon, 1989.

Torrey, E. Fuller. *Witchdoctors and Psychiatrists.* Harper & Row, New York. 1972. pp 107-108.

Tylor, Edward. **Primitive Culture.** 2nd Vol., Ist & 5th eds. London 1971-1913.

Wallace, A.F.C. "**The Institutionalization of Cathartic and Control Stategies in Iroquois Religious Psychotherapy**". In *Culture and Mental Health.* edited by MK.. Opler. New York: the Macmillan Company, 1959.

Wallace, Anthony, *CULTURE AND PERSONALITY.* Random House: New York, 1964.

Weber, Max. **The Protestant Ethic and the Spirit of Capitalism.** Charles Scribner's sons, New york, 1958.

Wentz Evans, editor. **The Tibetan Book of the Great Liberation.** Oxford University Press, London 1968.

West, D.J.. *Psychical Research Today.* London: Penguin Books, 1962

Wild Science: Mind and Body. Encyclopedia Britannica Film: 1977.

White, John. **"Exploration in Kundalin Research".** In "Kundalin, Evolution and Enlightenment". Ed. John White. doubleday: Garden City, New York, 1979.

White, John. **"Some Possibilities for Further Kundalini Research".** In "Kundalini, Evolution and Enlightenment. Ed. John White. Doubleday: Garden City, New York, 1979.

White, John **"Kundalini, Evolution and Enlightenment"** paper delivered at the 1978 American Anthropological Association meeting in Los Angeles, California.

White, Leslie A. **The Science of culture: A Study of Man's Civilization.** New York: Fal, Straus 7 Co., 1949.

White, Leslie A. **The Evolution of Culture.** New York: Mcgraw Hill, 1959.

Whorf Lee Benjamin. *Language thought & Reality.* M.I.T. Pewaa. Massachusetts Institute of Technology Cambridge, Massachusetts.

Whyte WLilliams Jr. **The Organization Man.** Doubleday Anchor Books, New York 1965.

Wilson, Colin, *The Occult: a History. Random House, New York 1971.*

Wolfenstein, Martha. **Fun Morality: An Analysis of Recent American Child-Training Literature.** in Childhood in Contemporary Cultures. 1964

Young, Louise B. **Evolution of Man.** Louise B. Young, editor, New York: Oxford University Press 1963

Yamaguchi, Gogen. "**Karate: Goju-ryu by the Cat.**"International Karate-do Goju-Kai Tokyo, Japan 1966.

Zukav, Gary. **The Dancing wu Li Masters: An Overview of the New Physics.** Bantam Books, New york, 1980.

[1] Chaudhuri, 1954, Philosophy of Integralism p. 157.

GRAY-JACKET 5.5 X 8.5

9 780738 811147